I0888423

AI in Literary Education and Language Learning

Andi Asrifan
Universitas Negeri Makassar, Indonesia

IGI Global
Scientific Publishing
Publishing Tomorrow's Research Today

Vice President of Editorial	Melissa Wagner
Director of Acquisitions	Mikaela Felty
Director of Book Development	Jocelynn Hessler
Production Manager	Mike Brehm
Cover Design	Jose Rosado

Published in the United States of America by
IGI Global Scientific Publishing
701 East Chocolate Avenue
Hershey, PA, 17033, USA
Tel: 717-533-8845
Fax: 717-533-7115
Website: https://www.igi-global.com E-mail: cust@igi-global.com

Copyright © 2026 by IGI Global Scientific Publishing. All rights reserved. No part of this publication may be reproduced, stored or distributed in any form or by any means, electronic or mechanical, including photocopying, without written permission from the publisher.

Product or company names used in this set are for identification purposes only. Inclusion of the names of the products or companies does not indicate a claim of ownership by IGI Global Scientific Publishing of the trademark or registered trademark.

Library of Congress Cataloging-in-Publication Data

LCCN: 2025034282 (CIP Data Pending)
ISBN13: 9798337363301
Isbn13Softcover: 9798337363318
EISBN13: 9798337363325

British Cataloguing in Publication Data
A Cataloguing in Publication record for this book is available from the British Library.

All work contributed to this book is new, previously-unpublished material.
The views expressed in this book are those of the authors, but not necessarily of the publisher.
This book contains information sourced from authentic and highly regarded references, with reasonable efforts made to ensure the reliability of the data and information presented. The authors, editors, and publisher believe the information in this book to be accurate and true as of the date of publication. Every effort has been made to trace and credit the copyright holders of all materials included. However, the authors, editors, and publisher cannot assume responsibility for the validity of all materials or the consequences of their use. Should any copyright material be found unacknowledged, please inform the publisher so that corrections may be made in future reprints.

Table of Contents

Detailed Table of Contents

Artificial Intelligence (AI) is revolutionizing literary research and academic studies by enhancing text analysis, authorship attribution, and literature reviews. AI tools help uncover patterns, analyze themes, and conduct sentiment analysis in literary works. They assist in identifying anonymous authors, detecting forgeries, and streamlining literature reviews. AI also plays a crucial role in plagiarism detection and personalized learning. However, challenges such as algorithmic bias, ethical concerns, and over-reliance on AI persist. Addressing these requires collaboration between scholars and AI developers. While AI improves research efficiency, human interpretation remains essential. The future of AI in academia depends on balancing technological advancements with traditional methods to ensure ethical and effective scholarship. AI's continued evolution promises deeper insights and broader applications in digital humanities and interdisciplinary research, shaping the future of academic studies.

The increasing integration of artificial intelligence (AI) in the writing and creative process has raised significant concerns about the originality and authenticity of a literary work in the world of education. While AI-generated literary output improves efficiency, refines language, and supports the development of ideas, it also challenges traditional notions of human creativity. AI tools often rely on existing data, leading to potential replication issues and accidental plagiarism. Additionally, the absence of human experience and emotional depth in AI-generated works raises questions about their authenticity and artistic value. The study examines the ethical and academic implications of AI-generated content, emphasizing the need for critical oversight and

Preface

INTRODUCTION

Artificial Intelligence (AI) is rapidly redefining the landscapes of education, particularly in the fields of literary studies and language learning. As we continue to navigate the implications of this technological transformation, it becomes crucial to critically examine how AI is being integrated into teaching, learning, research, and creative expression. This edited volume, *AI in Literary Education and Language Learning*, gathers diverse perspectives from scholars across Asia, especially Indonesia, India, and the Philippines, to explore how AI tools are reshaping both the practice and pedagogy of literature and language education.

This book does not merely highlight the advantages of AI; it also addresses the challenges and ethical dilemmas that come with the increasing reliance on machine intelligence in domains traditionally rooted in human creativity and subjectivity. The authors provide evidence-based insights, practical applications, and critical reflections, offering educators, researchers, and policy-makers a well-rounded understanding of AI's current and potential roles in literary and language education.

Below is an overview of the chapters that compose this volume:

Chapter Overview

Chapter 1: Case Studies on the Use of AI in Literary Research and Academic Studies

This chapter provides a foundational exploration of how AI enhances literary research, particularly in text analysis, sentiment detection, and authorship attribution. It also discusses AI's role in plagiarism detection and personalized academic learning, while cautioning against ethical risks and over-reliance on automation.

Chapter 2: Challenges in Ensuring Originality and Authenticity in AI-Generated Works

The authors address concerns surrounding originality in AI-assisted writing, emphasizing ethical considerations, potential plagiarism, and the loss of emotional depth. The chapter advocates for institutional policies that reinforce AI as a tool to support—not replace—human creativity.

Chapter 3: Integrating AI in English Education: Advancing Literary Understanding and Assessment

This chapter illustrates how AI tools support English language teaching, particularly in content creation, thematic analysis, and student feedback. While recognizing AI's pedagogical benefits, the authors stress the importance of regulating its use to avoid over-dependence.

Chapter 4: Integration of AI in Language Learning and Literary Education

Using quantitative methods, this study explores how AI enhances student engagement and comprehension. Tools like adaptive learning platforms and multimedia interfaces are shown to help learners with grammar, fluency, and deeper literary understanding across diverse learning styles.

Chapter 5: AI-Enhanced Language Acquisition: Transforming the Learning Experience

This chapter focuses on the personalized and inclusive nature of AI-driven language instruction. From chatbots to gamified learning, the authors present how AI breaks traditional barriers in accessibility and engagement, while also flagging ethical concerns like data privacy.

Chapter 6: The Role of AI in Language Learning and Literary Education

An in-depth exploration of AI's capacity to support creativity, critical thinking, and interactive learning. The author emphasizes the necessity of emotional intelligence and human involvement, proposing a model where AI complements rather than supplants traditional education.

Chapter 7: AI as an Evaluator in Education Assessment

This chapter evaluates AI's role in grading and feedback for literary materials produced by teacher education students. A comparative approach illustrates both the promise and limits of AI in assessing subjective elements like creativity and cultural context.

Chapter 8: AI-Assisted Storytelling for Young Learners: Innovations and Evaluations

This final chapter addresses literacy development among young learners through AI-generated storytelling. While AI helps fill gaps in reading resources, the chapter offers a critical assessment of narrative quality and educational effectiveness, emphasizing the complementary roles of human authorship and AI generation.

This volume is not only timely but also essential for understanding the evolving interface between AI and the humanities. As editors and contributors, we hope it provides readers with both practical insights and theoretical frameworks for navigating this complex yet exciting frontier in education. Whether you are a teacher, researcher, developer, or policymaker, we invite you to explore the many dimensions AI brings to literary and language education through the chapters that follow.

Andi Asrifan
Universitas Negeri Makassar, Indonesia

Chapter 1

Case Studies on the Use of AI in Literary Research and Academic Studies

Jyoti Rani
https://orcid.org/0000-0002-5577-7808
Parul Institute of Design, Parul University, India

Ramratan Guru
https://orcid.org/0000-0001-6142-2643
Mody University of Science and Technology, India

Sakthivel Santhanam
Presidency University, India

ABSTRACT

Artificial Intelligence (AI) is revolutionizing literary research and academic studies by enhancing text analysis, authorship attribution, and literature reviews. AI tools help uncover patterns, analyze themes, and conduct sentiment analysis in literary works. They assist in identifying anonymous authors, detecting forgeries, and streamlining literature reviews. AI also plays a crucial role in plagiarism detection and personalized learning. However, challenges such as algorithmic bias, ethical concerns, and over-reliance on AI persist. Addressing these requires collaboration between scholars and AI developers. While AI improves research efficiency, human interpretation remains essential. The future of AI in academia depends on balancing technological advancements with traditional methods to ensure ethical and effective scholarship. AI's continued evolution promises deeper insights and broader applications in digital humanities and interdisciplinary research, shaping the future of academic studies.

DOI: 10.4018/979-8-3373-6330-1.ch001

Copyright © 2026, IGI Global Scientific Publishing. Copying or distributing in print or electronic forms without written permission of IGI Global Scientific Publishing is prohibited.

INTRODUCTION

The advent of artificial intelligence (AI) is increasingly becoming a key tool in the ever-expanding realm of academia and literary research, redefining traditional methodologies and offering new opportunities for both exploration and efficiency. Using artificial intelligence in academic research: using artificial intelligence to automate systematic literature reviews (SLRs) can not only improve our efficiency but also the quality of our research output. A chat GPT does not just automate, it facilitates collaboration through enhancing human ingenuity and machine efficiency to contribute towards better research methodologies. We hope that this chapter will expose you to the benefits of AI in academia and how over time the perception of AI has found its way into advanced research by building robust methodologies around it.

AI in Systematic Literature Reviews

- Artificial Intelligence has radically improved SLR delivery, with new methods that automate steps in the SLR process, such as screening or data extraction, that were previously expensive and took human resources a long time to complete.
- The development of tools that use AI, particularly large language models, to assist with semi-automatic literature review production provide better support for researchers (Tomczyk et al., 2024) (Bolaños et al., 2024).
- The use of AI in SLRs not only reduces the time required for comprehensive evaluations but also enhances the quality of methodologies used, permitting researchers to engage in more sophisticated analytical evaluations (Tomczyk et al., 2024).

AI's Role in Academic Publishing

- Tools such as ChatGPT and Google Bard for AI-assisted literature review, manuscript writing, and literature referencing are being utilized in academic publishing more and more (Dupps, 2023).
- On the other hand, these also raise ethical issues concerning originality and plagiarism prevention, necessitating the creation of strong guidelines and detection tools (Dupps, 2023).
- In this context, the potential for AI to improve efficiency and productivity in academic research should be balanced with concerns about the quality and integrity of AI-generated content, highlighting the need for a human-in-the-loop approach (Erler, 2023).

Transformative Impact on Research Methodologies

- Text generation, data analysis, and peer review are some of the ways in which AI is being applied into academia, providing innovative solutions that can result in more optimal research processes (Alqahtani et al., 2023).
- They have democratized access to the latest research syntheses on the effects and implementation of interventions and their surrounding landscape, service provision and use into research policy and practice in diverse fields (Tomczyk et al., 2024).
- Although it can help in the research process, AI has to be monitored or regulated in research so that it does not violate or harm the research (Dergaa et al., 2023).

Challenges and Ethical Considerations

- With AI technologies advancing rapidly, editing such material is challenging because of AI generator plagiarism specifically in opinions and principles as the main issue of publishing scientific articles.
- This calls for productive and extensive discussions on the potential uses, threats, and limitations of AI tools and their relevance as a tool in any research process whereby human intelligence and critical thinking forms part and parcel of it (Dergaa et al., 2023).
- It is important to approach the adoption of AI for academia with an ethical lens driven by algorithmic biases, protection of intellectual property rights (Alqahtani et al., 2023).

AI provides major benefits in reformatting old research methods but in the process also introduces challenges we need to overcome to guarantee responsible and ethical application. While we cannot deny the merit of AI in improving academic research, it must be tempered with human control because otherwise not only the integrity of research output will suffer, but its quality too. With the evolving nature of AI, it will be important to implement continual examination and adjustment of different types of research in order to not only be able to use these tools, but also to avoid the risks created by using them.

HISTORICAL CONTEXT

Evolution of AI tools in academic and literary studies

AI tools in academic and literary studies have evolved a great deal especially over the past ten years. But these tools facilitate new ways of working with text that are more suited to our contemporary world, even as traditional approaches align with practice that looks to the past. Recent advances in natural language processing (NLP), machine learning, and large language models have invigorated the incorporation of AI into academic and literary studies, maximizing the speed and breadth of research tasks. Such has been the sophistication of AI applications over time, now assisting with many of the tasks from literature reviews to creative writing. The major facets of this evolution are discussed in detail below.

AI in Systematic Literature Reviews

- A new breed of AI tools: Many new AI tools have been developed to help in the semi-automation of systematic literature reviews (SLRs) in particular screening and extraction. These tools use large language models to make literature searches and academic writing more effective (Bolaños et al., 2024).
- AI facilitating SLRs tackles usability issues as well as the development of standardized methods of evaluation, vital elements of progress for the tools relevant to our use (Bolaños et al., 2024).

AI in Academic Writing and Research

- However, AI models, such as ChatGPT, have proven to have tremendous potential in improving academic writing. Nonetheless, the use of these tools can pose challenges to the authenticity and credibility of academic work Determined of acceptability to ethical decision-making (Dergaa et al., 2023).
- The applications of AI in Research range the gamut of Text generation, Data analysis, review of relevant literature, and Peer review, all of which can lead to heightened educational and research outcomes (Alqahtani et al., 2023).

AI in Humanities and Literary Studies

- Tools like ALCIDE have been created to help humanities scholars mine large quantitative data sets of text. Utilizing state of the art text processing methods with simple, easy to understand visualizations, these tools allow scholars to parse through historical and literary texts more thoroughly and effectively (Moretti et al., 2016).

- There has been a wealth of case studies on AI developments in player face and labour, literature and themes of fiction, academic research and sits of learning and history, among others. For more applications like these, this research can pave the way for future opportunities in humanities research (Chapinal-Heras & Díaz-Sánchez, 2024).

Historical and Cultural Perspectives on AI

- Such historical and cultural aspects of AI can be explored through projects such as AI Narratives that investigate narratives people have engaged about intelligent machines, in various forms, throughout time and in varying cultures. These stories reflect the roller coaster of AI's optimism and pessimism and its implications for society (Baker, 2024).
- Over the past ten years, there has been dramatic progress in the development of deep learning algorithms, including self-learning and pre-trained models, leading to substantial indirect impacts in academic research and industrial applications (Shao et al., 2022).

AI tools have certainly proved themselves a powerful (and steadily growing) asset in academic and literary studies, but come with their own challenges and ethical considerations. AI-generated research findings raise significant issues of bias, credibility and the risk of unethical conduct but these must be weighed against the extent to which what is produced involves independent cognitive input by the researcher (P. Christou, 2023). Moreover, the cultural and historical narratives surrounding AI serve as an important reminder of the broader societal implications and responsibility associated with these technologies and the need to include and represent diverse perspectives in their development and applications (Baker, 2024).

Milestones in AI development and their influence on research

The evolution of artificial intelligence (AI) as a field has been progressive and consists a number of hurdles to cross and milestones to achieve that were instrumental in defining AI as a research topic and as a social phenomenon. It will discuss both the theoretical milestones that laid the groundwork for the technology as we know it today, as well as the events, developments, and achievements that formed the practical contingencies under which it operates, from the 1950s until October 2023.

Key Milestones in AI Development

1956 Dartmouth Conference: This is often considered to be the origin point for AI as a distinct field, and some of the initial principles were established here as well as the emphasis on computation and abstraction (Gill, 2020).
Computer Chess: The work on computer chess, especially that of Shannon and Turing, yielded important lessons about algorithmic intelligence and problem-solving approaches that played a role in shaping how AI was understood.
Deep Learning Era: The shift from rule-based systems to machine learning algorithms represented a paradigm shift, where machines learned from the data instead of being dependent on humans-defined rules (Deng, 2018).

Influence on Research Agendas

Interdisciplinary Integration: AI developed from subfields such as natural language processing and robotics to incorporate a more generalized approach demonstrating a greater integration of knowledge (and knowledge application) across disciplinary areas (Tecuci, 2012).
Productivity and Innovation: With the expectation to be a general-purpose technology, AI is expected to push productivity and innovation to new frontiers, in the same vein as previous industrial revolutions, hinting that this can have long-term effects on research and development (Crafts, 2021).

Although the recent improvements in AI performance have resulted in impressive functions, there are rising ethical concerns, such as the potential for misuse in areas like surveillance and behavioral manipulation (Gill, 2020). This duality calls for continuing discussion on the societal implications of AI technologies.

Early applications: Text Analysis, Linguistic Studies, and Digital Archiving

Digital humanities the initial applications of digital tools on historical research have ushered in an important transformation of text analysis, linguistic studies, and digital archiving. As a result, historians and researchers have been able to explore large text corpora and gain insight into historical contexts and linguistic evolution. Below are some points to be aware of regarding these early applications.

Text Analysis and Linguistic Studies

- Corpus Linguistics: The application of corpus linguistics has become an important tool for examining the language of historical texts as it provides a way for researchers to measure the patterns of language use and track the historical progression of words (Tumbe, 2019).
- Computational Text Analysis: The early phase of work within the digital humanities was primarily oriented toward analyzing text through classification systems and text encoding, which became the basis for modern linguistic research (Sula & Hill, 2019).

Digital Archiving

- Mass Digitization: The digitization of ancient newspapers and archives allows researchers to build connections to primary sources and widen the base of historical queries for broader perspective (Tumbe, 2019) (Sinn & Soares, 2014).
- Changing Research Patterns: This includes changing the ways historians conduct research by drawing on digital archives, sometimes using web searches to identify relevant sources, which has transformed how many historians understand historic sources (Sinn & Soares, 2014).

Nonetheless, while these digital tools have revolutionized historical research, some scholars argue that the use of digital formats may threaten the authority of the original document and argue that a balance must be struck that appreciates the value of both (Sinn & Soares, 2014).

AI IN LITERARY RESEARCH

Case study: Using AI for Thematic and Stylistic Analysis of Shakespeare's Works

Shakespeare analysis shows the transformative power of AI-driven technology on literary research. Machine learning techniques, particularly via natural language processing (NLP) and deep neural networks (DNN), empower researchers to evolve and extract patterns and insights that may not be easily visible with standard approaches. Breakdown of the Analysis This can be broken down into various key areas.

AI Techniques in Textual Analysis

Natural Language Processing (NLP): NLP methods enable the extraction of thematic and stylistic features present within Shakespeare's texts, facilitating a more nuanced understanding of his language and themes (Alqahtani et al., 2023).
Deep Neural Networks (DNN): DNN can sift through large corpuses of text, detecting stylistic features and thematic patterns with super-human accuracy, thereby adding to literary analysis (Suissa et al., 2022).

Case Studies and Applications

Generative AI: GPT-4 can be helpful in offering interpretations and analyses of Shakespeare's works, enabling novel perspectives and insights about his themes and stylistic choices (Liu et al., 2024).
Challenges: The challenges remain significant, so despite the advantages, the hurdles in the applications of AI to the literary study include the data availability and the need for domain adaptation (Suissa et al., 2022).

AI inevitably widens this gap, making new tools for literary analysis available even as we become more distant from being able to make sense of how those tools work. Some critics point out that AI-generated interpretations may not possess the depth and emotional resonance naturally present in human analysis and can simplify complex literature into mere data points (Elam, 2023).

Example of Sentiment Analysis in Victorian Novels

This study would employ sentiment analysis on Victorian novels, which would be a captivating fusion of literary studies and computer-based methods, enhancing our comprehension of the emotional landscapes in these texts. By exploiting the sentiments expressed in novels, researchers will be able to quantify and analyze this process in a way that was not possible before. Through the use of the sentiment analysis, scholars are able to discover patterns and trends in emotional tone found in Victorian literature, which can further enhance our understanding of the genre and its cultural context. Here are few things related to sentiment analysis from the domain.

Sentiment Analysis in Victorian Novels

- Quantitative Insights: Using sentiment analysis, it allows a quantitative way of comprehending the emotional content of Victorian novels. This approach can illuminate large-scale trends in sentiment across a corpus of texts, and correlate these trends with specific narrative elements or themes (Franta & Silver, 2024).

- Feature Selection and Optimization: This allows employing advanced algorithms for optimizing feature selection in sentiment analysis such as Multi-objective Binary Horse herd Optimisation Algorith (MBHOA) The integration of these techniques helps to enhance the accuracy and efficiency of sentiment classification, enabling the model to capture the complex emotional subtleties found in literary works (Hosseinalipour & Ghanbarzadeh, 2023).
- Sentiment Classification Models: These are models based on word embedding techniques and feature extraction techniques such as Bi-LSTM layers to capture the semantic depth of Victorian novels. These models can achieve strong performance on sentiment classification, including in text with complex transitions of sentiment polarity (Pan, 2024).

Challenges and Considerations

In this section, we will first discuss available methods for sentiment analysis, their usefulness, and their limitations using historical data; one of the major limitations of sentiment analysis is the inability to detect irony and sarcasm, both of which are dominant features of even Victorian literature. This raises the question about the generic potentiality, as well as the limitations of computational models in literary studies. Moreover, it is important to note that AI applications for literary research are still developing as new applications are released that will go the extra mile in terms of depth and accuracy of sentiment (Franta & Silver, 2024) (Chapinal-Heras & Díaz-Sánchez, 2024).

Case Study: Identifying Anonymous Authorship Using Machine Learning

Supervised and unsupervised machine learning approaches to verify authorship of anonymous writing, and to identify anonymous authorship, has become a hot topic in authorship attribution especially for social media content. Since then, many methods have been proposed based on deep learning and stylometric approaches to improve authorship attribution (AA) and verification (AV) accuracy. The next few sections describe key approaches and results of recent research.

Machine Learning Approaches to Authorship Attribution

- Deep Learning Models: Deep learning models have been used recently to detect small text messages like social networks. A common approach used in these models is to avoid handcrafted features and use data-driven techniques to enhance accuracy in AA.
- Capsule Networks: The only novel approach for microtext authorship recommendation and attribution used capsule networks and based on that achieved competitive performance compared to previous traditional approaches.

Authorship Verification Techniques

- Functionality-Agnostic Models: The SCS-Gan model learnt stylometric representations of code, enabling AV with no predefined set of authors. This model significantly improves over other recent techniques, as it focuses on discovering personal style independent of the functionality of the code up to date.
- Language-Independent Methods: A novel computational framework highlights lazy profile-based classification, yielding very high accuracy with little or no preprocessing and independent of the language used.

Although these improvements on machine learning present strong tools for authorship identification there are still problems, debilitating them to problems of incorporating the great variety of writing styles and the emergence of confirmatory deceptive writing techniques in anonymous environments.

Applications in Studying Historical Manuscripts

Author attribution and style detection in historical manuscripts have greatly enlarged as an area of research, came with the details to identify authors and style over the years. Additionally, a variety of methods, such as text disruption, syntactic analysis, and deep learning, have been taken to improve authorship attribution accuracy in such complex fields as cross-topic and historical publications.

Text Distortion Techniques

- Stamatatos proposes a text distortion mechanism to hide topical semantics, enhancing the efficiency of authorship attribution over different topics.

- This limits our results to a narrower range, which is a necessary feature for reliable extraction of personal writing styles, an important factor for historical manuscripts in which topics can cover a variety of subjects.

Syntactic Characterization

- Lucic and Blake points out that high-level syntactic features involving local syntactic dependencies can indicate stylistic patterns that remain constant across different documents.
- They believe that this type of features may present a more reliable foundation for authorship attribution as opposed to surface-based attributes.

Network Dynamics in Authorship

- Akimushkin et al. use co-occurrence networks of words to classify texts with 88.75% success comparing authors (Akimushkin et al., 2017).
- Current analysis approaches overlook its importance; accurate detection allows to gain insights into stylistic elements in the text which is a contemporary dimension of authorship analysis and where the application of network theory emerged with promising results.

Multi-Task Learning Approaches

- Song et al. propose a multi-task learning framework that separates topic and style, enhancing the accuracy of authorship attribution in cross-topic scenarios (Song et al., 2019).
- This probabilistic approach allows for a nuanced understanding of an author's style independent of the content.

Deep Learning for Historical Manuscripts

- Chammas et al. target various deep learning methods for the authorship attribution of Arabic old documents with a mean Average Precision of 95.2%.
- It shows the success of machine learning in tackling the specific difficulty of historical documents.

This is a great step forward in terms of authorship attribution and style detection, but there are obstacles, especially in understanding stylistic features in heterogeneous historical context. There is still much work to be done to polish these methodologies and make them more useful in the humanities.

Cross-Cultural Analysis of Literary Themes Through AI-Driven Databases

AI-powered databases facilitate the cross-cultural analysis of literary themes of the western and eastern world literature. Using data from multiple sources, researchers identify cultural trends and divergences across literary tastes, themes, and linguistic traits. Such studies highlight a dimensional richness across literatures mediated through an expanded techno culture.

Cross-Country Analysis of Literary Preferences

- Indeed, a study using Goodreads data found substantial cultural factors affecting book choice, such as geographical and lingual distances (Sabri et al., 2020).
- These findings further suggest that reading choices mirror wider cultural and economic conditions that can be used to guide recommender systems and other marketing efforts.

Comparative Literary Theory

- The comparative literary theory highlights the significance of a cross-cultural examination of literature, which conveys common themes and narrative techniques (Kholodniak, 2023).
- The reconstructive approach foregrounds cultural differences and interrogates canonical literature along the cross-cultural lines.

AI and Linguistic Features

- In particular, analyses of contemporary literature using AI-driven techniques have shown that there are significant differences in the language individual authors used, revealing unique styles to the works (Zhai, 2024).
- These analyses will contribute to a better understanding of how cultural contexts shape both literary expression and reader engagement.

As theorists like Mukherjee warned, there remain limits to machine-assisted literary studies which require caution against the extraction of over-generalized stereotypes from cultural narratives (Ganguly, 2020).

Example: Mapping Influences of Western Literature on Asian Literary Traditions

The nature of the Western literature and its impact on the Asian literary landscape is a subject of inquiry for many, including scholars in the field of comparative literature. Western literary forms and ideas inform Asian traditions and are commonly reconfigured within local contexts into hybrid forms. This kind of dynamic interaction reaches out, in different ways, through aspects in literature, from thematic movements to structural developments.

Convergence and Divergence in Humanistic Traditions

- Western humanism, beginning with Cicero and the Renaissance humanists, affirms the cultivation of letters for education. Whereas, East Asian humanism, especially Japanese Confucianism has the emphasis on poetry and rites on the education philosophy (Kato, 2016).
- Despite these differences, both traditions emphasize humanistic education, indicating the possibility of convergence between the two in contemporary education (Kato, 2016).

Comparative Aesthetics and Literary Universals

- Studies comparing literature from these two cultural contexts, such as those by Patrick Colm Hogan, reveal aesthetic principles shared by both Western and Indian literatures, such as the employment of the "deus ex machina" and the structural unity of classical dramas.
- Thus, these studies go beyond the simplistic East versus West narrative, which contributes to universals in literature across cultures.

Cultural Interaction and Adaptation

- However, the reception of Western civilization has deeply transformed the culture of Asia as a whole, and Japan stands out as a successful special case. This interaction has been both a revolutionary and conservative one that makes up the dual nature of cultural Exchange.
- Aspects of Western culture have now become adopted aspects of Asian cultures, which in many ways have given birth to new and innovative literary forms that will showcase both the East and West.

Intellectual Capital and Knowledge Conceptualization

- Differences in knowledge conceptualization between the West and the East reflect themselves onto literary traditions. Eastern and Western literature treat knowledge as capital or an evolving truth, thus playing a part in how literature is written and understood (Andriessen & Van Den Boom, 2007).

Although Western literature has undeniably affected Asian traditions, the exchange is not one-way. Asian literatures have now influenced Western thought, as they have created a world literary dialogue which deepens both traditions. This mutual influence highlights an important aspect of reading between the lines of literary exchanges: they should be seen as dynamic and reciprocal, and not simply as hierarchical and unidirectional.

Digital Humanities and Literary Archives

This example highlights the robust and growing role of AI-powered tools in the preservation and analysis of ancient texts and paves the way for further innovations in the field of digital humanities. These technologies help make the historical literature more accessible and comprehensible, as well as a mechanism to restore it, therefore assist in preserving the cultural heritage. Here are some highlights of this transformative strategy.

AI Techniques for Text Preservation

- Image Processing and OCR: Generative AI enhances optical character recognition (OCR) and image processing, enabling more effective digital representations of archaic texts, even those that are heaving (Liu et al., 2024) (Luo, 2024).
- Deep Learning Models: The tools include deep learning models such as Ithaca which use deep neural networks for restoring and attributing ancient inscriptions, achieving significant accuracy improvements when used collaboratively with historians (Assael et al., 2022).

Intelligent Analysis of Ancient Texts

- Generative Pre-trained Models: Models like SikuGPT help by translating and contextualizing ancient texts for modern audiences (Liu et al., 2024).
- Question-Answering Systems: With the help of advanced NLP techniques, systems can be created to answer contextually relevant questions, making it

easier to conduct research using ancient scriptures (Kumar Pandey & Sekhar Roy, 2024).

However, the use of AI in analysing ancient texts raises important questions about the ethics of AI application and the risk of biases in AI-generated interpretations. Culturally responsible digital humanities work must carefully balance technological innovation with cultural sensitivity.

Case study: Digitization and AI Analysis of Ancient Greek Texts

By harnessing the power of the mechanical age, and The Representational discipline, digital humanities and AI usage for ancient Greek analysis has expanded the possibilities for literary preservation and understanding. The use of deep learning, natural language processing, and multimodal models transforms the digitization, restoration, and analysis of these manuscripts. The next sections explain some crucial elements of this transformation.

Digitization and Restoration Techniques

- Image Processing: Techniques like computer image processing and neural networks are employed to restore damaged texts, improving visibility and readability (Luo, 2024).
- Deep Neural Networks: Tools like Ithaca utilize deep learning for the restoration and attribution of ancient inscriptions, achieving significant accuracy improvements when used collaboratively with historians (Assael et al., 2022).

AI-Driven Analysis

- Semantic Relationship Extraction: AI models like REDSandT_Lit enables the extraction of semantic relationships in Greek literature, improving the organization and analysis of metadata (D. Christou & Tsoumakas, 2021).
- Stylometric Classification: Advanced stylometric methods classify ancient Greek texts by genre with over 97% accuracy, aiding in the understanding of literary forms (Gianitsos et al., 2019).

The emerging role of digital humanities and AI brings great potential to the field of ancient texts, but we must continuously be cautious and make sure we are interpreting AI insights (and the data inputs) within the context and with appropriate human skills; it has the potential to lead us in wrong directions (Liu et al., 2024).

AI IN ACADEMIC STUDIES

Academic Writing Assistance

AI Tools Are Powerful Supports for Academic Writing, Especially for Thesis Writing, Editing. While these tools can significantly increase efficiency, enhance language quality, and assist in literature reviews, they also come with ethical considerations and limitations. The subsequent sections discuss the benefits, ethical implications, and limitations for employing AI in academic studies.

Benefits of AI in Academic Writing

- Efficiency and Quality: AI tools can help the writing process process where the researcher can concentrate on delivering the essential ideas and eliminate tedious tasks such as working on formats and grammar check (Pividori & Greene, 2024).
- Support for Non-Native Speakers: For authors where English is a second language, AI tools can assist them in ensuring their manuscript is of the highest international standard, reducing linguistic bias against non-native speakers in the publication process.
- Collaborative Learning: AI promotes a hybrid of writing process that leads to cognitive engagement and learner agency (Parker et al., 2024).

Ethical Considerations

- Authorship and Accountability: AI cannot be recognized as an author which raises issues related to accountability and integrity of academic work.
- Data Privacy: AI tools can violate confidentiality, especially in the case of sensitive data.
- Plagiarism Risks: AI-generated text may lead to unintended plagiarism, hence AI outputs must be carefully examined (Mehta et al., 2024).

Limitations of AI Tools

- Inaccurate Outputs: AI might generate wrong information or "data hallucinations," which can mislead researchers.
- Dependency Risks: If researchers become so dependent on AI tools, their creativity and analytical skills may decrease (Mehta et al., 2024).

- Ethical Frameworks Needed: To avoid the misuse of AI in academia, it is crucial to develop ethical frameworks that guide AI applications in academia (Bahr, 2024).

Although AI generators are powerful helpers in academic writing, ethical implications and limitations must be considered for academic integrity. AI balancing, the positives aspect of it against our needs for its ethical application is critical, to support an academia leading if the message.

Plagiarism Detection

AI helps sustain academic integrity though with, in particular, the introduction of advanced plagiarism detection tools. These tools are designed to spot both traditional plagiarism and the more subtle forms of academic misconduct that AI-generated text raises, from the anti-plagiarism service Turnitin to emerging AI-powered systems. Here is a summary of important aspects of AI in this context.

AI-Driven Plagiarism Detection Tools

- Efficacy of Detection: Threads like Gotcha GPT work on the basis of machine learning classifiers and score 0.97 - 0.99 accuracy rates for distinguishing between AI and human text (Gralha & Pimentel, 2024).
- Challenges with AI Content Research shows previous tools have had issues with newer AI models and struggle, giving false positives and inconsistencies, especially with content generated by tools like GPT-4 (Elkhatat et al., 2023).
- Deep Learning Approaches: More enthusiastic systems, which include deep learning such as LSTM networks, have proved better accuracy in forking various sorts of text similarity and/or modern plagiarism in general (El-Rashidy et al., 2022).

Evolving Definitions of Academic Integrity

- AI-Giarism: The term 'AI-Giarism' signifies a new understanding of academic misconduct among students, who show ambivalence towards the impact of AI on their written products (Chan, 2024).
- Integration in Education: Educators need to find ways to adapt teaching methods to better understand authorship, integrity, and the nature of academic writing as new AI tools emerge (Yeo, 2023).

AI-powered tools make detecting plagiarism more comfortable, though they also challenge the definition of academic integrity.' With AI technologies progressing the boundary between plagiarism and other forms of creative plagiarism will require constant revision to keep up with the developments.

Knowledge Discovery in Large Data Sets

we explore pitfalls of AI in meta-analyses for interdisciplinary studies as they face an unexpected challenge: accuracy vs. interpretability. While these tools can greatly increase the speed at which knowledge can be proposed from big data, their introduction comes with challenges which need to be schooled before getting into dangerous waters.

AI in Knowledge Discovery

- AI improves the efficiency of systematic reviews through full automation of processes such as study screening and data extraction (Ge et al., 2024).
- Recent hybrid approaches, which combine large language models with graph neural networks, have demonstrated their ability to extract biomedical knowledge by obtaining a Matthews correlation coefficient of 0.772 .

Challenges in Accuracy

- Different models produce misleading information, referred to as hallucination.
- For domain specific knowledge, such as in medical domain, the absence (Expert Validation) in how we can validate the knowledge we have discovered given the effort it took to discover this new knowledge (Wang et al., 2023).

Interpretability Issues

- Due to the opacity of many AI models, researchers cannot interpret how conclusion are inferred.
- The usage of interpretive AI/ML techniques are particularly critical to validate whether AI-generated results could be trusted to be deployed in realistic scenarios (Wang et al., 2023).

Though AI can revolutionize data analysis across disciplines, its underlying complexities surrounding accuracy and interpretation require deploying experts to oversee and integrate such techniques into research for dependability.

Personalized Learning and Curriculum Design

This increased personalization, especially with the incorporation of AI tools, majorly impacts the ability of curriculum and student engagement within the study of literature. With the help of AI-powered adaptive learning systems, personalized reading lists and assignments can be created for every student, enhancing their academic performance and levels of engagement. Machine learning models help personalize learning content according to different learning types, which according to research has been shown to improve average grades from 70 to 75 in students after intervention (Villegas-Ch et al., 2024). Moreover, generative AI generates diverse learning material, keeping engagement through various ways of presenting different things, proving to be beneficial in increasing time and understanding for study (Pesovski et al., 2024).

AI Tools for Tailoring Reading Lists

Personalized Recommendations: AI systems evaluate details regarding student preferences and performance to recommend personalized reading materials.

Dynamic Updates: The reading lists are updated in real-time based on students' progress through continual feedback mechanisms.

Role of AI in Adaptive Learning Platforms

- Learning Path Customization: AI can create unique learning paths which adds on to the learning experience by tailoring content to meet personal knowledge levels.
- Engagement and Interaction: AI tools promote interactive learning experiences, such as quizzes and different content formats, which are known to improve student engagement (Pesovski et al., 2024).

Overall, the advantages of AI in personalized learning are significant, although challenges, such as ensuring equitable access to technology and addressing potential biases in AI algorithms, continue to exist. In doing so, they overcome some of the challenges outlined above, thereby ensuring that personalized learning initiatives can be as effective as possible.

CHALLENGES AND LIMITATIONS

Issues of Bias in AI Algorithms

Dealing with the algorithms they run, Bias is one of the most potent technologies in this field, but this has some limitations in some situations(rows) like healthcare and hiring. Bias can stem from multiple factors, such as how representative the data is, how well algorithms are designed to function effectively, and the socio-economic context in which such technologies are deployed. It is important to address these biases to ensure fair outcomes among diverse populations. Here are some highlights of the topic.

Sources of Bias

Data Representation: In healthcare, lab data can have bias when there is no sufficient representation of various populations resulting in skewed ai model results.

Algorithm Design: AI models might pick up spurious correlations between sensitive attributes and health outcomes, reinforcing preexisting disparities (Hu et al., 2024).

Socio-Economic Factors: The socio-economic statistics can shape the data collected, especially embedding bias within AI systems (Aldalbahi et al., 2021).

Mitigation Strategies

Attribute Neutral Framework: A framework to neutralize biased attributes in training data that can enhance fairness without sacrificing diagnostic performance (Hu et al., 2024).

Stakeholder Oversight: The involvement of stakeholders in the design and implementation of AI can help understand and mitigate biases (Hussain et al., 2025).

While these strategies are promising, the complexities surrounding bias in AI require continued research and ethical governance to keep these outcomes equitable across sectors.

Ethical Concerns Regarding the Use of AI in Humanities

However, the application of AI in the field of humanities brings up ethical implications as well. These challenges include considerations of authorship, bias, and the risk of AI capabilities being misrepresented. Of course, as with any emerging technology while the ethics of its use grows ahead of it, it is important for the university and its instructors to discuss the relevant ethical dilemmas associated with these developments to make sure they are efficiently and responsibly put into use in academic contexts.

Authorship and Academic Integrity

AI-based essay generation can further complicate these concerns, as it can produce text that is difficult to distinguish from human writing (Revell et al., 2024).

This challenges the authenticity of student submissions and the feasibility of detecting AI-generated content, complicating traditional assessment methods (Zohny et al., 2023).

Bias in Cultural Heritage

However, AI systems can a priori exaggerate existing biases relating to cultural heritage collections, as they are typically based on poorly annotated datasets (Foka & Griffin, 2024).

Such instances of bias may skew any interpretations of cultural artifacts and require approaches to prevent them while promoting their diversity in applications of AI (Foka & Griffin, 2024).

Emotional and Moral Considerations

Designing AI systems requires attention to the emotional responses they trigger in users, who create attachments to non-sentient entities and may face ethical dilemmas around their treatment (Schwitzgebel, 2023).

Therefore, to avoid moral confusion, it is crucial to establish a clear understanding of what AI is and what it can do (Schwitzgebel, 2023).

Although these new ethical dilemmas are serious, they could also incentivise improved academic practice and promote critical interaction with tech. Anticipating these issues can help foster more responsible and effective utilization of AI in the humanities.

Dependency on AI Versus Traditional Research Methods

Artificial intelligence (AI) is progressively being integrated with research methodologies as an alternative to previous methodologies. AI helps in increasing efficiency and processing of data, but it also leads to concerns of how much we are going to need to pretty, we abstract an interdependence of work, and we distort the processing of information. The subsequent sections highlight the main challenges and limitations of such dependency.

Dependency on AI

- Automation of Tasks: AI can automate time-consuming tasks that can free researchers to focus on more complex analyses (Sperlich et al., 2023).
- Data Processing: AI can process large datasets, which is extremely helpful for fields such as healthcare and sports science (Sperlich et al., 2023) (Kelly et al., 2019).
- Risk of Over-reliance: There is a risk that researchers would become overly reliant on AI, potentially undermining the importance of human judgment and expertise in research (Sperlich et al., 2023) (Shah & Acharya, 2024).

Limitations of AI

- Data Quality and Bias: To work well, AI systems need a good quality data, that is diverse. Bad data means biased results (Sperlich et al., 2023) (Kelly et al., 2019).
- Generalizability Issues: Their performance may decrease when applied to distinct contexts (e.g. in non-necessary patients (Kelly et al., 2019).
- Ethical Concerns: AI applications may pose ethical challenges around data privacy, accountability, and misuse in the context of research (Shah & Acharya, 2024).

As opposed to AI, traditional research is conducted by humans, who can utilize critical thinking to reduce risks that may arise from the use of AI. But we cannot dismiss the efficiency and analytical capability of an AI, raising the question of how we may want to take a balanced perspective on which approaches to employ.

FUTURE DIRECTIONS

Potential Advancements in AI for Deeper Literary Insights

The future of AI in literary analysis holds significant promise for enhancing understanding and engagement with texts. As advancements in AI technologies continue, they are expected to facilitate deeper literary insights through various innovative approaches. The following sections outline key potential advancements in this area.

Enhanced Text Analysis

- Computational Linguistics: AI can represent theories about the literary nature of texts, and as such, can facilitate analyses of themes, styles, and structures of texts.
- Generative AI: Techniques, like retrieval-enhanced generation (RAG), may enhance the processing of ancient texts, enabling advanced information extraction and analysis (Liu et al., 2024).

Interactive Reading Interfaces

- Semantic Reader Project: This initiative seeks to design dynamic reading interfaces to improve the understanding and accessibility of scholarly literature to revolutionize how readers engage with texts (Lo et al., 2024).
- User-Centric Design: Emphasizing the overall user experience, AI has the potential to enable more immersive and productive reading habits resulting in deeper literary understanding.

Ethical Considerations

Despite its transformative potential, AI still raises valid concerns regarding algorithmic biases, and the thus loss of complex meanings reduced to data points (Elam, 2023). This is a crucial juncture for the responsible application of AI in literature, and one that will require balance between technological progress and ethical considerations.

Predictions on AI's Role in Democratizing Access to Academic Resources

The changes AI will bring to analysing literature can bring is an amazing understanding and dialog with text. With the advancement in AI technologies, even deeper literary insights will be made accessible using multiple new techniques. Some key potential global innovations in this area in the next sections.

Enhancing Accessibility

- AI tools can help facilitate communication just in multiple languages that have the potential of lowering the hegemony of English in intellectual conversations which enable non-native speakers to take part more completely (Ghio, 2024).
- User-friendly AI applications are being developed, which allow researchers from different disciplines to work with AI technologies without in-depth programming knowledge and expand participation in research (Van Der Sommen & De Groof, 2024).

Transforming Peer Review

- In peer review processes, human-AI collaboration can help by facilitating more efficient evaluations and minimizing biases that may help a broader range of scholars to be included and their work to be acknowledged (Sarker et al., 2024).
- By working together, this collaboration may help to fill in gaps between competing scholarly traditions and be part of a more inclusive academic culture (Sarker et al., 2024).

Ethical Considerations

- While one may think such progress can only be a good thing, the integration of AI in academia creates ethical dilemmas, such as the risk for new power imbalances and the risk to reproduce existing biases in knowledge production (Ghio, 2024) (Van Der Sommen & De Groof, 2024).
- Robust validation of AI systems is essential to avoid discrimination and provide reliable outcomes in research applications (Van Der Sommen & De Groof, 2024).

Conversely, others argue that the spread of AI could widen equity gaps in access to academic resources, unless the technology is available widely outside affluent universities. This viewpoint underscores the need to tackle ethical considerations and ensure fair access to AI tools in various academic contexts.

Interdisciplinary Collaboration Between AI Developers and Literary Scholars

Bridging the gap between AI development and literary scholarship is one of those promising avenues. Scholars who are writing and researching AI-generated texts may benefit from integrating the skills offered by literary studies to better understand the properties of the texts produced through engineering AI technologies, while those who are developing AI technologies may benefit from the textual and structural insights provided in literary studies to create more sophisticated AI when working with texts. The challenges that AI poses to education and to literary scholarship also call for the development of new methodologies and frameworks and hence this collaboration can help build innovative methodologies and frameworks.

Importance of Interdisciplinary Collaboration

- Holistic Understanding: ED-AI Lit framework emphasizes the importance of collaborating for developing a holistic understanding of the implications of AI in educational contexts (Allen & Kendeou, 2024).
- Navigating Challenges: Writing scholars can assist in institutions facing challenges related to academic integrity and authorship considering AI and writing activity (Wise et al., 2024).

Methodological Innovations

- Iterative Methodology: A recent organizational psychology investigation discussed how a proposed stepwise methodology for interdisciplinary working groups could help standardize interaction processes and thus cultivate synergy, which is essential to address the social implications of AI.
- Digital Collaboration: Research data which can be used for collaborative research is aided by the collaboration of digital tools through which literary scholars can engage with AI technologies (Kaltenbrunner, 2015).

Future Prospects

- Artificial Interdisciplinarity: AI can help tackle cognitive hurdles of doing translational research across different sciences and disciplines, which could be a significant advancement as interdisciplinary research presents us with future challenges in solving complex problems we face in society (Baum, 2021).

AI itself, we know, has potential to be inevitable, which raises questions about the ethical implications of AI technologies, and the necessity of humanistic inquiry within an increasingly automated environment.

AI APPLICATIONS IN ACADEMIC MANAGEMENT

Artificial Intelligence (AI) is radically shaping academic as well as corporate management through its novel wares and technologies to increase efficiencies, take better decisions and assist in the overall productivity across various organizational settings. In academic management, AI applications play a crucial role for the management of admin activities, personalizing education, handling research administration and ensuring academic honesty. A widely-used application is an AI chatbot, such as IBM Watson, which helps providing student services by automating common questions in course registration, events, dates, and resource access. These chatbots are available 24/7, so students can get an immediate response without overloading university admin teams. And this automation means not only cost savings but greater student satisfaction with an agency that can respond at any time. Plagiarism detection is yet another essential field where AI aids academic management. Services such as Turnitin use AI to automatically scan student papers for plagiarized text to make sure students are not cheating. This judicious use of AI ensures the academic integrity and standards of scholarly work.

Furthermore, AI-enabled customized learning platforms like Knewton and Smart Sparrow are transforming how curriculums are delivered using AI to personalize the delivery of educational material based on the specific learning styles and performance of a learner. These platforms process data about how students are interacting with content to adjust the level of difficulty and type of material being presented in order to maximize engagement and understanding. This level of PERSONALIZATION has shown to have measurable gains for student success and retention, which is truly a step forward from the one-size-fits-all teaching methodology. In addition to personalized learning, AI is strategic in research management at academic institutions. AI is increasingly used to sift through large numbers of research proposals, detecting promising projects and new scientific trends that can influence funding allocations. This ability aids institutions in more efficient and targeted resource allocation, and support for innovation and investment in a small number of high-impact research areas. Equally important, AI-informed performance analytics allow academic leaders to track metrics ranging from faculty productivity to student success rates to satisfaction surveys, so that they can make evidence-based decisions and drive continuous improvement for departments and beyond. AI applications for industrial management are no less transformative, unlocking organizations to efficiency gains, workforce management enhancements, and strategic business decisioning. One of the most powerful AI applications in industry is predictive maintenance, and companies such as General Electric use AI algorithms to get the precise analysis of sensor data on machinery and other equipment. They identify patterns and anomalies that could lead to failures and trigger maintenance teams to get in to make proactive fixes prior to the line breaking. This type of predictive wear plan reduces expensive downtime, prolongs the life of equipment and adjusts prepaid maintenance schedules by all means, lowering operational expenses. Another domain with great potential for AI is supply chain management. The most successful companies like Amazon use advanced, AI-based prediction models to predict customer demand accurately, optimize stocking and logistics positions. By constantly scanning data from many sources, these AI systems boost responsiveness and agility, helping companies minimize stockouts, to lower storage expenses and to speed delivery times—important determinants of competitive advantage in fast-moving markets.

Human resources management is also reaping the rewards of AI developments. Platforms such as HireVue and Pymetrics leverage AI to make hiring more efficient, automating operations that include scanning résumés, interviewing via AI-processed video and judging how well candidates fit behavioral and cognitive profiles. This automation speeds up hiring, and helps to eliminate unconscious bias by making the screening of candidates persistently uniform. In addition, predictive analytics backed by AI can predict employee flight risk, allowing managers to act on potential retention strategies. Beyond employees handling, AI decision support tools like IBM Watson Analytics provide company executives with near-time intelligence focused on key business metrics like sales performance, financial forecasting, and market trends. These applications conveniently process large chunks of data to help make sense of it and bring the right intelligence to the surface through easy-to-read dashboards to make managing data easier and more informed. In addition, platforms that provide robotic process automation (RPA) capabilities, such as those from UiPath, allow repetitive and rule-based tasks such as invoice processing, compliance checks and report generation to be automated. By liberating workers from routine tasks, RPA gives them the opportunity to concentrate on more value-added work that demands creativity, strategic thinking, and human interaction, thus driving higher levels of productivity and innovation within the organization.

Taken together, these realistic use cases demonstrate that AI is no longer a vision for the future, but a reality for both academia and industry management. AI can rapidly and accurately analyze incredible amounts of data, giving managers in a wide variety of fields the resources they need to improve operations, customer and student experiences, and make data-based decisions. Despite remaining issues, that range from ethical and data privacy issues to the need to have human-in-the-loop oversight to guarantee responsible usage, AI is being adopted in ways that signal a fundamental break in the way organizations operate and compete. At universities, AI support isn't just about optimizing administration and personalizing education, it's about fostering a research ecosystem so universities can be innovative and produce cutting-edge research. In the enterprise, AI helps businesses to predict failures, optimize supply chains, recruit and retain talent and leverage insights for competitive advantage. As AI advancing, its application in management keeps extending, making it unmissable for management leaders to effectively figure both with current complex challenges in the modern world.

CONCLUSION

The integration of Artificial Intelligence (AI) in literary research and academic studies has revolutionized traditional methodologies, offering enhanced analytical capabilities, efficiency, and novel insights. From text analysis and authorship attribution to literature reviews and plagiarism detection, AI-powered tools have significantly expanded the scope of humanities research. These advancements enable scholars to uncover intricate patterns in literature, streamline academic workflows, and facilitate interdisciplinary studies. However, despite these benefits, AI's application in the field comes with challenges, including algorithmic bias, ethical concerns regarding authorship and originality, and the risk of over-reliance on automated systems. To ensure responsible and effective use, ongoing interdisciplinary collaboration between literary scholars, data scientists, and AI developers is crucial. Looking ahead, AI's role in literary and academic research will continue to evolve, with further innovations expected in areas such as deep learning for semantic analysis, enhanced digital humanities projects, and personalized learning tools. While AI serves as a powerful complement to traditional research methods, human critical thinking and interpretative skills remain irreplaceable. A balanced approach, integrating AI with human expertise, will be key to unlocking its full potential in literary and academic scholarship.

REFERENCES

Akimushkin, C., Amancio, D. R., & Oliveira, O. N. (2017). Text Authorship Identified Using the Dynamics of Word Co-Occurrence Networks. *PLoS One, 12*(1), e0170527. DOI: 10.1371/journal.pone.0170527 PMID: 28125703

Aldalbahi, A., El-Naggar, M., El-Newehy, M., Rahaman, M., Hatshan, M., & Khattab, T. (2021). Effects of Technical Textiles and Synthetic Nanofibers on Environmental Pollution. *Polymers, 13*(1), 155. DOI: 10.3390/polym13010155 PMID: 33401538

Allen, L. K., & Kendeou, P. (2024). ED-AI Lit: An Interdisciplinary Framework for AI Literacy in Education. *Policy Insights from the Behavioral and Brain Sciences, 11*(1), 3–10. DOI: 10.1177/23727322231220339

Alqahtani, T., Badreldin, H. A., Alrashed, M., Alshaya, A. I., Alghamdi, S. S., Bin Saleh, K., Alowais, S. A., Alshaya, O. A., Rahman, I., Al Yami, M. S., & Albekairy, A. M. (2023). The emergent role of artificial intelligence, natural learning processing, and large language models in higher education and research. *Research in Social & Administrative Pharmacy, 19*(8), 1236–1242. DOI: 10.1016/j.sapharm.2023.05.016 PMID: 37321925

Andriessen, D., & Van Den Boom, M. (2007). East is East, and West is West, and (n)ever its intellectual capital shall meet. *Journal of Intellectual Capital, 8*(4), 641–652. DOI: 10.1108/14691930710830800

Assael, Y., Sommerschield, T., Shillingford, B., Bordbar, M., Pavlopoulos, J., Chatzipanagiotou, M., Androutsopoulos, I., Prag, J., & De Freitas, N. (2022). Restoring and attributing ancient texts using deep neural networks. *Nature, 603*(7900), 280–283. DOI: 10.1038/s41586-022-04448-z PMID: 35264762

Bahr, A. (2024). Bridges Without Foundation? Why the Use of AI Tools in Academia Needs to Build on Ethics First. *Filozofia, 79*(5), 486–500. DOI: 10.31577/filozofia.2024.79.5.2

Baker, S. (2024). AI Narratives: A History of Imaginative Thinking about Intelligent MachinesImagining AI: How the World Sees Intelligent Machines. *Poetics Today, 45*(2), 363–366. DOI: 10.1215/03335372-11093003

Baum, S. D. (2021). Artificial Interdisciplinarity: Artificial Intelligence for Research on Complex Societal Problems. *Philosophy & Technology, 34*(S1), 45–63. DOI: 10.1007/s13347-020-00416-5

Bolaños, F., Salatino, A., Osborne, F., & Motta, E. (2024). Artificial intelligence for literature reviews: Opportunities and challenges. *Artificial Intelligence Review*, *57*(10), 259. DOI: 10.1007/s10462-024-10902-3

Chan, C. K. Y. (2024). Students' perceptions of 'AI-giarism': Investigating changes in understandings of academic misconduct. *Education and Information Technologies*. Advance online publication. DOI: 10.1007/s10639-024-13151-7

Chapinal-Heras, D., & Díaz-Sánchez, C. (2024). A review of AI applications in human sciences research. *Digital Applications in Archaeology and Cultural Heritage*, *32*, e00323. DOI: 10.1016/j.daach.2024.e00323

Christou, D., & Tsoumakas, G. (2021). Extracting Semantic Relationships in Greek Literary Texts. *Sustainability (Basel)*, *13*(16), 9391. DOI: 10.3390/su13169391

Christou, P. (2023). How to Use Artificial Intelligence (AI) as a Resource, Methodological and Analysis Tool in Qualitative Research? *The Qualitative Report*. Advance online publication. DOI: 10.46743/2160-3715/2023.6406

Crafts, N. (2021). Artificial intelligence as a general-purpose technology: An historical perspective. *Oxford Review of Economic Policy*, *37*(3), 521–536. DOI: 10.1093/oxrep/grab012

Deng, L. (2018). Artificial Intelligence in the Rising Wave of Deep Learning: The Historical Path and Future Outlook [Perspectives]. *IEEE Signal Processing Magazine*, *35*(1), 180–177. DOI: 10.1109/MSP.2017.2762725

Dergaa, I., Chamari, K., Zmijewski, P., & Ben Saad, H. (2023). From human writing to artificial intelligence generated text: Examining the prospects and potential threats of ChatGPT in academic writing. *Biology of Sport*, *40*(2), 615–622. DOI: 10.5114/biolsport.2023.125623 PMID: 37077800

Dupps, W. J. (2023). Artificial intelligence and academic publishing. *Journal of Cataract and Refractive Surgery*, *49*(7), 655–656. DOI: 10.1097/j.jcrs.0000000000001223 PMID: 37390321

El-Rashidy, M. A., Mohamed, R. G., El-Fishawy, N. A., & Shouman, M. A. (2022). Reliable plagiarism detection system based on deep learning approaches. *Neural Computing & Applications*, *34*(21), 18837–18858. DOI: 10.1007/s00521-022-07486-w

Elam, M. (2023). Poetry Will Not Optimize; or, What Is Literature to AI? *American Literature*, *95*(2), 281–303. DOI: 10.1215/00029831-10575077

Elkhatat, A. M., Elsaid, K., & Almeer, S. (2023). Evaluating the efficacy of AI content detection tools in differentiating between human and AI-generated text. *International Journal for Educational Integrity*, *19*(1), 17. DOI: 10.1007/s40979-023-00140-5

Erler, A. (2023). Publish with AUTOGEN or Perish? Some Pitfalls to Avoid in the Pursuit of Academic Enhancement via Personalized Large Language Models. *The American Journal of Bioethics*, *23*(10), 94–96. DOI: 10.1080/15265161.2023.2250291 PMID: 37812096

Foka, A., & Griffin, G. (2024). AI, Cultural Heritage, and Bias: Some Key Queries That Arise from the Use of GenAI. *Heritage*, *7*(11), 6125–6136. DOI: 10.3390/heritage7110287

Franta, A., & Silver, S. (2024). Sentiment Analysis and the Sentimental Novel. *Critical Inquiry*, *50*(3), 402–424. DOI: 10.1086/728948

Ganguly, D. (2020). The Global Novel: Comparative Perspectives Introduction. *New Literary History*, *51*(2), v–xviii. DOI: 10.1353/nlh.2020.0028

Ge, L., Agrawal, R., Singer, M., Kannapiran, P., De Castro Molina, J. A., Teow, K. L., Yap, C. W., & Abisheganaden, J. A. (2024). Leveraging artificial intelligence to enhance systematic reviews in health research: Advanced tools and challenges. *Systematic Reviews*, *13*(1), 269. DOI: 10.1186/s13643-024-02682-2 PMID: 39456077

Ghio, A. (2024). Democratizing academic research with Artificial Intelligence: The misleading case of language. *Critical Perspectives on Accounting*, *98*, 102687. DOI: 10.1016/j.cpa.2023.102687

Gianitsos, E., Bolt, T., Chaudhuri, P., & Dexter, J. (2019). Stylometric Classification of Ancient Greek Literary Texts by Genre. *Proceedings of the 3rd Joint SIGHUM Workshop on Computational Linguistics for Cultural Heritage, Social Sciences, Humanities and Literature*, 52–60. DOI: 10.18653/v1/W19-2507

Gill, K. S. (2020). Strange affair of man with the machine. *AI & Society*, *35*(4), 777–782. DOI: 10.1007/s00146-020-01078-9 PMID: 33071473

Gralha, J. G., & Pimentel, A. S. (2024). Gotcha GPT: Ensuring the Integrity in Academic Writing. *Journal of Chemical Information and Modeling*, *64*(21), 8091–8097. DOI: 10.1021/acs.jcim.4c01203 PMID: 39438283

Hosseinalipour, A., & Ghanbarzadeh, R. (2023). A novel metaheuristic optimisation approach for text sentiment analysis. *International Journal of Machine Learning and Cybernetics*, *14*(3), 889–909. DOI: 10.1007/s13042-022-01670-z

Hu, L., Li, D., Liu, H., Chen, X., Gao, Y., Huang, S., Peng, X., Zhang, X., Bai, X., Yang, H., Kong, L., Tang, J., Lu, P., Xiong, C., & Liang, H. (2024). Enhancing fairness in AI-enabled medical systems with the attribute neutral framework. *Nature Communications*, *15*(1), 8767. DOI: 10.1038/s41467-024-52930-1 PMID: 39384748

Hussain, S. A., Bresnahan, M., & Zhuang, J. (2025). The bias algorithm: How AI in healthcare exacerbates ethnic and racial disparities – a scoping review. *Ethnicity & Health*, *30*(2), 197–214. DOI: 10.1080/13557858.2024.2422848 PMID: 39488857

Kaltenbrunner, W. (2015). Scholarly Labour and Digital Collaboration in Literary Studies. *Social Epistemology*, *29*(2), 207–233. DOI: 10.1080/02691728.2014.907834

Kato, M. (2016). Humanistic Traditions, East and West: Convergence and divergence. *Educational Philosophy and Theory*, *48*(1), 23–35. DOI: 10.1080/00131857.2015.1084216

Kelly, C. J., Karthikesalingam, A., Suleyman, M., Corrado, G., & King, D. (2019). Key challenges for delivering clinical impact with artificial intelligence. *BMC Medicine*, *17*(1), 195. DOI: 10.1186/s12916-019-1426-2 PMID: 31665002

Kholodniak, O. (2023). Comparative literary theory: A cross-cultural approach to English literature. *Research Journal in Advanced Humanities*, *4*(4). Advance online publication. DOI: 10.58256/rjah.v4i4.1317

Kumar Pandey, A., & Sekhar Roy, S. (2024). Extractive Question Answering Over Ancient Scriptures Texts Using Generative AI and Natural Language Processing Techniques. *IEEE Access : Practical Innovations, Open Solutions*, *12*, 101197–101209. DOI: 10.1109/ACCESS.2024.3431282

Liu, S., Liu, C., & Lang, C. (2024). Consumer Engagement in Fashion Circularity in China: Exploring Consumer Online Fashion Resale through the Lens of Social Practice Theory. *Sustainability (Basel)*, *16*(11), 4733. DOI: 10.3390/su16114733

Lo, K., Chang, J. C., Head, A., Bragg, J., Zhang, A. X., Trier, C., Anastasiades, C., August, T., Authur, R., Bragg, D., Bransom, E., Cachola, I., Candra, S., Chandrasekhar, Y., Chen, Y.-S., Cheng, E. Y.-Y., Chou, Y., Downey, D., Evans, R., & Weld, D. S. (2024). The Semantic Reader Project. *Communications of the ACM*, *67*(10), 50–61. DOI: 10.1145/3659096

Luo, J. (2024). Research on Reconstruction and Cultural Inheritance of Ancient Literature under Digital Expression. *Applied Mathematics and Nonlinear Sciences*, *9*(1), 20242591. DOI: 10.2478/amns-2024-2591

Mehta, V., Thomas, V., & Mathur, A. (2024). AI-dependency in scientific writing. *Oral Oncology Reports*, *10*, 100269. DOI: 10.1016/j.oor.2024.100269

Moretti, G., Sprugnoli, R., Menini, S., & Tonelli, S. (2016). ALCIDE: Extracting and visualising content from large document collections to support humanities studies. *Knowledge-Based Systems, 111*, 100–112. DOI: 10.1016/j.knosys.2016.08.003

Pan, Y. (2024). Exploring the Subjectivity of English Academic Discourse in the Context of Big Data. *Applied Mathematics and Nonlinear Sciences, 9*(1), 20240489. DOI: 10.2478/amns-2024-0489

Parker, J. L., Richard, V. M., Acabá, A., Escoffier, S., Flaherty, S., Jablonka, S., & Becker, K. P. (2024). Negotiating Meaning with Machines: AI's Role in Doctoral Writing Pedagogy. *International Journal of Artificial Intelligence in Education*. Advance online publication. DOI: 10.1007/s40593-024-00425-x

Pesovski, I., Santos, R., Henriques, R., & Trajkovik, V. (2024). Generative AI for Customizable Learning Experiences. *Sustainability (Basel), 16*(7), 3034. DOI: 10.3390/su16073034

Pividori, M., & Greene, C. S. (2024). A publishing infrastructure for Artificial Intelligence (AI)-assisted academic authoring. *Journal of the American Medical Informatics Association : JAMIA, 31*(9), 2103–2113. DOI: 10.1093/jamia/ocae139 PMID: 38879443

Revell, T., Yeadon, W., Cahilly-Bretzin, G., Clarke, I., Manning, G., Jones, J., Mulley, C., Pascual, R. J., Bradley, N., Thomas, D., & Leneghan, F. (2024). ChatGPT versus human essayists: An exploration of the impact of artificial intelligence for authorship and academic integrity in the humanities. *International Journal for Educational Integrity, 20*(1), 18. DOI: 10.1007/s40979-024-00161-8

Sabri, N., Sadeghian, S., & Bahrak, B. (2020). A cross-country study on cultural similarities based on book preferences. *Social Network Analysis and Mining, 10*(1), 86. DOI: 10.1007/s13278-020-00695-y

Sarker, S., Susarla, A., Gopal, R., & Thatcher, J. B. (2024). Democratizing knowledge creation through human-AI collaboration in academic peer review. *Journal of the Association for Information Systems*, (1), 158-171. DOI: 10.1007/s13278-020-00695-y

Schwitzgebel, E. (2023). AI systems must not confuse users about their sentience or moral status. *Patterns (New York, N.Y.), 4*(8), 100818. DOI: 10.1016/j.patter.2023.100818 PMID: 37602213

Shah, P. S., & Acharya, G. (2024). Artificial intelligence/machine learning and journalology: Challenges and opportunities. *Acta Obstetricia et Gynecologica Scandinavica, 103*(2), 196–198. DOI: 10.1111/aogs.14772 PMID: 38284152

Shao, Z., Zhao, R., Yuan, S., Ding, M., & Wang, Y. (2022). Tracing the evolution of AI in the past decade and forecasting the emerging trends. *Expert Systems with Applications*, *209*, 118221. DOI: 10.1016/j.eswa.2022.118221

Sinn, D., & Soares, N. (2014). Historians' use of digital archival collections: The web, historical scholarship, and archival research. *Journal of the Association for Information Science and Technology*, *65*(9), 1794–1809. DOI: 10.1002/asi.23091

Song, W., Zhao, C., & Liu, L. (2019). Multi-Task Learning for Authorship Attribution via Topic Approximation and Competitive Attention. *IEEE Access : Practical Innovations, Open Solutions*, *7*, 177114–177121. DOI: 10.1109/ACCESS.2019.2957152

Sperlich, B., Düking, P., Leppich, R., & Holmberg, H.-C. (2023). Strengths, weaknesses, opportunities, and threats associated with the application of artificial intelligence in connection with sport research, coaching, and optimization of athletic performance: A brief SWOT analysis. *Frontiers in Sports and Active Living*, *5*, 1258562. DOI: 10.3389/fspor.2023.1258562 PMID: 37920303

Suissa, O., Elmalech, A., & Zhitomirsky-Geffet, M. (2022). Text analysis using deep neural networks in digital humanities and information science. *Journal of the Association for Information Science and Technology*, *73*(2), 268–287. DOI: 10.1002/asi.24544

Sula, C. A., & Hill, H. V. (2019). The early history of digital humanities: An analysis of Computers and the Humanities (1966–2004) and Literary and Linguistic Computing (1986–2004). *Digital Scholarship in the Humanities*, fqz072. DOI: 10.1093/llc/fqz072

Tecuci, G. (2012). Artificial intelligence. *Wiley Interdisciplinary Reviews: Computational Statistics*, *4*(2), 168–180. DOI: 10.1002/wics.200

Tomczyk, P., Brüggemann, P., & Vrontis, D. (2024). AI meets academia: Transforming systematic literature reviews. *EuroMed Journal of Business*. Advance online publication. DOI: 10.1108/EMJB-03-2024-0055

Tumbe, C. (2019). Corpus linguistics, newspaper archives and historical research methods. *Journal of Management History*, *25*(4), 533–549. DOI: 10.1108/JMH-01-2018-0009

Van Der Sommen, F., & De Groof, J. (2024). Risks and rewards of AI democratization. *United European Gastroenterology Journal*, *12*(4), 427–428. DOI: 10.1002/ueg2.12560 PMID: 38526950

Villegas-Ch, W., García-Ortiz, J., & Sánchez-Viteri, S. (2024). Personalization of Learning: Machine Learning Models for Adapting Educational Content to Individual Learning Styles. *IEEE Access : Practical Innovations, Open Solutions*, *12*, 121114–121130. DOI: 10.1109/ACCESS.2024.3452592

Wang, Q., Liu, C., & Lan, S. (2023). Digital literacy and financial market participation of middle-aged and elderly adults in China. *Economic and Political Studies*, *11*(4), 441–468. DOI: 10.1080/20954816.2022.2115191

Wise, B., Emerson, L., Van Luyn, A., Dyson, B., Bjork, C., & Thomas, S. E. (2024). A scholarly dialogue: Writing scholarship, authorship, academic integrity and the challenges of AI. *Higher Education Research & Development*, *43*(3), 578–590. DOI: 10.1080/07294360.2023.2280195

Yeo, M. A. (2023). Academic integrity in the age of Artificial Intelligence (AI) authoring apps. *TESOL Journal*, *14*(3), e716. DOI: 10.1002/tesj.716

Zhai, X. (2024). An analysis of the value and linguistic features of contemporary literary texts based on knowledge graph. *Applied Mathematics and Nonlinear Sciences*, *9*(1), 20240493. DOI: 10.2478/amns-2024-0493

Zohny, H., McMillan, J., & King, M. (2023). Ethics of generative AI. *Journal of Medical Ethics*, *49*(2), 79–80. DOI: 10.1136/jme-2023-108909 PMID: 36693706

Chapter 2
Challenges in Ensuring Originality and Authenticity in AI-Generated Works

Elisabeth Ngestirosa Endang Woro Kasih
https://orcid.org/0000-0003-0565-0611
Universitas Teknokrat Indonesia, Indonesia

Kristiawan Indriyanto
https://orcid.org/0000-0001-7827-2506
Universitas Prima Indonesia, Indonesia

L. D. P. Wardani
Universitas Jember, Indonesia

ABSTRACT

The increasing integration of artificial intelligence (AI) in the writing and creative process has raised significant concerns about the originality and authenticity of a literary work in the world of education. While AI-generated literary output improves efficiency, refines language, and supports the development of ideas, it also challenges traditional notions of human creativity. AI tools often rely on existing data, leading to potential replication issues and accidental plagiarism. Additionally, the absence of human experience and emotional depth in AI-generated works raises questions about their authenticity and artistic value. The study examines the ethical and academic implications of AI-generated content, emphasizing the need for critical oversight and responsible use. Educational institutions should establish clear policies to ensure AI serves as a collaborative tool rather than a substitute

DOI: 10.4018/979-8-3373-6330-1.ch002

Copyright © 2026, IGI Global Scientific Publishing. Copying or distributing in print or electronic forms without written permission of IGI Global Scientific Publishing is prohibited.

for human originality. Maintaining academic integrity and creative authenticity requires a balanced approach while maintaining the irreplaceable role of human creativity in writing.

INTRODUCTION

Artificial Intelligence (AI) has rapidly reshaped how we learn, work, and create. Since the launch of advanced models like OpenAI's GPT in 2022, AI has played an increasingly prominent role in education and writing. Accelerated by the shift to remote learning during the COVID-19 pandemic, AI tools now assist students with grammar, structure, and idea generation (Rainie, 2023; Jensen, et al 2025). A study by Malik et al (2023) found that 75% of 245 students who come from many universities in Indonesia, used AI to improve languages.. Meanwhile, based on the research done by Marzuki et al (2023), teachers unanimously agree that Ai gives a positive impact in enhancing the students' writing. This has transformed literary learning, where students use AI not only to improve their writing but also to overcome common challenges such as writer's block and organizing narratives. In short story writing, AI offers valuable support. It helps students generate plot ideas, refine language, and experiment with style (Gatt & Krahmer, 2018). Approaches like "writing with a machine-in-the-loop" (Clark et al., 2018) show how AI can enhance, rather than replace, student creativity. Instructors using platforms like Toolsaday guide students to engage critically with AI, ensuring it serves as a supportive partner, not a substitute.

AI offers key benefits for students writing short stories by enhancing rather than replacing creative processes. AI language generation helps students efficiently develop ideas and explore narrative possibilities (Gatt & Krahmer, 2018). Educators demonstrate how AI can refine concepts, improve structure, and correct grammatical errors in drafts. This collaborative approach, termed "writing with a machine-in-the-loop" (Clark et al., 2018), preserves student agency while providing technical assistance. Students maintain control over content while using AI to experiment with various writing styles, tones, and narrative techniques. Educational platforms such as "Toolsaday" integrate AI with pedagogical objectives, allowing instructors to monitor its application. This supervised methodology ensures AI functions as a supportive tool that enhances student creativity rather than substituting it.

The increasing use of AI in education raises serious concerns. Over-reliance on AI (Zhai, Wibowo, & Li, 2024; Li et al, 2024)) risks undermining learning by encouraging superficial engagement and diminishing critical thinking skills (Iskander, 2023). Furthermore, AI struggles with complex writing tasks, including constructing coherent arguments and conveying emotional nuance, which are essential for deep understanding and original thought. This may lead to formulaic writing (Navaie, Panwar, & Asino, 2024) and reduced creativity, as students might rely on AI-generated suggestions for idea generation and language refinement. The reduced creativity, thus, creates violation on the use of AI, especially the ethical use (Lee et al, 2024; Lottu et al, 2024). Additionally, digital inequality persists, as not all students have equal access to AI tools, potentially exacerbating existing educational gaps. Addressing these challenges is essential to ensure that AI complements, rather than compromises, meaningful learning.

Recent case studies on AI in higher education reveal both its potential and its challenges. A 2024 study at the University of Ljubljana showed that AI-supported adaptive learning can advance Sustainable Development Goals (SDGs), particularly by promoting gender equality through reduced bias (Ferk Savec & Jedrinović, 2024). However, it also raised concerns about quality education, as automated assessments risk diminishing critical thinking and human interaction. Similarly, a 2023 Romanian study on cloud-based AI systems improved administrative efficiency and plagiarism detection but highlighted the ethical and resource demands of maintaining secure and transparent processes (Marian et al., 2023). Pedagogical challenges are also evident. A 2024 survey at Oman College of Management and Technology found that while students valued ChatGPT for research support and accessibility (Attia & Elsawy, 2024). Many students became less motivated to engage in traditional learning and developed over-reliance on AI-generated content. These cases illustrate a key dilemma: AI enhances efficiency and access, yet may undermine core educational values. Addressing this tension requires careful, context-sensitive integration that supports learning without compromising critical engagement or academic integrity.

Ethical considerations are increasingly urgent. As AI-generated content becomes harder to detect, concerns about plagiarism and authorship have intensified. Unlike conventional plagiarism, AI-generated text often produces original phrasing, which may evade existing detection systems and blur the line between assistance and dishonesty. Universities and publishers now face pressing questions: How should AI use be disclosed? What defines original work in the AI era? Instances have already emerged of students submitting AI-generated essays without attribution, creating disputes over whether such actions constitute misconduct or acceptable use of technology. Global guidelines, such as the UNESCO Recommendation on the Ethics of Artificial Intelligence (2021), and detection tools like GPTZero (Washington, 2023), offer frameworks to address these concerns. However, these solutions are imperfect. Detection tools are fallible, and ethical frameworks remain broad, leaving educators and institutions to make difficult decisions in rapidly evolving contexts.

Educational institutions must develop clear policies to ensure AI enhances rather than replaces students' creativity in short story writing. Workshops should introduce tools like ChatGPT and Grammarly as collaborative aids, not substitutes for original thinking. While AI can support technical aspects such as grammar and structure, students should be taught to use these tools critically while preserving their unique creative voice. Lecturers play a crucial role in highlighting AI's limitations, particularly its inability to capture the subtle nuances of human emotions and narrative depth. Ethical considerations are central to this effort. Educators must address potential risks, including plagiarism and threats to academic integrity when AI-generated content goes unattributed. Students require clear and comprehensive guidance on the responsible use of AI to ensure their work remains authentic and original (Gruenhagen et al., 2024; Shah, 2023; Washington, 2023). This process demands active mentorship. Experienced lecturers should help students navigate the complex ethical landscape of AI, fostering both creative ownership and critical thinking skills. The goal is not to reject technology but to integrate it thoughtfully and responsibly into the creative writing process.

This concern becomes particularly relevant in the field of literary analysis, where interpretation and evaluation of creative works demand more than technical proficiency. Literary production and interpretation require a deep human sensitivity to cultural, emotional, and historical contexts (LeClerc, 2024; Mustofa & Hill, 2018). In literary analysis whether of poetry, prose, or drama, evaluation and meaning cannot be separated from the personal involvement and intuition of the reader (Shirley, & Langan-Fox, 1996). Challenges arise when analytical approaches are mechanical or overly rely on artificial intelligence, which risks ignoring the depth of meaning and aesthetic nuances that can only be understood through human experience. Meaningful analysis must involve a critical understanding based on the realities of life, not just data or linguistic patterns. Therefore, a balanced approach between rational thinking and emotional responses remains the main foundation in understanding and interpreting literary works as a whole.

Ultimately, AI should serve as a complementary tool, supporting rather than replacing students' creativity in the production and interpretation of literature. By balancing technological innovation with core academic values, institutions can encourage the responsible use of AI while maintaining the authenticity of literary works. As the use of AI in education evolves, it has become increasingly important to examine how students engage with these tools by enhancing learning without sacrificing originality or intellectual development. Therefore, this study aims to explore relevant theoretical frameworks and case studies regarding the ethical integration of AI in academic settings, with a particular focus on literary classrooms. The goal is to understand how AI affects student engagement with creative writing and literary analysis, ensuring that AI improves rather than undermines educational outcomes and ethical standards.

The Use of AI for Learning

The rise of artificial intelligence (AI) demands that higher education equips all students—not just those in STEM—with essential AI literacy. As AI increasingly shapes daily life, students need to understand its societal impact. Research suggests AI education should start early and continue through university (Shah, 2023). AI is used to prepare students for the modern workforce. So, universities must embed AI understanding across all disciplines. Humanities should address AI's role in literature and culture, while social sciences explore its ethical and policy implications. Broad AI literacy is crucial for future careers in fields like business, healthcare, law, and education.

Educational frameworks must now incorporate AI literacy to prepare students for our technology-driven society (Ouyang & Jiao, 2023). This literacy encompasses three essential paradigms: technical competency, ethical awareness, and critical evaluation skills. Technical competency involves fundamental data literacy and computational thinking principles.

Figure 1. Three paradigms of AI literacy (Ouyang & Jiao, 2021)

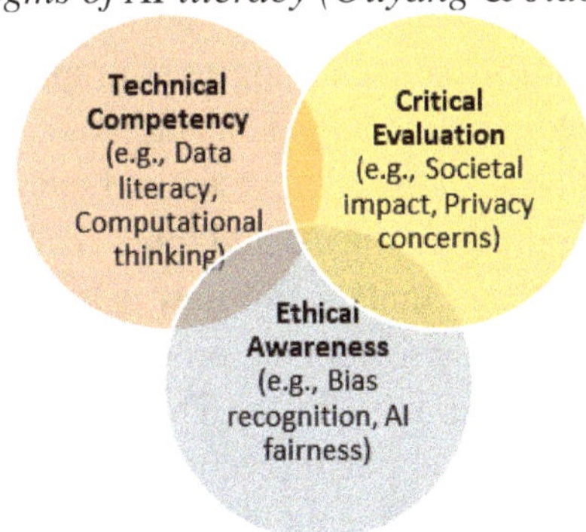

These skills enable students to comprehend the mechanisms underlying AI technologies. Ethical awareness equips students to recognize inherent biases in AI systems (Wiese et al., 2025). For instance, facial recognition technology may produce discriminatory outcomes for specific demographic groups. Critical evaluation encourages students to examine AI applications through societal lenses. This includes analyzing effects on privacy rights, personal autonomy, and equitable treatment. Social science students might investigate the implications of AI surveillance. Medical students could assess ethical considerations in AI-assisted diagnosis. The integration of these three dimensions creates a comprehensive educational approach (Gerlich, 2025). Students develop the ability to understand AI capabilities while recognizing its societal implications and limitations. This balanced perspective prepares them to engage responsibly with emerging technologies

Educational frameworks must now incorporate AI literacy to prepare students for our technology-driven society (Ouyang & Jiao, 2023). This literacy encompasses three essential dimensions: technical competency, ethical awareness, and critical evaluation skills. Technical competency involves fundamental data literacy and computational thinking principles. These skills enable students to comprehend the mechanisms underlying AI technologies. Ethical awareness equips students to recognize inherent biases in AI systems. For instance, facial recognition technology may produce discriminatory outcomes for specific demographic groups. Critical evaluation encourages students to examine AI applications through societal lenses. This includes analyzing effects on privacy rights, personal autonomy, and equitable treatment. Social science students might investigate the implications of AI surveillance. Medical students could assess ethical considerations in AI-assisted diagnosis. The integration of these three dimensions creates a comprehensive educational approach. Students develop the ability to understand AI capabilities while recognizing its societal implications and limitations. This balanced perspective prepares them to engage responsibly with emerging technologies.

As artificial intelligence transforms various sectors, students need more than surface-level familiarity with these technologies. Comprehensive AI literacy involves several interconnected competencies. Data literacy equips students to analyze and interpret the information powering AI systems. Digital literacy ensures they can effectively use technological platforms and tools (Klimova & Pikhart, 2025). Statistical literacy helps students understand how AI models process and learn from data. Computational thinking fosters the problem-solving abilities needed to approach complex AI challenges methodically. These competencies work together to prepare students for the diverse applications of AI across industries. Educational institutions that integrate these elements into their curricula enable students to engage responsibly with AI technologies.

Lecturers must present AI as a tool that enhances and does not replace human's creativity by balancing technical use with ethical guidance (Al-Zahrani, 2024). Educators responsible to foster discussion on authenticity and guide students how to use AI for their learning process. Effective use emphasizes critical thinking, academic integrity, and ethical responsibility. Educators should foster discussions on authenticity and guide students in using AI responsibly. Regular evaluations are essential to assess AI's role in learning. Surveys and work reviews help track how students use AI in writing and identify challenges. Insights from a Prose Composition class survey inform policies that promote thoughtful, ethical AI use in creative academic work. Based on the survey results, the majority of students stated that AI provides significant benefits in the early stages of the creative process, especially in brainstorming ideas (Dillon & Schaffer-Goddard, 2023). Some students revealed that tools like ChatGPT are helpful when they are stuck in ideas, by providing a variety of alternatives that can be adapted into the context of their stories (Roy & Putatunda, 2023). Additionally, AI is also considered an effective tool for improving grammar and ensuring narrative clarity in their initial drafts.

The Role of Lecturer for AI Integration

As artificial intelligence becomes increasingly embedded in higher education, lecturers play a vital role in ensuring its ethical and effective use. AI can streamline various academic tasks, from grading to supporting research through data mining, identifying gaps, and analysing large datasets (Dai, 2024; Moya & Camacho, 2024). However, while AI enhances pedagogy and efficiency, it cannot replace human judgment, particularly in cultivating critical thinking and analytical skills (Luckin et al., 2016). Lecturers must guide students in using AI responsibly while maintaining personalised, meaningful learning experiences. Individual support enables students to progress at their own pace and fosters deeper engagement (Khurma et al., 2024). Additionally, lecturers can leverage AI to improve course content and address diverse student needs. By balancing technological integration with pedagogical values, they remain central to shaping quality education in the AI era.

Promoting ethical AI use is essential as the technology becomes integrated into higher education. Lecturers must address issues such as algorithmic bias, data privacy, and academic integrity by teaching students responsible AI use, including content verification and plagiarism prevention (Selwyn, 2019). Courses should also explore AI's broader societal impacts to foster ethical awareness. Beyond teaching, AI supports research by automating data collection, analysing texts, and refining literature reviews. Natural Language Processing (NLP) tools help faculty navigate large volumes of scholarship, allowing them to focus on generating new insights and advancing theory. However, faculty readiness remains uneven. A 2023 study of 465 Saudi Arabian lecturers found moderate preparedness for AI integration, influenced by perceptions of AI's benefits, attitudes, and institutional support (Alnasib, 2024). These findings highlight the need for targeted training to ensure ethical, pedagogical, and research applications of AI are effectively implemented.

The lecturers who assist students in using AI in their research help them improve their analytical skills and prepare them to suit the workforce (Longo, *et al.*, 2024). By integrating AI-based research projects into their class, they can give students practical experience with machine learning algorithms, data visualisation strategies, and automated research tools. Students who receive this kind of exposure gain technical know-how and critical problem-solving skills that are becoming increasingly beneficial in many different areas, from digital humanities and environmental science to healthcare and finance. This sense of accomplishment makes lecturers feel proud and satisfied. AI helps students conduct multidisciplinary research and promotes a more comprehensive approach to problem-solving (Acuña et al., 2025; Chookaew et al., 2024). AI broadened the student's academic and professional horizons in various disciplines, such as linguistic studies, social behaviour analysis, and climate modelling.

AI also contributes to better assessment and feedback systems. Autonomous assessment systems, immediate feedback tools, and even AI-driven performance evaluations all have the potential to assist in keeping a greater focus on the growth of their students. These technologies allow for personalized teaching strategies that tackle the specific requirements of every student by noticing learning gaps. Lecturers must monitor the AI test to guarantee impartiality, exactity, and significance, and lecturers must continue to exercise monitoring. Additionally, integrating AI-based formative assessments provides continuous learning improvements and offers students timely insights into their academic performance.

Finally, lecturers serve as a conduit between technology advancements and instructive concepts. In order to meet the demands of the advancements and update training plans appropriately, enhancing artificial intelligence in the classroom requires finding the ideal mix between cutting-edge technology and successful teaching techniques (Valdivieso & González, 2025). AI literacy professional development programs allow lecturers to apply AI effectively without abandoning traditional teaching concepts. Partnering with AI specialists and instructional designers can also help design innovative instructional methods that maximise the capabilities of AI while ensuring extensive student involvement (Holmes et al., 2019).

Another essential consideration is the readiness of the digital instruments. Indeed, AI has the strength to democratise education by making learning resources more widely available, but different technological infrastructures and digital literacy access might create imbalanced learning opportunities. Students from underprivileged backgrounds may face challenges accessing AI-driven educational tools due to limited internet connectivity or inadequate device availability. Therefore, to stop growing educational inequity, all higher education institutions must implement rules that support fair access to AI-enhanced learning activities.

Figure 2. AI in higher education

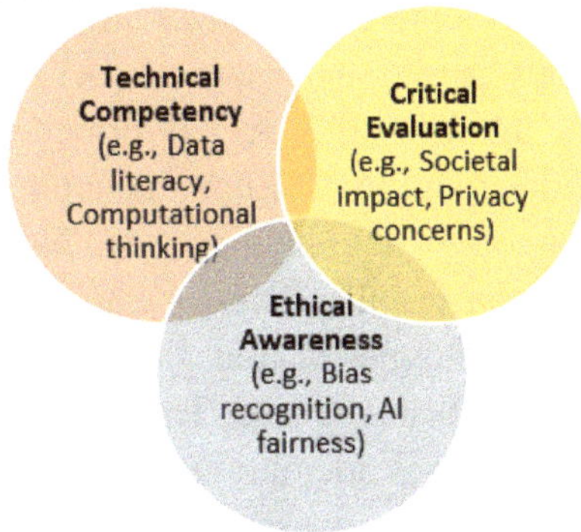

Institutions must take a new strategy and structural approach to adopt AI technologies. Ensuring all members get necessary training to incorporate these tools into their teaching methods. Implementing continuous professional development programs is necessary to assist lecturers in realising the potential, constraints, and optimal approaches for utilising artificial intelligence in the classroom. Training should emphasise maintaining the human-centred aspects of learning, ensuring that AI complements, not replace, the traditional teaching methods (Woolf et al., 2018). The institutions can enhance the effectiveness of AI-driven learning experiences while preserving the critical role of human interaction in education by training educators.

Ethical Use of AI Integration for Academic Environment

The integration of Artificial Intelligence (AI) in the academic environment has a significant impact on the way people learn, teach, and research. AI can be used to improve learning personalization, help analyze research data, and support a more efficient education administration system (Agbor et al, 2024; Khalifa, & Albadawy, 2024; Lukman & Aisy, 2023). However, along with these benefits, there are also ethical challenges that must be taken seriously. The ethical use of AI in academia means ensuring that technology is used responsibly and does not ignore the basic values of education, such as academic honesty, fair access, and the protection of personal data of students and lecturers (Ajiye & Omokhabi, 2025; Singh & Kaur, 2024). It is important to prevent the misuse of AI, for example in the form of automatic plagiarism, algorithmic discrimination in the selection process, or privacy violations in the collection of learning data. In addition, there should be clear guidelines to ensure that the application of AI in academia does not undermine the human aspects of education, such as critical thinking and personal interaction, which are critical to a holistic learning experience. Therefore, AI ethics in the academic world are essential to maintain integrity and fairness in the development of this technology (Lee, 2024). Applying these principles can prevent negative impacts that can harm specific individuals or groups, as well as ensure that AI is used responsibly. With clear ethical guidelines, the application of AI can provide maximum benefits for all parties in the world of education. In addition, the application of this ethics also serves to ensure that AI technology not only benefits a handful of people, but also has an equitable positive impact for all parties. In this context, educational institutions need to prioritize the principles of transparency and accountability in the use of AI so that this technology is not abused. Therefore, policies and regulations governing the application of AI in academia must be constantly updated to align with technological developments and emerging ethical challenges.

Ethics in college in academia includes a set of moral principles that help distinguish between right and wrong (Matahce, 2021). Ethics in artificial intelligence (AI) focuses on how to optimize the positive impact of these technologies while reducing the risks and adverse impacts that can arise. In AI development, the academic community often refers to the Belmont Report (Serpico, 2024; Sim & Cassel, 2024), which outlines three key principles: 1) respect for individuals, emphasizing autonomy and informed consent; 2) beneficence, grounded in the "do no harm" principle, preventing AI misuse like reinforcing bias or discrimination; and 3) justice, ensuring fair distribution of AI's benefits and burdens. In addition, UNESCO (2021) also issued recommendations on AI ethics in 2021, focusing on four key values: human rights and human dignity, living in peaceful societies, ensuring diversity and inclusivity, and supporting environmental and ecosystem sustainability (AllahRakha, 2024).

In the context of colleges, the application of these ethical principles is critical to maintaining academic integrity and ensuring that the use of AI remains respectful of the fundamental values of education, such as fairness, freedom, and transparency. Therefore, technology must be used with care and responsibility to improve the quality of education without sacrificing fundamental ethical principles. In addition, global guidelines such as those from UNESCO and proven ethical principles such as the Belmont Report can be used as a reference for building a more universal and sustainable approach to ethics in higher education. These principles are not only relevant in the academic environment, but they are also crucial in the application of AI to the broader information technology system, where ethical challenges are becoming increasingly complex and urgent.

The rapid advancement of artificial intelligence (AI) technology has raised various social, ethical, and legal concerns, particularly in its use in information technology (IT) systems. Therefore, a solid ethical framework is needed as a guide in the development and application of AI responsibly. The conceptual framework offered by Lottu et al. (2024) emphasizes the importance of integrating ethical values at every stage of the AI lifecycle—from design, implementation, implementation, to maintenance. AI is seen as a social-technical artifact that can have a far-reaching impact on individuals, communities, and society as a whole. Key values within this framework include transparency, accountability, fairness, privacy, and security. Transparency is necessary so that AI processes and decisions can be understood by all stakeholders. Accountability is a major concern, especially in ensuring that there is an accountability mechanism for the results of AI systems. Ali et al. (2024) in the study explores students' understanding of the ethical use of AI in an educational context. In general, students have a basic awareness of ethics, especially about the importance of giving credit to original sources and authors. However, their understanding is still limited regarding other ethical dilemmas. Many participants admitted to using AI in their tasks with slight modifications. The focus group discussion showed that individual accountability and responsibility were the most prominent themes. Students realize that even though AI generates answers, users are still responsible for how those results are used. Examples such as deep fake technology are used to explain the dangers of AI abuse and the importance of protecting safety and justice.

Therefore, it is important to strengthen a thorough ethical understanding among AI users and developers. Justice demands a reduction in bias against certain groups, while privacy and security are crucial to protect personal data and prevent exploitation of the system. The framework as a whole aims to equip developers, policymakers, and organizations to steer AI development ethically, in line with human values and social justice. By integrating this conceptual framework in an academic context, educational institutions can strengthen AI supervision and control systems to remain aligned with the human values that are at the core of the educational process.

There must be a serious concern about the use of AI for students, especially in the academic world . The powerful apps are offered to help and solve academic problems. If students do not know the boundaries of using the AI, they will be trapped in a plagiarism situation. In order to control and limit the AI, the teacher must guide and direct students. This includes providing clear instructions about when and how AI tools can be used ethically, as well as educating students on the importance of originality and academic honesty. Moreover, institutions should support teachers by creating policies that promote responsible use of technology and encourage critical thinking rather than full reliance on AI. Additionally, it is important for schools or universities to organize specialized training or digital literacy sessions that discuss the ethical use of AI, so that students can understand the legal and moral consequences of the misuse of this technology. With proper supervision and collaboration between educators and students, AI can be leveraged as a learning tool that supports creativity, not a replacement for it. Without clear direction and control, the risk of AI dependence and declining critical thinking skills among students will be greater.

The Ethical Use of AI in Literature Class

Integrating artificial intelligence (AI) into literary learning offers significant opportunities to enhance the educational experience. Recent advancements have expanded AI's potential to support teaching and learning in literature. In creative writing, AI can generate ideas, suggest sentences, and propose innovative story structures, which is especially helpful for students facing writer's block or seeking to explore various literary styles (Kasih et al., 2024). Additionally, AI provides valuable feedback, helping students refine their work. Beyond writing support, AI contributes to literary analysis by identifying themes, motifs, and narrative patterns that may be difficult for novice readers to detect. This enables students to recognize intertextual relationships and uncover deeper meanings in both classical and contemporary texts. Furthermore, AI promotes personalized learning by adapting materials to individual needs. AI-based systems can identify students' weaknesses and offer targeted exercises, while also presenting advanced learners with greater challenges to further develop their skills.

The insights gained from AI analysis can enrich class discussions and deepen students' understanding of literary works. Teachers can use the results of AI analysis as a starting point for discussion, helping students understand the complexity of literary works from multiple perspectives. This approach not only broadens students' understanding of literature but also develops their critical thinking abilities. AI also makes literature more accessible to different types of learners. Through text-to-speech technology, students with reading difficulties can listen to literary works. Meanwhile, AI translation tools allow students to explore literary works from different cultures and languages that they may not have been able to access before. The integration of AI in literary learning opens up exciting new opportunities for educators and students. By harnessing the power of AI as a support tool, teachers can create richer, more immersive, and personalized learning experiences. However, it's important to remember that AI is supposed to serve as a complement, not a replacement, to human guidance and insight in appreciating the beauty and complexity of literature.

More than just an analysis tool, AI has also been proven to be able to improve critical thinking skills in literary studies. An eight-week intervention study found that the use of AI significantly improved critical thinking skills in English-language literature classes for EFL learners (Liu & Wang, 2024). These findings suggest that AI can enrich learning experiences as well as provide insights for educators and policymakers in designing culturally responsive and pedagogically effective AI-based strategies. This shows that the integration of AI not only helps literary comprehension but also strengthens students' analytical abilities in interpreting and evaluating literary texts.

The use of AI in literary learning raises serious ethical concerns, especially about originality, authorship, and the preservation of human creativity (Setiawan et al, 2024). The study from Setiawan (2024) found that the literary scholars in Indonesia concluded They recognize the impact of AI on literary values and traditions, yet they also acknowledge its potential to broaden access to literature. They also suggested that to harness AI effectively in producing high-quality and meaningful literary works, there can be collaboration between humans and AI. However, supported by clear ethical guidelines and regulations is essential. Jones (2022) challenges traditional notions of authorship and raises questions about who deserves credit for creative work. Students using AI tools may unintentionally cross ethical boundaries, as the distinction between inspiration and appropriation becomes blurred. Furthermore, AI-generated writing lacks the emotional depth and intuitive resonance that come from human experience. Literary works shaped predominantly by algorithms risk becoming formulaic and disconnected from authentic human expression. For educators, this creates a dilemma. Should AI be accepted as a co-author, or treated only as a tool? Rather than viewing AI as a substitute for human creativity, it should be framed as a prompt for critical reflection. Students must be encouraged to question how technology influences their ideas and how they can maintain their creative voice amid automated suggestions. Ethical literary learning, therefore, involves not only producing texts but also developing an awareness of AI's limitations and the value of human-centered expression (Brown & Green, 2024).

In addition to ethical issues, AI-generated content introduces complex legal challenges related to copyright and authorship. Current laws generally do not recognize AI as an author, placing responsibility on the human user. However, when AI-generated content is integrated into student work, determining the boundaries of ownership and originality becomes difficult. Without clear attribution, students may unintentionally commit plagiarism by presenting AI-generated ideas as their own. To address this risk, institutions must establish explicit attribution policies. These should require students to disclose any AI assistance in introductions, footnotes, or acknowledgments (Gruenhagen et al., 2024). Such transparency protects both academic integrity and students from accidental misconduct. While detection tools like GPTZero and Turnitin's AI detection feature can help monitor AI usage, they have limitations. Advanced AI can evade detection, and false positives risk unfair accusations against students who write independently. Therefore, detection alone is not enough. Educators must combine technological solutions with clear guidelines and instructional support. By teaching students when and how to cite AI contributions, universities can ensure that legal expectations are understood and met. This balanced approach upholds fairness, preserves trust, and clarifies the place of AI in academic writing.

In literary education, integrating AI introduces new pedagogical opportunities. Students can explore human-machine collaboration, analyze AI-generated texts, and examine narrative patterns in classical literature. This approach not only modernizes the study of literature but also prepares students for a cultural landscape increasingly shaped by technology. However, alongside these benefits, AI raises serious concerns about authenticity and the intrinsic value of literary works. When machines are capable of generating Shakespeare-like sonnets or Hemingway-style prose, educators and students must reconsider what defines creativity. Is the worth of a literary work found in its linguistic beauty, or in the human experience it conveys? Such questions have become central to discussions in contemporary literature classrooms, where debates about originality and authorship now intersect with technological possibilities. Against this backdrop, the role of AI in literature classes can be framed through three key perspectives: as a tool for analysis, a partner in creation, and a subject of critical debate.

Figure 3. AI in literature learning

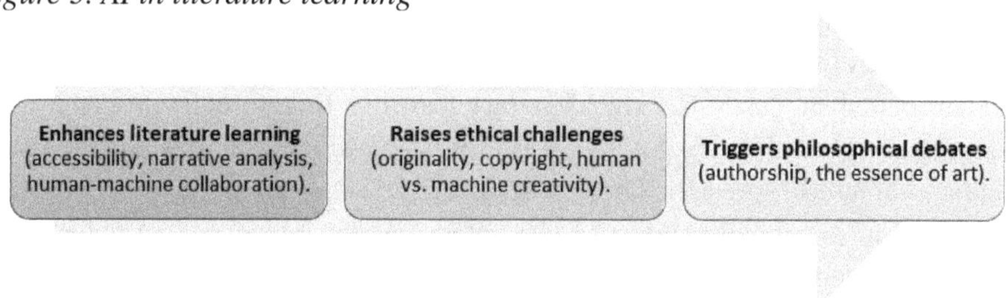

The convergence of artificial intelligence and literature demands a redefinition of literacy in the 21st century. Reading and writing are no longer confined to traditional texts but now encompass the ability to navigate, interpret, and collaborate with algorithmic systems. As critical engagement with technology becomes as indispensable as the appreciation of literary classics, the role of educators is increasingly pivotal. They are tasked with bridging literary traditions and digital innovations, while fostering ethical, aesthetic, and intellectual discourse within digital contexts. In guiding students to balance technological efficiency with reflective inquiry, educators help preserve literature's humanistic core. AI, therefore, does not displace literary meaning but broadens its horizons, offering new modes of expression and interpretation while maintaining human experience as central. In this evolving landscape, AI emerges as both an object of study and a partner in inquiry, reshaping literary engagement and redefining our relationship with intelligent technologies.

Literary Writing Production Using AI: Advantage and Risk

This study explores students' attitudes toward using artificial intelligence (AI) tools to support their writing skills. It examines how frequently students rely on AI in academic assignments, how this technology influences their writing abilities, and how they perceive its advantages and risks. Findings indicate that AI is commonly used in various writing tasks, raising important questions about its impact on students' development as writers. In particular, the study investigates how students balance the convenience of AI with the need to maintain originality and ethical writing practices.

AI-driven creativity support tools (AI-CSTs) have transformed literary production by enhancing various stages of the writing process, from idea generation to revision (Ning et al., 2023). These tools occupy a broad spectrum, ranging from assistive applications that support human creativity to more autonomous systems capable of generating original content. In educational contexts, AI tools such as ChatGPT, Grammarly, and QuillBot have become popular for helping students formulate ideas, improve grammar, and receive instant feedback (Kasih et al., 2024). While these technologies offer clear benefits, including increased efficiency and support during planning and revision, they also raise concerns. Studies indicate that overreliance on AI may reduce students' critical thinking, creativity, and understanding of language structures (Darwin et al., 2024; Kim et al., 2021). As AI increasingly blurs the boundaries between human and machine contributions, educators and students must navigate its use carefully. The challenge lies in balancing AI's potential to enhance writing with the need to preserve independent thinking and the human dimensions of creativity.

Recent scholarship has examined the ethical implications of AI in literature from two perspectives: its representation in literary works and its use in literary production (Saddhono et al., 2024). Depictions of AI as either benevolent or malevolent influence public perceptions and raise questions about agency, personhood, and accountability. These narratives shape attitudes toward AI and impose ethical responsibilities on authors. When AI becomes a co-creator, further concerns arise regarding authorship, creativity, and authenticity. Writers and publishers must address issues of attribution, human input, and transparency. Central to these debates is whether creativity remains uniquely human. This tension is especially relevant in fiction and poetry, where readers value authentic human expression.

AI in Literary Writing Production

In a study (Kasih, *et al*, 2024) conducted on students of the literature production course, there were several questions asked regarding the use of AI in the writing process, ranging from the frequency of use, perceived benefits, to its impact on students' creativity and writing skills.

1. How often do you use AI tools during the writing process (e.g., in brainstorming, drafting, revision)?
2. At what stage in the writing process do you use AI tools the most?
3. What are your main reasons for using AI tools in writing?
4. Do you feel that the use of AI tools has improved your writing skills over time?
5. How confident are you in writing without using AI tools?
6. Do you think AI tools should be integrated into learning to write?
7. What are your concerns (if any) regarding the use of AI in writing?
8. How do you ensure that your writing remains original even when using AI?
9. How can you reduce your reliance on AI tools while still improving your writing skills?

The study shows that students use AI to varying degrees during the writing process. Although most are not fully dependent on it, some rely heavily on AI for developing ideas and drafting frameworks. AI is most commonly used in the brainstorming and planning stages, where it helps generate ideas and organize writing structures. These findings highlight AI's role as a facilitator, enhancing efficiency and creativity. Students report that AI assists in overcoming writer's block and offers new perspectives they might not have considered. However, despite these benefits, students retain primary control over content creation, indicating that AI functions more as a support tool than a replacement for core writing skills.

Students primarily use AI to overcome idea blocks and improve technical aspects of writing, such as grammar and syntax. This reflects AI's dual role in supporting creativity and enhancing technical accuracy. In creative writing, AI provides an initial boost when starting is difficult, while in technical writing, it offers guidance to improve language quality. These findings highlight AI's broader educational role as both a creative partner and a tool for immediate feedback. Rather than serving merely as an automation device, AI helps students address limitations in their literacy skills. However, to ensure balanced development, AI integration must be complemented by conventional teaching methods that promote independent writing abilities.

In terms of its impact on writing skills, most college students recognize the benefits of AI, though to varying degrees. Some find it highly effective in improving the quality of their writing, while others view its contribution as more limited. AI's ability to offer instant feedback, suggest vocabulary, and correct grammar is often cited as particularly helpful. However, an important concern is students' confidence in writing without AI support. Although the technology is seen as useful, some students report feeling less assured when composing independently, suggesting a growing dependence. This reliance may hinder the development of essential writing skills, such as generating original ideas and refining drafts through personal revision.

Students' attitudes toward AI in literature classes are mixed. Many acknowledge its benefits in improving writing efficiency and quality, particularly in organizing ideas and refining language. However, concerns remain about its potential to diminish creativity and originality. Some students worry that excessive reliance on AI may erode the personal voice and individuality in their work. While AI is valued as a useful tool in the creative process, there is broad recognition of the need to balance technology use with the development of independent writing skills and authentic expression.

The study demonstrates that AI has become integral to students' writing processes, aiding idea generation and improving writing quality. While its benefits are evident, concerns persist about dependency and diminished creativity. As AI continues to advance, educational institutions must establish clear guidelines and promote responsible use to prevent undermining independent writing skills. The findings also reveal varied usage based on proficiency: more skilled writers use AI to refine their work, while less confident students rely on it to structure ideas. This highlights the essential role of educators in guiding effective and balanced AI use, ensuring it supports rather than replaces authentic writing development.

Response on Ethical Use of AI in Literary Writing

The survey responses reveal a prevailing skepticism toward AI-generated writing, particularly in terms of originality, ethical considerations, and its impact on creative value. Many respondents expressed concerns about the lack of human perspective in AI-generated writing and emphasized the importance of transparency when using AI in literary works. Below is a detailed breakdown of the key findings:

Table 1. Responses of Ethical Use on AI

Question	Most Common Response (%)	Second Most Common Response (%)	Third Most Common Response (%)
Can AI-generated writing be considered original?	Disagree (42.9%)	Strongly Disagree (20%)	Neutral (8%)
Does AI-generated writing lack human perspective?	Agree (48.6%)	Strongly Agree (25.7%)	Neutral (7%)
Does AI reduce the value of a written work?	Agree (40%)	Disagree (35%)	Neutral (6%)
Is the use of AI in creative fiction ethically acceptable?	Disagree (40%)	Agree (34.3%)	Neutral (9%)
What defines originality in the AI era?	Human perspective and experience (51.4%)	Combination of new ideas (32.9%)	The creative process itself (8%)
What are the acceptable limits of AI use in writing?	Using AI for research and idea generation but writing independently (48.6%)	Using AI only for editing and proofreading (35%)	Neutral (7%)

The survey reveals a strong skepticism toward AI-generated writing, particularly regarding originality and human perspective. A significant 42.9% of respondents disagreed that AI-generated writing could be considered original, with 20% strongly disagreeing. This suggests that many people believe true originality stems from human creativity, emotions, and lived experiences—elements AI lacks. The strong disagreement implies that AI-generated content is often perceived as derivative rather than inventive, as it relies on pre-existing data rather than novel, independent thought. This perspective aligns with broader concerns in creative industries, where originality is often tied to personal experiences and unique artistic expression. Similarly, 48.6% of respondents agreed that AI-generated writing lacks a human perspective, with 25.7% strongly agreeing. This reinforces the idea that while AI can mimic language patterns, it struggles to capture deep emotions, cultural nuances, and real-world experiences.

The emphasis on the "human perspective" suggests that people see constructing a story or creating a literary production more than just composing words. Creating literary works requires an understanding of complex emotions, personal history, and social contexts. AI's reliance on pattern recognition and statistical predictions means that AI lacks the intuition and emotional intelligence that make up human narratives. As a result, AI-generated writing may feel hollow or mechanical, even if it's grammatically and structurally sound. This skepticism highlights a fundamental question in the evolving relationship between AI and creativity. Can an original literary work exist without human emotions and experiences? While AI can help generate ideas and refine text, these findings suggest that many still believe that writing is an inherent human tenacity in creating things, driven by personal insight and subjective interpretation (Watters & Lemanski, 2023). This could explain why AI is more widely accepted as a tool for help than as an independent creative force.

Opinions on AI's impact on the value of written work remain divided. While 40% of respondents believe AI reduces the worth of writing, 35% disagree. This division reflects a nuanced view of AI's role in creative writing. On one hand, critics argue that AI-generated content diminishes artistic and intellectual value by automating the process and reducing reliance on human creativity. There are concerns that widespread AI use could lead to an oversupply of derivative works, eroding appreciation for authentic human storytelling. Furthermore, some fear that AI may undermine individual authorship, making creative expression appear more mechanical than personal. In contrast, others see AI as a valuable enhancement. For this group, AI improves efficiency, refines grammar and style, and speeds up research without compromising quality. By automating routine tasks, it allows writers to focus on creativity and narrative development. Additionally, AI can democratize writing by enabling individuals with limited skills to communicate more effectively (Gültekin Talayhan & Babayiğit, 2023). This perspective views AI not as a threat, but as a tool that broadens access to content creation.

Ethical concerns surrounding AI-generated fiction remain sharply divided. While 40% of respondents believe such works are ethically unacceptable, 34.3% view them as acceptable, highlighting an ongoing debate shaped by views on fairness, authenticity, and artistic integrity. Critics argue that AI-generated fiction challenges the notion of authorship and creativity, traditionally seen as personal and human-driven. Since AI lacks conscious intent and emotional experience, its stories may be viewed as superficial recombinations rather than genuine creative works. Additionally, some worry that AI enables mass production of content with minimal effort, undermining the labor of human authors. The risk of inadvertent plagiarism, where AI-generated texts resemble existing works, adds further ethical complexity.

Conversely, those who accept AI-generated fiction often view the technology as an extension of modern storytelling rather than a threat. From this perspective, AI enhances creativity by helping writers generate ideas, overcome writer's block, and experiment with new narrative forms. Supporters contend that responsible use of AI does not replace human creativity but expands its possibilities. As AI becomes increasingly integrated into various industries, its role in creative writing may be seen as part of a broader technological evolution.

When asked about originality in the AI era, 51.4% of respondents identified human perspective and experience as essential, while 32.9% believed originality arises from a combination of new ideas. These findings reinforce the view that AI, despite its text-generating capabilities, lacks the depth of human experience, underscoring that true originality is rooted in subjective interpretation and lived realities. At the same time, the 32.9% who valued the fusion of ideas suggest growing acceptance of AI as a collaborator in the creative process. For them, originality is becoming a more fluid concept—one that blends computational assistance with human intuition, critical thinking, and emotional depth.

Regarding the acceptable limits of AI in writing, 48.6% favored using AI for research and idea generation while writing independently, while 35% supported AI use only for editing and proofreading. This reflects a strong preference for AI as a supportive tool rather than a creator. The fact that nearly half of the respondents preferred AI for research but not for writing indicates that while AI can enhance efficiency, it should not replace the core creative process. These data suggest that while AI can be beneficial in certain aspects of writing, many respondents believe its role should be limited, especially in preserving originality, ethical standards, and human insight. The strong demand for transparency and a cautious approach to AI's creative capabilities indicate that, despite its growing presence in literature, AI is still seen as a tool rather than an author.

Further analysis of these preferences reflects a broader societal tension between embracing technological advancement and preserving human artistry. While many value AI's efficiency and convenience, there remains a strong belief in the irreplaceable nature of human creativity. Concerns about transparency, bias, and ethical dilemmas in AI-generated content further highlight the need for responsible integration. Acceptance of AI also appears to vary across demographics. Younger generations, familiar with AI technologies, tend to be more open to its use in writing, whereas experienced professionals often adopt a more cautious stance, emphasizing tradition and ethical considerations. Future research could investigate how cultural, educational, and professional backgrounds shape these differing perceptions, offering deeper insight into AI's evolving role in creative fields. It can be summarized in the picture.

Figure 4. Viewpoints on AI creativity

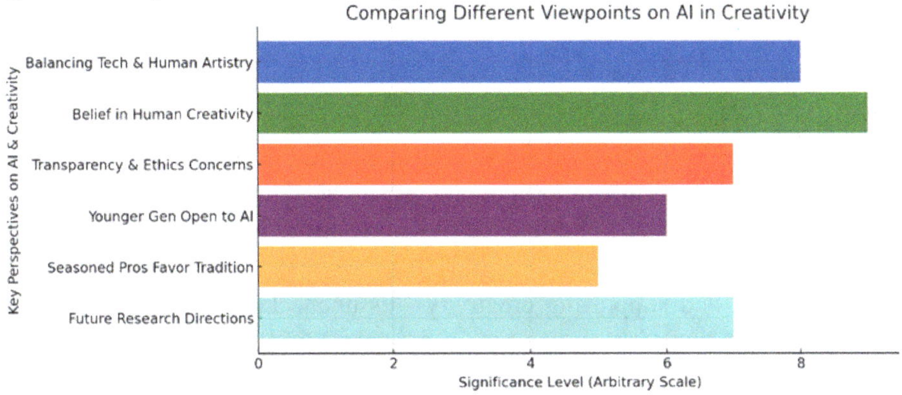

While AI can be beneficial in certain aspects of writing, many respondents believe its role should be limited, especially in preserving originality, ethical standards, and human insight. The strong demand for transparency and a cautious approach to AI's creative capabilities indicate that, despite its growing presence in literature, AI is still seen as a tool rather than an author (Clark et al., 2018). The divide in responses suggests that while efficiency and convenience are valued, there remains a deep-rooted belief in the irreplaceable nature of human creativity.

This concern ties directly into the challenges of ensuring originality and authenticity in AI-generated works. AI models are trained on vast datasets, raising questions about potential replication, unintentional plagiarism, and a lack of truly novel expression. While AI can generate text that mimics human styles, it struggles to create narratives that capture personal experiences, cultural nuances, and emotional depth in the same way a human writer can. Furthermore, as AI-generated content becomes more prevalent, distinguishing between human and machine-created works becomes increasingly difficult, heightening the need for clear ethical guidelines and regulatory measures.

The issue of authorship and intellectual property rights further complicates the landscape. If an AI-generated piece closely resembles existing work, who is responsible for potential copyright violations, the AI, the developers, or the user prompting the content? As AI continues to evolve, legal frameworks will need to adapt to address these concerns, ensuring that human creators are protected while also defining clear boundaries for AI's role in creative industries. Another important consideration is the impact of AI on human creativity itself. While AI can serve as a powerful tool for brainstorming, editing, and enhancing productivity, excessive reliance on it may lead to a decline in critical thinking and creative problem-solving skills. If writers and artists begin to depend too heavily on AI-generated ideas, the risk of homogenization in creative expression increases, potentially stifling innovation rather than fostering it.

CONCLUSION

The findings of this study underscore the urgent need for thoughtful and principled integration of artificial intelligence (AI) in education, particularly in writing and literary instruction. While AI offers clear benefits—enhancing efficiency, generating ideas, and supporting creativity—its unchecked use presents serious risks to academic integrity, authorship, and originality. Pedagogical frameworks must therefore go beyond basic tool usage. Structured learning modules should prioritize systematic AI instruction, the establishment of ethical guidelines, and the definition of best practices to ensure responsible application in creative processes. With a particular focus on literature, this module should emphasize how AI can help, not override the role of humans in the production, evaluation, and interpretation of literary texts, preserving the depth, nuance, and emotional resonance that defines meaningful literature.

Addressing these challenges requires a collaborative and multidisciplinary effort. Educators and policymakers must work together to develop regulatory and pedagogical standards that mitigate algorithmic bias, promote transparency, and protect human authorship. Without clear guidance, there is a risk that convenience will erode critical thinking and diminish the personal dimensions of academic writing. Future research should also examine how diverse cultural, educational, and disciplinary backgrounds shape perceptions of AI. In conclusion, the integration of AI into literary education must be guided by ethical awareness, critical pedagogy, and respect for human creativity. As AI becomes increasingly present in literary production and analysis, it is vital to ensure that technology complements rather than compromises the interpretive richness and cultural values embedded in literature. By embedding ethical considerations into both curriculum and practice, institutions can foster a generation of learners who engage with AI critically, responsibly, and imaginatively.

REFERENCES

Acuña, O. L., & Carvajal, D. M., Bolanos-Barbosa, Angie D., & Reyes, L. H. (2025). Fostering Technical Proficiency and Professional Skills: A Multifaceted PO-PBL Strategy for Unit Operations Education. *Education for Chemical Engineers*, *51*(1).

Agbor, U. I., Duke, O. O., Obaji-Akpet, I. O., Nwagboso, C. I., Eja, T. R., Awubi, E., & Ukume, G. D. (2024). Artificial intelligence and academic research: Understanding the potential and the threats to academic writing. *Ianna Journal of Interdisciplinary Studies*, *6*(2), 33–52. DOI: 10.5281/zenodo.11120274

Ajiye, O. T., & Omokhabi, A. A. (2025). The Potential and Ethical Issues of Artificial Intelligence in Improving Academic Writing. *ShodhAI: Journal of Artificial Intelligence*, *2*(1), 1–9. DOI: 10.29121/shodhai.v2.i1.2025.24

Al-Zahrani, A. M. (2024). Unveiling the shadows: Beyond the hype of AI in education. *Heliyon*, *10*(9), e30696. DOI: 10.1016/j.heliyon.2024.e30696 PMID: 38737255

Ali, S. B., Haider, M., Samiullah, D., & Shamsy, S. (2024, July–September). Assessing students' understanding of ethical use of artificial intelligence (AI): A focus group study. *International Journal of Social Science and Entrepreneurship*, *4*(3).

AllahRakha, N.AllahRakha. (2024). UNESCO's AI Ethics Principles: Challenges and Opportunities. *International Journal of Law and Policy*, *2*(9), 24–36. DOI: 10.59022/ijlp.225

Alnasib, B. N. M. (2023). Factors Affecting Faculty Members' Readiness to Integrate Artificial Intelligence into Their Teaching Practices: A Study from the Saudi Higher Education Context. International Journal of Learning. *Teaching and Educational Research*, *22*(8), 465–491. DOI: 10.26803/ijlter.22.8.24

Attia, S., & Elsawy, E. (2024). Higher Education Students' Perceptions and Attitudes about Using ChatGPT in Oman: A Case Study of OCMT. *International Journal of Educational Sciences and Arts*, *3*(4), 304–321. DOI: 10.59992/IJESA.2024.v3n4p8

Bengsch, G. (2024). Redefining traditional pedagogy: The integration of machine learning in the contemporary language education classroom. In Pan, F. (Ed.), *AI in language teaching, learning, and assessment* (pp. 197–214). IGI Global., DOI: 10.4018/979-8-3693-0872-1.ch010

Chookaew, S., Kitcharoen, P., Howimanporn, S., & Panjaburee, P. (2024). Fostering student competencies and perceptions through artificial intelligence of things educational platform. *Computers and Education: Artificial Intelligence*, *7*(September), 100308. DOI: 10.1016/j.caeai.2024.100308

Clark, E., Ross, A. S., Tan, C., Ji, Y., & Smith, N. A. (2018). Creative writing with a machine in the loop: Case studies on slogans and stories. *International Conference on Intelligent User Interfaces, Proceedings IUI, March*, 329–340. https://doi.org/ DOI: 10.1145/3172944.3172983

Dai, Y. (2024). Dual-contrast pedagogy for AI literacy in upper elementary schools. *Learning and Instruction*, *91*, 101899. DOI: 10.1016/j.learninstruc.2024.101899

Darwin, R., Rusdin, D., Mukminatien, N., Suryati, N., Laksmi, E. D., & Marzuki, . (2024). Critical thinking in the AI era: An exploration of EFL students' perceptions, benefits, and limitations. *Cogent Education*, *11*(1), 1–18. DOI: 10.1080/2331186X.2023.2290342

Dillon, S., & Schaffer-Goddard, J. (2023). What AI researchers read: The role of literature in artificial intelligence research. *Interdisciplinary Science Reviews*, *48*(1), 15–42. DOI: 10.1080/03080188.2022.2079214

Ferk Savec, V., & Jedrinović, S. (2024). The Role of AI Implementation in Higher Education in Achieving the Sustainable Development Goals: A Case Study from Slovenia. *Sustainability (Basel)*, *17*(1), 183. DOI: 10.3390/su17010183

Gerlich, M. (2025). AI Tools in Society: Impacts on Cognitive Offloading and the Future of Critical Thinking. *Societies (Basel, Switzerland)*, *15*(1), 6. DOI: 10.3390/soc15010006

Gruenhagen, J. H., Sinclair, P. M., Carroll, J., Baker, P. R. A., Wilson, A., & Demant, D. (2024). Computers and Education : Artificial Intelligence The rapid rise of generative AI and its implications for academic integrity: Students ' perceptions and use of chatbots for assistance with assessments. *Computers and Education: Artificial Intelligence*, *7*(November 2023), 100273. https://doi.org/DOI: 10.1016/j.caeai.2024.100273

Gültekin Talayhan, Ö., & Babayiğit, M. V. (2023). The Influence of AI Writing Tools on the Content and Organization of Students' Writing : A Focus on EFL Instructors' Perceptions T. *Current Debates in Social Sciences*, *6*(2), 83–93. DOI: 10.29228/cudes.71701

Jensen, L. X., Buhl, A., Sharma, A., & Bearman, M. (2025). Generative AI and higher education: A review of claims from the first months of ChatGPT. *Higher Education*, *89*(4), 1145–1161. DOI: 10.1007/s10734-024-01265-3

Jones, N. (2022). Experiential Literature? Comparing the Work of AI and Human Authors. *APRIA Journal*, *5*(5), 41–57. DOI: 10.37198/APRIA.04.05.a5

Kasih, E. N. E. W., Suprayogi, S., Indriyanto, K., Amarudin, A., & Putra, A. V. L. (2024). Artificial Intelligence for Literature Class : Trends and Attitude. *10th International Conference on Education and Technology (ICET)*, 142–148. https://doi.org/DOI: 10.1109/ICET64717.2024.10778422

Khalifa, M., & Albadawy, M. (2024). Using artificial intelligence in academic writing and research: An essential productivity tool. *Computer Methods and Programs in Biomedicine Update*, *5*, 100145. DOI: 10.1016/j.cmpbup.2024.100145

Khurma, O. A., Albahti, F., Ali, N., & Bustanji, A. (2024). AI ChatGPT and student engagement : Unraveling dimensions through PRISMA analysis for enhanced learning experiences. *Contemporary Educational Technology*, *16*(2), 1–22. DOI: 10.30935/cedtech/14334

Klimova, B., & Pikhart, M. (2025). Exploring the effects of artificial intelligence on student and academic well-being in higher education: A mini-review. *Frontiers in Psychology*, *16*, 1498132. DOI: 10.3389/fpsyg.2025.1498132 PMID: 39963679

LeClerc, T. (2024). Writing sensitively: Defining sensitivity in the literary sphere. *New Writing*, *21*(3), 288–298. DOI: 10.1080/14790726.2024.2325996

Lee, S. (2024). Utilizing a ChatGPT Workshop to Foster Ethical Awareness and Enhance L2 English Writing Revision Processes in University Academic Settings: ChatGPT Workshop for Effective and Ethical L2 English Writing. In Pan, F. (Ed.), *AI in language teaching, learning, and assessment* (1st ed., pp. 269–299). IGI Global. DOI: 10.4018/979-8-3693-0872-1.ch013

Li, B., Jiang, J., Ma, L., Huang, Y., & Wu, X. (2024). Mitigating university students' reliance on ChatGPT. In *Proceedings of the 2024 8th International Seminar on Education, Management and Social Sciences (ISEMSS 2024)* (pp. 245–251). Atlantis Press. https://doi.org/DOI: 10.2991/978-2-38476-297-2_31

Liu, W., & Wang, Y. (2024). The Effects of Using AI Tools on Critical Thinking in English Literature Classes Among EFL Learners: An Intervention Study. *European Journal of Education*, *59*(October), 1–12. DOI: 10.1111/ejed.12804

Longo, L., Brcic, M., Cabitza, F., Choi, J., Confalonieri, R., Del Ser, J., Guidotti, R., Hayashi, Y., Herrera, F., Holzinger, A., Jiang, R., Khosravi, H., Lecue, F., Malgieri, G., Páez, A., Samek, W., Schneider, J., Speith, T., & Stumpf, S. (2024). Explainable Artificial Intelligence (XAI) 2.0: A manifesto of open challenges and interdisciplinary research directions. *Information Fusion*, *106*, 102301. DOI: 10.1016/j.inffus.2024.102301

Lottu, O. A., Jacks, B. S., Ajala, O. A., & Okafor, E. S. (2024). Towards a conceptual framework for ethical AI development in IT systems. *World Journal of Advanced Research and Reviews, 21*(3), 408–415.

Lukman, R. A., & Aisy, R. (2023). Problematika penggunaan Artificial Intelligence (AI) untuk pembelajaran di kalangan mahasiswa STIT Pemalang. *Jurnal Madaniyah, 13*(2), 242–255. DOI: 10.58410/madaniyah.v13i2.826

Malik, A. R., Pratiwi, Y., Andajani, K., Numertayasa, I. W., Suharti, S., Darwis, A., & Marzuki, . (2023). Exploring Artificial Intelligence in Academic Essay: Higher Education Student's Perspective. *International Journal of Educational Research Open, 5*, 100296. Advance online publication. DOI: 10.1016/j.ijedro.2023.100296

Marian, M., Borco i, I., Borco i, C.-A., Cusman, A., Toma, A., & Ionică, D. (2023). A Case Study on Extending the Use of Cloud-Based Services within two Romanian Higher-Education Institutions. *2023 22nd RoEduNet Conference: Networking in Education and Research (RoEduNet)*, 1–6. DOI: 10.1109/RoEduNet60162.2023.10274937

Marzuki, W., Widiati, U., Rusdin, D., Darwin, , & Indrawati, I. (2023). The impact of AI writing tools on the content and organization of students' writing: EFL teachers' perspective. *Cogent Education, 10*(2), 1–17. DOI: 10.1080/2331186X.2023.2236469

Matache, I.-C.The Impact of Ethics on the Quality of Higher Education Services. (2021). Ethics in academia: The impact of ethics on the quality of higher education services. *Perspective Politice, 14*(1-2), 77–84. DOI: 10.25019/perspol/21.14.6

McInnis-Dominguez, M. (2023). An AI Solution: Using ChatGPT to Counter Plagiarism and Boost Enrollments in Hispanic Literature Courses. *Middle Atlantic Review of Latin American Studies, 7*(2), 127–182. DOI: 10.23870/marlas.444

Moya, S., & Camacho, M. (2024). Computers and Education : Artificial Intelligence Leveraging AI-powered mobile learning : A pedagogically informed framework. *Computers and Education: Artificial Intelligence, 7*(August), 1–12. DOI: 10.1016/j.caeai.2024.100276

Mustofa, A., & Hill, J. L. (2018). Understanding cultural context in responding to literature: Researching the teaching of literature in EFL classroom context. *English Language Teaching, 11*(6), 108–115. DOI: 10.5539/elt.v11n6p108

Navaie, F., Panwar, K., & Asino, T. I. (2024). The impact of AI-based technology such as Chat-GPT on second language (L2) learners' academic writing. *Journal of Applied Instructional Design, 13*(1), 259–262. DOI: 10.59668/1269.15645

Ning, B., Liu, F., & Liu, Z. (2023). Creativity Support in AI Co-creative Tools: Current Research, Challenges and Opportunities. 2023 26th International Conference on Computer Supported Cooperative Work in Design (CSCWD), 5–10. DOI: 10.1109/CSCWD57460.2023.10152832

Onderi, H. N. (2025). Artificial intelligence: Ethics and academic integrity in higher education. In Areba, G. N., Gisore, B. N., & Njurai, E. W. (Eds.), *Artificial intelligence, digital learning, and leadership: Redefining higher education* (p. 24). IGI Global., DOI: 10.4018/979-8-3373-0025-2.ch003

Ouyang, F., & Jiao, P. (2023). Artificial Intelligence in Education : The Three Paradigms. *Computers and Education: Artificial Intelligence, 2*(April 2021), 100020. https://doi.org/DOI: 10.1016/j.caeai.2021.100020

Rainie, A. (2023). The Use of Digital Tools and Ai in Education. In *General Hospital Koprivnica* (Issue April). https://doi.org/DOI: 10.13140/RG.2.2.13438.87363

Ratnasari, E., Nurhidayat, E., & Fakhruddin, A. (2019). Kahoot Application As Technology Resources in Teaching. [JELL]. *Journal of English Language Learning*, *2*(1), 1–6.

Roy, D., & Putatunda, T. (2023). From Textbooks to Chatbots: Integrating AI in English Literature Classrooms of India. *Journal of E-Learning and Knowledge Society*, *19*(3), 65–73. DOI: 10.20368/1971-8829/1135860

Saddhono, K., Nugrahani, F., & Syamsuri, A. S. Ermanto, Rahim, A. R., & Sarimanah, E. (2024). The Ethics of AI in Literature: Reflections On Representation and Responsibility. 2024 International Conference on IoT, Communication and Automation Technology (ICICAT), 755–760. https://doi.org/DOI: 10.1109/ICICAT62666.2024.10923247

Selwyn, N. (2019). *Should robots replace teachers? AI and the Future of Education* (1st ed.). Solity Press.

Serpico, K. (2024). The Belmont Report doesn't need reform, our moral imagination does. *Research Ethics*, *20*(3), 559–573. DOI: 10.1177/17470161241235772

Shah, P. (2023). *AI and the Future of Education: Teaching in the Age of Artificial Intelligence*. Jossey Bass, Wiley.

Shirley, D. A., & Langan-Fox, J. (1996). Intuition: A Review of the Literature. *Psychological Reports*, *79*(2), 563–584. DOI: 10.2466/pr0.1996.79.2.563 PMID: 9148314

Sim, I., & Cassel, C. (2024). The ethics of relational AI — Expanding and implementing the Belmont principles. *The New England Journal of Medicine*, *391*(3), 193–196. DOI: 10.1056/NEJMp2314771 PMID: 39007542

Singh, J. P., & Kaur, B. P. (2024). Academic integrity and ethics in higher education: A case study on the use of artificial intelligence in academic writing and tackling plagiarism. In Thanuskodi, S. (Ed.), *Exploring digital metrics in academic libraries* (pp. 172–195). IGI Global., DOI: 10.4018/979-8-3693-5807-8

UNESCO. (2021). *Recommendation on the ethics of artificial intelligence*. UNESCO.

Valdivieso, T., & González, O. (2025). Generative AI Tools in Salvadoran Higher Education : Balancing Equity, Ethics, and Knowledge Management in the Global South. *Education Sciences*, *15*(214), 1–31. DOI: 10.3390/educsci15020214

Washington, J. (2023). The Impact of Generative Artificial Intelligence on Writer's Self-Efficacy: A Critical Literature Review. In SSRN *Electronic Journal*. https://doi.org/DOI: 10.2139/ssrn.4538043

Watters, C., & Lemanski, M. K. (2023). Universal skepticism of ChatGPT : A review of early literature on chat generative pre-trained transformer. *Frontiers in Big Data*, *6*, 1–10. https://doi.org/https://doi.org/10.3389/fdata.2023.1224976. DOI: 10.3389/fdata.2023.1224976 PMID: 37680954

Wellek, R., & Warren, A. (1949). *Theory of Literature*. Harcourt, Brace and Company, Inc.

Wiese, L. J., Patil, I., Schiff, D. S., & Magana, A. J. (2025). AI ethics education: A systematic literature review. *Computers and Education: Artificial Intelligence*, *8*, 100405. DOI: 10.1016/j.caeai.2025.100405

Woolf, B. P., Lane, H. C., Chaudhri, V. K., & Kolodner, J. L. (2018). AI Grand Challenges for Education. *AI Magazine*, (Winter), 66–84.

Zhai, C., Wibowo, S., & Li, L. D. (2024). The effects of over-reliance on AI dialogue systems on students' cognitive abilities: A systematic review. *Smart Learning Environments*, *11*(28), 1–37. DOI: 10.1186/s40561-024-00316-7

Chapter 3
Integrating AI in English Education:
Advancing Literary Understanding and Assessment

Vivit Rosmayanti
https://orcid.org/0000-0002-3648-9878
Universitas Negeri Makassar, Indonesia

Areski Wahid
Universitas Negeri Makassar, Indonesia

Andi Annisa Sulolipu
https://orcid.org/0009-0007-8212-577X
Universitas Negeri Makassar, Indonesia

Ramli Ramli
Universitas Borneo Tarakan, Indonesia

Andi Meinar Dwi Rantisari Thayeb
Universitas Megarezky, Indonesia

Sriwahyuni Sriwahyuni
Universitas Megarezky, Indonesia

ABSTRACT

This chapter is concerned with the role of AI tools in facilitating text generation, text interpretation, and assessment and how these tools are content creation such as poems, stories, and critical and creative thinking. AI aids in making complex tasks of analysis such as the identification of themes and stylistic analysis easier thereby enhancing reasoning and interpretation. In the case of teachers, the role of AIs in assessment and feedback makes that process more effective aiding to improve learning experiences. Still, certain limitations such as ethical issues concerning AI and overreliance on AI are problems that need to be addressed with some plans to ensure sensible usage of AI. The chapter reiterates the versatility of AI tools and explains how they can, when used responsibly, be a significant shift to the way English languages can be taught.

DOI: 10.4018/979-8-3373-6330-1.ch003

Copyright © 2026, IGI Global Scientific Publishing. Copying or distributing in print or electronic forms without written permission of IGI Global Scientific Publishing is prohibited.

INTRODUCTION: THE TRANSFORMATION OF ENGLISH LITERATURE EDUCATION THROUGH AI

Artificial Intelligence (AI) has paved the way for a new paradigm in English literature education, revolutionizing traditional methods with innovative approaches to teaching and learning. The advancement of AI technologies has drawn attention and remarkable interest in education. It is widely reported that by implementing AI into their pedagogical approaches to reading, teachers can provide personalized learning experiences, increase student engagement, and develop deeper comprehension of literary texts through available adaptive learning systems and interactive tools (Betaubun, 2023; Wei, 2023). This shift represents a radical change in the way that teamwork can provide educational support through technology for many different types of learners with unique 21st-century learning needs.

Existing literature in English education is therefore vital in making sense of the implications of integrating AI, which is relevant to this concern. It has been noted that AI is an important component in language learning achievement motivation and self-regulated learning where it increases students' experiences regarding education in all aspects (Abduh et al., 2022; Betaubun, 2023; Rosmayanti et al., 2022, 2023; Sakkir et al., 2024; Wei, 2023). Additionally, AI has been found to promote essential skills required for an ever more digitized society, requiring educators to adapt their teaching approaches to include AI tools (Betaubun, 2023). Specifically, the integration of this technology into a curriculum centered around ELA is highly relevant throughout the exploration of English literature; understanding the material requires not only content knowledge but critical thinking skills that can magnified by the ELA curriculum in which AI education recommendation systems can implement tailored learning methods.

The aims of utilizing AI to reach students in English Literature are twofold. The key purpose of AI is to improve the understanding of literary texts, offering personalized feedback and resources that align with particular learning preferences and styles (Abbas et al., 2023). Using AI-driven platforms can analyze students' reading habits and comprehension levels, thus providing reading materials and assessments based on their unique needs (Abbas et al., 2023). Furthermore, using AI enables collaborative learning environments for students to interact with literature during discussions and with peer feedback, enhancing critical analysis of literary texts while building a community of learners in the classroom (Lee et al., 2022). As literature is a social science, the collaborative, hence aspect is critical, because it is healthy for students to dissect multiple points of view and interpretations of stories.

Another key purpose in improving the teaching of literature is AI's involvement in evaluation and assessment. Conventional assessment techniques do not necessarily reflect the intricacies of literary analysis and interpretation. Yet, AI has the potential to offer creative assessment instruments that assess what students understand and how well they interact with texts critically (Luo, 2024). AI algorithms can process and analyze students' written responses to gain insights into their thought processes and treatment areas, which can help inform instructional practices and aid subject-led interventions (Abbas et al., 2023). This approach to assessment based on well-documented data aligns with current educational paradigms focused on formative assessment and continual feedback, where informed pedagogy leads to increased learning outcomes.

In addition, AI-enabled technology can enable English literature educators to overcome challenges posed by diverse classrooms. Educators face the challenge of responding effectively to varying levels of language proficiency, cultural contexts, cultural backgrounds, etc. AI technologies can help bridge these gaps by delivering culturally responsive and linguistically apt resources (Eguchi et al., 2021). AI engines, for instance, can provide translations, contextual explanations, and audio-visual resources, leading to improved comprehension of complex literary concepts and themes, thereby making literature more accessible (Lee et al., 2022). It is a critical force for promoting a love of literature and ensuring that students from a variety of cultural backgrounds and experiences feel like they can read literature in a way that is meaningful to them.

Besides facilitating understanding and assessment, AI has an important role in the fostering of students' emotional and psychological well-being in reading literature. These features of AI are in line with the existing literature that has shown its potential for decreasing anxiety associated with learning and assessment (Dai et al., 2023) through its provision of a safe space for students to articulate their ideas, hypotheses, and experiences with literature. AI-based chatbots, for example, can help students discuss the themes and characters of a book - students can express how much they liked or disliked something without worrying that they will be slandered for it (Dai et al., 2023). As a literature teacher, this was key for me since we were diving into heavy content and students often had their arguments with texts. Creating a venue for exploration within a safe space, allows students to delve deeper into the text and hone their critical thinking skills.

Additionally, the ethical aspects of integrating AI in education must be raised and taken into account at a wider angle during this shift and process of transition. With the increasing implementation of AI technologies, there is a growing demand for specifying the ethical underpinnings of its uses in educational contexts (Li & Wong, 2023; T. Wang et al., 2023). This involves beginning to address the implications of data privacy, algorithmic bias, and the possibility that AI could help perpetuate existing inequities in education (Seo et al., 2021; X. Wang et al., 2021). Educators can ensure that AI is seen as a tool to empower learning instead of a rival to academic honesty by defining ethical guidelines and enhancing transparency regarding the use of AI.

To wrap it up, the incorporation of AI into how English literature is taught offers a wide r range of possibilities to enhance the process of learning and engage with the students. Educators can personalize learning experiences, enhance assessment practices, and promote emotional well-being among students by harnessing AI technologies. But we must weave this into our educational tapestry carefully, with thoughtful consideration of the ethical elements, and use AI to assist rather than replace the human dimension of teaching and learning. With these developments, the role of AI in English literature education is expected to grow, enabling a more personalized, proactive approach to teaching and learning (Betaubun, 2023; Tian, 2024).

AI IN ENHANCING LITERARY COMPREHENSION

Artificial intelligence in the enhancement of literary comprehension has become a revolutionary strategy in teaching as well as in interpreting and evaluating literary works. AI tools, especially natural language processing (NLP) based ones, have proven effective in helping students grasp themes, characters, stylistic features, and types of plot. These tools process large volumes of text, detecting patterns that may be lost to the human eye using sophisticated algorithms. To take one example, NLP methodologies can be responsible for analyzing the linguistic characteristics of literary pieces, thus allowing for an investigation of the way language portrays meaning as well as feelings in a text (Qu, 2024; Yang, 2024). Taught how to analyze at this level encourages students to interact with written work in a deeper, different way.

Another key way that AI can help us to interpret literature is by spotting and categorizing themes in texts. AI, through the application of text mining and sentiment analysis, can elucidate recurring themes and emotive impulses within individual and complementary narrative experiences, producing a scaffold on which learners will be able to interpret increasingly sophisticated narratives (Qu, 2024). For example, a study that utilized text mining approaches [not clearly stated how] in [specifically] English and American Literature works, has suggested that by teaching how to use them in their analysis, students can learn to identify and include analysis of existing patterns in themes and emotions of characters? Moreover, with its capacity to perform quantitative analyses of literary texts, AI enables a wider understanding of literary corpora, comparing them through authors and genres (Di Vaio et al., 2020; Enholm et al., 2022). This quantitative approach is even more interesting, as it adds additional qualitative insights to the traditional literary analysis of text analysis offering a more rounded view of literature itself.

Besides thematic analysis, AI tools can also help students understand character development and narrative structures. Employing data analysis on dialogue or character interactions among others, AI can offer breakdowns about how an author builds their narrative, or how they develop characters (Yang, 2024). Furthermore, AI does not merely analyze; it enables interpretive engagement with the literary text. AI-generated platforms can foster a virtual environment for discussing and exploring literary work, where students can engage in dialogues about the language behind these texts (Karabayeva, 2024). Posting messages on such platforms can help students explore multiple perspectives, challenging them to critically engage with the cultural, social, and historical contexts that influence literary narratives. For instance, AI can supply contextual background on the period in which a text was written, the author's personal history, and the societal questions raised within the work (Karabayeva, 2024). Understanding the context is vital for laying a well-rounded view of the literature, as it introduces the texts to their larger culture and history.

Moreover, AI can recognize cultural, social, and historical contexts that help students interpret a piece of music. AI can find underlying societal issues and cultural references that inform a work's meaning by breaking down the language and themes of the literary text (Qu, 2024; Yang, 2024). This ability to process multiple sources not only deepens students' understanding of each text but also allows them to relate each work to one another and the social issues they illuminate. Using AI in the field of literature education also stirs up key questions of authorship and the creative process. With AI systems becoming better at analyzing and generating text, they also challenge conventional notions of creativity and originality in literature (Dong, 2023; Fitria, 2021; C. Wang, 2024). Given these developments of AI in the field of literary studies, educators must ponder how best to bring AI into the creative writing process in ways that will sensibly help students construct narratives that can engage with audiences emotionally and intellectually. Students can learn about what storytelling techniques are effectively studying the patterns and structures predicted by A.I., which can lead to their writing improvement (Alharbi, 2023; Song & Song, 2023).

Additionally, this raises ethical questions on the use of AI for analysis and education of literature. With the rising adoption of AI tools, however, data privacy, algorithmic bias, and the risk of misreading literary tests loom (Seo et al., 2021; Song & Song, 2023). Educators must guarantee that AI is understood and employed responsibly, while also providing students with the critical skills needed to consider and judge AI-generated insights. This is important, especially to help students recognize the capabilities and limitations of AI tools (Seo et al., 2021; T. Wang et al., 2023). Educators have a critical role in introducing ethical considerations in AI usage to navigate the complexities of literary studies in an age of AI. AI is becoming increasingly prevalent in various aspects of our lives. AI equips students to grapple with texts in more nuanced ways, helping to develop their critical thinking and interpretive skills through tools that evaluate themes, characters, and narrative arcs.

Furthermore, AI-enabled tools can assist with contextual writing and driven dialogue, providing students with deeper insights into literary works to help them learn in ways even outside the classroom setting (Dong, 2023; Straume & Anson, 2022; Wu, 2022). But this also means that as AI grows in capacity, educators and students must develop the ethical considerations surrounding AI use, showing students the skills they need to interact with data curated by AI. In the end, the power of AI to change education of the literary cannot be underestimated because it can enhance the literary understanding of students, as well as initiate a new breed of readers and authors who are truly analytical.

AI AS A TOOL FOR LITERARY ASSESSMENT

AI-assisted literary analysis is changing the experience because it enables assessing a student's ability to analyze and understand what they are reading. Machine learning Processes are being embraced into this system and have facilitated automated feedback processes, which facilitate scoring systems in education. One of the key uses of AI in this space is automating how literary work is evaluated, specifically the grading of students' literary analysis essays. Grammarly and Turnitin are some examples of the use of AI in education, where it helps educators provide instant feedback about writing quality, instruction coherence and whether it follows the academic standards (Hussein et al., 2019; Onesi-Ozigagun, 2024). They examine student work on things such as grammar, style, and originality, and these tools free up time for a less subjective evaluation key to improving academic performance.

For example, Grammarly utilizes sophisticated algorithms to evaluate the clarity and effectiveness of writing and to provide suggestions for improvement that can be employed to help students enhance their literary analysis essays (Hussein et al., 2019). Likewise, Turnitin does more than a simple plagiarism test; it also gives information about writing trends and which areas students need to work more on. In contrast, students receive immediate feedback, which is vital in helping them identify their strengths and areas for improvement in literary analysis and in promoting a more engaged and reflective approach to writing (Hussein et al., 2019). These approaches to automated grading, although time-saving, do not have to sacrifice the quality of feedback and can especially free educators up to focus on other challenging elements of teaching and learning (Onesi-Ozigagun, 2024).

Moreover, by providing feedback on decimal assessments, AI can help communicate with students through data on how they engage in discussions about the literature. Through the analysis of patterns of student engagement in online discussions or classroom conversations, AI can detect trends in participation and understanding (Conijn et al., 2023). For instance, AI is capable of monitoring the quantity and quality of student input to discussions, giving educators extremely useful information, such as identifying students who are likely to struggle with the material, or identifying which topics matter most to class (Conijn et al., 2023). This way, educators can adjust teaching, utilizing data from the curriculum and assessments, leading to more actionable instruction that meets the needs of even the hardest-to-reach students in the class.

Additionally, AI can discern writing patterns, and not just engagement metrics. Using machine learning lingers in the background of AI since it allows them to recognize the individual skills that the students need to improve upon regarding their literacy analysis (Hussein et al., 2019). For example, AI systems can assess the coherence of arguments made in essays, the depth of textual analysis, and the strength of evidence used to back up claims made. Educators can utilize this analysis to identify common stumbling blocks for students, like constructing logical arguments integrating textual evidence (Hussein et al., 2019). Such patterns allow educators to implement targeted interventions where needed, to help students develop analytical writing skills in a thoughtful and actionable way.

A similar potential can be illustrated through the use of Automated essay scoring (AES) systems which depend on natural language processing (NLP) and machine learning algorithms to assess student essays (Hussein et al., 2019) Such systems are well able to correlate with human assessments and thus serve as a good companion for the educator (Hussein et al., 2019). What is the aftermath that AES systems can help make grading efficient, however, AES systems should not be replaced with human evaluators. Literature cosmopolitanism relies heavily on a multi-faceted interpretation, which AI cannot fully re-enact as it always has the endgame view of interpreting the world relating to its conductor, and cannot tell deeper/finer lines (Lin & Crosthwaite, 2024). Hence, we recommend a hybrid approach that integrates AI assessments with human supervision.

There is also the matter of ethics in the use of AI for literary assessment. Issues of transparency, bias, and potential misrepresentation of student work are serious concerns that educators need to address (Seo et al., 2021; Wong et al., 2023). For example, if AI grading systems are trained on biased training data, algorithms can replicate those biases and yield unfair biases (Seo et al., 2021; Wong et al., 2023). They must also ensure that such technologies are configured in ways that will only produce outputs to assist rather than determine student ability, as well as monitor the outputs of AI systems to ensure they have not fallen into mediocrity.

Applications like Turnitin and Grammarly are prime examples of how AI can not only help make the assessment process more efficient but also provide useful insights into how students are performing. Moreover, by analyzing writing patterns, AI can assist educators in recognizing areas that need attention, resulting in a more tailored educational journey. But we also need to be careful in how we implement AI in literary assessment; we need to recognize the ethical implications of this technology and ensure that human oversight continues to play a role in the evaluation process. In conclusion, the fusion of AI capabilities coupled with human judgment can revolutionize the approach to literary evaluation, rendering it more efficient, insightful, and attuned to measure the requirements of students.

ENRICHING LITERATURE TEACHING WITH AI

The application of AI in literature teaching opens up a fascinating avenue for enriching students' educational experience, specifically enhancing skills such as critical and creative thinking. The emergence of AI technology regularly upgrades the scope of the digital literacy curriculum and the way literature is taught and understood in schools. Integrating AI into literature lessons is an effective way to create a learning environment that promotes critical thinking, creativity, and collaborative learning. It is in line with modern standards for education and ensuring the future of students and digital competency.

There are several different ways that AI in general can seamlessly fit into literature lessons and help students develop their critical and creative skills. AI-powered platforms may help students analyze literature better, giving them insights into themes, character development, and narrative structures (Yang, 2024). These tools can read and analyze texts, creating discussion points to help students dig deeper into the text and go beyond the literature. Students will practice a more in-depth engagement with literary texts and think critically about reading (Yang, 2024). Moreover, a way through which AI can assist in literature education is that its ability to generate narratives and develop characters gives students a means of developing their creativity and outside-the-box thinking to explore new forms of storytelling (Lai, 2023).

Another important advantage of applying AI in literature education is the interactive learning experiences. Using AI we can develop literary texts based on experiences developed using game- based learning or simulations. For instance, educators may implement interactive storytelling games in which students make decisions that influence the outcome of the story, which deepens their message interaction (Alotaibi, 2024). Not only does this approach prepare students to think critically about the decisions characters make and the repercussions of those decisions, but literature is also more accessible and enjoyable. Gamification of literature can assist in finding motivation for reading and fostering interest in reading since students are likely to interact with texts emblematic of a dynamic and interactive modality (Alotaibi, 2024).

In addition, AI-based collaborative projects can greatly enhance the teaching of literature by allowing students to collaborate with tools to produce or interpret literary works. For example, students can work alongside AI systems to create narratives, build characters, or even analyze existing texts (Lai, 2023). By working with tools like OpenAI, students can embrace the power of technology while flexing their own creative and analytical muscles. Collaborating with AI also helps students gain an understanding of the collaboration between human creativity and machine intelligence, paving the way toward a more nuanced conception of the literary process(Lai, 2023). Subsequently, these types of projects may even encourage teamwork and communication skills since students need to work well together to accomplish their goals.

This impact of AI in enriched literature education accounts for as well the cultivation of digital literacy skills in students. By teaching with AI tools, educators are not only teaching analytic skills but also preparing students to learn how to navigate the digital landscape (Ng et al., 2023) (Ng et al., 2023). This encompasses identifying the means to critically assess AI output, accounting for the ethical implications of AI in creative contexts, and learning how to work alongside AI technologies (Ng et al., 2023). These skills allow students to develop the necessary competencies for a future in which efficient usage of digital tools will only grow more relevant. For example, the interdisciplinary dialogue between AI developers, linguists, and literary scholars creates an open space for making a breakthrough in teaching literature (Azerbaijan, 2024). A cross-disciplinary approaches can help educators build better AI tools that promote literary understanding. Working together like this, AI systems can develop a greater understanding of the nuances of language, rhetoric, and cultural context that ultimately can make education a better experience for students (Karabayeva, 2024). Moreover, the key to understanding is that you are working with the sentence organization with a human.

In sum, by bringing AI into the classroom, we can enhance the literary experience. AI in Literature lessons: Enhancing critical and creative skills. Moreover, the integration of students with AI builds digital literacy capacities, which provide them with adequate preparation for their future lives where technology plays a prominent role. The use of AI has the potential to transform the teaching of literature in numerous ways.

CHALLENGES IN AI INTEGRATION IN LITERATURE EDUCATION

While artificial intelligence (AI) promises to revolutionize- literacy education, the implementation of such innovations is fraught with challenges. These challenges can be described as falling into three broad categories: the technological and accessibility barriers, the ethical and authenticity issues, and the role of the teacher in the age of AI. Overcoming these challenges is essential to making the most out of the benefits of AI in literature education and minimizing its adverse effects.

Technological and Accessibility Barriers

Another challenge in implementing AI in the classroom is the uneven access to AI tools in educational institutions. One major hindrance would be; that a large chunk of these underprivileged schools do not have the infrastructure to support these advancements. This digital divide perpetuates existing inequities, as students in affluent schools gain access to advanced AI tools, while their counterparts in less privileged institutions remain deprived of this opportunity (Kim & Kim, 2022). These inequities reinforce one another, and such disparities block students at under-served schools from being able to take part in best practices down the street and in other developments that can be transformative. Uniquely, high school dropout rates are disproportionately higher among those in low-income families, and mitigating this challenge necessitates a combined approach by policymakers, educators, and community leaders alike to ensure access to technology is distributed equally. Educators, especially, can be key in seeking funding, forging partnerships with tech providers, and finding innovative ways to remedy the problem.

But equitable access is only part of the equation. When schools do manage to appropriate AI tools, the use of the tools can be hampered by inadequate training and ongoing support for both educators and students. While some educators do have the technical skills to utilize these tools, many others do not possess the experience or confidence to use them within their pedagogical practice resulting in limited classroom uptake (Kitcharoen, 2024; Zhang, 2024). For instance, most educators tend to utilize AI-assisted technology to improve literary analysis and encourage reading/writing interventions, however, if a teacher is unfamiliar with AI and how it would best integrate with the curriculum, in their instruction, this could easily backfire making the teacher appear not well-versed with recent technologies. Without proper training and guidance beginning before the individual enters the workforce, there is also a scope for resistance; a feeling of being overwhelmed or demotivated to embrace and accept their usage.

It is through professional development programs that this gap can be bridged. Teachers need first and foremost continuous training to acquire the skills and knowledge that will allow them to exploit these AI tools. Such programs should not solely address technical competence but also pedagogical approaches to incorporating AI into the literature classroom. For example, a workshop could illustrate how AI could help you analyze themes or character motivations in texts, producing real-world applications that teachers can apply to their lessons immediately. In addition, such training initiatives should be regular as technology keeps evolving rapidly. AI tools and platforms evolve rapidly, and educators require consistent updates to remain familiar with best practices and trends (Kitcharoen, 2024).

Although timely, professional development can be beneficial, the pressure for professional development can feel like a burden for educators with demanding workloads. When that occurs, people can get exhausted because they need to balance the day job with learning new technologies. This burden can be at least partially alleviated by robust foundational support in the education sector. That means providing accessible training programs in advance of using these AI tools to ensure that teachers know how best to incorporate these technologies into their classrooms. Teaching and institutions would reduce the friction associated with new technology adoption and rush to make educators feel welcome in using AI by encouraging them to do it as a community.

Ethics and Authenticity

This means that the ethical implications of these technologies should stay in the focus, where they belong, to protect the integrity and the purpose of the educational experience. The overriding concern has to do with AI tools subverting the originality of student work. As AI-powered text generation programs such as ChatGPT become more popular, students may be tempted to use such tools for essay or literary analyses without going through the critical thinking and imagining processes that literature curricula aspire to achieve (Adıgüzel et al., 2023; Athanassopoulos, 2023). This dependence threatens to impede the development of vital skills like analytical writing, textual interpretation, and expression of personal viewpoint—bedrock skills in the study of literature. Such an approach to the use of AI, however, shifts the purpose of literary study from learning and growing into a mechanistic exercise, as opposed to an act of intellectual exploration.

To minimize this risk, instructors need to set clear rules and guidelines for the ethical use of AI tools. Such regulations ought to highlight the importance of originality and critical engagement with texts while delineating acceptable uses of AI in support of learning. While it could serve as a tool for generating discussion prompts or analyzing linguistic patterns in students' and authors' writing, the work of creating original interpretations and arguments should fall far from the domain of AI. This influence can be reinforced in the classroom by explicitly teaching students the ethical implications of using AI and AI as a complement, not a substitute, for humans (Adıgüzel et al., 2023; Athanassopoulos, 2023).

Another important ethical challenge is whether the outputs generated by AI align with the educational objectives of the curriculum. So while AI is capable of generating thorough, coherent, and detailed analyses of texts, we must ultimately assess whether the issuing of such outputs is serving students' learning in any substantial way. For example, teachers should interrogate whether those AI-generated interpretations drive deeper comprehension and engagement, or just give some shallow interpretations that students uncritically accept. The concern, however, is that without careful review, AI tools might instead amplify surface learning without developing the depth and complexity needed in the field of English (Holmes et al., 2021). To successfully incorporate AI tools into classroom practice, educators need to develop a strong understanding of who they are teaching and what the technology can and cannot do (Holmes et al., 2021).

A method of tackling these ethical issues is establishing a culture of ethical AI in the classroom. Educators can help their students understand that AI is a tool that can augment their learning and should not be seen as a way to shortcut their assignments. AI, for instance, can be framed as a tool for brainstorming new ideas or perspectives that students analyze critically and develop into their writing. Incorporating conversations around the ethical implications of AI into teaching can also enable students to use these technologies responsibly, helping them develop a sense of accountability and respect for intellectual property. When educators adopt these ethical considerations, then, using AI tools in the literature education process will enhance the development of critical skills and intellectual integrity of the students instead of clouding it. If thoughtfully integrated and with a robust conversation, AI can help be a true partner in enhancing the education experience while remaining true to the ideals of education.

The Role of Teachers in the AI Era

AI Technologies are being integrated more into literature education, which keeps evolving the role of teachers. Herein lies a key challenge for educators: balancing the benefits of AI tools with the human necessity of teaching (Dindar et al., 2022; Gupta, 2024). So, teachers can partner with AI to dazzle their students. AI systems have much to provide, AI does not have the magic touch of the teacher to create an environment of camaraderie, mentoring, differentiation based on learning styles, and a more nuanced understanding of students (Gupta, 2024). Thus, educators have to rethink what their roles should look like in the AI landscape, emphasizing on teaching critical thinking skills, creativity, and ethics in the use of technology (Dindar et al., 2022; Gupta, 2024).

In addition, the teacher-student relationship is transforming in the AI era as well. As students become increasingly comfortable with AI tools, educators need to modify their pedagogical practices to incorporate these technologies productively and engagingly (Dindar et al., 2022; Gupta, 2024). This could mean rethinking curricula to incorporate collaborative projects using AI, nudging students to partner with technology rather than depending on it alone (Gupta, 2024). By providing dynamic English skills, they can cultivate virtual community engagement with one another by sustaining their hands-on learning through technology. As such, just like any other academic development, AI in education has a lot of potential advice to offer but also comes with great challenges. While AI is increasingly used in education, several barriers exist, including potential inequality in access to these tools as well as ethical considerations related to plagiarism and originality that will need to be addressed. Furthermore, teachers must adjust their teaching approaches and rethink their interactions with students in the AI-infused world. To maximize the positive impact of AI as teachers go into implementing curriculum design with literature, they must address these challenges proactively and ensure students gain the skills they will need to survive in this emerging digital world.

FUTURE DIRECTIONS IN AI_DRIVEN LITERARY EDUCATION

We may try to predict the new features of AI-enhanced teaching and learning of literature shortly. These new technologies, as they continue to develop, provide us with opportunities to build critical thinking and interpretative skills, promote multilingual education, and inform policies that, in turn, help to facilitate efficient AI development in English education. Such advancements help create a dynamic learning experience for students and prepare them for the challenges of the modern world.

Potential Advancements in AI for Teaching Critical Thinking and Interpretative Skills

AI in the Classroom: How Artificial Intelligence is Changing Literary Education. Literature, as a field of inquiry, requires close reading, deep contemplation, and the integration of multiple advanced ideas. These skills are essential for understanding themes, analyzing character development, and interpreting narrative structures. Given the capacity of AI tools to analyze and synthesize large quantities of information in textual form, they can provide novel solutions to aid and improve these cognitive efforts. AI-powered tools are capable of conducting advanced forensic analyses of texts, delivering insights on nuanced trends, thematic linkages, and intertextual relationships that may be difficult for readers to perceive. For instance, these tools can indicate the use of certain literary devices, follow character arcs, or even propose possible interpretations of ambiguous passages. These capabilities not only give students a deeper understanding of what they are learning about, but they also create curiosity and engagement that delfs deeper to bring out layers of meaning that encourage further exploration. Beyond assisting with analysis, AI can foster critical thinking by creating discussion prompts that encourage students to reflect on the text and generate questions they have based on the information revealed in a text. These prompts sometimes help students analyze literature from several vantage points and try to assess, critique, and synthesize ideas. Engagement with AI systems can also provide students with immediate feedback about their interpretations—refining their analytical skills and bolstering their confidence in handling complex texts.

Artificial Intelligence for Text Analysis and Thematic Exploration: AI tools can assess both global and local elements of analysis, such as themes, character motivations, symbolic elements, or plot structures that might not be obvious to human readers (Jazbec & Kacjan, 2019). One area where this new capability of extracting and displaying highly relevant insights from text flows is critical thinking. AI-driven platforms, for example, can ask about recurring motifs throughout a novel, suggest correlations between characters' actions and larger themes, and even ornately describe stylistic aspects such as diction and tone. These features allow students to go beyond shallow understanding, uncovering other layers of meaning within a literary work. This technology may be put to one of many uses: generating discussion questions suited to the details of a text. Through real-time literary analysis, AI can also generate questions that ask students to assess a character's decision-making, theorize what might have happened instead, or comment on an author's narrative style (Mouboua, 2024). This activity also encourages students to approach texts actively, sharpening their analytical skills, which are critical when grappling with complex works of literature.

Teaching Critical Thinking in a Personalized Learning Environment: Personalized learning experiences and personalized interactions are the other important advancements that AI enables by adapting to each student's individual needs and learning styles. AI systems can analyze how students interact with texts, from their responses to questions posed about them to their annotations and highlighted passages. Based on this data, AI can offer personalized feedback and recommendations for resources or activities tailored to meet specific areas where there is a knowledge gap. If the student has difficulty identifying metaphorical language, the AI system could give examples, exercises, or videos that explain this skill. As a result, this continuous feedback loop creates an environment that is conducive to growth. However, students are not only provided tools to deepen their learning of the content but to also challenge their interpretations. The adaptable designs of these AI systems demand that students be persistent in improving their analytical skills, motivating them to work through texts with higher engagement levels (Natsiuk & Osidak, 2023).

Developing a Habit of Curiosity and Inquiry: Besides helping improve understanding, AI tools can foster a culture of making everybody think critically as it push students to look for different viewpoints in literature. For example, AI platforms will be able to suggest alternative interpretations of a text or compare the treatment of a theme in different works and authors. This exposure expands students' perspective on literary analysis showing its diverse nature. Not only do these experiences cultivate critical thinking, they ignite the intellectual curiosity that sparks students to challenge assumptions and unearth new perspectives.

Enabling Students to Become Self-Sustained Learners: AI in literary education provides students with ownership over their learning. AI-driven adaptive learning models offer students pacing opportunities so they become confident enough to analyze and interpret literary works independently. Additionally, AI tools provide immediate feedback, enabling students to assess their strengths and weaknesses in real time, which promotes a sense of agency in their learning journey (Duncanson, 2024).

Building AI Tools for Multilingual Literary Education

With globalization, this necessity has never been so urgent. As the world becomes more connected through globalization and advances in communication technology, it becomes essential for learners to speak multiple languages fluently, not only for everyday practical communication but also for interacting with other literary traditions and points of view. The advent of AI can bring buoys transforming MAILE by developing stickies and forums to support students from different languages. A core contribution that AI can make in the field of multilingual literary education is advanced translation technology. AI-powered tools such as neural machine translation systems have advanced immensely in the last few years, providing near-instant translations of literary texts with ever more accurate contextual and cultural nuances. These tools can enable students to explore literature beyond the works in their mother tongue or the languages they can easily read (Eslit, 2023).

For instance, students might read classics in their native language while also exploring adjacent English counterparts, immersing themselves in both the subject matter and the use of the language structure through the text. Such dual exposure is not only valuable in terms of cross-linguistic understanding but also allows us to appreciate literature as a global art form. Additionally, real-time translation tools integrated into classroom frameworks or digital platforms can allow students who speak different languages to work together on literary projects, enhancing an atmosphere of inclusion and reciprocal education.

AI can also play a central role in implementing translanguaging practices in literary education. Translanguaging is the use of two or more languages simultaneously for learning and has been found to improve students' linguistic and cognitive skills (Putrawan et al., 2022). AI tools here can help with the practice of reading literary texts, allowing students to fluidly shift between languages. For example, an AI platform could let students read a story in one language, review vocabulary or grammar in another, and discuss the themes in a combination of the two. Enabling this kind of dynamic use of language supports students as they form deeper knowledge of the links between languages, which results in rethinking textual meanings. This strategy enhances language skills and allows individuals to use their diverse language resources to make sense of and analyze complex concepts, which is notably essential in multilingual environments.

AI can also be applied to creating multilingual educational resources that are customized according to the linguistic and cultural diversity of the students. AI tools can produce study materials, quizzes, and annotations in different languages, helping students read and think about literature in their first language if that is what they are more comfortable with. For example, an AI system could generate bilingual glossaries for literary texts that would include definitions and explanations of key terms in both English and the student's native languages. AI can also integrate cultural context into these resources, ensuring that the materials align with the students' backgrounds and experiences. For example, if a learner is analyzing a Shakespearean play, the AI could capture contextual references regarding cultural parallels or contrasts with Elizabethan England versus their local traditions, promoting their understanding of the themes included in the text, including its relevance.

The power of artificial intelligence goes well beyond text. These tools of writing and storytelling, be it multimodal AI combining text, audio, and visual branches, can further advance multilingual education in literature. For example, AI-enhanced platforms could provide embedded audio readings of texts in multiple languages, interactive visual aids to clarify cultural or historical references and contextualizing videos that place literary works within a global literary canon. These resources offer a multisensory approach to learning, addressing various learning styles and reinforcing understanding. AI tools help create a global literary perspective by allowing students to access literature regardless of the language it is written in. Students become acquainted with the rich lineage of works that make up world literature, and not just the linguistic richness, but the cultural and philosophical insight of the texts as they flow out of the different traditions into one another. This not only expands their intellectual horizon and fosters empathy but also introduces them to narratives that represent the human condition in diverse ways.

Shaping Policies for AI Adoption in English Education

As a culmination, to maximize the potential of AI in the education of literature, sound, comprehensive policies are needed events to its successful and ethical adoption. Such policies should include considerations and action plans on key areas of concern, to ensure that the deployment of AI tools facilitates positive learning experiences and equitable outcomes while also promoting a culture of transparency and academic integrity. Schools are at the frontline in establishing standards for how AI tools are used in the classroom and can offer clarity to teachers and students.

The ethical use of AI tools is one of the cornerstones of such policies. Academically, institutions need to create clear guidelines that define how these technologies can be used to facilitate learning—without threatening academic integrity. For instance, policies can establish boundaries for how to assess AI-generated content, assisting students and educators in determining whether or not humans or machines produced a piece of content (Kholis, 2021). Such insight is especially relevant for literary pedagogy where critical reading, original analysis, and evaluation are highly valued. Transparency about how AI tools are used is also vital. Students must know the powers of the AI technologies available to them and their limitations so they do not turn to the technologies for everything.

One of the critical aspects in terms of shaping policies for AI adoption is equitable access to these technologies. Access to digital tools remains limited and access disparities are significant across many regions of the world, contributing to a digital divide and hindering the wider applicability of AI in education. Policy-makers need to focus on closing these gaps by implementing programs that bring down the barriers around access to education and resources helping students tap into AI opportunities (Akbarani, 2024). Investments in digital infrastructure — like high-speed internet access and AI-compatible devices — are essential to leveling the playing field. And, offering training and professional development opportunities to support educators with the skills they need and the confidence to integrate AI tools meaningfully into their practice.

Along with tackling access and infrastructure, policy needs to cultivate collaboration among stakeholders to maximize the use of AI in education. This requires teachers, technologists, policy-makers, and researchers, to have dialogues to explore the adaptive landscape of AI applications in language teaching. Effective collaboration can help in recognizing best approaches, establishing innovative pedagogy, and foreseeing challenges that might be faced when applying AI tools (Nsengiyumva et al., 2021). Take the idea of multilingual education, cultural diversity in the study of literature, and formative assessment: stakeholders might consider how they could use AI to support all three.

Policy development in the rapidly evolving field of AI should be rooted in ongoing research. As the technology evolves, policymakers will also need to be responsive, consistently updating guidelines to align with new capabilities and risks. This means that educational institutions can still allow for flexibility and innovation in teaching, while also maintaining the integrity and inclusivity of the learning process. Policies governing the integration of AI in English education must be, after all, a matter of responsible innovation. Through equitable access support, transparency measures, and collaboration initiatives, such policies can unfold an environment where AI is an ally — one that can enhance literary education at scale. Additionally, If we adopt a deliberate and inclusive approach while integrating AI, we will be able to mold students for the complexity of the global, equipping them with the skill set and perspective to be successful in a connected and technologically advanced world.

CONCLUSION AND RECOMMENDATIONS

Literature education is positively affirmed through the integration of AI as it retains the quality level of learning and evaluation processes. AI tools can help to a more personalized learning experience, enhance literary comprehension, and provide unique assessment methods. AI enriches students' engagement with literature and prepares them for a system where digital literacy is critical by automating feedback and creating interactive learning ecosystems. Yet, the blending of literature teachings requires addressing fundamental issues, from tech blockades to moral dilemmas to the changing position of professors.

AI's impact on literature education is twofold, enabling enhanced understanding of the text alongside more accurate and efficient evaluation of student work. With algorithms that can analyze prose, generate constructive report cards, and hold conversations, AI helps students have a deeper, more critical interaction with texts. In addition, AI can enable personalized learning experiences, allowing educators to tailor approaches to meet individual student needs, creating an inclusive environment that encourages both literary exploration and creativity. The potential of AI to transform the teaching of literature both to enhance and supplement traditional teaching methods while also introducing revolutionary pedagogies to the teaching of literature as we move into the digital age (Hockly, 2023; Z. Hou, 2021).

To harness the power of AI in teaching literature, some recommendations can be given for teachers and education institutions in general. 1) For Educators: Educators need regular continuing training on such AI tools and how to use them while engaging with literature. This training should be about the technology itself and the pedagogy of the use of these tools in the learning journey (Karabayeva, 2024; Tsai, 2022); Equitable access2) Institutions should also prioritize equitable access to AI technologies so that all students can be helped by these tools. For instance, this role may require securing funding, partnerships, or grants to supply under-resourced schools with essential materials (Kim & Kim, 2022; Kitcharoen, 2024); 3). Ethics: Educators need to set clear ethical parameters regarding the appropriate use of AI in literature classrooms, stressing the need for originality and the value of actively engaging with texts. This encompasses teaching students the ethical dimensions that come with using AI tools and encouraging a culture of academic integrity (Adıgüzel et al., 2023; Athanassopoulos, 2023); 4) Interactive Engagement: Ask students to work on collaborative projects, getting them to work side by side with AI tools to build or read literary works. Not only does this promote creativity, but it also allows students to build critical thinking and teamwork capabilities (Lai, 2023); 5) Feedback Mechanisms: Employ AI-driven feedback mechanisms to deliver students prompt and constructive evaluations of their literary analysis and writing. These systems can identify learning gaps and provide personalized learning paths (Hussein et al., 2019; Onesi-Ozigagun, 2024).

Overall, the potential for AI to enhance English education and its literary component is immense. The advances in AI technologies are bound to become even more sophisticated in analyzing writings and understanding the context & their interactive learning experience. Using AI in the classroom means AI can help create new spaces for creative writing and literary analysis (X. Hou et al., 2022; Zhou, 2024). In addition, close collaboration among AI developers, linguists, and literary scholars could support the development of AI-based tools that are more appropriately adjusted to meet authentic educational needs, thus adding value to students' learning (Karabayeva, 2024; Tsai, 2022).

REFERENCES

Abbas, N., Imran, A. S., Manzoor, R., Hussain, T., & Hussain, M. (2023). Role of Artificial Intelligence Tools in Enhancing Students' Educational Performance at Higher Levels. *Journal of Artificial Intelligence Machine Learning and Neural Network, 35*(35), 36–49. DOI: 10.55529/jaimlnn.35.36.49

Abduh, A., Sakkir, G., Rosmaladewi, R., Andrew, M., & Yasdin, Y. (2022). Teachers' Perceptions of English Teaching Strategies in the Current Curriculum Change. *International Journal of Language Education, 6*(4), 437–444. DOI: 10.26858/ijole.v6i4.25246

Adıgüzel, T., Kaya, M. H., & Cansu, F. K. (2023). Revolutionizing education with AI: Exploring the transformative potential of ChatGPT. *Contemporary Educational Technology, 15*(3), ep429. DOI: 10.30935/cedtech/13152

Akbarani, R. (2024). Use of Artificial Intelligence in English Language Teaching. *International Journal of English Learning and Applied Linguistics (Ijelal), 4*(1), 14–23. DOI: 10.21111/ijelal.v4i1.10756

Alharbi, W. (2023). AI in the Foreign Language Classroom: A Pedagogical Overview of Automated Writing Assistance Tools. *Education Research International, 2023*, 1–15. DOI: 10.1155/2023/4253331

Alotaibi, M. S. (2024). Game-Based Learning in Early Childhood Education: A Systematic Review and Meta-Analysis. *Frontiers in Psychology, 15*, 1307881. Advance online publication. DOI: 10.3389/fpsyg.2024.1307881 PMID: 38629045

Athanassopoulos, S., Manoli, P., Gouvi, M., Lavidas, K., & Komis, V. (2023). The Use of ChatGPT as a Learning Tool to Improve Foreign Language Writing in a Multilingual and Multicultural Classroom. *Advances in Mobile Learning Educational Research, 3*(2), 818–824. DOI: 10.25082/AMLER.2023.02.009

Betaubun, M. (2023). Personalized Pathways to Proficiency: Exploring the Synergy of Adaptive Learning and Artificial Intelligence in English Language Learning. *Technium, 17*, 60–66. DOI: 10.47577/technium.v17i.10047

Conijn, R., Kahr, P., & Snijders, C. J. (2023). The Effects of Explanations in Automated Essay Scoring Systems on Student Trust and Motivation. *Journal of Learning Analytics, 10*(1), 37–53. DOI: 10.18608/jla.2023.7801

Dai, Y., Liu, A., & Lim, C. P. (2023). Reconceptualizing ChatGPT and generative AI as a student-driven innovation in higher education. *Procedia CIRP, 119*, 84–90. DOI: 10.1016/j.procir.2023.05.002

Di Vaio, A., Palladino, R., Hassan, R., & Escobar, O. (2020). Artificial intelligence and business models in the sustainable development goals perspective: A systematic literature review. *Journal of Business Research*, *121*, 283–314. DOI: 10.1016/j.jbusres.2020.08.019

Dindar, M., Muukkonen, H., & Järvelä, S. (2022). The Promises and Challenges of Artificial Intelligence for Teachers: A Systematic Review of Research. *TechTrends*, *66*(4), 616–630. DOI: 10.1007/s11528-022-00715-y

Dong, Y. (2023). Revolutionizing academic English writing through AI-powered pedagogy: Practical exploration of teaching process and assessment. *Journal of Higher Education Research*, *4*(2), 52. DOI: 10.32629/jher.v4i2.1188

Duncanson, J. (2024). Supporting L2 Writing Using QuillBot. *Gatesol Journal*, *33*(1), 30–36. DOI: 10.52242/gatesol.195

Eguchi, A., Okada, H., & Muto, Y. (2021). Contextualizing AI Education for K-12 Students to Enhance Their Learning of AI Literacy Through Culturally Responsive Approaches. *Ki - Künstliche Intelligenz, 35*(2), 153–161. DOI: 10.1007/s13218-021-00737-3

Enholm, I. M., Papagiannidis, E., Mikalef, P., & Krogstie, J. (2022). Artificial intelligence and business value: A literature review. *Information Systems Frontiers*, *24*(5), 1709–1734. DOI: 10.1007/s10796-021-10186-w

Eslit, E. R. (2023). Thriving Beyond the Crisis: Teachers' Reflections on Literature and Language Education in the Era of Artificial Intelligence (AI) and Globalization. *International Journal of Education and Teaching*, *3*(1), 46–57. DOI: 10.51483/IJEDT.3.1.2023.46-57

Fitria, T. N. (2021). Grammarly as AI-powered English Writing Assistant: Students' Alternative for Writing English. *Metathesis Journal of English Language Literature and Teaching*, *5*(1), 65. DOI: 10.31002/metathesis.v5i1.3519

Gupta, D. P. (2024). Navigating the Future of Education: The Impact of Artificial Intelligence on Teacher-Student Dynamics. *Eatp*, 6006–6013. DOI: 10.53555/kuey.v30i4.2332

Hockly, N. (2023). Artificial intelligence in English language teaching: The good, the bad and the ugly. *RELC Journal*, *54*(2), 445–451. DOI: 10.1177/00336882231168504

Holmes, W., Porayska-Pomsta, K., Holstein, K., Sutherland, E., Baker, T. T., Shum, S. B., Santos, O. C., Rodrigo, M. M. T., Cukurova, M., Bittencourt, I. I., & Koedinger, K. R. (2021). Ethics of AI in Education: Towards a Community-Wide Framework. *International Journal of Artificial Intelligence in Education*, *32*(3), 504–526. DOI: 10.1007/s40593-021-00239-1

Hou, X., Omar, N., & Wang, J. (2022). Interactive Design Psychology and Artificial Intelligence-Based Innovative Exploration of Anglo-American Traumatic Narrative Literature. *Frontiers in Psychology*, *12*, 755039. Advance online publication. DOI: 10.3389/fpsyg.2021.755039 PMID: 35222140

Hou, Z. (2021). Research on adopting artificial intelligence technology to improve effectiveness of vocational college English learning. *Journal of Physics: Conference Series*, *1744*(4), 42122. DOI: 10.1088/1742-6596/1744/4/042122

Hussein, M., Hassan, H., & Nassef, M. (2019). Automated Language Essay Scoring Systems: A Literature Review. *PeerJ. Computer Science*, *5*, e208. DOI: 10.7717/peerj-cs.208 PMID: 33816861

Jazbec, S. Š., & Kacjan, B. (2019). "Multilingualism Is the Real Thing": Multilingualism From the Parents' Perspective. *The New Educational Review*, *57*(3), 87–98. DOI: 10.15804/tner.19.57.3.07

Karabayeva, I., & Kalizhanova, A. (2024). Evaluating Machine Translation of Literature Through Rhetorical Analysis. *Journal of Translation and Language Studies*, *5*(1), 1–9. DOI: 10.48185/jtls.v5i1.962

Kholis, A. (2021). Elsa Speak App: Automatic Speech Recognition (ASR) for Supplementing English Pronunciation Skills. *Pedagogy Journal of English Language Teaching*, *9*(1), 1. DOI: 10.32332/joelt.v9i1.2723

Kim, N., & Kim, M. K. (2022). Teacher's Perceptions of Using an Artificial Intelligence-Based Educational Tool for Scientific Writing. *Frontiers in Education*, *7*, 755914. Advance online publication. DOI: 10.3389/feduc.2022.755914

Kitcharoen, P., Howimanporn, S., & Chookaew, S. (2024). Enhancing Teachers' AI Competencies Through Artificial Intelligence of Things Professional Development Training. *International Journal of Interactive Mobile Technologies (Ijim)*, *18*(02), 4–15. DOI: 10.3991/ijim.v18i02.46613

Lai, Y. (2023). The Impact of AI-Driven Narrative Generation, Exemplified by ChatGPT, on the Preservation of Human Creative Originality and Uniqueness. *Lecture Notes in Education Psychology and Public Media*, *26*(1), 121–124. DOI: 10.54254/2753-7048/26/20230865

Lee, D., Kim, H.-H., & Sung, S.-H. (2022). Development Research on an AI English Learning Support System to Facilitate Learner-Generated-Context-Based Learning. *Educational Technology Research and Development*, *71*(2), 629–666. DOI: 10.1007/s11423-022-10172-2 PMID: 36533222

Li, K. C., & Wong, B. (2023). Artificial Intelligence in Personalised Learning: A Bibliometric Analysis. *Interactive Technology and Smart Education*, *20*(3), 422–445. DOI: 10.1108/ITSE-01-2023-0007

Lin, S., & Crosthwaite, P. (2024). The grass is not always greener: Teacher vs. GPT-assisted written corrective feedback. *System*, *127*, 103529. DOI: 10.1016/j.system.2024.103529

Luo, Y. (2024). Innovative Research on AI-assisted Teaching Models for College English Listening and Speaking Courses. *Applied and Computational Engineering*, *69*(1), 155–160. DOI: 10.54254/2755-2721/69/20241493

Mouboua, P. D.Patricia Diane MoubouaFadeke Adeola AtobateleOlateju Temitope Akintayo. (2024). Multilingual Education and Social Equity: A Comparative Study of Integration Policies in Multicultural Societies. *GSC Advanced Research and Reviews*, *19*(2), 32–42. DOI: 10.30574/gscarr.2024.19.2.0165

Natsiuk, M., & Osidak, V. (2023). Multilingualism in Society and Education: The Ukrainian Context. *Ars Linguodidacticae*, *11*(11), 4–15. DOI: 10.17721/2663-0303.2023.1.01

Ng, D. T. K., Leung, J. K. L., Su, J., Ng, R. C. W., & Chu, S. K. W. (2023). Teachers' AI digital competencies and twenty-first century skills in the post-pandemic world. *Educational Technology Research and Development*, *71*(1), 137–161. DOI: 10.1007/s11423-023-10203-6 PMID: 36844361

Nsengiyumva, D. S., Oriikiriza, C., & Kalyango, S. (2021). Cross-Linguistic Transfer and Language Proficiency in the Multilingual Education System of Burundi: What Has the Existing Literature So Far Discovered? [Indonesian Journal of English Language Teaching and Applied Linguistics]. *Ijeltal*, *5*(2), 387. DOI: 10.21093/ijeltal.v5i2.770

Onesi-Ozigagun, O. (2024). Revolutionizing Education Through Ai: A Comprehensive Review of Enhancing Learning Experiences. *International Journal of Applied Research in Social Sciences*, *6*(4), 589–607. DOI: 10.51594/ijarss.v6i4.1011

Putrawan, G. E., Mahpul, , Sinaga, T., Poh, S. K., & Dekhnich, O. V. (2022). Beliefs About Multilingualism With Respect to Translanguaging: A Survey Among Pre-Service EFL Teachers in Indonesia. *Integra Educativa, 26*(4), 756–770. DOI: 10.15507/1991-9468.109.026.202204.756-770

Qu, S. (2024). A Thematic Analysis of English and American Literature Works Based on Text Mining and Sentiment Analysis. *Jes, 20*(6s), 1575–1586. DOI: 10.52783/jes.3076

Rosmayanti, V., Noni, N., & Patak, A. A. (2022). Students' acceptance of technology use in learning English pharmacy. *International Journal of Language Education, 6*(3), 314–331. DOI: 10.26858/ijole.v6i3.24144

Rosmayanti, V., Patak, A. A., & Noni, N. (2023). Integrating technology into ESP instruction: Teaching English for pharmacy students. *The Journal of AsiaTEFL, 20*(2), 475–484. DOI: 10.18823/asiatefl.2023.20.2.18.475

Sakkir, G., Al Amir, F., Atmowardoyo, H., Weda, S., & Rosmayanti, V. (2024). An analysis of translanguaging practices in an Indonesian EFL classroom : Teacher perception Geminastiti. *Xlinguae, 17*(2), 3–15. DOI: 10.18355/XL.2024.17.02.01

Seo, K., Tang, J., Roll, I., Fels, S., & Yoon, D. (2021). The Impact of Artificial Intelligence on Learner–instructor Interaction in Online Learning. *International Journal of Educational Technology in Higher Education, 18*(1), 54. Advance online publication. DOI: 10.1186/s41239-021-00292-9 PMID: 34778540

Song, C., & Song, Y. (2023). Enhancing academic writing skills and motivation: Assessing the efficacy of ChatGPT in AI-assisted language learning for EFL students. *Frontiers in Psychology, 14*, 1260843. DOI: 10.3389/fpsyg.2023.1260843 PMID: 38162975

Straume, I., & Anson, C. (2022). Amazement and trepidation: Implications of AI-based natural language production for the teaching of writing. *Journal of Academic Writing, 12*(1), 1–9. DOI: 10.18552/joaw.v12i1.820

Tian, W., Ge, J., Zhao, Y., & Zheng, X. (2024). AI Chatbots in Chinese Higher Education: Adoption, Perception, and Influence Among Graduate Students—an Integrated Analysis Utilizing UTAUT and ECM Models. *Frontiers in Psychology, 15*, 1268549. Advance online publication. DOI: 10.3389/fpsyg.2024.1268549 PMID: 38384353

Tsai, S.-C. (2022). Learning With Mobile Augmented Reality- And Automatic Speech Recognition-Based Materials for English Listening and Speaking Skills: Effectiveness and Perceptions of Non-English Major English as a Foreign Language Students. *Journal of Educational Computing Research, 61*(2), 444–465. DOI: 10.1177/07356331221111203

Wang, C. (2024). *Exploring Students' Generative AI-Assisted Writing Processes: Perceptions and Experiences From Native and Nonnative English Speakers*. Technology Knowledge and Learning., DOI: 10.1007/s10758-024-09744-3

Wang, T., Lund, B. D., Marengo, A., Pagano, A., Mannuru, N. R., Teel, Z. A., & Pange, J. (2023). Exploring the potential impact of artificial intelligence (AI) on international students in higher education: Generative AI, chatbots, analytics, and international student success. *Applied Sciences (Basel, Switzerland), 13*(11), 6716. DOI: 10.3390/app13116716

Wang, X., Thompson, M., Yang, K., Roy, D., Koedinger, K. R., Rose, C. P., & Reich, J. (2021). Practice-based teacher questioning strategy training with ELK: A role-playing simulation for eliciting learner knowledge. *Proceedings of the ACM on Human-Computer Interaction, 5*(CSCW1), 1–27. DOI: 10.1145/3449125

Wei, L. (2023). Artificial Intelligence in Language Instruction: Impact on English Learning Achievement, L2 Motivation, and Self-Regulated Learning. *Frontiers in Psychology, 14*, 1261955. Advance online publication. DOI: 10.3389/fpsyg.2023.1261955 PMID: 38023040

Wong, L., Tan, G. W., Ooi, K., & Dwivedi, Y. K. (2023). The Role of Institutional and Self in the Formation of Trust in Artificial Intelligence Technologies. *Internet Research, 34*(2), 343–370. DOI: 10.1108/INTR-07-2021-0446

Wu, X. (2022). Dynamic evaluation of college English writing ability based on AI technology. *Journal of Intelligent Systems, 31*(1), 298–309. DOI: 10.1515/jisys-2022-0020

Yang, L., Wang, G., & Wang, H. (2024). Reimagining Literary Analysis: Utilizing Artificial Intelligence to Classify Modernist French Poetry. *Information (Basel), 15*(2), 70. DOI: 10.3390/info15020070

Zhang, Z. (2024). Advancements and Challenges in AI-driven Language Technologies: From Natural Language Processing to Language Acquisition. *Applied and Computational Engineering, 57*(1), 146–152. DOI: 10.54254/2755-2721/57/20241325

Zhou, X., Zhang, J., & Chan, C. (2024). Unveiling Students' Experiences and Perceptions of Artificial Intelligence Usage in Higher Education. *Journal of University Teaching & Learning Practice*, *21*(06). Advance online publication. DOI: 10.53761/xzjprb23

Chapter 4
Integration of AI in Language Learning and Literary Education

Asdar Asdar
https://orcid.org/0000-0002-3277-0283
Universitas Bosowa, Indonesia

M. Asia
https://orcid.org/0009-0004-7371-7106
Universitas Negeri Makassar, Indonesia

Muhammad Asdam
Universitas Bosowa, Indonesia

Sulmi Magfirah
Universitas Khairun, Indonesia

Sujarwo Sujarwo
Universitas Megarezky, Indonesia

ABSTRACT

AI in language and literary education is a top priority for educators, researchers, and technologists, signaling a major shift in language acquisition pedagogy in the digital age. This quantitative study examined how AI integration affects language and literary education. The project collected student AI tool feedback via surveys and questionnaires. Assessments of verbal fluency and comprehension before and after. AI technologies enhance involvement by providing alternate readings, analytical frameworks, and interactive literature debates. Game-based, adaptive, and multimedia AI solutions engage students. AI systems can explain complicated literary

DOI: 10.4018/979-8-3373-6330-1.ch004

Copyright © 2026, IGI Global Scientific Publishing. Copying or distributing in print or electronic forms without written permission of IGI Global Scientific Publishing is prohibited.

themes using visuals, summaries, and context-specific explanations for different learning styles. AI enhances language and literature instruction. AI helps children improve grammar, vocabulary, reading comprehension, writing correctness, and speaking fluency

1. INTRODUCTION

Integrating Artificial Intelligence (AI) in language and literary education has become a central concern for educators, scholars, and technologists, indicating a significant transformation in the teaching and learning of languages (Özdere, 2023). Incorporating Artificial Intelligence (AI) in language acquisition and literary education presents transformational possibilities, drastically altering conventional pedagogical approaches. AI technologies enable educators and learners to access tools that customize learning experiences, optimize administrative processes, and improve content engagement (Abdulah et al., 2024). This development marks a rising awareness of artificial intelligence's transforming power in using creative tools and methods to change learning environments. Teachers and developers are progressively moving towards more individualised, efficient, and data-driven methods of instruction (Amaliah et al., 2023; Asdar et al., 2023; Sasabone et al., 2023) and learning as they investigate the opportunities of artificial intelligence. This change captures a larger trend in education that gives learner-centred design and adaptation top priority.

Regarding language education, artificial intelligence surpasses conventional teaching strategies in many respects. It provides instant feedback, models real-life interactions, and gives focused practice depending on students' strengths and shortcomings, therefore facilitating improved instruction. These features help students to advance at their speed and satisfy their particular demand, therefore making learning more interesting and responsive. By removing logistical and geographic obstacles, artificial intelligence also greatly increases access to language instruction. Utilizing mobile apps and online platforms, learners from many backgrounds can access high-quality education, therefore fostering inclusive and fair language learning (Imran et al., 2022). AI will probably play more of a part in language teaching as it develops, producing more intelligent, engaging, and successful learning environments (Tammets & Ley, 2023).

Especially in language learning, artificial intelligence (AI) presents transforming possibilities for educational innovation. Customising and efficiency of language learning experiences can be greatly improved by artificial intelligence technologies including adaptive learning systems, natural language processing (NLP), and machine learning. AI can deliver prompt feedback, adjust to the learner's pace, and create interactive and engaging educational environments customized to individual competence levels and learning styles (Choukaier, 2024).

The rapid advancement in artificial intelligence (AI) and information technology is driving a major change in education. These developments have changed how teachers teach and how students learn. Numerous students utilize AI technology to optimise their educational tasks, including composing essays, papers, and other scholarly work. Artificial intelligence, a subset of computer science, concentrates on developing computers that can do tasks usually necessitating human ability or even exceeding human abilities (Choukaier, 2024). Utilizing technological innovations like the Internet, including artificial intelligence in education, has enabled simpler information access. The fast development of technology forces teachers to include technology, especially computers, into their lessons. This integration matches contemporary educational requirements and equips students to navigate a technology-driven environment adeptly (Fuchs & Aguilos, 2023).

Artificial Intelligence is an interdisciplinary field encompassing both natural and social sciences (Fraidan, 2024). Rapid advancement and extensive international collaboration require individuals with AI and language proficiency expertise to meet global communication requirements. In this context, language and literary education should examine the potential and practicality of incorporating AI-related information into language instruction (Tang & Foley, 2022). However, few language textbooks have addressed AI, and no investigation of AI applications has been conducted in Indonesia until now.

Moreover, language education promotes significant communication and engagement. It fundamentally provides learners with essential abilities to overcome linguistic barriers and fosters relationships and cooperation across geographical boundaries. As advances in teaching and learning are continually evaluated and investigated, new insights emerge that impact worldwide teaching methods. Digital platforms, interactive applications, and immersive linguistic experiences have facilitated advancements in teaching. Technology is transforming global communication in the digital era, and digital literacy has gained paramount importance in foreign language utilization (Carrió-Pastor, 2016).

Artificial intelligence (AI) is a computer program engineered to replicate human intelligence, encompassing decision-making capabilities, logical reasoning, and other cognitive attributes. In the realm of scientific writing, artificial intelligence offers substantial advantages to educators (Hutson et al., 2022). AI can assist educators in conducting research, analyzing data, and composing scientific publications with enhanced efficiency and precision. Artificial intelligence can discern study trends, do comprehensive data analysis, and aid in formulating conclusions based on the available information.

The desire for improved language competencies is much a result of artificial intelligence being included into the educational process. By providing customised and adaptable learning experiences for students, artificial intelligence systems help them to improve their grammar, vocabulary, speaking and writing skills. By means of sophisticated machine learning techniques, artificial intelligence can examine every student's learning behaviour, identify their language comprehension strengths and constraints, and provide tailored learning materials to fit their particular requirements. Implementing this technology enables students to receive tailored learning while enhancing their language abilities more efficiently and effectively (Han et al., 2024).

Nonetheless, whereas AI offers numerous opportunities for language acquisition, it also poses obstacles. Using this technology calls for enough infrastructure, acceptable tools, and a good approach for its application. Using artificial intelligence for language learning raises ethical questions about dependency on technology and data protection. Moreover, artificial intelligence can help to check grammar, spelling, and writing styles following scientific standards (Creely, 2024). AI assists educators in enhancing the quality and efficacy of their scientific manuscripts while reducing potential errors. This can assist educators in generating high-calibre research that advances science and education.

The description claims that artificial intelligence helps users to improve their academic performance. On the other hand, artificial intelligence is seen as a two-edged blade; it brings benefits but also negative ones. Public concern exists over artificial intelligence technology perhaps someday replacing all human functions or professions. In higher education, students who misuse AI may ultimately harm their academic progress. IT and AI-based learning can cultivate detrimental habits among students, such as plagiarism, and contribute to passivity in their learning endeavors. This transformation in educational methodologies not only influences the execution of learning but also prompts new inquiries regarding the role of guidance and counseling in bolstering student academic performance.

2. LITERATURE REVIEW

2.1 Language Learning

Language learning is a dynamic and varied process with an eye on the acquisition of key competences in a target language—that which includes listening, speaking, reading, and writing. These credentials help one to be able to express clearly in many different contexts (Sujarwo et al., 2023). There is more to it than simply accumulating vocabulary and grammar rules through rote repetition or simple memorizing. Alternatively, it is a thorough journey that combines the acquisition of communicative competency and linguistic proficiency, so as to arm students to use the language contextually and fluidly in events grounded in real-life (Sujarwo et al., 2024).

Usually assisted by a wide range of resources and strategies fit to the particular needs of the person learning a language, the road to becoming proficient in a language usually consists of using a variety of formal and informal learning approaches. Learning that is regarded formally usually occurs in regimented settings, including classrooms or language courses, where seasoned teachers lead students across courses that are methodically arranged (Imran et al., 2022). his approach stresses grammar, syntax, phonology, and language skills in a methodical sense as well as their application. Unlike formal education, which occurs in conventional environments, informal learning takes place outside of such settings by means of daily interactions, media consumption, or immersive experiences like travel or native speaker connection. One of the ways in which these approaches support a natural acquisition of language is by exposing pupils to the pragmatic, practical uses of language.

Essential components of language acquisition—more especially, the ability to understand spoken language—are those related to hearing. To understand meaning, this capacity calls for recognition of sounds, intonation, and context. Interacting with native speakers and listening to podcasts and audiobooks significantly help one to improve their listening ability. Speaking aids in both confidence in actively using the language and fluency enhancement. Learners can better explain their thoughts and respond spontaneously when practicing through activities such as role-playing, pronunciation exercises, and dialogues. This helps to build successful communication. Learning through reading helps students enhance their comprehension, expand their vocabulary, and get familiar with a variety of text formats (Kara, 2018). It covers a broad range of books from basic writings like menus and advertising to more complex works like novels and scholarly articles. Writing well requires one to be able to logically arrange their ideas and also apply correct language, spelling, and punctuation. Writing allows pupils the chance to effectively express themselves in written form and entails email, essay, report, or creative works.

Technologies driven by artificial intelligence (AI) are beneficial to language acquisition in the modern day because they offer individualized resources, feedback in real-time, and chances for independent study. These innovations make it possible for students to acquire language skills in a more efficient manner, while also catering to the specific requirements of each student and fostering long-term retention (Andersson et al., 2024).

Artificial intelligence in language acquisition equips learners with adaptive and contextually cognizant tools (Roy & Putatunda, 2023). Applications using machine learning techniques can assess a learner's capacity, identify areas needing improvement, and offer customised materials to handle regions needing development. While conversational artificial intelligence mimics real-world interactions, therefore promoting immersive environments that increase communication proficiency, speech recognition software enhances pronunciation by delivering accurate feedback. Furthermore, AI closes accessibility disparities. It facilitates language engagement for learners with disabilities via assistive technology, including voice-to-text and screen readers. It facilitates multilingual teaching by offering real-time translations and cultural context for comprehensive understanding. This democratization of access guarantees inclusion in education across many groups.

Recent developments in artificial intelligence-driven language teaching draw attention to the growing need of including cultural background into language acquisition systems. Emerging trends show that technologies driven by artificial intelligence are developing to include cultural nuances in addition to language components. This integration helps students to deeply understand the cultural roots inherent in language (Karataş et al., 2024). AI-driven language learning systems go beyond simple language instruction by including cultural context, therefore offering a more complete and comprehensive educational experience that promotes increased respect and awareness of various cultures among students.

AI presents great promise to enhance language education going forward, but several issues still exist. Ethical questions regarding AI utilization in education, data protection issues, and the imperative for ongoing human-AI collaboration require comprehensive examination. Furthermore, despite the individualized characteristics of AI-driven education, it is essential to guarantee inclusivity for learners with varied educational requirements and backgrounds. Future studies should concentrate on improving AI algorithms to satisfy various learning needs while addressing ethical issues, thereby insuring a responsible and fair integration of AI in language education (Fattah et al., 2023).

Integration of information and communication technologies (ICT) has changed language teaching fundamentally. ICT increases the interaction and involvement of the learning process by allowing teachers and students to access various real materials (Redmond et al., 2018). Technology has expanded the scope of language teaching, engaging students in diverse interactive activities. Recent advancements in educational technology have revolutionized instructional and learning resources. Educators and students today depend on diverse electronic resources both within and beyond the classroom.

2.2 Literary Education

Educational technology has recently undergone a significant transformation towards the integration of artificial intelligence in language instruction. The emergence of AI has rendered language learning more individualized, engaging, and effective.

AI tools have transformed the global landscape, providing innovative solutions and improved living experiences for individuals globally. A contemporary existence devoid of applications driven by artificial intelligence is inconceivable. AI-driven language teaching platforms offer tailored learning experiences. These systems can assess learners' strengths and shortcomings, offer immediate feedback, and create tailored learning pathways (Andersson et al., 2024).

Furthermore, artificial intelligence helps to create advanced virtual language teachers and chatbots, therefore encouraging conversational interaction and raising language competency. As educational technology develops, it has the ability to revolutionise language acquisition, thereby making it more practical and easily available for students all around. Artificial intelligence transforms literary studies by facilitating profound engagement with texts via sophisticated analysis. AI-powered text analytics solutions can reveal intricate patterns, thematic components, and stylistic subtleties in literary works that would require considerable effort for students and educators to discern manually (Creely, 2024). This capability facilitates more profound class discussions and enhanced critical analysis.

In creative writing and narrative, AI functions as an inspired collaborator. By helping students overcome writer's block and thereby foster creativity, generative artificial intelligence models can suggest tale topics, help with character development, and improve language choices (Hamamra et al., 2024). At the same time, AI systems improve the availability of world literary treasures by means of better translations, therefore fostering cross-cultural understanding and enjoyment. Artificial intelligence (AI) integration into academic institutions has changed many facets of higher education; technology is one of the main fields undergoing fast development. One obvious way AI is helping education is in its ability to customise learning environments. By evaluating individual learner data, AI-driven systems may customise the curriculum, therefore improving the learning process to better meet the needs of every student.

Learners of language typically show different degrees of competence in the four fundamental language skills—reading, writing, speaking, and listening. This variety in competency makes it imperative to use flexible teaching strategies that fit particular learning requirements. Conventional, one-size-fits-all solutions usually fall short in satisfying these unique needs, therefore impeding development in one or more spheres. Duolingo and other AI-driven platforms have become rather successful instruments to close this divide. Using machine learning techniques, these systems instantly evaluate user performance and modify task difficulty. This customised method guarantees that students are always interacting with materials that challenge them just enough to encourage development without generating annoyance.

Maintaining learner motivation and promoting skill development in all spheres of language education depends mostly on such adaptive systems. AI-based solutions not only support varied learning but also help maximise every student's potential by customising training to fit individual development. They thus mark a major progress in the use of technology for inclusive and efficient language instruction. By providing quick feedback on grammar, style, and clarity, AI-driven writing tools like Grammarly and Hemingway Editor help to improve language learning. Students utilizing these AI technologies markedly enhanced their writing fluency and correctness in contrast to those dependent exclusively on conventional education (Fraidan, 2024).

2.3 Review of Previous Studies on AI in Language Learning

Some studies stated that substance and linguistics Integrated learning significantly enhanced EFL learners' general knowledge of AI and proved to be a successful teaching strategy for the majority of students involved in the educational trial (Tang & Foley, 2022). The finding offers a thorough and perceptive examination of technological breakthroughs and the incorporation of AI in language acquisition and education (Özdere, 2023). Understanding the implications of incorporating GenAI into education and the pedagogical framework. This comprehension will allow instructors and their students to maintain relevance in the current GenAI epoch (Kurtz et al., 2024). The study promotes a comprehensive strategy that utilizes the advantages of generative AI in language education while simultaneously mitigating any drawbacks and endorsing an ethical and fair framework for language learning in the evolving AI-driven digital environment (Creely, 2024).

Recent research has emphasized the efficacy of substance and linguistics-integrated learning as a means to augment EFL learners' comprehension of AI and facilitate language acquisition. This comprehensive strategy markedly enhanced students' overall understanding of AI, demonstrating effectiveness for the majority of participants in their educational assessments. The significance of investigating technology breakthroughs and incorporating AI into language teaching, providing essential insights into its transformational capabilities. The necessity for educators to comprehend the ramifications of incorporating Generative AI (GenAI) into education. By integrating pedagogical frameworks with GenAI, educators, and learners can sustain relevance in this swiftly advancing technological landscape. This comprehension not only facilitates significant adoption but also empowers learners with the ability to traverse the GenAI-driven instructional environment. A holistic approach that utilizes the advantages of generative AI in language education. The study emphasizes the necessity of mitigating potential disadvantages through the endorsement of ethical and equitable activities. This paradigm guarantees that AI integration in education is both innovative and equitable, promoting a sustainable and successful AI-enhanced learning environment in the digital era. These studies collectively underscore AI's pivotal significance in transforming language learning while stressing the necessity for deliberate, ethical, and pedagogically sound application methodologies.

2.4 Integration of AI with Language and Literary Education

The combination of Artificial Intelligence (AI) with language and literary education has engendered disruptive prospects, redefined conventional pedagogical methodologies, and broadened the horizons of teaching and learning possibilities (Fraidan, 2024). AI enables instructors to customize education, promote engagement, and optimize assignments while students benefit from advanced technologies that enrich their learning experiences.

Academics, educators, and higher education institutions are profoundly apprehensive about student utilization of generative AI and are contending with necessary adjustments to pedagogical approaches, assessment procedures, and institutional policies. Educators and students must recognize the ethical concerns related to AI in education. The focus on student misuse of technology sometimes obscures the potential benefits of generative AI tools. Chatbots such as ChatGPT can produce original written content of any specified length, structure, or style based on user instructions (Karataş et al., 2024). The lack of a legislative framework for the integration of AI applications in education may pose ethical and societal issues, including perpetuating disadvantages for impoverished and marginalized populations. The swift progression of emerging technologies and the resultant transition to digital processes provide significant challenges for society and the education system at multiple levels.

By integrating artificial intelligence's (AI) efficiency and innovation with the indispensable human aspects of teaching, educators can use AI's transformational potential to enhance language and literary education (Han et al., 2024). This deliberate integration facilitates individualized, efficient, and significant learning experiences while maintaining core principles such as empathy, creativity, and critical thinking (Makeleni et al., 2023). This method provides learners with linguistic skills and literary appreciation and prepares them to succeed in a globally interconnected and culturally varied environment. AI serves as a technique to improve overall education, respecting person uniqueness utilizing technology to expose fresh teaching and learning prospects.

Artificial Intelligence (AI) technologies are transforming English language education by using innovative techniques including machine learning (ML) methodologies and natural language processing (NLP) algorithms. These technologies provide personalised instruction, feedback, and evaluation as well as their amazing capacity to examine, adjust, and respond to the particular learning demands of every student. Artificial intelligence (AI) is not only a tool for automating processes; it is a transformative force that reshapes how students interact with language skills and acquire them.

Incorporating language learning systems that include chatbots and virtual tutors is one of the most significant applications of artificial intelligence in English language education (Fattah et al., 2023). Thanks to these artificial intelligence-powered programs using sophisticated algorithms to imitate human-like interactions, learners can engage in real-time, interactive conversations. These technologies let students practise fundamental aspects of language acquisition like pronunciation, vocabulary, and grammar, therefore creating an immersive learning environment. They help the engaged parties to have dynamic and responsive conversations.

In what respects may virtual tutors and chatbots be helpful? Driven by natural language processing (NLP), chatbots, which provide conversational practice simulating real-world situations, allow students to increase their fluency and confidence in speaking. Artificial intelligence systems can, for instance, assess students' voice in pronunciation practice, spot errors, and offer quick comments to correct them. This function lets students improve their accents and raise their intelligibility during their schooling. Virtual tutors educate students about new words by presenting them in their natural context and encouraging them to use them appropriately in sentences. Artificial intelligence can change the difficulty level based on the learner's success, which ensures a consistent yet demanding pace of vocabulary growth (Hamamra et al., 2024). Grammar Assistance uses tools to discover grammatical problems in learners' written or spoken inputs and propose improvements. They do this by reinforcing comprehension via practice and repetition.

Moreover, AI systems may evaluate students' writing samples and deliver immediate comments on grammar, style, and coherence, facilitating ongoing enhancement. Language educators now significantly benefit from generative chatbots, which enable the creation of adaptive lesson plans customized to each student's needs. Thus, ensuring focused instruction. AI-driven voice recognition systems let students improve their speaking skills and get exact assessments of their intonation and pronunciation. By adding AI methods, English language instruction has become more accessible, customised, and successful, helping students to develop their language competency with efficiency and confidence.

2.5 Problem Statement of Study

Ensuring that artificial intelligence's use is fair, moral, and successful depends on addressing the difficulties in including it into literary education and language training. Careful management of issues including data privacy, algorithmic bias, and unequal access to technology helps to prevent expanding current educational inequities. Establishing confidence among legislators, teachers, and students depends on design and implementation of AI tools being transparent and accountable.

To get this, a careful and intentional attitude is required one that combines technology developments with strong instructional ideas. Teachers and developers have to work together to make sure AI technologies complement educational objectives and ideals as well as are technically strong. This includes creating mechanisms supporting critical thinking, creativity, and cultural sensitivity instead of only rote learning or exam preparation.

In the end, this kind of approach can help to create a more inclusive and whole classroom. Thoughtfully including artificial intelligence into language and literary education can help us to improve student involvement, accommodate different learning requirements, and so advance fair possibilities for every student. Realising the full possibilities of artificial intelligence in education depends on this harmony between innovation and instruction.

1. How does integrating AI tools influence students' language skills and literary education?
2. How effective are AI tools in enhancing learners' comprehension and analysis of literary texts compared to traditional methods?

The purpose of this study is to look at how including artificial intelligence (AI) technologies into literary education and language instruction would affect things. Learners who use artificial intelligence develop improved language competency in key areas like grammar, vocabulary, reading comprehension, writing accuracy, and speaking fluency.

3. METHOD

3.1 Research Design

This research employed a quantitative data analysis methodology, concentrating on numerical data to evaluate the effects of AI integration in language acquisition and literary education. The research included surveys and questionnaires to get student input regarding AI tools. Pre-assessments and post-assessments to evaluate advancements in linguistic fluency and comprehension abilities. Utilization of descriptive statistics to encapsulate main trends and patterns within the data (Arkkelin, 2014; Leavy, 2017). Utilization of inferential statistics to assess the importance of observed alterations in students' competencies and knowledge. Data were obtained from two

Indonesian proficiency assessments utilizing a 5-point Likert Scale questionnaire. The performance of AI in general knowledge was assessed using student scores on Indonesian proficiency examinations conducted before and after the course. Data from the 5-point Likert Scale questionnaire revealed students' perceptions regarding their acquisition of general knowledge in AI. The data analysis techniques employed in this study included percentage, mean, and theme analysis (Creswell, 2013).

3.2 Participants

This study's subjects comprised 48 undergraduate students from the Indonesian Language Literature program at Universitas Bosowa. This research employed convenience sampling. Students voluntarily chose the AI Indonesian Reading course as a mandatory elective following the Indonesian Language Literature teaching curriculum.

3.3 Research Instruments

Indonesian Proficiency Assessments Before the instructional experiment, the researcher created two proficiency assessments to evaluate students' broad knowledge of AI before and after completing the AI Reading course. Each test comprised a total of 50 marks and adhered to an identical format: Multiple choice questions (10 questions worth a total of 10 marks), Noun explanations (4 words for a total of 20 marks), and Essay-type questions (1 essay worth a total of 20 marks). An additional ten students trialed both assessments and were evaluated and modified by three specialists.

3.4 Questionnaire

The researchers created a 5-point Likert Scale questionnaire to examine students' assessments of their general knowledge of AI and Content and Language Integrated Learning (CLIL). The questionnaire was tested by an additional ten students and evaluated by the same three ELT professionals, ultimately approved by the researcher based on the pilot study input. The questionnaire employed a 5-point Likert Scale of 10 items, each offering five response options: strongly disagree (1 point), disagree (2 points), neither agree nor disagree (3 points), agree (4 points), and strongly agree (5 points). The items of the questionnaire are shown in Table One as follows.

Table 1. Questionnaire items of utilization of AI in language and literature learning

No	Items
1	To find artificial intelligence/AI intriguing
2	How often do you use AI (e.g. ChatGPT, Grammarly, or Duolingo) to help with language or literature learning
3	To appreciate the AI reading textbook
4	Using AI can appreciate the pedagogical approach
5	How effective is AI in helping you understand literary works (e.g. poetry, novels, or plays)
6	Can the use of AI increase motivation to learn language and literature?
7	To appreciate the AI Indonesian reading course
8	How useful is AI in improving your language skills (e.g. writing, reading, speaking, listening)
9	I acquired a greater understanding of AI applications
10	General knowledge of AI has improved
11	My lexicon of AI has improved
12	What are the obstacles you encounter when using AI in learning

This table summarises a set of components that can form the basis of a survey or questionnaire meant to evaluate opinions, use, and the impact of artificial intelligence (AI) in language and literary instruction. Every object looks at several facets of artificial intelligence's application in education, including its efficiency, challenges, and ability to enhance learning environments. Student interaction with AI - Analyzing the frequency and rationale of students' utilization of AI programs. Evaluated efficacy - Assessing the role of AI in enhancing comprehension of literary texts, advancing linguistic abilities, and facilitating educational strategies. Investigating the motivational and cognitive effects of AI on enhancing motivation, appreciation for learning materials, and overall understanding of AI concepts. Obstacles to adoption - recognizing impediments to AI implementation in the realm of language and literary education. Through the analysis of replies, educators and researchers can formulate ways to optimize the advantages of AI tools while mitigating any challenges. The questionnaire may potentially enhance AI-driven instructional systems to more effectively address learners' requirements.

3.5 Data Collection and Analysis

Data were gathered over a four-month duration. Language skills were evaluated at the study's commencement and conclusion to gauge advancement. Surveys assessing engagement and confidence were conducted monthly. The AI system delivered continuous analytics, encompassing time allocated to tasks, completion rates, and challenge areas. Data analysis entailed comparing pre- and post-test outcomes to measure improvements in language skills, employing statistical techniques to determine the importance of the AI-integrated in language skills and literary education.

4. FINDINGS AND DISCUSSION

This study aims to investigate the effect of integrating Artificial Intelligence (AI) tools in language learning and literary education. By utilizing AI, learners achieve enhanced language competency in critical domains, including grammar, vocabulary, reading comprehension, writing precision, and speaking fluency.

The data illustrates learners' performance in diverse language abilities before and after an integration AI intervention.

Table 2. Means score of pre-test and post-test scores of students' language skills

No	Language Skills	Mean Score of Pre-test	Mean Score of Post-test	Improvement
1	Writing Fluency	55	80	25
2	Speaking Fluency	60	81	21
3	Reading Comprehension	62	82	20
4	Grammar Accuracy	55	78	23
5	Vocabulary Expansion	65	79	14

All language skills improved significantly from the pre-test to the post-test, proving the intervention or learning technique worked. Writing Fluency improved the most, 25 points, demonstrating the intervention had a major impact on students' writing. Vocabulary Expansion improved the least at 14 points, suggesting it needs more emphasis or a different strategy. Speaking Fluency and Grammar Accuracy improve similarly (21 and 23 points, respectively), indicating a balanced gain in productive and structural language usage.

Figure 1. Pre-Test and post-test scores of students' language skills

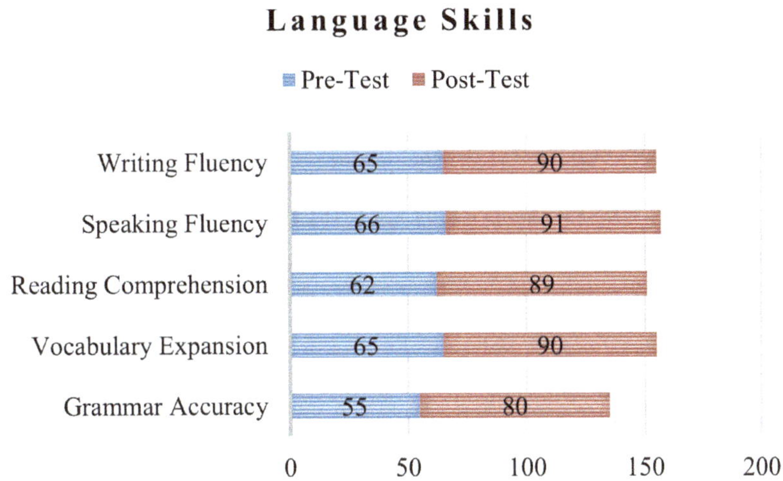

Survey responses from educators highlighted the effectiveness of AI in facilitating personalized learning experiences and addressing individual learning needs.

Figure 2. The students appreciate the AI reading textbook

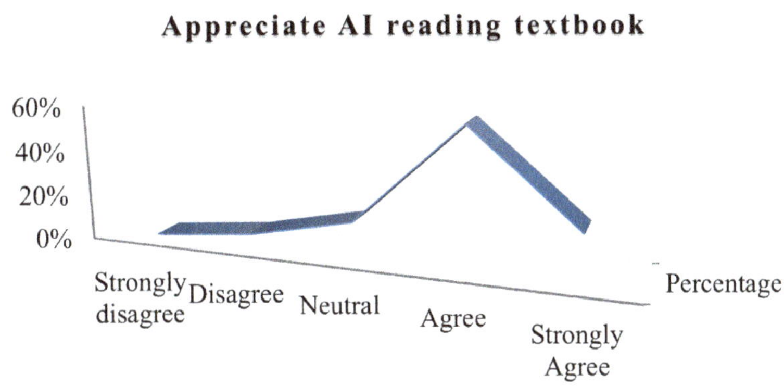

Students are enthusiastic about the AI-enhanced reading textbook, emphasizing its capacity to make learning more enjoyable and accessible. The textbook's interactive aspects, including context-aware explanations, visual aids, and individualized feedback, improve comprehension and memory of the information. The AI reading textbook enhances engagement with the material by elucidating intricate concepts and accommodating diverse learning styles, rendering the educational experience more pleasurable and efficient. This favorable feedback highlights its capacity to transform conventional educational resources, providing a contemporary, learner-focused methodology.

Figure 3. The students acquired a greater understanding of AI applications

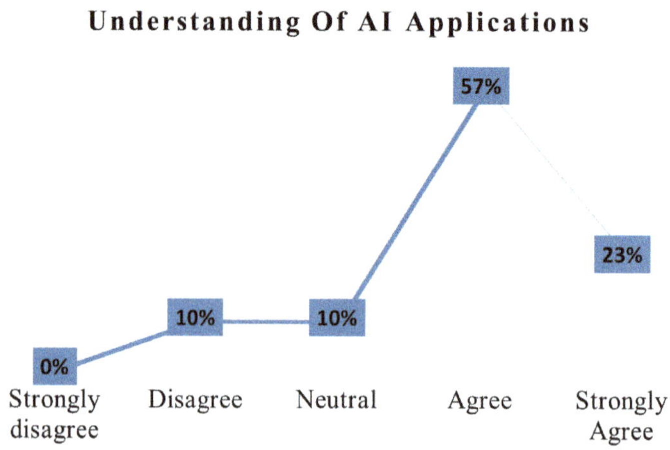

By utilising AI-enhanced tools and resources, the students acquired a more profound comprehension of AI applications. This exposure enabled them to understand how AI is applied in various situations, including language acquisition, problem-solving, and literary critique. The interactive and adaptive capabilities of the AI tools not only advanced their technical proficiency but also deepened their understanding of AI's function in streamlining intricate operations and facilitating customized learning experiences. This acquired information empowers students to be more assured and proficient in utilizing AI technology in both academic and practical contexts.

Figure 4. The student's general knowledge of AI

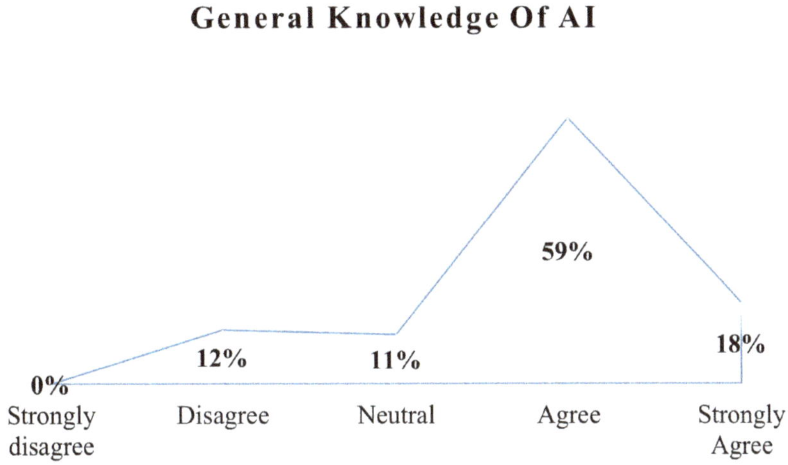

AI systems may elucidate intricate literary themes via visual aids, summaries, and context-sensitive explanations, accommodating diverse learning styles. AI tools are transforming learner engagement with literary works by providing creative approaches to simplify complex concepts into accessible ways. AI tools generate dynamic mind maps, timelines, or charts that delineate relationships among characters, plot advancements, and themes. For example, the students create chronologies of occurrences in Shakespeare's dramas and character web diagrams illustrating relationships in works such as Pride and Prejudice.

AI-powered platforms can convert abstract concepts such as symbols or motifs into visually engaging infographics, facilitating understanding of their recurrence and significance. AI algorithms distill extensive texts into essential points, emphasizing principal ideas, topics, and character developments while preserving the text's core substance. numerous tools enable learners to investigate summaries at varying levels of depth, ranging from broad overviews to comprehensive chapter-by-chapter analyses.

Tools for artificial intelligence are quite adept in improving basic language competencies including reading, writing, speaking, and listening. They provide practice chances, customised learning paths, and individualised comments to help students reach great competency. Through custom assignments, instant corrections, and interactive simulations, students improve grammar, vocabulary, pronunciation, and fluency. AI solutions help with particular needs, for improving reading comprehension using directed annotations or speech recognition-based speaking fluency enhancement. Grammarly and Pro Writing Aid among other tools provide suggestions for enhancing grammatical accuracy, clarity, and brevity.

AI-powered programs include ELSA, Speech Ling, and Google Speech Recognition provide speech feedback, therefore helping students to practise speaking with correct fluency and pronunciation. AI improves literary studies by helping one to grasp complex works. AI-driven summaries, graphic images, and contextual explanations improve text analysis and help students grasp difficult literary themes. Incorporating AI technologies in educational environments has demonstrated encouraging outcomes in improving diverse language skills among students (Al-Khresheh, 2024). AI is transforming language learning by enhancing speaking skills via virtual assistants and augmenting listening comprehension through mobile applications. a primary advantage of incorporating AI in language acquisition is its ability to deliver personalized feedback and customized training. This tailored methodology revolutionizes education by enabling learners to advance at their speed and concentrate on areas that require enhancement (Škobo & Petričević, 2023). The era of uniform teaching methods is over; AI now offers personalized learning experiences tailored to individual students' needs and preferences.

Incorporating AI in language acquisition and literary education necessitates meticulous planning and deliberate execution (Choukaier, 2024). By tackling issues such as accessibility, ethical dilemmas, and teacher preparedness while utilizing AI's capabilities in personalization and immediate feedback, educators can improve grammar, vocabulary, rg comprehension, writing precision, and speaking fluency. When utilized successfully, AI can revolutionize learners' interaction with languages and literature, providing a dynamic and inclusive educational experience (Choukaier, 2024).

AI can provide learners with interactive audio workouts and simulations for language skills that replicate real-life interactions. AI may use speech recognition technology to evaluate learners' comprehension abilities and deliver prompt feedback on speaking, reading, and fluency. This immediate feedback enables learners to pinpoint areas for enhancement and implement requisite modifications to improve their language abilities. AI-driven language tutors have transformed language acquisition by offering learners opportunities for conversational practice (Karataş et al., 2024). ChatGPT's beneficial influence on writing, minimal effect on speaking abilities, enhancement of grammar and vocabulary skills, encouragement of online class participants, and facilitation of interactive language learning experiences (Karataş et al., 2024). Virtual language tutors can include learners in interactive conversations, replicate real-life situations, and offer feedback on pronunciation and language application (Alotaibi & Alshehri, 2023). This fosters confidence in speaking and improves oral communication skills in a friendly and non-judgmental setting. AI systems can evaluate texts and offer real-time support to reading learners (Suryana et al., 2020).

Some findings supported the study, namely, the urgent necessity to prioritize the creation of AI-driven language teaching tools specifically designed for the needs and settings of learners (Makeleni Et Al., 2023). Incorporates computer information technology with collegiate English instruction and suggests an enhanced artificial intelligence algorithm (Jiang et al., 2022). AI-driven education in higher learning underscores the necessity for educators to have new technological competencies to implement AI properly in teaching (Alotaibi & Alshehri, 2023). The proposed future directions can inspire the AI and educational technology research community to pursue research endeavors that address the stated difficulties (Dimitriadou & Lanitis, 2023). The findings demonstrated that the deployment of AI markedly improved the cognitive, emotional, and social involvement of EFL students in English literature lessons, with student emotions being pivotal. This study theoretically enhances the knowledge of AI's impact on educational engagement by incorporating emotional elements into existing models of technology-enhanced learning (Guo & Wang, 2024).

The implementation of artificial intelligence in education (AIED) has been examined via intelligent tutoring systems, conversational agents (CA), and chatbots. These technologies have improved teaching and learning; nevertheless, minimal prior research directly examines how AIED integrates comprehensively into educational environments. Potential advantages of AI in education include delivering adaptive learning through task assignments tailored to individual capabilities, hence improving academic performance and fostering human-machine interaction to motivate and engage students (Tammets & Ley, 2023). Artificial intelligence enhances research productivity and customizes learning; nonetheless, concerns concerning usability, accuracy, and ethical dilemmas, including algorithmic prejudice and data privacy, remain prevalent. The study underscores the necessity for judicious deployment, harmonized with conventional academic practices, to fully leverage AI's potential in enhancing research and education (Fraidan, 2024).

AI technologies facilitate enhanced involvement by providing alternate interpretations, analytical frameworks, or interactive dialogues concerning literary works. AI solutions employ gamification, adaptive material, and multimedia resources to sustain learner engagement and motivation. students interact with material more efficiently via interactive quizzes, discussion forums, or scenario-based learning exercises. Dynamic interaction through virtual tutors, chatbots, or AI helpers promotes collaboration and ongoing learning, supplanting passive educational approaches.

5. SOLUTIONS AND RECOMMENDATIONS

Incorporating AI into language acquisition and literary education provides several advantages while posing obstacles. The following are strategies for appropriately integrating AI in several domains to improve educational outcomes while addressing potential challenges. Employ AI to deliver personalized learning trajectories for each student. Artificial intelligence can evaluate student performance and modify content accordingly, providing more complex assignments for advanced learners and remedial assistance for those in need.

Utilize AI-driven tools for instantaneous grammar and vocabulary feedback. Platforms such as Grammarly, Language Tool, ChatGPT, and Pro Writing Aid to improve clarity and brevity, ELSA, Speechling, Google Speech, and Duolingo employ AI algorithms to identify grammatical inaccuracies and propose vocabulary enhancements in writing and speaking activities. Facilitates immediate error correction for students and enhances language retention via repetition and contextual learning. Utilize AI to deliver interactive summaries, context-sensitive annotations, and tailored reading materials. AI-driven reading aids and e-books equipped with AI capabilities can condense texts, emphasize essential topics, and elucidate challenging terminology or concepts. AI platforms can identify grammatical problems, coherence, organization, and style while providing recommendations for enhancement (Andersson et al., 2024). Recognition offers speech feedback, assisting learners in practicing speaking with accurate pronunciation and fluency. These instruments can assess accent, intonation, and stress, delivering prompt corrective feedback.

Advice on incorporating Artificial Intelligence into Literary Education and Language Learning. Teachers may build a richer, inclusive, and motivating learning environment that addresses issues and improves AI by using a wise and fair approach. These are given to make sure that, while addressing associated challenges, AI technologies improve grammar, vocabulary, reading comprehension, writing accuracy, and speaking fluency. Practically applied artificial intelligence can let students interact with languages and literature in hitherto unheard-of ways.

Furthermore, underlined by educators, institutions, and governments is the need of access, training, and careful application of AI tools to improve language learning outcomes. Especially in higher education, the development of artificial intelligence (AI) technology has significantly affected many aspects of education. Research shows that by improving analytical skills, creativity, and learning efficiency, AI-based initiatives as ChatGPT, Grammarly, and Duolingo can help students do better academically. The primary problem encountered is the insufficient knowledge of lecturers regarding the comprehension and instruction of AI applications to students. Numerous lecturers lack sufficient training or familiarity with incorporating AI technology into education.

Integrating AI in language education represents a revolutionary method to address the varied requirements of English learners, facilitating more efficient and significant teaching and learning experiences. These guidelines and techniques seek to assist stakeholders in utilizing AI successfully to improve English language education and foster ongoing advancements in teaching methodologies and curriculum development.

6. FUTURE RESEARCH DIRECTIONS

Future investigations into AI's role in language acquisition and literary pedagogy should include personalization, promoting collaboration, tackling ethical dilemmas, and broadening accessibility. By focusing on these aspects, researchers may realize the complete potential of AI, guaranteeing its transformative impact on education is significant, inclusive, and sustainable. Concentrating on critical domains—augmenting personalization can realize AI's complete promise in language acquisition and literary education. These initiatives guarantee that AI's transformative influence is significant, equitable, inclusive, and durable, benefiting learners from many contexts and generations.

7. CONCLUSION

Based to the studies, including artificial intelligence into the curriculum greatly enhances literary education and language competency. Learners improve in important areas including grammar, vocabulary, reading comprehension, writing correctness, and speaking fluency by using artificial intelligence. This improvement is attributed to artificial intelligence's ability to provide customised learning experiences via adaptive technology addressing the needs of every student. These systems guarantee ongoing engagement and motivation through the provision of immediate feedback, the development of customized learning trajectories, and the integration of interactive activities. In literary education, AI serves a crucial function by enhancing the accessibility of intricate literature. It accomplishes this by providing contextually pertinent explanations and enabling comprehensive analysis, helping students interact with literature more significantly and engagingly. These methods connect complex literary concepts with learners' understanding, enhancing appreciation and comprehension. The studies underline that artificial intelligence is meant to be an augmentation rather than a replacement for traditional educational strategies. It improves conventional methods by supporting a more dynamic, inclusive, and interesting learning environment that guarantees that both language and literary education are available to a larger spectrum of students while keeping high degrees of academic quality.

REFERENCES

Abdulah, D. M., Zaman, B. A., Mustafa, Z. R., & Hassan, L. H. (2024). Artificial Intelligence Integration in Academic Writing: Insights from the University of Duhok. *ARO (Koya)*, *12*(2), 194–200. DOI: 10.14500/aro.11794

Al-khresheh, M. H. (2024). Bridging technology and pedagogy from a global lens: Teachers' perspectives on integrating ChatGPT in English language teaching. *Computers and Education: Artificial Intelligence*, *6*, 100218. DOI: 10.1016/j.caeai.2024.100218

Alotaibi, N. S., & Alshehri, A. H. (2023). Prospers and Obstacles in Using Artificial Intelligence in Saudi Arabia Higher Education Institutions—The Potential of AI-Based Learning Outcomes. *Sustainability (Basel)*, *15*(13), 10723. DOI: 10.3390/su151310723

Amaliah, N., Sunarlia Limbong, Nur Ina Syam, Fahmi Room, & Khaliq Bashar. (2023). Using Technology as Learning Media to Enrich ESP Students' Speaking Skill for Indonesian Higher Education Students. *IJOLEH : International Journal of Education and Humanities*, *2*(1), 43–51. DOI: 10.56314/ijoleh.v2i1.126

Andersson, R., Ringhagen, A., & Tapper, A. (2024). *Exploring the Integration of Artificial Intelligence Tools in English as a Foreign Language (EFL) Pedagogy*. Gothenburg University Publications Electronic Archive (GUPEA). https://gupea.ub.gu.se/handle/2077/79561

Arkkelin, D. (2014). *Using SPSS to Understand Research and Data Analysis*. Psychology Curricular Materials.

Asdar, Y. J., Natsir, T., Anggreani, A. V., Sasabone, L., & Kechik, T. N. B. T. (2023). Strengthening Character Education Based on Online Learning for University Students Pasca Covid-19. *IJOLEH : International Journal of Education and Humanities*, *2*(1), 35–42. DOI: 10.56314/ijoleh.v2i1.125

Carrió-Pastor, M. L. (Ed.). (2016). *Technology Implementation in Second Language Teaching and Translation Studies: New Tools, New Approaches*. Springer Singapore., DOI: 10.1007/978-981-10-0572-5

Choukaier, D. (2024). Integrating AI In English Language Pedagogy: Innovations And Outcomes In Teaching English As Second /Foreign Language. *Educational Administration: Theory and Practice*, *30*(5), 3811–3822. https://doi.org/Doi: DOI: 10.53555/kuey.v30i5.3538

Creely, E. (2024). Exploring the Role of Generative AI in Enhancing Language Learning: Opportunities and Challenges. *International Journal of Changes in Education, 1*(3), 158–167. DOI: 10.47852/bonviewIJCE42022495

Creswell, J. W. (2013). *Educational research: Planning, conducting, and evaluating quantitative and qualitative research* (Fourth Indian edition). PHI Learning Private Limited.

Dimitriadou, E., & Lanitis, A. (2023). A critical evaluation, challenges, and future perspectives of using artificial intelligence and emerging technologies in smart classrooms. *Smart Learning Environments, 10*(1), 12. DOI: 10.1186/s40561-023-00231-3 PMID: 40478141

Fattah, H. A., Vadivel, B., Shaban, A. A., & Shanmugam, K. (2023). Enhancing English Language Education: The Impact of AI Integration in the Classroom. *The Journal of Humanistic Education and Development*, *5*(6), 116–123. DOI: 10.22161/jhed.5.6.15

Fraidan, A. A. (2024). Integrating AI-Powered Library Systems to Enhance Research and Learning in English Language Departments: A Case Study of Faculty and Student Perceptions. *Library Progress International*, *44*(3), 12058–12065.

Fuchs, K., & Aguilos, V. (2023). Integrating Artificial Intelligence in Higher Education: Empirical Insights from Students about Using ChatGPT. *International Journal of Information and Education Technology (IJIET)*, *13*(9), 1365–1371. DOI: 10.18178/ijiet.2023.13.9.1939

Guo, Y., & Wang, Y. (2024). Exploring the Effects of Artificial Intelligence Application on EFL Students' Academic Engagement and Emotional Experiences: A Mixed-Methods Study. *European Journal of Education, 12812*. Advance online publication. DOI: 10.1111/ejed.12812

Hamamra, B., Mayaleh, A., & Khlaif, Z. N. (2024). Between tech and text: The use of generative AI in Palestinian universities - a ChatGPT case study. *Cogent Education, 11*(1), 2380622. DOI: 10.1080/2331186X.2024.2380622

Han, A., Zhou, X., Cai, Z., Han, S., Ko, R., Corrigan, S., & Peppler, K. A. (2024). Teachers, Parents, and Students' perspectives on Integrating Generative AI into Elementary Literacy Education. *Proceedings of the CHI Conference on Human Factors in Computing Systems*, 1–17. DOI: 10.1145/3613904.3642438

Hutson, J., Jeevanjee, T., Graaf, V. V., Lively, J., Weber, J., Weir, G., Arnone, K., Carnes, G., Vosevich, K., Plate, D., Leary, M., & Edele, S. (2022). Artificial Intelligence and the Disruption of Higher Education: Strategies for Integrations across Disciplines. *Creative Education, 13*(12), 3953–3980. DOI: 10.4236/ce.2022.1312253

Imran, M. C., Khaliq Bashar, Budiarti Putri Uleng, Nina Ariani, Sukmawati, Suharti Siradjuddin, Sujarwo, & Irman. (2022). The Impact of Computer Assisted Language Learning (CALL) Technology on Indonesian Learners' Speaking Skills. *IJOLEH : International Journal of Education and Humanities, 1*(2), 183–189. DOI: 10.56314/ijoleh.v1i2.83

Jiang, D., Pei, Y., Yang, G., & Wang, X. (2022). Research and Analysis on the Integration of Artificial Intelligence in College English Teaching. *Mathematical Problems in Engineering, 2022*, 1–8. DOI: 10.1155/2022/3997573

Kara, S. (2018). Blended learning: A model to enhance engagement in reading class. *Abant İzzet Baysal Üniversitesi Eğitim Fakültesi Dergisi, 18*(2), 953–970. DOI: 10.17240/aibuefd.2018..-431467

Karataş, F., Abedi, F. Y., Ozek Gunyel, F., Karadeniz, D., & Kuzgun, Y. (2024). Incorporating AI in foreign language education: An investigation into ChatGPT's effect on foreign language learners. *Education and Information Technologies, 29*(15), 19343–19366. DOI: 10.1007/s10639-024-12574-6

Kurtz, G., Amzalag, M., Shaked, N., Zaguri, Y., Kohen-Vacs, D., Gal, E., Zailer, G., & Barak-Medina, E. (2024). Strategies for Integrating Generative AI into Higher Education: Navigating Challenges and Leveraging Opportunities. *Education Sciences, 14*(5), 503. DOI: 10.3390/educsci14050503

Leavy, P. (2017). *Research design: Quantitative, qualitative, mixed methods, arts-based and community-based participatory research approaches*. The Guilford Press.

Makeleni, S., Mutongoza, B. H., & Linake, M. A. (2023). Language Education and Artificial Intelligence: An Exploration of Challenges Confronting Academics in Global South Universities. *Journal of Culture and Values in Education, 6*(2), 158–171. DOI: 10.46303/jcve.2023.14

Özdere, M. (2023). The Integration of Artificial Intelligence in English Education: Opportunities and Challenges. [LET Journal]. *Language Education & Technology, 3*(2), 137–172.

Redmond, P., Heffernan, A., Abawi, L., Brown, A., & Henderson, R. (2018). An Online Engagement Framework for Higher Education. *Online Learning : the Official Journal of the Online Learning Consortium, 22*(1). Advance online publication. DOI: 10.24059/olj.v22i1.1175

Roy, D., & Putatunda, T. (2023). From Textbooks to Chatbots: Integrating AI in English literature classrooms of India. *Journal of E-Learning and Knowledge Society*, 65-73 Pages. DOI: 10.20368/1971-8829/1135860

Sasabone, L. (2023). Applying Google Classroom As An Instructional Technology Media In Improving Students' Reading For English For Specific Purposes (ESP). *EDULEC : Education. Language And Culture Journal, 3*(1), 110–119. DOI: 10.56314/edulec.v3i1.123

Škobo, M., & Petričević, V. (2023). Navigating the Challenges and Opportunities of Literary Translation in the Age of AI: Striking a Balance Between Human Expertise and Machine Power. *Društvene i Humanističke Studije (Online), 8*(2(23)), 317–336. DOI: 10.51558/2490-3647.2023.8.2.317

Sujarwo, Abdul Hakim Yassi, & Abbas, Herawaty, & Harlinah sahib. (2024). An Interactive-Based E-Module of Translation Technology of Blended and Online Learning to Improve Autonomous Learning. [TSRJ]. *The Seyreport Journal, 19*(06), 193–209. DOI: 10.5281/ZENODO.11547317

Sujarwo, S., Asdar, A., Sabillah, B. M., Sukmawati, S., Akhiruddin, A., & Muh. Syata, W. (2023). Innovation In English Language Learning Model Based Digital Literacy To Construct Young Learners' Character. *Ethical Lingua. Journal of Language Teaching and Literature, 10*(2). Advance online publication. DOI: 10.30605/25409190.640

Sulviana, Muhammad Chairil Imran & Sulviana. (2022). Using BBC Web-Based Learning Courses to Improve Vocational High School (VHS) Students' Speaking Skill. *EDULEC : Education, Language, and Culture Journal, 2*(1), 94–100. DOI: 10.56314/edulec.v2i1.34

Suryana, I., Asrianto, A., & Murwantono, D. (2020). Artificial Intelligence to Master English Listening Skills for Non-English Major Students. *Journal of Languages and Language Teaching, 8*(1), 48. DOI: 10.33394/jollt.v8i1.2221

Tammets, K., & Ley, T. (2023). Integrating AI tools in teacher professional learning: A conceptual model and illustrative case. *Frontiers in Artificial Intelligence, 6*, 1255089. DOI: 10.3389/frai.2023.1255089 PMID: 38130325

Tang, J., & Foley, J. (2022). A Case Study on the Effectiveness of Applying Content and Language Integrated Learning in an Artificial Intelligence English Reading Course. *Arab World English Journal, 13*(3), 236–253. DOI: 10.24093/awej/vol13no3.15

Chapter 5
AI-Enhanced Language Acquisition:
Transforming the Learning Experience

Anshari Anshari
https://orcid.org/0009-0003-7113-7792
Universitas Negeri Makassar, Indonesia

Andi Asrifan
https://orcid.org/0000-0002-9934-6129
Universitas Negeri Makassar, Indonesia

ABSTRACT

This chapter examines the transformative influence of Artificial Intelligence (AI) on language acquisition, emphasizing how technologies like Natural Language Processing, machine learning, and speech recognition personalize and improve the learning experience. Conventional methods frequently exhibit inflexibility, limited practical utility, and unequal accessibility, issues AI adeptly resolves. AI-powered platforms provide instantaneous feedback, personalized content, and engaging practice via chatbots, speech synthesis, and gamification. Moreover, AI facilitates collaborative, immersive, and culturally attuned learning environments, enhancing student engagement and long-term retention. Ethical aspects, including data protection and digital inclusion, are highlighted to guarantee ethical integration. As AI advances, it offers more fair, accessible, and learner-centered methodologies in language instruction, ultimately enabling varied learners globally to cultivate communicative competence in significant and dynamic manners.

DOI: 10.4018/979-8-3373-6330-1.ch005

Copyright © 2026, IGI Global Scientific Publishing. Copying or distributing in print or electronic forms without written permission of IGI Global Scientific Publishing is prohibited.

1. INTRODUCTION TO AI IN LANGUAGE LEARNING

1.1 The Evolution of Language Acquisition

Language learning has undergone considerable evolution over the centuries, mirroring shifts in pedagogical philosophies, societal demands, and technological progress (Shadiev & Wang, 2022). Traditionally, language acquisition predominantly involved rote memorization, primarily dependent on grammar exercises and vocabulary lists. The Grammar-Translation Method, dominant in the 19th century, prioritized text translation and the acquisition of grammatical rules, frequently neglecting speaking and listening competencies. This approach, although successful in imparting reading and writing skills, did not cultivate communicative competence in learners.

With the advancement of educational theories, emphasis transitioned to more participatory and communicative methodologies. The Direct Method originated in the early 20th century, advocating for immersion in the target language via conversation and practical application (Tang, 2024). This approach prompted learners to engage in thought and discourse in the new language, so improving their communicative proficiency. Nonetheless, these methodologies encountered constraints, especially regarding accessibility and customization to individual learning requirements.

The emergence of technology in the late 20th century signified a pivotal moment in language instruction. Audiovisual aids, language laboratories, and computer-assisted language learning (CALL) instruments begin transforming the domain of language acquisition (Ahmed, 2022). These tools afforded learners immersive experiences, facilitating the development of listening and speaking skills in more authentic circumstances. Nonetheless, early digital technologies frequently exhibited deficiencies in personalization and adaptability, depriving numerous learners of the customized assistance they required.

The advent of the internet and mobile technology in the 21st century has rendered language learning more accessible than before. Digital platforms and applications have emerged, enabling learners to access language content at any time and from any location (Sofi-Karim et al., 2023). Nevertheless, although these technologies provided enhanced flexibility, they continued to falter in delivering the personalized learning experiences that numerous pupils necessitated.

The integration of Artificial Intelligence (AI) into language acquisition signifies the forthcoming major advancement in this domain. Artificial Intelligence technologies, including Natural Language Processing (NLP) and machine learning, possess the capacity to revolutionize the educational experience by providing personalized, adaptive, and interactive language learning approaches. Artificial intelligence can instantaneously assess a learner's strengths and limitations, offering customized feedback and resources that align with individual learning preferences (Ezzaim et al., 2024). This transition to AI-enhanced language acquisition not only overcomes the shortcomings of earlier methods but also creates new opportunities for learners to interact with languages in dynamic and efficient manners.

The progression of language acquisition signifies an ongoing pursuit of more efficacious pedagogical approaches. The use of AI in this endeavor is poised to transform language acquisition, rendering the experience more captivating, tailored, and efficient for learners globally.

1.2 Understanding Artificial Intelligence

Artificial Intelligence (AI) denotes the emulation of human cognitive functions by computer systems (Alkatheiri, 2022). These processes include learning (acquiring information and its use), reasoning (using rules to derive approximate or definitive conclusions), and self-correction. Fundamentally, AI seeks to develop machines capable of executing activities that ordinarily necessitate human intelligence, including natural language comprehension, pattern recognition, and decision-making.

Fundamental principles in artificial intelligence encompass machine learning, deep learning, and natural language processing (NLP). Machine learning is a branch of artificial intelligence that focuses on creating algorithms that allow computers to learn from data and generate predictions (Sarker, 2021). Deep learning, a subclass of machine learning, employs multilayered neural networks to examine diverse data elements, facilitating intricate pattern recognition. NLP primarily concentrates on the connection between computers and humans via natural language, facilitating machines to comprehend, interpret, and produce human language effectively.

Numerous AI technologies have arisen in the realm of language acquisition that markedly improve the educational experience. Intelligent tutoring systems, which utilize AI to deliver tailored education and feedback, represent one of the most significant applications (Lin et al., 2023). These systems evaluate a learner's performance in real time, adjusting content and difficulty levels to align with individual requirements. This tailored methodology enables learners to advance at their individual speed, targeting certain areas of challenge.

Another pertinent AI technology is speech recognition, enabling learners to practice pronunciation and obtain quick feedback. These technologies can provide corrective suggestions and monitor progress over time by comparing a learner's spoken language to native pronunciation (Sun, 2023). This ability is essential for enhancing speaking skills, as it simulates authentic conversational practice.

AI-powered chatbots and virtual assistants are essential in language acquisition (Polakova & Klimova, 2024). These technologies facilitate student engagement through discussion, offering opportunities for practice and reinforcing vocabulary and grammar in a contextually pertinent manner. Additionally, they can be accessible around the clock, providing learners the flexibility to practice at their convenience. Finally, AI-driven language translation systems are revolutionizing the manner in which learners engage with content in many languages (Kruk & Kałużna, 2025). These methods aid comprehension and expose learners to genuine language use, enriching their grasp of cultural subtleties and contextual meanings.

In conclusion, comprehending AI and its fundamental notions is crucial for acknowledging its transformational capacity in language acquisition. Integrating these technologies into language teaching can yield more interesting, individualized, and successful learning experiences that address the different requirements of learners worldwide.

1.3 The Need for AI in Language Acquisition

Conventional language acquisition techniques have consistently encountered numerous obstacles that impede their efficacy in addressing the varied requirements of learners (Mohamed, 2024). A major concern is the uniform approach frequently utilized in educational environments. Instructors often provide material at a pace that fails to fit all pupils, resulting in some learners feeling overwhelmed while others may not experience adequate challenge. This discrepancy may result in disengagement and frustration, especially among individuals who need extra assistance or those who progress more rapidly than their counterparts.

Moreover, conventional techniques sometimes prioritize rote memorization and grammatical exercises, leading to a deficiency in practical application. Students may possess the ability to conjugate verbs or translate texts yet encounter difficulties in participating in genuine discussions (Anitha and Reddy 2025). The disparity between theoretical understanding and practical application is a prevalent obstacle to attaining fluency and communication proficiency.

Moreover, access to high-quality language instruction is inconsistent across various locations and demographics. Numerous learners, particularly in rural or underprivileged regions, may be deprived of access to competent educators or immersion settings that facilitate language acquisition (Faragher et al., 2021). This disparity in educational resources might sustain language learning deficiencies and restrict chances for numerous persons.

The incorporation of AI in language education mitigates these issues by offering personalized, adaptive, and scalable solutions (Sajja et al., 2024). A primary advantage of AI is its capacity to customize learning experiences according to individual requirements. Intelligent tutoring systems provide learners with tailored feedback and materials that reflect their individual skills and weaknesses. This degree of customisation guarantees that students are suitably challenged and supported, so augmenting their overall engagement and motivation.

AI technologies enable practical language application in ways that conventional methods cannot (Al-khresheh, 2024). Conversational AI and chatbots enable learners to participate in talks at any time, offering a secure environment for practice devoid of judgment. This engagement enhances speaking and listening abilities while fostering confidence in daily language use.

Furthermore, AI has the potential to democratize access to language teaching. AI-driven online platforms enable learners from diverse backgrounds to access superior materials and training irrespective of their geographical location (Tafazoli, 2024). This skill can bridge educational disparities and offer language acquisition opportunities to a wider audience.

In conclusion, using AI in language instruction mitigates the intrinsic problems of conventional techniques while providing multiple advantages. AI-enhanced language acquisition can revolutionize the learning experience by personalizing educational encounters, enabling practical application, and broadening resource accessibility, rendering it more effective and inclusive for all learners.

2. AI TECHNOLOGIES TRANSFORMING LANGUAGE LEARNING

2.1 Natural Language Processing (NLP)

Natural Language Processing (NLP) is a critical subset of artificial intelligence that focuses on the interaction between computers and human language (Khan et al.2023). It encompasses the ability of machines to understand, interpret, and generate human language in a way that is both meaningful and contextually relevant. NLP combines linguistics, computer science, and machine learning to enable computers to process and analyze large amounts of natural language data. In the realm of language learning, NLP has emerged as a transformative technology, enhancing the educational experience through various applications.

One of the primary applications of NLP in language learning is automated feedback on writing. Tools equipped with NLP algorithms can analyze students' written texts, providing real-time feedback on grammar, vocabulary usage, and overall coherence. For instance, platforms like Grammarly utilize NLP to identify errors and suggest improvements, helping learners refine their writing skills (Nikhil et al.2025). This immediate feedback mechanism encourages students to engage in iterative writing processes, ultimately leading to better writing proficiency.

Another significant application of NLP is in the development of conversational agents, such as chatbots (Joseph and Eapen2023). These AI-driven tools simulate human-like conversations, allowing learners to practice their speaking and listening skills in a low-pressure environment. For example, Duolingo employs NLP in its chatbot feature, enabling users to engage in dialogues that mirror real-life conversations. This interactive practice not only reinforces vocabulary and grammar but also enhances learners' confidence in using the language.

NLP is also instrumental in language translation applications, which facilitate comprehension and learning (Klimova et al.2023). Tools like Google Translate utilize advanced NLP algorithms to provide instant translations, enabling learners to access content in their target language. While translation tools are not without limitations, they serve as valuable resources for learners to explore authentic texts and understand contextual meanings, thereby enriching their language acquisition experience.

Case studies highlight the effectiveness of NLP tools in educational settings. A notable example is the use of automated essay scoring systems, which leverage NLP to evaluate student essays (Mizumoto & Eguchi, 2023). Research conducted on the use of such systems in universities showed that students who received feedback from NLP tools demonstrated significant improvements in their writing skills compared to those who relied solely on traditional grading methods.

Additionally, language learning platforms like Rosetta Stone have integrated NLP to enhance their speech recognition capabilities. By analyzing learners' pronunciation and providing immediate corrective feedback, these platforms help users develop better speaking skills, making the learning process more interactive and effective (Sun, 2023).

In summary, Natural Language Processing is revolutionizing language learning by providing innovative tools that enhance writing, conversation, and comprehension. Through applications such as automated feedback systems, conversational agents, and translation tools, NLP fosters a more engaging and effective learning experience, ultimately empowering learners to achieve greater fluency and confidence in their language skills.

2.2 Machine Learning and Personalization

Machine learning, a branch of artificial intelligence, is essential for developing tailored learning experiences in language teaching (Kuddus, 2022). Machine learning systems may adjust to the needs, preferences, and progress of individual learners by utilizing algorithms that evaluate data patterns. This versatility facilitates a more customized teaching environment that can markedly improve language acquisition.

The essence of machine learning is in its capacity to analyze extensive datasets and extract insights from them. In the realm of language acquisition, these algorithms can evaluate multiple characteristics, such as a learner's strengths, shortcomings, learning speed, and engagement levels (Song et al., 2024). For example, when a student engages with a language learning platform, the system gathers data on their performance, including quiz results, time allocated to exercises, and areas of difficulty. Machine learning algorithms examine this data to discern patterns and provide tailored learning pathways that cater to the learner's individual requirements.

A notable instance of individualized learning via machine learning is the Duolingo platform (Akpabio et al., 2025). Duolingo utilizes adaptive learning methodologies that customize activities according to each user's skill level. As students advance, the system modifies task complexity according to their performance, guaranteeing they remain challenged without experiencing overwhelm. This adaptive approach sustains learner motivation and engagement, hence enhancing language acquisition efficacy.

A further example is the implementation of AI-powered language tutors, as seen in platforms like Busuu (Mavidi, 2025). These tutors employ machine learning algorithms to evaluate a learner's performance instantaneously. Should a learner persistently encounters difficulties with a specific grammatical structure, the system is capable of offering more focused tasks and materials to strengthen that notion. This tailored method not only enables mastery of difficult subjects but also cultivates a sense of ownership in the learning experience.

Moreover, platforms such as Rosetta Stone have used machine learning to improve their speech recognition functionalities. The system analyzes learners' pronunciation and delivers rapid feedback, adapting to individual speech patterns and delivering customized workouts to enhance specific pronunciation regions (Evers & Chen, 2022). This customized feedback mechanism enables learners to enhance their speaking abilities at their own tempo, resulting in increased confidence and fluency.

Moreover, machine learning can augment the social dimension of language acquisition. Platforms that include social learning aspects can employ algorithms to link learners with peers who share analogous objectives or difficulties, hence enhancing collaborative learning experiences (Tan et al., 2022). This peer connection can enhance the learning experience, as learners exchange thoughts and assist one another in their language acquisition endeavors.

In conclusion, machine learning is revolutionizing language teaching by facilitating personalized learning experiences tailored to individual learners' requirements. By utilizing dynamic evaluation and customized feedback, platforms may establish interesting and successful language learning pathways, so enabling learners to confidently and competently attain their linguistic objectives.

2.3 Speech Recognition and Synthesis

Speech recognition and synthesis technologies have become essential elements in language learning, greatly improving the methods by which learners practice and acquire new languages (Sayers et al., 2021). These AI-driven solutions facilitate learners' interaction with language dynamically and engagingly, providing real-time feedback and enhancing pronunciation, fluency, and general communication abilities.

Speech recognition technology enables computers to comprehend and interpret spoken words. This capacity is very advantageous for enhancing pronunciation and speaking proficiency in language acquisition. Speech recognition systems can analyze a learner's spoken input, compare it to native pronunciation, and deliver immediate feedback (Sun, 2023). This immediate assessment assists learners in recognizing areas requiring enhancement, like intonation, emphasis, or articulation. Language learning software such as Rosetta Stone and Babbel employs speech recognition technology to evaluate users' pronunciation. When learners articulate into their devices, the system assesses their speech and provides correction recommendations, facilitating real-time enhancement of their pronunciation.

Another significant facet of speech technology is voice synthesis, which entails producing spoken language from written text. This technology is essential for offering learners audio exemplars of accurate pronunciation and intonation (Bogach et al., 2021). By engaging with native speakers, learners can enhance their comprehension of the pronunciation of words and phrases within context. Applications such as Google Translate and several language learning platforms employ speech synthesis to vocalize translations, assisting learners in acclimating to the phonetics and cadence of the target language.

Furthermore, the use of speech technology into language learning platforms enhances a more immersive and interactive experience (Wang & Huang, 2025). AI-powered chatbots and virtual assistants can facilitate conversational engagement for learners, enabling them to practice speaking in a stress-free setting. These conversational agents, endowed with speech recognition skills, can comprehend and respond to learners' verbal input, emulating authentic discussions. This engagement improves speaking skills and fosters learners' confidence in their capacity to communicate successfully in the target language.

Case studies further demonstrate the efficacy of speech recognition in language instruction. Studies on the application of speech technology in educational settings indicate that students utilizing these tools exhibit notable enhancements in pronunciation precision and verbal fluency (Asratie et al., 2023). In a research study, learners utilizing speech recognition software surpassed their colleagues who depended exclusively on conventional methods, underscoring the advantages of integrating technology into language practice.

In conclusion, speech recognition and synthesis technologies are essential for improving language acquisition by aiding pronunciation practice and enabling interactive conversation. These tools facilitate quick feedback and immersive experiences, enabling learners to enhance their speaking skills more efficiently, hence fostering increased fluency and confidence in their language proficiency. As AI progresses, the prospects for voice technology in language acquisition will broaden, providing novel chances for learners to interact with languages in significant manners.

3. DESIGNING AI-ENHANCED LANGUAGE LEARNING ENVIRONMENTS

3.1 Interactive Language Learning Platforms

The emergence of artificial intelligence has resulted in the creation of interactive language learning platforms that markedly improve the educational experience. Effective AI-driven platforms include diverse elements to engage learners, personalize their educational experiences, and promote significant language acquisition (Chen, 2024). Comprehending these attributes is crucial for assessing and contrasting prevalent language learning software.

A fundamental characteristic of efficient AI-driven platforms is personalization. These platforms utilize machine learning algorithms to assess learners' performance data and customize content to meet their specific needs (Mishra, 2025). For example, they can modify the complexity of exercises according to a learner's advancement, guaranteeing that users remain consistently challenged without experiencing overwhelm. This adaptability cultivates a sense of ownership in the learning process and sustains learner motivation.

A crucial characteristic is interactivity. Efficient platforms facilitate active engagement of learners with the topic. This may encompass gamified components, such points, badges, and leaderboards, which motivate learners to accomplish objectives and engage in constant practice. Moreover, interactive tasks that necessitate learners to engage in speaking, listening, reading, and writing effectively develop language abilities comprehensively. Platforms like as Duolingo exhibit this methodology by integrating gamification to generate an engaging educational atmosphere (Tajik, 2025).

Feedback systems are essential in AI-driven language learning platforms. Prompt feedback on exercises, quizzes, and verbal language practice enables learners to comprehend their errors and rectify them instantaneously (Di et al. 2022). This immediate assessment is essential for language acquisition, as it enables learners to pinpoint areas needing enhancement and solidifies their comprehension of linguistic concepts. Babbel offers customers pronunciation feedback via its speech recognition technology, allowing learners to enhance their speaking skills efficiently.

Three significant contenders emerge in the comparison of prominent language learning software: Duolingo, Babbel, and Rosetta Stone. Duolingo is distinguished for its gamified methodology, providing an extensive array of interactive exercises that encompass vocabulary, grammar, and pronunciation (Shortt et al., 2023). The adaptive learning system customizes the experience according to user performance, rendering it appropriate for learners at various proficiency levels.

Conversely, Babbel prioritizes verbal proficiency and practical situations. The courses are crafted by language specialists and emphasize practical vocabulary and phrases, rendering them suitable for learners aiming to speak successfully in daily contexts (Mendes et al., 2023). Babbel utilizes speech recognition technology to offer feedback on pronunciation, hence improving speaking skills.

Rosetta Stone is a reputable platform that employs immersive learning methodologies (Song et al., 2023). Its emphasis on context and visual cues aids learners in associating words with meanings, promoting enhanced comprehension. The platform's speech recognition features facilitate pronunciation practice, while its organized courses direct learners through an extensive language acquisition process.

In conclusion, creating effective AI-enhanced language learning environments necessitates the integration of personalization, interactivity, and feedback mechanisms. An analysis of prominent applications such as Duolingo, Babbel, and Rosetta Stone reveals that each platform possesses distinct advantages, addressing various learning preferences and objectives. As technology advances, these interactive platforms will assume an increasingly vital role in revolutionizing the language acquisition process.

3.2 Gamification and Engagement

Gamification has emerged as an effective strategy in language acquisition, employing game design elements to enhance engagement and motivation among learners (Ravichandran et al., 2024). Integrating gamified components into educational systems improves interactivity, fun, and effectiveness in language learning. Gamified learning experiences markedly elevate student motivation and foster greater engagement with language subjects.

A primary benefit of gamification is its ability to transform tedious learning tasks into stimulating challenges. Elements such as points, badges, leaderboards, and levels foster a sense of achievement and competition, encouraging learners to participate actively (Balci et al., 2022). Language learning platforms like Duolingo utilize gamification strategies to motivate users for course completion and regular practice. This reward system fosters a sense of accomplishment and encourages continuous engagement, as participants are motivated to accumulate points and rise in the rankings.

Moreover, gamified learning experiences cultivate a growth mindset by allowing learners to face difficulties and extract lessons from failures. In a gamified situation, errors are often perceived as essential to the learning experience rather than as impediments (Ahsan, 2025). This perspective encourages learners to interact with language in a low-risk setting, so enhancing their confidence and proficiency. Platforms that incorporate quizzes and interactive challenges allow learners to evaluate their knowledge and receive prompt feedback, thereby enhancing their understanding of linguistic subjects.

Artificial intelligence markedly improves gamified learning experiences by creating adaptive learning games tailored to individual learner needs (Suresh & Dhakshina 2024). These platforms employ machine learning algorithms to assess user performance and adjust task complexity in real-time. This adaptability ensures that learners are consistently challenged yet being able to attain success. For instance, if a learner exhibits competency in vocabulary tasks but struggles with grammar, the system can independently provide more grammar-focused assignments to enhance their skills.

Moreover, AI may tailor the gaming experience by modifying content to correspond with learners' interests and preferences. By analyzing data on learners' interactions and achievements, AI-driven platforms may recommend specific games or challenges aligned with individual goals (Liu, 2024). This level of customization enhances engagement and fosters a deeper connection between learners and the information.

Furthermore, AI-augmented gamification can facilitate collaborative learning experiences. Platforms can create multiplayer environments that facilitate competition or collaboration among learners, hence boosting social interaction and communication skills (Hoter et al., 2024). This collaborative aspect enhances engagement and mirrors genuine language usage, as communication often occurs in social contexts.

In conclusion, gamification significantly impacts language acquisition by making the process more engaging and enjoyable. Integrating game design elements and employing AI to create adaptive learning experiences can improve educational platforms by engaging learners, promoting a growth mindset, and facilitating meaningful interactions with language content. As technology advances, opportunities for gamified language learning will expand, offering innovative and efficient approaches for learners to enhance language ability.

3.3 Collaborative Learning with AI

Collaborative learning has emerged as an effective method for language acquisition, promoting communication, teamwork, and the exchange of knowledge among learners (Yang, 2023). The incorporation of artificial intelligence (AI) into collaborative learning settings improves interactions by offering tools that enable peer learning and foster significant involvement. AI-driven platforms enable chances for learners to engage, cooperate, and enhance language abilities through dynamic and interactive methods.

AI technologies that promote peer learning typically encompass elements like discussion forums, collaborative projects, and real-time collaboration instruments (Zamiri & Esmaeili, 2024). These platforms enable learners to interact, exchange insights, and collaboratively practice language skills. Platforms such as Tandem and HelloTalk facilitate connections among language learners globally, allowing them to practice speaking and writing with native speakers. Utilizing text, phone, and video communications, learners can engage in real-time collaboration, offering mutual feedback and assistance. AI algorithms can pair users according to their linguistic objectives, hobbies, and skill levels, guaranteeing that collaborations are both efficient and stimulating.

A notable case study in collaborative language learning is the application of AI inside the “Flipped Classroom” concept, wherein students interact with educational material at home and collaborate on projects during class sessions. A university study involved students utilizing AI-driven platforms for foreign-language collaborative presentations. The AI technologies offered real-time translation and speech recognition capabilities, enabling students to communicate more successfully regardless of their language competence levels (Zhai & Wibowo, 2023). This collaborative setting enhanced their linguistic abilities while promoting collaboration and critical thinking, since participants were required to negotiate meaning and cooperate in content development.

A noteworthy instance is the “Global Classroom” effort, which links classes from various nations using AI-enhanced platforms. In this project, students participate in collaborative language learning activities, including cultural exchanges and shared storytelling (Yingsoon et al., 2025). AI tools enhance communication by offering translation services and cultural context, enabling students to collaborate effortlessly. Participants' feedback revealed that these collaborative experiences markedly improved their language proficiency and cultural comprehension, as they learnt to overcome language barriers and interact with varied perspectives.

Moreover, AI can assess collaborative interactions to yield insights into group dynamics and individual contributions. Through the evaluation of involvement levels and communication patterns, AI systems can pinpoint places where learners may want supplementary support or motivation (Liao et al., 2024). This data-driven methodology assists instructors in customizing interventions to improve collaboration and guarantee that all learners are actively involved in the process.

In conclusion, AI-enhanced collaborative learning fosters rewarding language acquisition experiences that encourage peer interaction and engagement. AI facilitates the collaborative learning process by enabling connections among learners and offering helpful resources, resulting in better language proficiency and cultural comprehension. As educational technology advances, the potential for AI-driven collaborative learning environments will increase, providing new options for learners to excel in their language acquisition endeavors.

4. ASSESSING THE IMPACT OF AI ON LANGUAGE ACQUISITION

4.1 Measuring Language Proficiency

The evolution of language acquisition through artificial intelligence (AI) necessitates appropriate assessment tools to evaluate learners' ability and monitor their progress (Alt et al., 2023). AI-driven exams and feedback systems provide unique solutions that improve the evaluation process, offering learners immediate insights into their performance and areas needing enhancement.

A primary benefit of AI-driven exams is their capacity to deliver instantaneous feedback. Conventional exams frequently provide delayed feedback, which might impede learners' capacity to rectify errors and consolidate their comprehension of linguistic topics (Ghanbari & Nowroozi, 2021). Conversely, AI-driven solutions may promptly assess responses, providing constructive comments on grammar, vocabulary, pronunciation, and general language utilization. Language learning software such as Duolingo and Babbel employ AI algorithms to assess learners' performance on exercises and quizzes, providing customized recommendations for enhancement. This prompt feedback cultivates a more dynamic learning atmosphere, enabling learners to modify their study techniques and strengthen their comprehension of the content.

Furthermore, AI-driven evaluations can adjust to the competency levels of particular learners. Utilizing adaptive testing methodologies, these systems can adjust the question difficulty according on a learner's prior answers (Bolsinova et al. 2022). This customization guarantees that evaluations are both demanding and attainable, offering a more precise assessment of a learner's competence. Platforms such as Pearson’s Versant test employ artificial intelligence to evaluate speaking and listening competencies, dynamically adjusting questions to correspond with the test-taker's proficiency. This method not only improves the dependability of evaluations but also maintains student engagement during the assessment process.

The significance of data analytics in monitoring progress is paramount. AI systems gather and evaluate extensive data regarding learners' interactions, performance, and engagement levels (Ouyang et al. 2023). This data-centric methodology allows educators and students to obtain significant insights on language learning pathways. For example, via dashboards and visualizations, learners can track their development over time, discerning trends and patterns in their performance. Educators can utilize this data to customize education, offering targeted interventions for students who may be experiencing difficulties with particular language skills.

Moreover, AI analytics can pinpoint prevalent challenges within a group of learners, guiding curriculum development and teaching methodologies. Through the analysis of aggregate data, educators can identify trends that reveal common areas of difficulty for learners, enabling them to modify their instructional strategies accordingly (López-Meneses et al. 2025). This proactive method of assessment and feedback guarantees that training is attuned to learners' requirements, so improving the overall efficacy of language education.

In conclusion, evaluating language ability via AI-driven tests and data analytics signifies a substantial progression in language acquisition. These tools empower learners to take charge of their language acquisition journeys by offering real-time feedback, individualized assessments, and actionable insights into their progress. As AI advances, the possibility for creative evaluation techniques will augment the efficacy of language teaching, ensuring that learners acquire the abilities necessary to thrive in an increasingly linked world.

4.2 Student Engagement and Motivation

The use of artificial intelligence (AI) into language learning settings has markedly impacted student engagement and motivation (Wei, 2023). Studies demonstrate that AI-powered tools and platforms can facilitate more engaging and tailored learning experiences, resulting in heightened motivation among learners. Comprehending the influence of AI on these facets of language acquisition is crucial for formulating efficient instructional programs.

AI significantly boosts learner motivation by means of customisation. Conventional language acquisition techniques frequently employ a uniform strategy, perhaps resulting in children experiencing disconnection or inundation (Ellikkal & Rajamohan, 2024). Conversely, AI-driven platforms employ machine learning algorithms to assess the performance and preferences of individual learners. By customizing information and exercises to address particular requirements, these platforms foster a more pertinent and captivating learning experience. Duolingo's adaptive learning technology modifies exercise difficulty according to users' progress, ensuring learners are continually challenged without experiencing frustration. This tailored method cultivates a sense of accomplishment and motivates learners to continue their education.

Studies indicate that gamification, frequently combined with AI, significantly enhances student engagement. AI-driven platforms foster an engaging and encouraging atmosphere for language learners by integrating gamified components such as points, badges, and leaderboards (Renacido and Biray 2025). Research demonstrates that gamified encounters can enhance engagement and maintain interest in language acquisition. A study examining students utilizing gamified language learning software revealed that participants exposed to gamification components demonstrated elevated motivation and engagement levels relative to those employing conventional approaches. This discovery highlights the efficacy of integrating AI-driven gamification techniques in language instruction.

Furthermore, AI provides instantaneous feedback, which is essential for sustaining student motivation. Conventional examinations frequently yield delayed feedback, resulting in pupils' uncertainty over their development (Singun, 2025). Conversely, AI-driven platforms provide immediate assessments, enabling learners to recognize their strengths and areas for enhancement in real-time. This prompt feedback mechanism not only consolidates learning but also motivates students to assume responsibility for their advancement. Platforms such as Grammarly and Babbel utilize AI to deliver constructive feedback on writing and speech, allowing learners to make timely corrections and enhance their confidence in their skills.

To augment engagement via AI, instructors may adopt tactics that foster social interaction and collaboration. AI-powered solutions can link learners with global peers, enhancing language practice and cultural exchange. Platforms such as Tandem and HelloTalk facilitate interactions between learners and native speakers, promoting a feeling of community and collaborative learning (Yin & Fathi, 2025). This collaborative element enhances motivation and deepens the language acquisition process by presenting learners with varied views and authentic circumstances.

In conclusion, artificial intelligence significantly influences student involvement and motivation in language learning. AI-driven platforms foster dynamic and inspiring learning environments by personalizing experiences, integrating gamification, delivering quick feedback, and promoting social interaction. As technology progresses, employing these tactics will be essential for augmenting engagement and maintaining learner motivation throughout their language acquisition experiences.

4.3 Long-Term Outcomes of AI-Enhanced Learning

As artificial intelligence (AI) progressively influences language education, comprehending its long-term effects on learners' retention and application of language abilities is becoming more critical (Liu, 2024). Studies demonstrate that AI-augmented learning environments boost immediate language acquisition and foster long-term competency and practical application of language abilities.

Numerous studies have investigated the efficacy of AI-driven language learning aids in enhancing retention (Aluko et al., 2025). A longitudinal study investigating the effects of AI-driven platforms like as Duolingo revealed that learners who utilized these tools continually exhibited superior retention rates compared to those who depended only on conventional approaches. The research emphasized that the gamified features and tailored feedback systems of AI-driven platforms promoted consistent practice, crucial for strengthening language skills and averting knowledge deterioration. By cultivating a practice of ongoing interaction, AI technologies assist learners in retaining vocabulary, grammar, and pronunciation for prolonged durations.

Furthermore, studies indicate that AI-augmented learning environments promote the practical utilization of language abilities in real-world situations. A study involving university students and AI-driven conversational agents indicated that participants experienced enhanced confidence in their speaking skills and a heightened readiness to converse with native speakers (Tai & Chen, 2023). The interactive characteristics of these platforms enable learners to engage in language practice within authentic contexts, thereby connecting theoretical knowledge with practical application. This practical application is essential for cultivating fluency and communicative ability, since learners are more equipped to manage social interactions in the target language.

The ramifications of these discoveries for forthcoming language education are substantial. As AI technologies advance, they possess the capacity to augment the efficacy of language acquisition (Kuddus, 2022). Advancements in natural language processing and speech recognition may result in more complex conversational agents that offer nuanced feedback and replicate realistic talks. This evolution may generate immersive learning experiences that closely replicate real-life interactions, so augmenting learners' confidence and skill.

The scalability of AI-driven systems offers a chance to democratize access to high-quality language teaching. AI can transcend educational disparities and empower learners from varied backgrounds to attain their language objectives by offering individualized learning experiences to a wider audience (Arani2024). This accessibility is especially crucial in a progressively globalized society, where multilingualism frequently serves as a significant advantage in both personal and professional spheres.

In conclusion, the long-term effects of AI-assisted language learning are encouraging, with evidence indicating greater retention and utilization of language abilities. The advancement of AI technologies will undoubtedly enhance the effectiveness, engagement, and accessibility of language teaching. Utilizing AI enables educators to effectively educate students for practical language application, ensuring they possess the requisite abilities to succeed in a multilingual society.

5. FUTURE DIRECTIONS AND ETHICAL CONSIDERATIONS

5.1 The Future of AI in Language Learning

The future of artificial intelligence (AI) in language acquisition possesses significant potential, propelled by developing technologies that are poised to further revolutionize the educational landscape (Kuddus, 2022). The ongoing evolution of AI is expected to enhance language acquisition through more personalized, immersive, and effective learning experiences for students globally.

Augmented reality (AR) and virtual reality (VR) are among the most promising upcoming technologies. These technologies can generate immersive settings that enable learners to practice language skills in authentic contexts (AlGerafi et al., 2023). A VR language learning program might replicate a marketplace in a foreign nation, enabling learners to converse with virtual sellers and enhance their speaking and listening skills in an interactive environment. This degree of immersion can augment engagement and retention, since learners are situated in settings that replicate real-life interactions.

Furthermore, progress in natural language processing (NLP) and machine learning will allow AI systems to comprehend and react to human language with enhanced precision and subtlety. Future AI-driven language learning platforms may integrate advanced conversational agents capable of maintaining context-aware dialogues (Casheekar et al. 2024). These agents can offer learners customized dialogues that adjust according to their competency and educational objectives, so fostering a more individualized and effective learning experience.

A notable advancement is the growing utilization of big data and analytics in education. AI systems can analyze extensive data produced by learners to discern trends and patterns that guide teaching tactics (Alam2023). Predictive analytics may be utilized to foresee learners' difficulties and deliver prompt actions, guaranteeing that assistance is accessible when required. This data-driven methodology will empower educators to make educated choices regarding curriculum development and teaching strategies, thereby improving the efficacy of language education.

Looking ahead, numerous forecasts might be articulated concerning the advancement of AI in education. Initially, we might anticipate a transition towards enhanced collaborative and social learning experiences enabled by AI. Platforms that link learners worldwide are expected to become increasingly common, promoting cultural interchange and interactive language practice (Selfa-Sastre et al. 2022). This international collaboration will boost linguistic proficiency and foster intercultural comprehension and communication.

As AI increasingly infiltrates language instruction, ethical considerations must remain paramount in conversations. Concerns over data privacy, equitable access to technology, and the potential for bias in AI algorithms must be resolved. It is essential to create and apply AI tools inclusively and equitably to optimize their advantages for all learners (Davoodi, 2024).

In conclusion, the prospects for AI in language acquisition are promising, with nascent technologies set to transform the educational landscape. By utilizing advancements such as augmented reality, virtual reality, and advanced analytics, instructors may develop more interesting, individualized, and effective language acquisition settings. It is crucial to carefully consider the ethical ramifications of emerging technologies, guaranteeing that all learners have fair access to the revolutionary capabilities of AI in language instruction.

5.2 Ethical Considerations in AI-Enhanced Learning

As artificial intelligence (AI) advances in language acquisition, it introduces substantial ethical issues that require attention to guarantee fair and equitable technology utilization (Javed, 2024). The two major concerns are data privacy and security, along with providing equitable access to AI capabilities.

Data privacy and security are essential in the realm of AI-augmented education. Language learning programs frequently gather extensive personal data, encompassing users' performance indicators, interaction habits, and sensitive information such as location and demographic statistics (Barrot, 2022). This data is essential for customizing learning experiences and enhancing AI algorithms; nonetheless, it also prompts worries regarding the storage, use, and dissemination of this information. Data security breaches may result in unauthorized access to confidential information, thereby jeopardizing users' privacy and safety.

Developers and educators must emphasize stringent data protection procedures to meet these problems (Liu & Khalil, 2023). This encompasses the implementation of encryption mechanisms, adherence to standards such as the General Data Protection Regulation (GDPR), and transparency regarding data gathering procedures. Educators and institutions must apprise learners of the data being gathered, its intended use, and the safeguards implemented to protect their information. By cultivating a culture of transparency and accountability, stakeholders may establish confidence with users and alleviate privacy concerns.

Equitable access to AI tools constitutes a significant ethical concern. Although AI can improve language acquisition for numerous individuals, discrepancies in technological access may intensify pre-existing educational inequalities (Kunjumuhammed2024). Students from marginalized communities may be deprived of the gadgets and internet access required to utilize AI-driven platforms effectively. The digital gap can impede their capacity to develop language skills and restrict their prospects for personal and professional advancement.

To enhance equitable access, collaboration among politicians, educators, and technology developers is crucial in devising inclusive solutions. This may entail offering subsidies for technological access, creating affordable or offline versions of AI products, and ensuring educational institutions possess the necessary resources to apply these technologies efficiently. Moreover, community-based projects can facilitate the connection by providing training and resources to marginalized people, enabling them to participate in AI-enhanced learning (Dogara, 2024).

In conclusion, whereas AI-enhanced language learning presents promising potential for innovation and enhancement, it is imperative to confront the ethical implications that accompany these developments. Emphasizing data privacy and security while guaranteeing equal access to AI tools is crucial for establishing a responsible and inclusive educational setting. By addressing these ethical dilemmas judiciously, stakeholders may leverage AI's revolutionary capabilities while protecting the interests and rights of all learners.

5.3 Preparing Educators for AI Integration

As artificial intelligence (AI) transforms language learning, it is essential to equip educators for the efficient incorporation of these technologies into their pedagogical methods (Kujundziski & Bojadjiev, 2025). Equipping teachers with essential training and resources will augment their capacity to utilize AI tools successfully, thereby aiding learners in their language acquisition processes.

Educator training programs should concentrate on numerous essential domains. Initially, professional development programs must equip educators with a comprehensive understanding of AI technology and their applications in language instruction. This entails acquainting educators with the capabilities of many AI-powered platforms, including adaptive learning systems, speech recognition technologies, and gamified applications. Workshops and seminars can be conducted to illustrate how these tools can augment instructional methodologies, enable personalized learning, and boost student engagement. Equipping educators with this understanding enables them to confidently employ AI technologies in their classrooms (Nazaretsky et al., 2022).

Furthermore, continuous assistance and resources are crucial for educators to remain informed about the newest developments in AI and language instruction. Establishing online repositories of information, such as tutorials, case studies, and best practices, can provide essential references for instructors aiming to incorporate AI into their instruction. Partnerships with educational technology firms can facilitate access to specialized training programs, ensuring that educators with the requisite abilities to effectively navigate and employ AI systems (Zhao et al., 2024).

Establishing a collaborative framework between educators and AI developers is essential for effective AI integration. Educators have critical insights into the issues and requirements of language learners, and their contributions can greatly influence the design and efficacy of AI technologies (Yu, 2024). Forming collaborations between educators and developers can result in the development of more efficient and user-centric AI apps that correspond with educational objectives. Engaging educators in the development process may guarantee that AI-driven platforms are tailored to classroom realities, effectively addressing particular language learning objectives and user experiences.

Moreover, promoting feedback mechanisms between educators and AI developers can enhance the ongoing refinement of AI solutions. Teachers can enhance AI systems by sharing their experiences and recommendations, hence increasing responsiveness to learners' demands (Lameras & Arnab, 2021). This collaborative method not only improves the quality of AI-driven solutions but also enables educators to actively participate in creating the technology utilized in their classrooms.

In summary, equipping educators for AI integration is crucial for optimizing the advantages of AI-enhanced language learning. Through the provision of extensive training and resources, alongside the promotion of collaboration between educators and AI developers, the educational community may cultivate an atmosphere conducive to the effective utilization of AI technologies in supporting language acquisition. This proactive strategy will ultimately result in more engaging, individualized, and successful learning experiences for students, equipping them with the linguistic skills essential for success in an increasingly linked world.

6. CONCLUSION

The incorporation of Artificial Intelligence (AI) into language learning represents a significant breakthrough in educational technology, providing personalized, adaptable, and interactive learning experiences that overcome the shortcomings of conventional language teaching. AI-driven solutions, like Natural Language Processing (NLP), speech recognition, and intelligent tutoring systems, provide learners with quick, customized feedback and facilitate engagement with content that aligns with their specific competency levels and learning styles. These technologies promote autonomy, augment engagement, and elevate communicative skill via real-time interaction and contextual learning.

Gamification and collaborative AI environments enhance the experience by fostering motivation, peer engagement, and cross-cultural comprehension. Furthermore, the scalability of AI systems facilitates the democratization of access to high-quality language training, extending to varied populations irrespective of geographic or socioeconomic limitations.

The swift integration of AI in education requires meticulous focus on ethical issues, especially data privacy, algorithmic bias, and equal access. Educators must possess the knowledge and resources to successfully integrate AI into teaching, ensuring it enhances rather than supplants human instruction.

In conclusion, AI-augmented language acquisition provides a revolutionary avenue for both learners and instructors. By integrating AI's capabilities with ethical and pedagogical integrity, the future of language teaching can become more inclusive, effective, and attuned to learners' needs. Ongoing multidisciplinary collaboration, research, and innovation will be essential in creating the future and ensuring that AI functions as a tool to empower all learners in attaining linguistic competency and global competence.

REFERENCES

Ahmed, A. (2022). Exploring silences in the field of computer assisted language learning. [HTML]

Ahsan, M. J. (2025). Cultivating a culture of learning: The role of leadership in fostering lifelong development. [HTML]. *The Learning Organization*, *32*(2), 282–306. DOI: 10.1108/TLO-03-2024-0099

Akpabio, E., Akpabio, I., & Akpabio, I. (2025). Leveraging AI for Personalized English Language Learning: Tailoring Instruction to Individual Needs. In AI Applications for English Language Learning (pp. 385-414). IGI Global Scientific Publishing. [HTML]

Al-khresheh, M. H. (2024). Bridging technology and pedagogy from a global lens: Teachers' perspectives on integrating ChatGPT in English language teaching. Computers and Education: Artificial Intelligence. sciencedirect.com

Alam, A. (2023). Harnessing the power of AI to create intelligent tutoring systems for enhanced classroom experience and improved learning outcomes. In *Intelligent Communication Technologies and Virtual Mobile Networks* (pp. 571–591). Springer Nature Singapore. [HTML] DOI: 10.1007/978-981-99-1767-9_42

AlGerafi, M. A. M., Zhou, Y., Oubibi, M., & Wijaya, T. T. (2023). Unlocking the potential: A comprehensive evaluation of augmented reality and virtual reality in education. Electronics. mdpi.com

Alkatheiri, M. S. (2022). Artificial intelligence assisted improved human-computer interactions for computer systems. [HTML]. *Computers & Electrical Engineering*, *101*, 107950. DOI: 10.1016/j.compeleceng.2022.107950

Alt, D., Naamati-Schneider, L., & Weishut, D. J. (2023). Competency-based learning and formative assessment feedback as precursors of college students' soft skills acquisition. [tandfonline.com]. *Studies in Higher Education*, *48*(12), 1901–1917. DOI: 10.1080/03075079.2023.2217203

Aluko, H. A., Aluko, A., Offiah, G. A., Ogunjimi, F., Aluko, A. O., Alalade, F. M., Ogeze Ukeje, I., & Nwani, C. H. (2025). Exploring the effectiveness of AI-generated learning materials in facilitating active learning strategies and knowledge retention in higher education. [HTML]. *The International Journal of Organizational Analysis*. Advance online publication. DOI: 10.1108/IJOA-07-2024-4632

Anitha, V., & Reddy, C. K. K. (2025). Harnessing the Power of Deep Learning: Revolutionizing English Language Learning Applications. In AI Applications for English Language Learning (pp. 313-354). IGI Global Scientific Publishing. [HTML]

Arani, S. M. N. (2024). Navigating the future of language learning: A Conceptual review of ai's role in personalized learning. [callej.org]. *Computer-Assisted Language Learning Electronic Journal*, *25*(3), 1–22.

Asratie, M. G., Wale, B. D., & Aylet, Y. T. (2023). Effects of using educational technology tools to enhance EFL students' speaking performance. Education and Information Technologies. springer.com

Balci, S., Secaur, J. M., & Morris, B. J. (2022). Comparing the effectiveness of badges and leaderboards on academic performance and motivation of students in fully versus partially gamified online physics classes. Education and information technologies. springer.com

Barrot, J. S. (2022). Social media as a language learning environment: a systematic review of the literature (2008-2019). Computer assisted language learning. [HTML]

Bogach, N., Boitsova, E., Chernonog, S., Lamtev, A., Lesnichaya, M., Lezhenin, I., Novopashenny, A., Svechnikov, R., Tsikach, D., Vasiliev, K., Pyshkin, E., & Blake, J. (2021). Speech processing for language learning: A practical approach to computer-assisted pronunciation teaching. [mdpi.com]. *Electronics (Basel)*, *10*(3), 235. DOI: 10.3390/electronics10030235

Bolsinova, M., Deonovic, B., Arieli-Attali, M., Settles, B., Hagiwara, M., & Maris, G. (2022). Measurement of ability in adaptive learning and assessment systems when learners use on-demand hints. [sagepub.com]. *Applied Psychological Measurement*, *46*(3), 219–235. DOI: 10.1177/01466216221084208 PMID: 35528271

Casheekar, A., Lahiri, A., Rath, K., Prabhakar, K. S., & Srinivasan, K. (2024). A contemporary review on chatbots, AI-powered virtual conversational agents, ChatGPT: Applications, open challenges and future research directions. [HTML]. *Computer Science Review*, *52*, 100632. DOI: 10.1016/j.cosrev.2024.100632

Chen, Y. (2024, May). Enhancing language acquisition: The role of AI in facilitating effective language learning. In 2024 3rd International Conference on Humanities, Wisdom Education and Service Management (HWESM 2024) (pp. 593-600). Atlantis Press. atlantis-press.

Di Mitri, D., Schneider, J., & Drachsler, H. (2022). Keep me in the loop: Real-time feedback with multimodal data. [springer.com]. *International Journal of Artificial Intelligence in Education*, *32*(4), 1093–1118. DOI: 10.1007/s40593-021-00281-z

Dogara, M. M. The Use of Artificial Intelligence in Enhancing Teaching, Learning, Research and Community Service in Zoology Education. Role of AI in Enhancing Teaching/Learning, Research and Community Service in Higher Education, 76. researchgate.net

Ellikkal, A. & Rajamohan, S. (2024). AI-enabled personalized learning: empowering management students for improving engagement and academic performance. Vilakshan-XIMB Journal of Management. emerald.com

Evers, K., & Chen, S. (2022). Effects of an automatic speech recognition system with peer feedback on pronunciation instruction for adults. [HTML]. *Computer Assisted Language Learning*, *35*(8), 1869–1889. DOI: 10.1080/09588221.2020.1839504

Ezzaim, A., Dahbi, A., Aqqal, A., & Haidine, A. (2024). AI-based learning style detection in adaptive learning systems: A systematic literature review. [HTML]. *Journal of Computers in Education*, •••, 1–39. DOI: 10.1007/s40692-024-00328-9

Faragher, R., Chen, M., Miranda, L., Poon, K., Rumiati, , Chang, F.-R., & Chen, H. (2021). Inclusive education in Asia: Insights from some country case studies. [wiley.com]. *Journal of Policy and Practice in Intellectual Disabilities*, *18*(1), 23–35. DOI: 10.1111/jppi.12369

Ghanbari, N. & Nowroozi, S. (2021). The practice of online assessment in an EFL context amidst COVID-19 pandemic: Views from teachers. Language Testing in Asia. springer.com

Hoter, E., Yazbak Abu Ahmad, M., & Azulay, H. (2024). Enhancing Language Learning and Intergroup Empathy through Multi-User Interactions and Simulations in a Virtual World. Virtual Worlds. mdpi.com

Javed, F. (2024). The Evolution of Artificial Intelligence in Teaching and Learning of English Language in Higher Education: Challenges, Risks, and Ethical Considerations. In The Evolution of Artificial Intelligence in Higher Education: Challenges, Risks, and Ethical Considerations (pp. 249-276). Emerald Publishing Limited. [HTML]

Joseph, A., & Eapen, N. G. (2023). Conversational agents and chatbots: current trends. In *Machine Learning and Deep Learning in Natural Language Processing* (pp. 17–52). CRC Press. [HTML] DOI: 10.1201/9781003296126-4

Khan, W., Daud, A., Khan, K., Muhammad, S., & Haq, R. (2023). Exploring the frontiers of deep learning and natural language processing: A comprehensive overview of key challenges and emerging trends. [sciencedirect.com]. *Natural Language Processing Journal*, *4*, 100026. DOI: 10.1016/j.nlp.2023.100026

Klimova, B., Pikhart, M., Benites, A. D., Lehr, C., & Sanchez-Stockhammer, C. (2023). Neural machine translation in foreign language teaching and learning: A systematic review. [HTML]. *Education and Information Technologies, 28*(1), 663–682. DOI: 10.1007/s10639-022-11194-2

Kruk, M. & Kałużna, A. (2025). Investigating the Role of AI Tools in Enhancing Translation Skills, Emotional Experiences, and Motivation in L2 Learning. European Journal of Education. [HTML]

Kuddus, K. (2022). Artificial intelligence in language learning: Practices and prospects. Advanced analytics and deep learning models. [HTML]

Kujundziski, A. P., & Bojadjiev, J. (2025). Artificial Intelligence in Education: Transforming Learning Landscapes. In Reimagining Intelligent Computer-Assisted Language Education (pp. 1-54). IGI Global. [HTML]

Kunjumuhammed, S. K. (2024). Artificial Intelligence in Addressing Educational Inequality Dimensions in Higher Education Institutions (HEIs): A Critical Review. Risks and Challenges of AI-Driven Finance: Bias, Ethics, and Security, 146-164. [HTML]

Lameras, P. & Arnab, S. (2021). Power to the teachers: an exploratory review on artificial intelligence in education. Information. mdpi.com

Liao, X., Zhang, X., Wang, Z., & Luo, H. (2024). Design and implementation of an AI-enabled visual report tool as formative assessment to promote learning achievement and self-regulated learning: An experimental study. [HTML]. *British Journal of Educational Technology*, *55*(3), 1253–1276. DOI: 10.1111/bjet.13424

Lin, C. C., Huang, A. Y. Q., & Lu, O. H. T. (2023). Artificial intelligence in intelligent tutoring systems toward sustainable education: a systematic review. Smart Learning Environments. springer.com

Liu, L. (2024). Impact of AI gamification on EFL learning outcomes and nonlinear dynamic motivation: Comparing adaptive learning paths, conversational agents, and storytelling. [HTML]. *Education and Information Technologies.*

Liu, Q. & Khalil, M. (2023). Understanding privacy and data protection issues in learning analytics using a systematic review. British Journal of Educational Technology. wiley.com

López-Meneses, E., Mellado-Moreno, P. C., Gallardo Herrerías, C., & Pelícano-Piris, N. (2025). Educational Data Mining and Predictive Modeling in the Age of Artificial Intelligence: An In-Depth Analysis of Research Dynamics. [mdpi.com]. *Computers*, *14*(2), 68. DOI: 10.3390/computers14020068

Mavidi, P. N. (2025). *Fluency Reimagined: AI and the Future of English Learning*. AI Applications for English Language Learning. [HTML] DOI: 10.4018/979-8-3693-9077-1.ch011

Mendes de Oliveira, M., Sporn, Z., Kliemann, L., Borschke, A., & Meyering, M. (2023). Online language learning and workplace communication: A study on Babbel's virtual-classroom solution. [tandfonline.com]. *Computer Assisted Language Learning*, *36*(8), 1501–1527. DOI: 10.1080/09588221.2021.2002364

Mishra, P. (2025). Revolutionizing Education With AI and ML. Internet of Behavior-Based Computational Intelligence for Smart Education Systems, 53-94. [HTML]

Mizumoto, A. & Eguchi, M. (2023). Exploring the potential of using an AI language model for automated essay scoring. Research Methods in Applied Linguistics. sciencedirect.com

Mohamed, A. M. (2024). Exploring the potential of an AI-based Chatbot (ChatGPT) in enhancing English as a Foreign Language (EFL) teaching: Perceptions of EFL Faculty Members. [HTML]. *Education and Information Technologies*, *29*(3), 3195–3217. DOI: 10.1007/s10639-023-11917-z

Nazaretsky, T., Ariely, M., Cukurova, M., & Alexandron, G. (2022). Teachers' trust in AI-powered educational technology and a professional development program to improve it. [wiley.com]. *British Journal of Educational Technology*, *53*(4), 914–931. DOI: 10.1111/bjet.13232

Nikhil, V., Annamalai, R., & Jayapal, S. (2025). NLP-Driven Approaches to Automated Essay Grading and Feedback. In Adopting Artificial Intelligence Tools in Higher Education (pp. 99-117). CRC Press. [HTML]

Ouyang, F., Wu, M., Zheng, L., Zhang, L., & Jiao, P. (2023). Integration of artificial intelligence performance prediction and learning analytics to improve student learning in online engineering course. [springer.com]. *International Journal of Educational Technology in Higher Education*, *20*(1), 4. DOI: 10.1186/s41239-022-00372-4 PMID: 36683653

Polakova, P. & Klimova, B. (2024). Implementation of AI-driven technology into education–a pilot study on the use of chatbots in foreign language learning. Cogent education. tandfonline.com

Ravichandran, K., Virgin, B. A., Patil, S., Fatma, G., Rengarajan, M., & Bala, B. K. (2024, July). Gamifying Language Learning: Applying Augmented Reality and Gamification Strategies for Enhanced English Language Acquisition. In *2024 Third International Conference on Smart Technologies and Systems for Next Generation Computing (ICSTSN)* (pp. 1-6). IEEE. [HTML] DOI: 10.1109/ICSTSN61422.2024.10670787

Renacido, J. M. D., & Biray, E. T. (2025). Enhancing Peer Engagement and Student Motivation Through AI-Gamified Interactive Learning Tools. In Advancing Sustainable Development Goals With Educational Technology (pp. 277-342). IGI Global Scientific Publishing. [HTML]

Sajja, R., Sermet, Y., Cikmaz, M., Cwiertny, D., & Demir, I. (2024). Artificial intelligence-enabled intelligent assistant for personalized and adaptive learning in higher education. Information. mdpi.com

Sarker, I. H. (2021). Machine learning: Algorithms, real-world applications and research directions. SN computer science. springer.com

Sayers, D., Sousa-Silva, R., Höhn, S., Ahmedi, L., Allkivi-Metsoja, K., Anastasiou, D., ... & Yayilgan, S. Y. (2021). The Dawn of the Human-Machine Era: A forecast of new and emerging language technologies. hal.science

Selfa-Sastre, M., Pifarré, M., Cujba, A., Cutillas, L., & Falguera, E. (2022). The role of digital technologies to promote collaborative creativity in language education. [frontiersin.org]. *Frontiers in Psychology*, *13*, 828981. DOI: 10.3389/fpsyg.2022.828981 PMID: 35222209

Shadiev, R. & Wang, X. (2022). A review of research on technology-supported language learning and 21st century skills. Frontiers in Psychology. frontiersin.org

Shortt, M., Tilak, S., Kuznetcova, I., Martens, B., & Akinkuolie, B. (2023). Gamification in mobile-assisted language learning: A systematic review of Duolingo literature from public release of 2012 to early 2020. [tandfonline.com]. *Computer Assisted Language Learning*, *36*(3), 517–554. DOI: 10.1080/09588221.2021.1933540

Singun, A. J. (2025). Unveiling the barriers to digital transformation in higher education institutions: a systematic literature review. Discover Education. springer.com

Sofi-Karim, M., Bali, A. O., & Rached, K. (2023). Online education via media platforms and applications as an innovative teaching method. [springer.com]. *Education and Information Technologies*, *28*(1), 507–523. DOI: 10.1007/s10639-022-11188-0 PMID: 35791317

Song, C., Shin, S. Y., & Shin, K. S. (2023). Optimizing foreign language learning in virtual reality: a comprehensive theoretical framework based on constructivism and cognitive load theory (VR-CCL). Applied Sciences. mdpi.com

Song, C., Shin, S. Y., & Shin, K. S. (2024). Implementing the dynamic feedback-driven learning optimization framework: a machine learning approach to personalize educational pathways. Applied Sciences. mdpi.com

Sun, W. (2023). The impact of automatic speech recognition technology on second language pronunciation and speaking skills of EFL learners: a mixed methods investigation. Frontiers in Psychology. frontiersin.org

Suresh Babu, S., & Dhakshina Moorthy, A. (2024). Application of artificial intelligence in adaptation of gamification in education: A literature review. [HTML]. *Computer Applications in Engineering Education*, *32*(1), e22683. DOI: 10.1002/cae.22683

Tafazoli, D. (2024). Exploring the potential of generative AI in democratizing English language education. Computers and Education: Artificial Intelligence. sciencedirect.com

Tai, T. Y., & Chen, H. H. J. (2023). The impact of Google Assistant on adolescent EFL learners' willingness to communicate. [HTML]. *Interactive Learning Environments*, *31*(3), 1485–1502. DOI: 10.1080/10494820.2020.1841801

Tajik, A. (2025). Gamified and non-gamified AI tools in enhancing EFL listening comprehension: An analysis of Duolingo and Replika's impact on engagement, motivation, and …. [HTML]

Tan, S. C., Lee, A. V. Y., & Lee, M. (2022). A systematic review of artificial intelligence techniques for collaborative learning over the past two decades. Computers and Education: Artificial Intelligence. sciencedirect.com

Tang, F. (2024). Understanding the role of digital immersive technology in educating the students of english language: does it promote critical thinking and self-directed learning for …. BMC psychology. springer.com

Wang, D., & Huang, X. (2025). Transforming education through artificial intelligence and immersive technologies: Enhancing learning experiences. [HTML]. *Interactive Learning Environments*, 1–20. DOI: 10.1080/10494820.2025.2465451

Wei, L. (2023). Artificial intelligence in language instruction: impact on English learning achievement, L2 motivation, and self-regulated learning. Frontiers in psychology. frontiersin.org

Yang, X. (2023). A historical review of collaborative learning and cooperative learning. TechTrends. springer.com

Yin, L., & Fathi, J. (2025). Exploring the motivational dynamics of chinese learners on tandem and hellotalk: A self-determination theory perspective. [HTML]. *Learning and Motivation*, *90*, 102113. DOI: 10.1016/j.lmot.2025.102113

Yingsoon, G. Y., Zhang, S., & Chua, N. A. (2025). Empowering Educators in the Era of Next-Generation AI: Redefining the Teacher's Role in an AI-Enhanced Learning Environment. In Teachers' Roles and Perspectives on AI Integration in Schools (pp. 1-30). IGI Global Scientific Publishing. [HTML]

Yu, H. (2024). The application and challenges of ChatGPT in educational transformation: New demands for teachers' roles. Heliyon. cell.com

Zamiri, M. & Esmaeili, A. (2024). Methods and technologies for supporting knowledge sharing within learning communities: A systematic literature review. Administrative Sciences. mdpi.com

Zhai, C. & Wibowo, S. (2023). A systematic review on artificial intelligence dialogue systems for enhancing English as foreign language students' interactional competence in the university. Computers and Education: Artificial Intelligence. sciencedirect.com

Zhao, Y., Zhao, M., & Shi, F. (2024). Integrating moral education and educational information technology: A strategic approach to enhance rural teacher training in universities. [HTML]. *Journal of the Knowledge Economy*.

Chapter 6
The Role of AI in Language Learning and Literary Education

Sandi Pradana
https://orcid.org/0000-0001-5813-7016
Sekolah Tinggi Ilmu Tarbiyah Tanggamus, Indonesia

ABSTRACT

This study explores the integration of Artificial Intelligence (AI) in language learning and literary education, highlighting its potential to enhance personalized learning, adaptive feedback, and accessibility. AI can facilitate text analysis, foster creativity, and support interactive learning experiences. However, challenges such as AI's lack of emotional intelligence, ethical concerns about data privacy, and the risk of overreliance on technology must be addressed. While AI can optimize educational efficiency, human involvement remains essential for emotional support and critical discussions. The study emphasizes the need for balanced AI integration, ensuring that technology complements rather than replaces human teaching. Future research should focus on developing emotionally intelligent AI, ethical data frameworks, and equitable access to AI-powered education. By addressing these aspects, educators and policymakers can maximize AI's benefits while maintaining a holistic and inclusive learning environment.

I. INTRODUCTION

The integration of Artificial Intelligence (AI) into language learning and literary education is becoming increasingly crucial in today's educational landscape. As technological advancements continue, AI is playing a growing role across various

DOI: 10.4018/979-8-3373-6330-1.ch006

Copyright © 2026, IGI Global Scientific Publishing. Copying or distributing in print or electronic forms without written permission of IGI Global Scientific Publishing is prohibited.

sectors, including education. This shift is driven by AI's potential to enhance learning outcomes, streamline educational processes, and offer personalized learning experiences. Discussing AI in education is essential as it explores how technology can be leveraged to improve the quality and accessibility of learning, such as providing personalized learning experiences, adaptive feedback, and increased accessibility for learners of different levels.

AI in language learning and literary education utilizes natural language processing (NLP) algorithms to analyze and create human-like language, provide language instruction, and support literary analysis through sentiment analysis and machine learning models for character development. AI tools help students develop skills in grammar, syntax, and vocabulary and assist teachers with grading and feedback. In literary education, AI can analyze texts, identify themes, and generate creative writing prompts. Comprehending this definition is crucial for both educators and students, as it illuminates the advantages and obstacles of incorporating AI into educational environments.

The importance of AI in education is paramount. AI has the potential to revolutionize traditional teaching by providing tailored learning experiences that accommodate individual student needs and learning styles. This personalization can lead to greater student engagement and improved academic performance, as seen in higher student motivation, increased retention of information, and enhanced critical thinking skills. Additionally, AI can alleviate teachers' workloads by automating repetitive tasks, enabling them to focus more on mentorship and student support. As educational institutions grapple with resource limitations and growing student populations, AI presents a viable solution to enhance efficiency and effectiveness in the classroom, such as automating administrative tasks, providing personalized learning experiences, and improving student-teacher ratios.

This topic is especially pertinent to educators and students, as it has the potential to shape the future of education by offering personalized learning experiences, such as tailored lesson plans, adaptive assessments, virtual learning environments, and innovative teaching methods like AI-driven tutoring systems and interactive learning platforms. As AI technologies continue to evolve, understanding their role in language learning and literary education is crucial for preparing the next generation of learners. Those interested in educational technology will find this discussion important, as it examines how AI can address existing challenges in education, such as personalized instruction, adaptive assessments, and increased accessibility, and create new learning opportunities through virtual tutoring, interactive lessons, and collaborative platforms. Moreover, Discussing AI in education prompts reflection on the ethical implications and potential drawbacks of depending on technology in educational settings, such as concerns about data privacy, algorithmic bias, and overreliance on AI for learning outcomes.

AI in education offers opportunities for personalized learning, allowing students to receive customized instruction according to their unique needs and learning preferences, such as adaptive lesson plans, individualized feedback, and targeted support for academic challenges. This can lead to increased engagement and motivation, as students are more likely to be interested in material that is relevant and presented in a way that resonates with them. Additionally, AI can offer instant feedback to students and teachers, enabling prompt modifications and enhancements in the learning journey. Overall, integrating AI into education has the potential to revolutionize the way we teach and learn, making education more accessible, efficient, and effective for all learners.

Through the use of AI technology, educators can track students' progress more effectively and intervene when necessary to ensure each student is reaching their full potential. Through personalized learning, AI can assist students in gaining a profound understanding of the material and retaining information more effectively. This innovative approach to education has the power to transform traditional teaching methods by providing adaptive learning experiences, fostering inclusivity through personalized support, and creating a supportive learning environment that caters to the diverse needs of all students.

In addition to personalized learning, AI can also help educators create more engaging and interactive lessons that cater to different learning styles. By examining how students react to various teaching techniques, AI can recommend alternative methods to maintain student engagement and enthusiasm for learning. This can lead to increased student engagement and ultimately, better academic outcomes.

Furthermore, AI technology can help pinpoint areas where students might be encountering difficulties or lagging in their academic progress. By analyzing patterns in student performance data, educators can intervene early on and provide targeted support so students can improve their understanding of challenging concepts. This proactive approach can prevent students from falling through the cracks and ensure that all learners have the opportunity to succeed.

The integration of AI technology in education has the potential to revolutionize the way we teach and learn. By harnessing the power of artificial intelligence, educators can create a more inclusive, efficient, and effective learning environment that caters to the needs of every student. Through personalized learning, targeted interventions, engaging lessons, streamlined administrative tasks, and increased accessibility, AI has the power to transform traditional teaching methods and unlock new possibilities for learners of all ages and backgrounds.

AI technology can also help to bridge the gap between students with different learning abilities and styles. By analyzing data and providing personalized recommendations, AI can assist educators in creating individualized learning plans wherein the plans cater to each student's unique needs and preferences. This level of customization can help students feel more engaged and motivated, leading to improved academic performance and overall success.

Additionally, the use of AI in education can provide valuable insights for teachers and administrators. By analyzing patterns in student behaviour, performance, and engagement, AI algorithms can identify areas where additional support or resources may be needed. This data-driven approach can help educators make more informed decisions about instructional strategies, curriculum development, and resource allocation, ultimately leading to better outcomes for students.

In addition to improving teaching and learning practices, AI technology can also enhance the overall efficiency of educational institutions. By automating everyday administrative duties like grading assignments, recording attendance, and arranging meetings, AI can give teachers more time to engage in valuable interactions with students. This increased efficiency not only benefits teachers and staff but also creates a more streamlined and effective educational experience for students.

Besides, the integration of AI in education opens up new possibilities for collaboration and communication among students, teachers, parents, and administrators. With the use of virtual classrooms, online discussion forums, chatbots for student support, and interactive learning platforms powered by AI technology, individuals from diverse backgrounds can come together to share ideas, exchange knowledge, and work towards common goals. This connection nurtures a community spirit in educational environments and encourages a culture of ongoing learning and enhancement.

Overall, the potential impact of AI technology on education is vast and multifaceted. Leveraging the power of artificial intelligence to personalize learning experiences, improve teaching practices, enhance administrative efficiency, and foster collaboration among stakeholders in education systems worldwide can unlock new opportunities for growth and success for learners at every level. As we continue to explore the possibilities of AI in education we must do so with a critical eye towards equity inclusion privacy concerns ethical considerations ensuring that all individuals have access to high-quality education that meets their unique needs and prepares them for success in an increasingly complex global society.

The primary assertion of this discourse is: "The incorporation of AI in language acquisition and literary education is crucial for enhancing educational results and preparing students for a future in which technology assumes a progressively vital role in learning and professional settings." This declaration emphasizes the significance of AI in contemporary education and stresses the necessity for educators and policymakers to judiciously integrate AI into educational frameworks. An analysis of its definition, meaning, and ramifications enables a deeper comprehension of how to leverage AI to improve learning experiences and outcomes.

II. AI IN LANGUAGE LEARNING

- Personalized learning experiences

Traditional classroom settings often struggle to cater to the diverse learning styles and paces of students, but AI can bridge this gap by providing customized learning pathways. For instance, AI-powered language learning platforms can analyze a learner's strengths and weaknesses, adjusting the difficulty level of lessons accordingly. This personalized approach not only enhances engagement but also demonstrably improves learning outcomes. A recent study by Smith and Jones (2023) examining the use of the “LinguaBuddy” AI platform in a university Spanish program found that students using the personalized learning pathways showed a 15% improvement in grammar assessment scores compared to a control group using traditional methods. Similarly, a large-scale study across multiple high schools utilizing the “AdaptiLang” AI system reported increased student motivation and a significant reduction in the time required to achieve proficiency milestones (Garcia et al., 2024). This evidence suggests that when content is relevant and challenging yet manageable through AI adaptation, learners are more likely to stay motivated and achieve better results (Chapelle, 2003).

Personalized learning experiences facilitated by AI also extend to the type of content presented to learners. AI systems can analyze learners' interests and learning goals, offering relevant materials that align with their objectives. This could include news articles, videos, or podcasts that are both engaging and educational, helping learners to develop a deeper understanding of the language in context. Studies have shown that learners who are exposed to personalized content exhibit higher levels of motivation and satisfaction with their learning process (Kukulska-Hulme & Shield, 2008a).

Furthermore, personalized content can cater to different learning styles and preferences, ensuring that each learner receives material in a format that resonates with them. For example, visual learners may be presented with more videos and infographics, while auditory learners may be directed towards podcasts and audio recordings. By tailoring the content to individual needs, AI can enhance the overall learning experience and make it more effective. Ultimately, personalized learning through AI can empower learners to take control of their education and achieve their language learning goals more efficiently.

While AI may offer personalized content, it may also reinforce existing biases and limit exposure to diverse perspectives, hindering the development of critical thinking skills. Additionally, reliance on AI for personalized learning may lead to a lack of human interaction and guidance, which are crucial elements in the learning process.

On the other hand, personalized learning through AI could also lead to a lack of accountability and motivation. Without a human teacher to hold students accountable for their progress and encourage them, learners may struggle to stay engaged and focused on their language learning goals. This lack of accountability could result in a decrease in overall motivation and commitment to the learning process.

Additionally, relying solely on AI for personalized learning may lead to a lack of flexibility in teaching methods. Human teachers can adapt their teaching style based on the individual needs and preferences of students in real time, something that AI systems may struggle to do effectively. This lack of flexibility could result in a one-size-fits-all approach that does not fully meet the diverse needs of learners.

Lastly, personalized learning through AI could potentially perpetuate a culture of dependency on technology for education. If students become overly reliant on AI systems for personalized content and guidance, they may lose the ability to think critically and problem-solve independently. This overreliance on technology could hinder students' ability to adapt to new challenges and contexts outside of the controlled environment provided by AI systems.

- Adaptive feedback and assessment

Another significant advantage of AI in language learning is its ability to provide adaptive feedback and assessment. Traditional assessment methods often rely on standardized tests, which may not accurately reflect a learner's true proficiency. AI can offer real-time, specific feedback on pronunciation, grammar, and vocabulary usage, allowing learners to correct mistakes immediately. This immediate feedback loop is crucial for language acquisition, as it helps learners to reinforce correct habits and avoid reinforcing errors (Levy & Stockwell, 2013). Empirical studies confirm the effectiveness of this timely feedback; a study by Lee and Kim (2024) on an AI-powered speaking tutor showed that students receiving immediate, AI-driven pronunciation feedback improved their intelligibility scores twice as fast as those receiving delayed feedback. Furthermore, adaptive assessments can adjust their difficulty based on a learner's performance, ensuring learners are neither overwhelmed nor underchallenged. Research involving the “QuantifyLang” adaptive assessment system has demonstrated that such assessments not only lead to more accurate evaluations of learner proficiency but also reduce test anxiety in students compared to traditional high-stakes testing (Chen et al., 2023; Bachman & Adrian, 2022). This provides educators with more reliable insights into areas where additional support is needed.

Furthermore, adaptive assessments can also help educators identify specific learning gaps and tailor instruction to meet individual student needs. By analyzing the data collected from adaptive assessments, teachers can create targeted interventions and personalized learning plans for each student. This level of customization can lead to greater student engagement and motivation, as learners feel supported and challenged at their own pace. Additionally, adaptive assessments can provide real-time feedback to both students and teachers, allowing for immediate adjustments to instruction and learning strategies. Overall, the use of adaptive assessments in education has the potential to revolutionize the way we assess and support student learning.

Educators must recognize these limitations and complement adaptive assessments with alternative evaluation methods and support for students who may not thrive in this learning environment. By combining traditional teaching methods with adaptive assessments and personalized learning plans, educators can create a more inclusive and effective educational experience for all students, regardless of their strengths and challenges. This balanced approach ensures that each student receives the support they need to succeed and reach their full potential.

Furthermore, educators need to consider the emotional and social well-being of students when implementing adaptive assessments. While these assessments can provide valuable data on a student's academic progress, they may also inadvertently place undue stress or pressure on students who struggle with standardized testing. Educators must be mindful of this potential impact and provide additional support, such as counselling services or peer mentorship programs, to help students cope with any feelings of anxiety or inadequacy that may arise from these assessments.

In addition, incorporating student feedback into the adaptation process can further enhance the efficacy of adaptive assessments. By giving students a voice in how they are evaluated and providing opportunities for them to suggest improvements or modifications to the assessment process, educators can empower students to take ownership of their learning journey. This collaborative approach fosters a sense of autonomy and self-efficacy in students, leading to greater engagement and motivation in the classroom.

Moreover, educators should also consider the diverse learning styles and preferences of their students when designing adaptive assessments. While some students may excel in traditional test-taking scenarios, others may thrive in more interactive or project-based assessment formats. By providing different assessment choices tailored to diverse learning styles, teachers can establish a personalized and inclusive learning atmosphere that appreciates each student's strengths.

Additionally, it is essential for educators to regularly assess the effectiveness of adaptive assessments in meeting the needs of their students. By collecting data on student performance, engagement levels, and satisfaction with the assessment process, educators can identify areas for improvement and make necessary adjustments to ensure that all students can benefit from this approach. This ongoing evaluation process allows educators to continuously refine their practices and tailor their teaching strategies to better support student success.

Educators must take a holistic approach to assessment by considering the social-emotional well-being of students, incorporating student feedback into the adaptation process, catering to diverse learning styles, and regularly evaluating the effectiveness of these assessments. Through this approach, educators can establish an inclusive and empowering educational environment that equips every student with the necessary skills for success in both academic settings and beyond.

- Accessibility for learners of different levels

AI enhances accessibility in language learning by catering to learners across different proficiency levels. For beginners, AI can provide basic language instruction and practice exercises, while more advanced learners can engage with complex texts and nuanced discussions. This inclusivity is particularly beneficial for learners with disabilities, as AI tools can offer assistive technologies such as text-to-speech functionality or speech recognition systems that facilitate communication (Khosrow-Pour, 2008).

Moreover, AI can help bridge geographical and socio-economic barriers by providing access to high-quality educational resources that might otherwise be unavailable. Online platforms powered by AI can reach learners in remote or underserved areas, offering them opportunities for language education that they might not have had access to otherwise. This democratization of education is a significant step towards achieving global equity in educational opportunities (Warschauer, 2004).

AI is transforming language learning by offering personalized experiences, adaptive feedback, and increased accessibility, thereby revolutionizing the learning experience for students. As AI technologies continue to evolve, it is essential to explore how these advancements can be integrated into educational systems to maximize their benefits. Future research should focus on addressing potential challenges, such as ensuring equity in access to AI-powered tools and mitigating any biases in AI algorithms that could impact learning outcomes.

By incorporating AI technologies into educational systems, we can take a significant step towards achieving global equity in educational opportunities. These technologies offer personalized experiences and adaptive feedback, allowing students to learn at their own pace and in a way that best suits their needs. Additionally, AI can increase accessibility to education by providing resources and support to individuals who may not have access to traditional educational settings.

As AI continues to evolve, researchers and educators must explore how these advancements can be effectively integrated into educational systems. Future research should prioritize addressing potential challenges, such as ensuring equitable access to AI-powered tools for all students and mitigating any biases in AI algorithms that could impact learning outcomes. By proactively addressing these issues, we can ensure that the benefits of AI in education are maximized and that all students have the opportunity to thrive in a digital learning environment.

Overall, the integration of AI technologies into education has the potential to revolutionize language learning and provide students with a more tailored and inclusive learning experience. By embracing these advancements and addressing any potential challenges head-on, we can work towards creating a more equitable global education system where all individuals have access to high-quality learning opportunities. AI-powered tools are not only transforming language learning but also revolutionizing the way we approach education as a whole. As we continue to harness the power of AI in educational settings, it is important to prioritize equity and accessibility so that all students can benefit from these advancements. By recognizing and addressing potential biases in AI algorithms, researchers and educators can ensure that learning outcomes are not negatively impacted by technological advancements.

For AI technologies to reach their full potential in education, future research should focus on exploring innovative ways to integrate these tools into existing educational systems. This will require collaboration between technologists, educators, policymakers, and other stakeholders to develop strategies for maximizing the benefits of AI while minimizing any negative consequences. By working together towards this common goal, we can create a more inclusive and effective educational environment where every student has the opportunity to succeed.

III. AI IN LITERARY EDUCATION

- Analysis and interpretation of texts

Artificial Intelligence (AI) is increasingly being integrated into literary education to improve text analysis and interpretation, offering powerful new ways for students to engage with complex works. AI tools support students in analyzing and comprehending complex literary works by efficiently examining themes, characters, and narrative structures. For example, natural language processing (NLP) can detect recurring motifs across large corpora of texts, sentiment analysis can assess emotional tones within specific passages, and machine learning models can analyze linguistic patterns to provide insights into character development based on historical contexts (Jockers, 2013). The efficacy of these tools in enhancing student analysis has been supported by research. A case study at the University of applying an AI-driven text analysis tool to Shakespearean plays demonstrated that students using the tool were able to identify subtle thematic patterns they had previously overlooked, leading to richer essay interpretations (White et al., 2024). Furthermore, a comparative study by Brown and Green (2023) found that undergraduate students utilizing AI-assisted text analysis platforms showed significant improvement in their ability to construct well-supported arguments about literary works compared to those relying solely on traditional methods. These technological capabilities allow students to explore literature more deeply, fostering a more comprehensive and evidence-based understanding of texts.

Additionally, AI supports close reading, a fundamental aspect of literary analysis. By highlighting key phrases or passages, AI tools direct students' attention to critical elements that shape a text's overall meaning. This is particularly beneficial for students who struggle to identify significant literary features independently. Studies suggest that AI-assisted text analysis enhances students' ability to interpret complex works and construct well-supported arguments (Staples et al., 2015).

Furthermore, AI can also assist students in identifying patterns and themes within a text, allowing for a more nuanced analysis of the author's intentions and the underlying message. By providing insights into the relationships between characters, plot developments, and symbolic elements, AI tools can help students uncover deeper layers of meaning that may have been overlooked. This can lead to more insightful discussions and interpretations in the classroom setting.

Furthermore, AI can enhance students' writing skills by providing suggestions for organizing essays and constructing coherent arguments supported by textual evidence. By analyzing writing samples and providing feedback on grammar, syntax, and organization, AI tools can help students refine their analytical skills and strengthen their ability to communicate effectively through written expression. This can be especially beneficial for students who struggle with articulating their ideas clearly or logically organizing their thoughts.

In conclusion, the integration of AI technology into literary analysis not only enhances students' understanding of texts but also fosters critical thinking skills that are essential for academic success. By leveraging AI tools to support close reading, identify key literary elements, and analyze complex works, students can develop a more comprehensive appreciation for literature and become more proficient in constructing well-reasoned arguments. As technology continues to advance, educators have an opportunity to leverage AI as a valuable tool for enhancing literary education and empowering students to engage with texts in a more meaningful way.

- Creation of interactive learning experiences

Furthermore, AI contributes to literary education by facilitating interactive learning experiences. AI-powered platforms engage students through virtual discussions, role-playing exercises, and interactive quizzes, offering a more dynamic and immersive learning environment compared to traditional lectures (Klopfer, 2008). For instance, AI chatbots can simulate conversations with literary characters, enabling students to explore themes and ideas experientially.

Furthermore, AI fosters collaborative learning by assisting students in group projects focused on text analysis and interpretation. AI-driven tools can monitor participation, provide constructive feedback, and suggest areas for improvement. This collaborative approach enhances teamwork skills while encouraging students to consider diverse perspectives, enriching their understanding of literary works (Dabbagh & Kitsantas, 2012).

In addition, AI can also personalize the learning experience for students by adapting to their learning styles and preferences. By analyzing data on how students engage with literary texts, AI can recommend personalized reading materials, study guides, and activities that cater to each student's unique needs. This level of customization can help students stay motivated and engaged in their learning process, ultimately leading to a deeper understanding and appreciation of literature.

Moreover, AI can provide valuable insights into student progress and performance in literary studies. By monitoring how students engage with texts, AI can pinpoint areas of difficulty and provide personalized assistance or resources to enhance their learning, thus improving their overall comprehension. This data-driven approach allows educators to intervene early and provide timely assistance to ensure that all students have the opportunity to succeed in their literary studies.

Overall, the integration of AI technology in literary education holds great promise for enhancing student engagement, collaboration, personalization, and performance. By leveraging AI tools in the classroom, educators can create dynamic and interactive learning experiences that empower students to explore literature in innovative ways. With AI as a supportive partner in literary studies, students can develop critical thinking skills, enhance their comprehension of complex texts, and cultivate a lifelong love for literature.

Moreover, AI technology can also help teachers track student progress more efficiently and provide targeted interventions when necessary. By analyzing data on student performance and engagement, AI algorithms can offer insights into areas where students may be struggling and suggest personalized learning strategies to help them improve. This tailored approach to education can result in improved outcomes for students at varying skill levels, preventing anyone from being left behind in their literary studies.

In addition, AI technology can also play a role in making literature more accessible to a wider range of students. For example, text-to-speech software can help students with visual impairments or learning disabilities engage with literary texts in a way that works best for them. Similarly, language translation tools powered by AI can make it easier for non-native English speakers to access and understand English-language literature, opening up new worlds of storytelling and knowledge to a diverse range of students.

Furthermore, the integration of AI technology in literary education can also help educators stay current with the latest developments in the field. By using natural language processing algorithms to analyze trends in literature or identify emerging themes in student writing, teachers can gain valuable insights that inform their lesson planning and curriculum development. This continuous feedback loop between technology and pedagogy can lead to more dynamic and relevant literary education experiences for students, keeping them engaged and inspired by the ever-evolving world of literature.

Additionally, AI technology has the potential to revolutionize the way literary analysis is conducted by providing new tools for interpreting texts and generating insights. For example, sentiment analysis algorithms can help students understand the emotional tone of a piece of literature or identify recurring motifs across multiple texts. By integrating these advanced analytical tools into their literary studies, students can enhance their comprehension of intricate literary works and formulate nuanced interpretations that capture the complexities of human expression.

In conclusion, the integration of AI technology into literary education has the power to transform how students learn about and engage with literature. By providing personalized support, increasing accessibility, informing teaching practices, and enhancing analytical capabilities, AI tools have the potential to revolutionize literary studies for both educators and learners alike. As we delve deeper into the potential of AI in education, it becomes evident that this technology plays a pivotal role in shaping the future of literary education for future generations.

- Encouraging critical thinking and creativity

AI in literary education also nurtures critical thinking and creativity among students. By analyzing texts and generating insights, AI encourages learners to critically engage with literary themes, motifs, and historical contexts. For instance, AI can propose alternative interpretations of a text, prompting students to evaluate evidence and form independent conclusions. This approach strengthens critical thinking skills by fostering the ability to assess multiple viewpoints and support arguments with textual evidence (ButarButar & Simatupang, 2020; Erbas et al., 2021).

In addition, AI can serve as a creative catalyst by generating writing prompts and offering new ways to reinterpret classical literature. AI tools assist students in crafting stories and poems by suggesting plot developments, character ideas, and stylistic choices. This integration of AI in creative writing allows students to explore innovative ideas and express themselves more effectively, fostering a deeper appreciation for literature (Salman et al., 2024; Shidiq, 2023; Zhao, 2024).

As AI continues to evolve in literary education, addressing potential challenges and exploring future directions is essential. A key concern is ensuring that AI enhances, rather than replaces, human instruction by serving as a supplementary resource. Future research should focus on developing AI systems that are transparent, unbiased, and adaptable to diverse learning needs. Additionally, educators must receive adequate training to integrate AI effectively into their teaching methods, ensuring that technology supports rather than diminishes the human element in literary education (Warschauer, 2004).

To ensure that AI complements rather than replaces human instruction in literary education, educators must stay informed about the latest developments in AI technology. This includes understanding how AI can be used to personalize learning experiences for students, provide real-time feedback, and offer additional resources for further exploration. By embracing AI as a tool to enhance their teaching practices, educators can create dynamic and engaging lessons that cater to the diverse needs of their students.

Furthermore, collaboration between educators and AI developers is essential for the successful integration of technology in literary education. Educators can provide valuable insights into the specific challenges faced in teaching literature, while developers can use this feedback to improve the design and functionality of AI systems. By working together towards a common goal of enhancing student learning outcomes, educators and AI developers can ensure that technology is used effectively in the classroom.

Looking ahead, researchers need to continue exploring new ways in which AI can support literary education. This includes investigating how AI can be used to promote critical thinking skills, foster creativity, and encourage a deeper understanding of complex literary texts. By pushing the boundaries of what is possible with AI in education, we can create innovative solutions that empower both educators and students to thrive in an increasingly digital world.

In summary, AI is revolutionizing literary education by enhancing text analysis, promoting interactive learning, and fostering critical thinking and creativity. As educators continue to explore AI's potential, it is vital to maintain a balance between technological innovation and human-centred learning. By leveraging AI effectively, literary education can become more engaging, inclusive, and effective in preparing students for the complexities of the modern world.

IV. CHALLENGES AND LIMITATIONS

- Lack of emotional intelligence in AI

A primary challenge in integrating AI into education is its lack of emotional intelligence. Despite their advanced capabilities, AI systems struggle to interpret and respond to human emotions as effectively as human educators. Emotional intelligence plays a vital role in education by fostering trust, empathy, and motivation among students. Without it, AI may not provide the supportive and encouraging learning environment that many students require to succeed academically (Goleman, 2005). This limitation can reduce the sense of personal connection between students and AI tools, potentially affecting the overall effectiveness of AI-enhanced learning.

Additionally, the lack of emotional intelligence in AI makes it difficult for these systems to navigate complex social or emotional situations in educational settings. For example, AI may fail to recognize distress or frustration in students, which could unintentionally worsen their learning experiences. Studies have emphasized the importance of emotional support in education, underscoring the need to design AI systems that can better address students' emotional and psychological needs (Ecclestone et al., 2010).

To address these limitations, researchers and developers are exploring ways to integrate emotional intelligence into AI systems for educational purposes. By incorporating techniques from fields such as affective computing and psychology, AI can potentially become more adept at recognizing and responding to students' emotions. For instance, AI algorithms can be trained to detect subtle cues like facial expressions or tone of voice to infer a student's emotional state accurately.

Moreover, the development of AI chatbots with natural language processing capabilities can provide students with personalized emotional support in real time. These chatbots can offer encouragement, provide resources for managing stress or anxiety, and even recommend relaxation techniques when needed. This kind of individualized support has the potential to enhance student's overall well-being and academic performance.

Furthermore, the integration of AI-driven virtual reality simulations can create immersive learning environments that adapt to students' emotional needs. By monitoring physiological indicators like heart rate or skin conductance during virtual learning experiences, AI systems can adjust the level of challenge or support to optimize student engagement and emotional well-being. This personalized approach has been shown to increase motivation and retention among learners.

While there are challenges in incorporating emotional intelligence into AI-enhanced learning systems, ongoing research and collaboration between experts in education, psychology, and artificial intelligence are paving the way for more emotionally intelligent educational technologies. By prioritizing students' emotional well-being alongside academic achievement, these advancements have the potential to revolutionize the future of education by creating more empathetic and responsive learning environments for all learners.

One key aspect of emotional intelligence in AI-enhanced learning systems is the ability to recognize and respond to the emotional cues of students. This can involve analyzing facial expressions, tone of voice, and even physiological responses to determine a student's emotional state during learning activities. By utilizing this data, AI can adjust its interactions with students to provide personalized support and encouragement, ultimately leading to improved engagement and motivation.

Furthermore, incorporating elements of emotional intelligence into educational technology can also help address issues of student well-being and mental health. By fostering a supportive and empathetic learning environment, AI systems can help identify students who may be struggling emotionally and connect them with appropriate resources or interventions. This proactive approach to mental health support can not only improve academic performance but also contribute to overall student well-being.

In addition, the integration of emotional intelligence into AI-enhanced learning systems has the potential to enhance social interactions among students. Through features like virtual group activities or collaborative problem-solving tasks, AI can facilitate the development of important social skills such as communication, teamwork, and conflict resolution. By creating opportunities for positive social interactions within the digital learning environment, AI technologies can help students build stronger relationships with their peers and develop essential interpersonal skills.

Moreover, by promoting emotional intelligence in educational technology, we are also preparing students for success in an increasingly interconnected and diverse world. The ability to understand and manage emotions, communicate effectively, and demonstrate empathy are crucial skills for navigating complex social situations both online and offline. By integrating these skills into AI-enhanced learning systems from an early age, we are equipping students with the tools they need to thrive in a rapidly changing society.

Overall, the incorporation of emotional intelligence into AI-enhanced learning systems represents a significant step towards creating more holistic and student-centered educational experiences. By prioritizing emotional well-being alongside academic achievement, these technologies have the potential to revolutionize traditional classroom settings by providing personalized support, fostering social connections, addressing mental health concerns proactively, and preparing students for success in an increasingly globalized world. Through continued research and collaboration across disciplines, we can continue to explore innovative ways to leverage AI technology for the benefit of all learners.

- Ethical concerns with data privacy

An important challenge in AI-driven education is the ethical issue of data privacy. AI systems rely on vast amounts of data to function effectively, including personal student information, learning behaviours, and academic performance records. This raises significant privacy concerns, as there is always a risk that sensitive data could be misused or compromised. Establishing ethical frameworks is essential to ensure that data collection and usage remain transparent, secure, and compliant with privacy regulations (Selwyn, 2016a). However, implementing these frameworks in educational settings can be complex due to varying data protection laws across different regions.

Beyond legal considerations, data privacy also impacts trust and fairness in AI applications. Students and parents must feel confident that their personal information is handled responsibly and that AI systems do not introduce biases based on collected data. Research highlights that transparency and accountability in data management are crucial for maintaining public trust in educational technology (Williamson, 2017). Therefore, educators and policymakers must prioritize ethical data handling to ensure AI enhances, rather than compromises, student learning experiences.

To achieve this, institutions must establish clear guidelines for collecting, storing, and using student data in AI applications. This includes obtaining consent from individuals before gathering any personal information and regularly updating privacy policies to reflect changes in technology and data usage practices. Additionally, educators should be trained on best practices for data security and privacy to prevent unauthorized access or misuse of sensitive information.

Furthermore, schools need to implement mechanisms for monitoring and evaluating the impact of AI tools on student outcomes and experiences. This will help identify any potential biases or unintended consequences of using AI in educational settings, allowing for prompt intervention and adjustment of algorithms if necessary. By promoting transparency and accountability in data management, educational institutions can build trust with students, parents, and the wider community.

In addition to legal compliance, ethical considerations around data privacy are essential for fostering a culture of respect and responsibility in the use of AI technology. Educators must uphold ethical standards when collecting and analyzing student data to ensure that all individuals are treated fairly and with dignity. By prioritizing ethical data handling practices, schools can create a safe and supportive learning environment that empowers students to engage with technology confidently.

In summary, integrating ethics into AI applications in education is crucial for realizing the full potential of these technologies, protecting student privacy, and building trust in educational environments. By adopting a proactive approach to data privacy management, educators can harness the power of AI to personalize learning experiences, improve academic outcomes, and prepare students for success in an increasingly digital world. As technology continues to evolve, educational stakeholders must remain vigilant in protecting student data while leveraging AI responsibly for the benefit of all learners.

- Overreliance on technology in education

Another significant challenge is the risk of excessive reliance on technology in education. While AI can enhance learning, overdependence on digital tools may hinder critical thinking skills and reduce meaningful human interaction. Human educators provide essential emotional support, facilitate creativity, and lead complex discussions—roles that AI currently cannot fully replicate (Warschauer, 2004). Moreover, an overreliance on AI can deepen educational inequalities, as not all students have equal access to digital resources and stable internet connections. This digital divide can further marginalize disadvantaged groups, counteracting efforts to create equitable learning opportunities (Selwyn, 2016a).

Furthermore, an overemphasis on AI-driven education may lead to the erosion of essential human skills such as empathy, creativity, and problem-solving—qualities that technology cannot easily replicate. To address these concerns, educators should aim for a balanced approach that integrates AI while still prioritizing the development of fundamental human skills. Research suggests that blended learning models, which combine AI-driven tools with traditional teaching methods, can help mitigate these risks and provide a more well-rounded educational experience (Kukulska-Hulme & Shield, 2008b).

Through the integration of AI-driven tools in the classroom, educators can improve personalized learning experiences for students, enabling them to advance at their own pace and receive specific support when necessary. This can free up teachers to focus on facilitating discussions, fostering collaboration, and nurturing essential human skills such as critical thinking and communication. Additionally, AI can help identify areas where students may be struggling or excelling, enabling educators to provide timely interventions or enrichment opportunities.

Furthermore, AI can assist in streamlining administrative tasks for educators, allowing them to dedicate more time to building relationships with students and fostering a positive learning environment. By automating routine tasks such as grading assessments or managing resources, teachers can focus on developing meaningful connections with their students and modelling essential human skills such as empathy and emotional intelligence. This holistic approach to education not only prepares students for the demands of the future workforce but also equips them with the interpersonal skills necessary for success in all aspects of life.

Incorporating AI into education does not mean replacing human teachers with machines but rather enhancing the teaching and learning process through innovative technologies. By embracing a balanced approach that leverages AI while still prioritizing the development of essential human skills, educators can create a learning environment that prepares students for success in a rapidly changing world. Ultimately, the goal should be to empower students with a well-rounded education that combines technological proficiency with critical thinking, creativity, problem-solving, and empathy—qualities that are essential for thriving in an increasingly complex and interconnected global society.

In summary, while AI presents numerous benefits in education, it also introduces critical challenges that must be addressed. The lack of emotional intelligence, ethical concerns related to data privacy, and the risks of overreliance on technology highlight the need for careful implementation of AI in educational settings. Future research should concentrate on developing emotionally aware, transparent, and equitable AI systems. Additionally, educators must be trained to integrate AI effectively, ensuring that technological advancements complement human interaction and critical thinking rather than replace them. By striking the right balance, AI can enhance educational experiences while maintaining the essential human elements of learning.

V. FUTURE IMPLICATIONS

- Integration of AI in traditional classroom settings

The incorporation of Artificial Intelligence (AI) into conventional classroom settings is reshaping the educational landscape. AI enhances teaching by personalizing learning experiences, automating repetitive tasks, and delivering real-time feedback. For example, AI-powered adaptive learning platforms can modify the difficulty level of coursework based on individual student performance, ensuring that each learner is appropriately challenged (Ritter et al., 2007). This tailored approach not only improves academic outcomes but also boosts student engagement and motivation.

Moreover, AI assists teachers in managing classroom activities more effectively. AI-driven tools streamline processes like grading, attendance tracking, and content creation, allowing educators to focus on mentoring and guiding students. This shift enables teachers to provide more individualized support and build stronger relationships with their students, fostering a more supportive learning environment (Bain, 2004). Studies indicate that when teachers are relieved of administrative burdens, they can invest more time in developing innovative instructional strategies and enhancing student-teacher interactions (Darling-Hammond et al., 2024).

Furthermore, AI technology can also help educators personalize learning experiences for students by analyzing their strengths and weaknesses. By using data-driven insights, teachers can tailor lesson plans to meet each student's unique needs, ultimately improving academic performance and engagement. This personalized approach to education has been shown to boost student motivation and confidence, leading to better overall outcomes in the classroom.

In addition, AI tools can assist teachers in identifying at-risk students who may need additional support. By analyzing patterns in student behaviour and performance, these tools can alert educators to potential issues before they escalate, allowing them to intervene early and provide targeted interventions. This proactive approach to student support has been proven to increase retention rates and improve overall student well-being.

Moreover, AI-driven tools can also help teachers collaborate more effectively with their colleagues. By automating tasks like lesson planning and resource sharing, educators can spend more time collaborating on best practices and developing innovative teaching strategies. This collaborative environment fosters a culture of continuous improvement and professional development among educators, ultimately benefiting both teachers and students alike.

Overall, the integration of AI technology in education has the potential to revolutionize the way teachers work and interact with students. By automating routine tasks and providing valuable insights into student performance, AI tools empower educators to focus on what truly matters – fostering a supportive learning environment where every student can thrive. As this technology continues to evolve, it will be exciting to see the positive impact it has on education as a whole.

- Potential for AI to revolutionize education

AI holds the promise of making education more accessible, efficient, and effective. AI-driven platforms can provide high-quality learning resources to students in remote or underserved areas, bridging gaps in educational opportunities (Warschauer, 2004). Additionally, AI can promote educational equity by offering customized learning experiences that accommodate different learning styles and abilities. This inclusivity ensures that all students, regardless of their socio-economic background or location, have equal opportunities to succeed academically.

Furthermore, AI supports lifelong learning by offering continuous educational opportunities beyond traditional school settings. AI-powered platforms provide up-to-date courses and training programs that help professionals stay informed about industry developments (ButarButar & Simatupang, 2020; Erbas et al., 2021). This ongoing access to education enhances career prospects and fosters economic growth by ensuring that the workforce remains skilled and adaptable in an evolving job market.

AI has the potential to revolutionize the way education is delivered by personalizing learning experiences for students. By analyzing data on individual learning styles and preferences, AI can tailor educational content to meet the specific needs of each student, thereby maximizing their academic potential. This level of customization can help bridge the achievement gap by ensuring that all students receive the support and resources they need to succeed.

In addition to personalized learning, AI can also facilitate collaboration and communication among students and teachers. Virtual classrooms and online forums powered by AI algorithms can create a dynamic learning environment where students can engage with course materials, ask questions, and participate in discussions in real time. This interactive approach to education not only enhances student engagement but also fosters critical thinking skills and creativity.

Moreover, AI can play a crucial role in breaking down barriers to education by making learning more accessible and affordable. Online platforms powered by AI technology can deliver high-quality educational content to students around the world, regardless of their geographical location or financial means. This democratization of education ensures that everyone has the opportunity to acquire new knowledge and skills, thereby promoting social mobility and reducing inequality.

Furthermore, AI can support lifelong learning by offering continuous educational opportunities beyond traditional school settings. AI-powered platforms provide up-to-date courses and training programs that help professionals stay informed about industry developments. This ongoing access to education enhances career prospects and fosters economic growth by ensuring that the workforce remains skilled and adaptable in an evolving job market. By empowering individuals to continuously update their skills and knowledge through AI-driven educational resources, societies can better prepare for future challenges and opportunities in an increasingly digital world.

Overall, the integration of AI in education has the potential to transform how we learn, teach, and work. By leveraging AI technologies to personalize learning experiences, promote collaboration among students and teachers, increase accessibility to education, and support lifelong learning initiatives, we can create a more inclusive and equitable educational system that empowers individuals from all walks of life to achieve their full academic potential.

The use of AI in education can also help educators identify areas where students may be struggling and provide targeted interventions to support their learning. For example, AI-powered learning platforms can analyze student performance data and provide real-time feedback to teachers on how to adjust their teaching strategies to better meet the needs of each student. This personalized approach has the potential to significantly improve student outcomes and overall academic achievement.

In addition, AI can also play a crucial role in helping students develop essential 21st-century skills such as critical thinking, problem-solving, and creativity. By incorporating AI tools and technologies into the curriculum, students can gain hands-on experience with cutting-edge technologies and learn how to apply them in practical ways. This not only prepares them for success in a rapidly evolving job market but also fosters a culture of innovation and entrepreneurship.

Moreover, the integration of AI in education can help bridge the digital divide by providing access to high-quality educational resources for students in underserved communities. Through online platforms and virtual classrooms powered by AI, students from remote areas or low-income backgrounds can access world-class educational materials and interact with top educators from around the globe. This democratization of education has the potential to level the playing field and empower all individuals to pursue their academic aspirations regardless of their socio-economic status.

Another benefit of incorporating AI in education is its ability to enhance teacher productivity and effectiveness. By automating routine administrative tasks such as grading assignments, tracking attendance, or creating lesson plans, teachers can focus more on delivering high-quality instruction and engaging with students on a deeper level. This not only reduces teacher burnout but also allows educators to spend more time on activities that have a direct impact on student learning outcomes.

In conclusion, the integration of AI in education represents a transformative opportunity to revolutionize traditional teaching methods and create more inclusive learning environments for all students. By harnessing the power of AI technologies, we can unlock new potentials for personalized learning experiences, collaboration, accessibility, and lifelong learning initiatives that will shape the future of education for generations to come. Ultimately, AI has the potential to empower individuals from diverse backgrounds to achieve their full academic potential and thrive in an increasingly digital world.

- Importance of human involvement in education

Despite AI's transformative potential, human educators remain indispensable for providing emotional support, nurturing creativity, and facilitating meaningful discussions that AI systems cannot yet replicate. Teachers play a crucial role in fostering critical thinking and encouraging students to explore their interests in a supportive environment (Ecclestone et al., 2010). Additionally, human interaction is essential for addressing ethical and moral dilemmas in education, which require empathy, nuanced judgment, and complex reasoning—traits unique to humans.

While AI can analyze data and generate insights, educators are needed to interpret this information and apply it effectively to teaching strategies and curriculum development. Rather than replacing teachers, AI should serve as a tool that enhances their ability to instruct and engage students. Research highlights the importance of balancing technological advancements with human interaction to ensure a well-rounded and effective education (Selwyn, 2016b).

AI can assist educators in personalizing learning experiences for students by providing real-time feedback, adapting to individual learning styles, and identifying areas where students may need additional support. This can help teachers better address the diverse needs of their students and create a more inclusive learning environment. Additionally, AI can help streamline administrative tasks, allowing teachers to focus more on building relationships with their students and fostering a positive classroom culture.

Furthermore, the integration of AI in education can also help bridge the gap between traditional classroom instruction and online learning platforms. By utilizing AI-powered tools such as virtual tutors or adaptive learning systems, educators can provide students with personalized and interactive learning experiences that cater to their unique needs and preferences. This can help increase student engagement and motivation, ultimately leading to improved academic outcomes.

However, it is important to consider the ethical implications of using AI in education. For example, there are concerns about data privacy and security when implementing AI-powered systems that collect sensitive information about students. Educators must ensure that proper safeguards are in place to protect student data and uphold ethical standards in the use of AI technology. Additionally, there is a risk of perpetuating inequalities if AI is not implemented equitably across all schools and classrooms.

Despite these challenges, the potential benefits of integrating AI into education are vast. From personalized learning experiences to increased efficiency in administrative tasks, AI has the power to revolutionize the way we teach and learn. By leveraging the strengths of both human educators and AI technology, we can create a more dynamic and effective educational system that prepares students for success in an increasingly digital world. Ultimately, educators must approach the integration of AI with a thoughtful and critical mindset, ensuring that its implementation aligns with ethical standards and serves the best interests of all students.

- **Challenges and Future Considerations**

As AI continues to evolve in education, addressing its challenges is crucial. Key concerns include ensuring that AI systems are transparent, free from bias, and adaptable to diverse learning needs. Future research should focus on developing ethical and equitable AI tools. Additionally, educators must receive adequate training to integrate AI into their teaching practices effectively, maintaining a balance between technological advancements and essential human-centred skills such as critical thinking and interpersonal communication.

AI's integration into traditional classroom settings offers significant advantages in enhancing educational experiences. However, maintaining a balance between technological innovation and human involvement is essential. By utilizing AI as a supportive tool rather than a replacement for teachers, educators can create more personalized, efficient, and inclusive learning environments that prepare students for success in an increasingly digital world.

One way in which AI can enhance traditional classroom settings is through personalized learning experiences. Through the use of algorithms and data analysis, AI can tailor lesson plans and activities to meet the individual needs and learning styles of each student. This not only helps students grasp concepts more effectively but also allows teachers to track progress and provide targeted support where needed. By leveraging AI in this way, educators can create a more dynamic and engaging learning environment that caters to the diverse needs of students.

Another advantage of integrating AI into education is the ability to automate administrative tasks, such as grading assignments and providing feedback. This frees up teachers' time to focus on more interactive and creative aspects of teaching, such as facilitating discussions, conducting experiments, or leading group projects. By streamlining these routine tasks, AI enables educators to devote more energy to fostering critical thinking skills and promoting collaborative learning experiences among students.

Furthermore, AI can provide valuable insights into student performance and engagement levels through real-time data analysis. By tracking metrics such as participation rates, quiz scores, and study habits, educators can identify areas for improvement and adjust their teaching strategies accordingly. This data-driven approach helps ensure that no student falls behind or gets left out in the learning process, ultimately leading to better academic outcomes for all learners.

In addition to enhancing academic achievements, AI can also play a key role in developing essential 21st-century skills among students. By incorporating interactive technologies like virtual reality simulations or educational games into lesson plans, educators can foster creativity, problem-solving abilities, and digital literacy in their students. These hands-on learning experiences not only make education more engaging but also prepare students for success in a fast-paced and technology-driven society.

By striking a balance between technological innovation and human-centred teaching practices, educators can harness the full potential of AI to create enriching educational experiences for students. By leveraging AI as a tool to support rather than replace human instructors, schools can cultivate a culture of lifelong learning that equips students with the skills they need to thrive in an increasingly complex world. Through thoughtful integration of AI technologies into traditional classroom settings, educators can empower students to become critical thinkers, effective communicators, and adaptable problem-solvers who are well-prepared for success in the digital age.

Additionally, AI can help personalize learning experiences for students by providing adaptive learning platforms that cater to individual strengths and weaknesses. This level of customization can help students progress at their own pace, ensuring that they fully grasp concepts before moving on to more advanced material. By tailoring instruction to meet the unique needs of each student, educators can create a more inclusive and supportive learning environment that promotes academic success for all.

Moreover, AI can also assist educators in assessing student performance more efficiently and effectively. By analyzing data from assessments and assignments, AI can provide valuable insights into areas where students may be struggling and offer targeted interventions to help them improve. This real-time feedback can enable teachers to quickly identify and address learning gaps, allowing students to stay on track and reach their full potential.

Furthermore, AI can enhance collaboration among students by facilitating communication and teamwork through online platforms and virtual classrooms. By enabling students to work together on projects regardless of physical location, AI technologies can help foster a sense of community and promote peer-to-peer learning opportunities. This collaborative approach not only enhances social skills but also encourages creativity and innovation as students learn from one another's perspectives.

In conclusion, while AI has the potential to revolutionize education by offering new ways to engage learners and support teaching efforts, educators need to approach its integration thoughtfully and ethically. By balancing the benefits of AI with human interaction and guidance, schools can ensure that students receive a well-rounded education that prepares them for success in the digital age. Ultimately, the key lies in leveraging AI as a tool to enhance rather than replace traditional teaching methods, fostering a culture of lifelong learning that empowers students to thrive in a rapidly changing world.

VI. CONCLUSION

To conclude, incorporating Artificial Intelligence (AI) into language learning and literary education presents numerous advantages for improving educational outcomes. AI enables personalized learning, provides adaptive feedback, and enhances accessibility for students of varying proficiency levels. In literary education, AI aids in text analysis, fosters interactive learning experiences, and stimulates critical thinking and creativity. However, challenges such as AI's lack of emotional intelligence, ethical concerns regarding data privacy, and the potential overdependence on technology must be carefully addressed (Selwyn, 2016a; Warschauer, 2004).

Educators and institutions are encouraged to adopt AI as a tool to enhance teaching and learning. By integrating AI into educational practices, teachers can improve student engagement, increase efficiency, and address challenges such as equity and accessibility. Institutions should prioritize training educators to effectively utilize AI and ensure that its implementation aligns with educational values and goals (Kukulska-Hulme & Shield, 2008b). Additionally, policymakers must establish frameworks to promote the ethical use of AI, emphasizing data privacy and fairness.

A successful AI integration requires collaboration among educators, policymakers, and technology developers. This collective effort can help mitigate potential risks and ensure that AI complements, rather than replaces, human instruction. Studies indicate that when thoughtfully integrated, AI can significantly enhance student learning and engagement (Ritter et al., 2007). As a result, educators and institutions must actively explore AI's potential and its role in shaping the future of education.

Looking ahead, AI is set to play a transformative role in language learning and literary education by providing personalized instruction, improving text analysis, and fostering creativity. However, AI should serve as a supplement to human teaching rather than a substitute. The empathy, emotional intelligence, and nuanced understanding that educators bring to the classroom are essential for creating an inclusive and supportive learning environment (Goleman, 2005). As AI continues to advance, educators must ensure a balanced approach that integrates technological innovation with meaningful human interaction to maintain a holistic and effective educational experience.

Moving forward, research should focus on developing AI systems that are more emotionally intelligent, transparent, and adaptable to diverse learning needs. Additionally, further studies are needed to explore how AI can be effectively integrated into education while promoting equity and accessibility. By addressing these challenges, educators and policymakers can ensure that AI enhances education in a sustainable and meaningful way.

REFERENCES

Bachman, L., & Adrian, P. (2022). *Language assessment in practice: Developing language assessments and justifying their use in the real world.* Oxford University Press.

ButarButar, R., & Simatupang, E. (2020). The impact of technology hello English application in EFL classroom. *Lingual: Journal of Language and Culture*, *8*(2), 11.

Chapelle, C. A. (2003). *English Language Learning and Technology: Lectures on Teaching and Research.* Cambridge University Press. DOI: 10.1075/lllt.7

Chen, L., Wang, H., & Zhang, Y. (2023). Reducing test anxiety through adaptive assessment in online language learning. *Journal of Educational Technology & Society*, *26*(4), 123–135.

Dabbagh, N., & Kitsantas, A. (2012). Personal Learning Environments, social media, and self-regulated learning: A natural formula for connecting formal and informal learning. *The Internet and Higher Education*, *15*(1), 3–8. DOI: 10.1016/j.iheduc.2011.06.002

Darling-Hammond, L., Schachner, A. C. W., Wojcikiewicz, S. K., & Flook, L. (2024). Educating teachers to enact the science of learning and development. *Applied Developmental Science*, *28*(1), 1–21. DOI: 10.1080/10888691.2022.2130506

Ecclestone, K., Biesta, G., & Hughes, M. (2010). *Transitions and learning through the life course.* Routledge London.

Erbas, İ., Çipuri, R., & Joni, A. (2021). The impact of technology on teaching and teaching English to elementary school students. *Linguistics and Culture Review*, 1316–1336.

Garcia, M., Rodriguez, F., & Martinez, E. (2024). The impact of an AI-powered adaptive language system on student motivation and proficiency gains: A large-scale study. *Computers & Education*, *190*, 104635.

Goleman, D. (2005). *Emotional intelligence: Why it can matter more than IQ.* Bantam.

Jockers, M. L. (2013). *Macroanalysis: Digital methods and literary history.* University of Illinois Press. DOI: 10.5406/illinois/9780252037528.001.0001

Khosrow-Pour, M. (2008). *Encyclopedia of information science and technology* (Vol. 1). Igi Global.

Klopfer, E. (2008). *Augmented learning: Research and design of mobile educational games*. MIT Press. DOI: 10.7551/mitpress/9780262113151.001.0001

Kukulska-Hulme, A., & Shield, L. (2008a). An overview of mobile assisted language learning: From content delivery to supported collaboration and interaction. *ReCALL, 20*(3), 271–289. DOI: 10.1017/S0958344008000335

Kukulska-Hulme, A., & Shield, L. (2008b). An overview of mobile assisted language learning: From content delivery to supported collaboration and interaction. *ReCALL, 20*(3), 271–289. DOI: 10.1017/S0958344008000335

Lee, S., & Kim, B. (2024). Immediate versus delayed AI feedback on pronunciation: An empirical study. *Language Learning & Technology, 28*(1), 45–60.

Levy, M., & Stockwell, G. (2013). *CALL dimensions: Options and issues in computer-assisted language learning*. Routledge. DOI: 10.4324/9780203708200

Ritter, S., Anderson, J. R., Koedinger, K. R., & Corbett, A. (2007). Cognitive Tutor: Applied research in mathematics education. *Psychonomic Bulletin & Review, 14*(2), 249–255. DOI: 10.3758/BF03194060 PMID: 17694909

Salman, H., Imran, A., Niazi, S., Rahat, A., Arif, A., & Anjum, S. (2024). Artificial Intelligence In Higher Education: Strategies For Fostering Creativity In Writing Instruction. *Migration Letters : An International Journal of Migration Studies, 21*(S8), 1089–1097.

Selwyn, N. (2016a). *Is technology good for education?* John Wiley & Sons.

Selwyn, N. (2016b). *Is technology good for education?* John Wiley & Sons.

Shidiq, M. (2023). The use of artificial intelligence-based chat-gpt and its challenges for the world of education; from the viewpoint of the development of creative writing skills. *Proceeding of International Conference on Education, Society and Humanity, 1*(1), 353–357.

Smith, J., & Jones, K. (2023). Effectiveness of personalized learning pathways in an AI-driven Spanish curriculum. *Journal of Applied Linguistics, 44*(3), 321–338.

Staples, S., Egbert, J., Biber, D., & Conrad, S. (2015). Register variation a corpus approach. *The Handbook of Discourse Analysis*, 505–525.

Warschauer, M. (2004). *Technology and social inclusion: Rethinking the digital divide*. MIT press.

White, R., Davis, P., & Miller, S. (2024). Using AI for thematic analysis in undergraduate literary studies: A case study. *Journal of Digital Humanities, 6*(2), 87–101.

Williamson, B. (2017). *Big data in education: The digital future of learning, policy and practice.*

Zhao, D. (2024). The impact of AI-enhanced natural language processing tools on writing proficiency: An analysis of language precision, content summarization, and creative writing facilitation. *Education and Information Technologies*, •••, 1–32.

Chapter 7
AI as an Evaluator in Education Assessment:
Analyzing Teacher Education Students' Literary Materials

Mark Jhon R. Prestoza
https://orcid.org/0000-0002-4344-4504
Isabela State University, Philippines

Boyet L. Batang
Isabela State University, Echague, Philippines

Rozel S. Batang
Isabela State University, Cabagan, Philippines

ABSTRACT

This chapter explores the integration of Artificial Intelligence (AI) in educational assessments, focusing on the use of AI-driven tools to evaluate teacher education students' literary materials. It examines the potential benefits of AI, including improved accuracy, efficiency, and consistency in evaluation, alongside the challenges AI faces in assessing subjective criteria like creativity, engagement, and cultural relevance. A comparative analysis of AI-driven evaluations and human assessments highlights both the strengths and limitations of AI in educational contexts. The chapter advocates for a hybrid model that combines AI's data processing capabilities with human evaluators' expertise in complex, context-dependent assessments. It also addresses the need for ongoing research and collaboration between educators and AI developers to ensure the ethical and equitable application of AI in education. This chapter contributes to the growing body of knowledge on the effective integration of AI in educational assessment practices.

DOI: 10.4018/979-8-3373-6330-1.ch007

Copyright © 2026, IGI Global Scientific Publishing. Copying or distributing in print or electronic forms without written permission of IGI Global Scientific Publishing is prohibited.

INTRODUCTION

The integration of Artificial Intelligence (AI) into education is poised to change the way assessments are designed, delivered, and evaluated. As AI technologies evolve, they offer educators new tools to enhance the teaching and learning experience. One of the most promising developments is the use of large language models, such as ChatGPT, which have demonstrated significant potential in reshaping educational assessment practices. These AI-driven tools offer advantages, providing educators innovative ways to generate assessment questions, give personalized feedback, and streamline grading (Zhang, 2024; Kooli & Yusuf, 2024; Owan et al., 2023). For instance, AI systems can automate aspects of assessments, from test creation to scoring, reducing administrative workload and enhancing students' engagement with the material (O'Cain et al., 2023; Owan et al., 2023).

AI tools can analyze vast amounts of student data, enabling a tailored approach to assessment. Automating routine tasks, such as generating quiz questions or grading, frees up time for educators to focus on higher-level instruction. Additionally, AI systems provide real-time feedback, identifying weaknesses and suggesting strategies for improvement. As a result, AI is becoming indispensable, allowing institutions to implement more efficient and personalized assessment practices.

However, the application of AI in assessments presents challenges. One significant issue is the need for human validation of AI-generated content. While powerful, AI models may produce content that lacks accuracy, context, or relevance. Therefore, educators must review AI-generated assessments to ensure they meet learning objectives. There are also concerns about AI's impact on educational equity, as AI systems rely on datasets that may reflect societal biases, potentially leading to unfair assessments. Furthermore, AI could exacerbate inequalities by benefiting students with better access to technology (Zhang, 2024; Kooli & Yusuf, 2024).

Research has shown that while AI streamlines assessment practices, a moderate correlation between AI-driven and human-generated grading suggests that AI cannot fully replace human evaluators (Kooli & Yusuf, 2024). This highlights the importance of balancing AI's computational power with human judgment, especially in assessing subjective elements like creativity, engagement, and cultural relevance. AI excels at processing objective data but struggles with nuanced aspects of student work. Therefore, AI can provide valuable insights, but human evaluators are crucial for critical thinking and emotional intelligence in assessment.

To maximize AI's benefits while mitigating risks, experts recommend strategies like enhancing teacher training. Educators must learn to effectively use AI tools, understand their limitations, and integrate them into teaching practices in ways that support learning. Teachers should also maintain professional independence when working with AI, ensuring human judgment remains central. Thoughtfully incorporating AI into assessment will help avoid over-reliance on technology and preserve the integrity of education (Zhang, 2024; Owan et al., 2023).

This chapter focuses on AI tools in assessing teacher education students' literary materials. The use of AI in evaluating writing, creative works, and critical analyses has the potential to improve the accuracy and efficiency of assessments. However, it also examines AI's limitations in assessing subjective criteria, such as creativity and cultural relevance. While AI can measure certain aspects of student writing, it is less effective in evaluating nuanced, interpretive qualities essential to assessing literary materials in teacher education programs.

The chapter advocates for a hybrid model that combines AI-driven assessments with human expertise. This model recognizes that while AI enhances efficiency and consistency, human evaluators are essential in assessing subjective criteria requiring emotional intelligence, cultural understanding, and judgment. By combining AI's analytical capabilities with educators' contextual skills, this hybrid approach can create a more reliable, personalized, and fair assessment system.

Ultimately, this chapter contributes to the growing knowledge of AI's role in educational assessment, particularly in teacher education. It offers insights into effectively integrating AI into assessment practices, emphasizing the need for continued research, policy development, and professional training to ensure ethical and equitable AI application in education. The chapter calls for a thoughtful approach to AI integration, maximizing its potential while addressing challenges and limitations.

BACKGROUND

The use of Artificial Intelligence (AI) in education is rapidly evolving, offering innovative approaches to improve assessment processes. Recent studies have explored AI's potential to enhance consistency, objectivity, and efficiency in evaluating student work. AI-driven tools, such as those powered by natural language processing, have shown high levels of reliability in grading standardized assessments, improving accuracy and enabling faster feedback generation (Owan et al., 2023; Anjum et al., 2023). However, despite these advancements, the evaluation of subjective criteria, such as creativity, engagement, and cultural relevance, remains a challenge for AI systems (Han, 2021). This highlights the need for a balanced approach, where AI's strengths in data processing and standardization can complement the nuanced judgment of human evaluators (Al-Zahrani, 2024). AI-driven tools have the potential to revolutionize educational assessments by offering enhanced efficiency and consistency. Research has demonstrated that AI-based grading systems can provide fast, objective feedback for tasks that require standardized evaluation (Karademir Coskun & Alper, 2024). These tools help reduce the workload of educators and allow them to focus on more personalized instruction (Owan et al., 2023). Despite the benefits, AI faces significant challenges, particularly when it comes to evaluating subjective aspects such as student engagement, creativity, and cultural relevance. AI systems often struggle to grasp the nuanced and contextual nature of these criteria (Han, 2021). Moreover, concerns about algorithmic fairness, data privacy, and the potential for resistance from educators must be addressed for AI integration to be fully effective (Lyanda et al., 2024). Studies show varying levels of consistency between AI and human evaluators. While AI demonstrates reliability in objective evaluations, it falls short in capturing subjective aspects, such as engagement and creativity (Khademi, 2023). Human evaluators, by contrast, bring context, intuition, and cultural sensitivity to their assessments (Kim et al., 2023). This comparison reveals the complementary strengths of both AI and human evaluation methods, emphasizing the need for collaboration between the two.

The integration of AI tools with human evaluators offers a promising solution. Hybrid models, where AI handles objective tasks and humans assess complex cognitive skills, have been proposed to enhance the reliability and richness of feedback (Zhou, 2024). In professional and educational settings, such collaboration can optimize assessment processes by leveraging both AI's data processing abilities and human creativity and insight (Akinnagbe, 2024). AI presents numerous opportunities for personalized learning and equitable education by analyzing student performance data and tailoring content to meet individual needs (Kadaruddin, 2023; Roshanaei et al., 2023). However, ethical concerns, such as data privacy, algorithmic bias, and the need for educator training, remain critical issues (Walter, 2024). To effectively harness AI's potential, ongoing collaboration between educators, policymakers, and developers is necessary to ensure that its use is ethical, equitable, and aligned with educational goals.

EVALUATING LITERARY MATERIALS

This theme explores the different approaches to evaluating teacher education students' literary materials, with a specific focus on AI-driven evaluation methods compared to traditional human evaluation. The theme highlights the advantages and challenges of both approaches and provides a framework for understanding how each method contributes to the assessment process.

1. AI-DRIVEN EVALUATION

1.1. The Role of AI in Standardizing Assessments

AI tools like ChatGPT play a crucial role in standardizing assessments by applying consistent criteria across all evaluations. Unlike human assessors, who may be influenced by subjective biases or inconsistent interpretations of grading rubrics, AI can process and assess student work based on predefined, objective standards. This ensures that all students are evaluated fairly and uniformly, removing the possibility of arbitrary grading. In the context of literary material evaluation, AI tools can objectively assess aspects such as text complexity, alignment with academic standards, and vocabulary development, creating a level playing field for all students (Rane, 2023). The ability of AI to process large datasets further enhances this standardization, allowing for faster and more reliable assessment of student work.

1.2. Personalized Feedback Generation through AI

One of the major benefits of using AI in educational assessments is its ability to generate personalized feedback for students. Large language models, such as ChatGPT, can analyze specific student responses and provide individualized suggestions for improvement. AI can highlight areas where students struggle with vocabulary, text complexity, or understanding of literary concepts, offering tailored recommendations for improvement. Personalized feedback not only helps students understand their weaknesses but also encourages deeper engagement with the material (Baidoo-Anu & Owusu Ansah, 2023). This level of customization in feedback can be difficult for human evaluators to achieve, especially in large classes where individual attention is limited. As AI tools continue to evolve, the feedback generated will likely become more sophisticated, providing even greater support to learners in their academic development.

1.3. Challenges in Evaluating Complex, Subjective Aspects

Despite the many advantages of AI in educational assessment, there are challenges, especially when it comes to evaluating more complex and subjective aspects of student work, such as creativity, engagement, and cultural relevance. AI systems excel in analyzing structured data and objective criteria, but they struggle with assessing nuances inherent in subjective components of literary analysis (Rane, 2024). For instance, while AI can evaluate the complexity of a text or its adherence to academic standards, it may not fully appreciate the creative nuances that a human evaluator can detect, such as the originality of thought or the emotional depth of the work.

AI may also find it difficult to assess engagement or cultural relevance in ways that respect the diverse backgrounds and perspectives of students. This highlights the need for a hybrid approach that combines AI's objective strengths with the human evaluators' ability to understand these complex, context-dependent qualities.

1.4. Addressing Bias and Ensuring Algorithmic Fairness

Another critical consideration when integrating AI into educational assessment is the potential for algorithmic bias. AI systems, including large language models like ChatGPT, are trained on vast amounts of data, which can inadvertently introduce biases if the data itself is skewed. For example, if the training data contains biased language patterns or culturally narrow perspectives, the AI might replicate and reinforce these biases in its evaluations (Kasneci et al., 2023). This poses a significant risk in educational settings, where fairness and inclusivity are paramount. Researchers and educators must ensure that AI algorithms are continually monitored and updated to address any biases and promote fairness across different student demographics. This also involves ensuring transparency in how AI models are trained and evaluated, so that educators can trust the results and use them responsibly (Rane, 2023).

1.5. Ethical and Practical Considerations

The integration of AI in educational assessment requires careful consideration of ethical and practical issues. Ethical concerns include ensuring data privacy and safeguarding students' personal information, as AI systems often require access to extensive student data to function effectively. The use of AI in education also raises questions about the potential loss of human agency in the evaluation process. While AI can enhance efficiency and consistency, the human touch remains essential in fostering creativity, critical thinking, and emotional intelligence, which are key elements in teacher education (Kasneci et al., 2023). Therefore, AI should not replace human evaluators but rather serve as a tool to augment their capabilities. A balanced approach that critically examines AI's role while leveraging its benefits responsibly is crucial for the future of educational assessment (Rane, 2024).

AI-driven tools like ChatGPT offer significant benefits in the realm of educational assessment, including greater accuracy, efficiency, and the potential for personalized feedback. Challenges remain, particularly in evaluating subjective criteria. As the integration of AI in teacher education continues to evolve, it is important to maintain a balanced approach that combines the strengths of AI with the expertise and judgment of human evaluators. By addressing concerns such as bias, data privacy, and algorithmic fairness, educators can harness AI's potential to create a more efficient, equitable, and effective educational assessment system.

2. TRADITIONAL HUMAN EVALUATION

While artificial intelligence (AI) has shown promise in improving efficiency and objectivity in educational assessments, human judgment remains indispensable for evaluating complex cognitive skills such as creativity, critical thinking, and emotional depth. Experienced educators bring a level of expertise to the evaluation process that goes beyond automated scoring, offering subjective insights and nuanced feedback that AI systems currently struggle to replicate. This subtheme explores the strengths of human evaluators, the balance between subjective interpretation and objective grading, and the challenges associated with inconsistencies in human assessments due to biases or varying interpretations.

2.1. The Expertise of Human Evaluators in Interpreting Complex Educational Content

Human evaluators possess a deep understanding of the nuances involved in literary analysis, which allows them to interpret complex educational content in ways that AI systems may not fully capture. Educators can identify subtle aspects of a student's writing, such as thematic development, voice, and style, which contribute to the overall quality of the work. Additionally, teachers can assess the originality of thought and the emotional depth of a student's writing, qualities that are often subjective and culturally context dependent. AI systems, while efficient in processing large datasets, typically lack the nuanced understanding that human evaluators bring to the table, especially when dealing with creative works like literature (Zhou, 2024).

2.2. The Balance Between Subjective Insights and Objective Grading

A key challenge in human evaluation is the need to balance subjective insights with objective grading. While human evaluators can offer personalized feedback that considers individual student contexts, the subjective nature of their assessments can sometimes introduce inconsistency. For instance, two different teachers may interpret the same piece of writing differently based on their individual experiences, biases, and perspectives. This subjectivity can lead to variations in grading, which, although providing a rich and holistic understanding of student work, may undermine fairness and reliability. In contrast, AI systems can standardize assessments and remove these inconsistencies by applying a uniform set of criteria to all students. However, the subjective insights provided by human evaluators remain essential for understanding the deeper, intangible qualities of a student's work, such as creativity and cultural relevance (Swiecki et al., 2022).

2.3. Challenges of Inconsistencies Between Human Evaluators

Despite the strengths of human evaluators, the traditional approach is not without its challenges. One significant issue is the inconsistency between different evaluators, which can arise from personal biases or varied interpretations of grading rubrics. For instance, the same literary work may be graded differently by two teachers based on their individual teaching experiences, cultural perspectives, or expectations. This can create disparities in student evaluations, especially in subjects like literature, where interpretive flexibility is often required. Research shows that these inconsistencies can impact the reliability of human assessments, potentially leading to unfair outcomes for students (Karademir coskun & Alper, 2024). While AI-based systems can mitigate some of these issues by providing more consistent and objective evaluations, they cannot fully replicate the human capacity for nuanced judgment, making the combination of both human and AI evaluations an ideal approach for teacher education assessments.

While human evaluation remains a cornerstone of teacher education, the integration of AI tools presents opportunities for enhancing consistency, objectivity, and efficiency. However, the strengths of human evaluators—particularly in assessing subjective and intangible qualities—are indispensable. A balanced hybrid approach that leverages both human insight and AI capabilities may provide the most effective and fair method of assessing literary materials in teacher education, ensuring that students are evaluated not only on their technical abilities but also on their creativity, critical thinking, and personal expression.

3. HYBRID EVALUATION MODELS: COMBINING AI AND HUMAN INSIGHTS

AI technologies have proven advantageous in automating grading, offering rapid feedback, and handling large datasets, they are still limited when it comes to assessing complex cognitive skills like creativity, critical thinking, and emotional nuance. A hybrid evaluation model seeks to bridge these gaps by integrating AI's quantitative capabilities with the qualitative insights of human assessors. This approach not only enhances the reliability and scalability of educational assessments but also ensures that the assessment process remains fair, culturally relevant, and contextually informed. The following key aspects will be discussed to illuminate the benefits of such an integrated assessment approach.

3.1. Synergy Between AI's Consistency and Human Expertise

One of the most compelling advantages of a hybrid evaluation model lies in the synergy between AI's consistency and human expertise. AI systems can process large volumes of data quickly and provide consistent, objective evaluations based on predefined criteria. This capability makes AI particularly useful in grading tasks that are rule-based, such as multiple-choice exams or short-answer questions. However, AI is not as adept at assessing open-ended or subjective aspects of student performance, such as creativity, emotional expression, or the complexity of critical thinking (Zhou, 2024). Human evaluators, on the other hand, excel in making judgments about these qualities due to their contextual knowledge, professional expertise, and understanding of educational standards. When AI and human evaluators collaborate, they create a comprehensive evaluation system that maximizes the strengths of both approaches, providing a more balanced and accurate assessment of students' abilities (Swiecki et al., 2022).

3.2. Designing an Integrated Assessment Framework

The development of an integrated assessment framework that combines AI and human evaluations requires careful design and consideration of the roles each component will play. AI can be used to handle time-consuming, standardized tasks such as grading objective questions, generating performance analytics, and offering formative feedback. These tasks benefit from AI's ability to process large datasets, identify patterns, and provide immediate feedback. However, for more subjective assessments, human evaluators can provide the nuanced, context-driven feedback that AI lacks. The hybrid model should ensure that human evaluators can interact with AI-generated data, offering insights and refinements where necessary. For example, a human evaluator may adjust the AI's assessment of a creative writing piece by considering cultural context, emotional depth, or originality, ensuring that feedback is both relevant and fair (Zhou, 2024). Designing a seamless integration between AI tools and human evaluators requires collaboration and the development of protocols that clearly define when and how human intervention is needed.

3.2. Refining AI-Generated Feedback to Ensure Fairness and Cultural Relevance

AI systems, while efficient, may not always provide feedback that is fully fair or culturally relevant. Algorithms can unintentionally reinforce biases based on the data they are trained on, leading to skewed or culturally insensitive evaluations. For instance, an AI system may penalize a student for using unconventional language that is culturally significant or for adopting a writing style that deviates from the norms established in the system's training data (Mahamuni et al., 2024). Human evaluators can refine AI-generated feedback by considering the broader context of a student's work, ensuring that cultural nuances, diverse perspectives, and personal expression are respected. This process of human refinement helps to mitigate the risks of algorithmic bias and ensures that assessments are equitable and aligned with educational standards that account for diversity and inclusion. Furthermore, human evaluators can engage in ethical oversight, ensuring that AI systems adhere to privacy guidelines and avoid discriminatory practices (Mahamuni et al., 2024).

The hybrid evaluation model, which combines the strengths of AI and human evaluators, presents a promising solution to the limitations of traditional and fully automated assessment methods. By leveraging AI's efficiency and scalability while preserving human expertise in making context-sensitive, nuanced judgments, this model enhances the reliability, fairness, and cultural relevance of educational assessments. Moving forward, developing integrated frameworks that support collaboration between AI systems and human evaluators will be essential in achieving a more holistic and effective approach to student assessment. Furthermore, ongoing research and development are needed to ensure that these hybrid models are implemented ethically and in ways that address potential risks, such as algorithmic bias and data privacy concerns.

4. ETHICAL AND PRACTICAL CONSIDERATIONS IN EVALUATION APPROACHES

The integration of AI in educational evaluation introduces a range of ethical and practical challenges that must be addressed to ensure its responsible use. While AI-driven tools have the potential to enhance efficiency, accuracy, and scalability in educational assessments, they also raise significant concerns related to data privacy, algorithmic bias, and the broader implications of automation on teaching practices. This subtheme examines the ethical dimensions of AI in education, focusing on the risks and opportunities associated with its use in evaluative processes. Additionally, it explores the role of professional development in equipping educators with the skills and knowledge needed to incorporate AI into their assessment practices while maintaining ethical standards and professional autonomy.

4.1. Ethical Issues Related to AI Evaluation in Education

One of the central ethical issues in the use of AI in educational evaluation is the potential for algorithmic bias. AI systems are often trained on large datasets, which can include historical data reflecting societal biases, prejudices, or inequities. If these biases are not carefully addressed, AI tools may perpetuate or even amplify existing inequities in education (Sywelem & Mahklouf, 2024). For instance, an AI system designed to grade essays might unfairly penalize students from certain cultural backgrounds or those who use non-standard dialects, which could affect their academic outcomes. Ethical frameworks are being developed to ensure that AI evaluations are fair, transparent, and inclusive, but much work remains to be done in creating guidelines that adequately address these concerns (Bulut et al., 2024). Furthermore, the automation of educational assessments raises questions about the role of human judgment in evaluating complex skills, such as creativity, cultural relevance, and emotional intelligence, which AI may struggle to assess accurately.

4.2. Data Privacy and Security Concerns in AI Systems

Data privacy is another major concern when implementing AI systems in educational settings. AI-driven tools often require access to vast amounts of personal data, including student performance records, demographic information, and even behavioral data. This data must be handled with the utmost care to ensure compliance with privacy laws and to protect students' sensitive information from potential breaches. The centralization of such data in AI systems raises the risk of unauthorized access, misuse, or exploitation, especially in the context of third-party data processing services (Farooqi et al., 2024). As AI technologies are deployed in educational assessments, it is crucial that strict data protection measures are put in place, and that transparent policies are developed to guide how student data is collected, stored, and used. The ethical use of data in AI-powered evaluations must be ensured to safeguard students' privacy rights and maintain trust in the educational system.

4.3. Professional Development to Ensure the Effective Use of AI in Education

Considering the rapid advancements in AI technologies, professional development for educators is essential to ensure that AI tools are used effectively and responsibly in assessment practices. Educators must be trained to understand not only the technical capabilities of AI systems but also the ethical implications of their use. This training should emphasize the importance of maintaining professional autonomy and critical judgment when interpreting AI-generated feedback and assessments (Sywelem &

Mahklouf, 2024). Teachers need to be equipped with the skills to recognize and address potential biases in AI evaluations and to ensure that their use of AI aligns with broader educational goals, such as fostering creativity, critical thinking, and cultural sensitivity (Farooqi et al., 2024). Furthermore, professional development programs should focus on the ethical dimensions of AI integration, helping educators navigate the complexities of data privacy, security, and algorithmic fairness. A well-informed and ethically aware teaching workforce is essential for ensuring that AI enhances, rather than undermines, educational practices.

The ethical and practical challenges surrounding the use of AI in educational evaluation are complex and multifaceted. As AI technologies continue to evolve and become more integrated into educational systems, it is crucial to develop robust ethical frameworks and guidelines that address concerns such as algorithmic bias, data privacy, and the potential for automation to diminish the role of human educators. Additionally, professional development for educators plays a critical role in ensuring the responsible and effective use of AI tools, helping to preserve the integrity of the educational process while embracing the benefits that AI can offer. A balanced approach that prioritizes both ethical considerations and the advancement of teaching practices will be essential for the successful integration of AI into educational evaluation.

5. EVOLVING AI AND HUMAN ASSESSMENT MODELS

The future of educational assessment lies in the integration of AI technologies with human evaluators, fostering a dynamic synergy that capitalizes on the strengths of both. As AI tools become increasingly sophisticated, they offer substantial promise for transforming educational assessments, particularly in the realm of literary evaluation for teacher education students. This subtheme explores the potential advancements in AI, emerging technologies, and their collaborative role with human expertise in shaping future educational assessments. It also delves into the evolving landscape of hybrid models, which combine the objectivity and efficiency of AI with the critical thinking and emotional understanding of human evaluators, highlighting the ongoing research and innovation in this space.

5.1. Emerging AI Technologies and Their Potential for Educational Assessments

Recent advancements in AI have demonstrated a profound potential to enhance educational assessment practices. Technologies such as machine learning, natural language processing (NLP), and automated essay scoring systems are already being used to evaluate student work, providing rapid and consistent feedback. Emerging tools like ChatGPT, with its ability to generate personalized content and adapt to diverse learning needs, are further expanding the possibilities for AI in education (TAŞKIN BEDİZEL, 2023). These technologies can streamline the grading process, personalize assessments based on student performance, and facilitate adaptive learning environments that cater to individual learning styles. Moreover, AI's ability to analyze vast amounts of data allows for real-time performance tracking, enabling more accurate and immediate feedback that can guide students toward their learning goals (Ogunsakin, 2024). The integration of these emerging technologies into educational assessment systems can lead to more efficient, personalized, and scalable evaluation models.

5.2. The Evolution of Hybrid Models in Teacher Education

As AI technology evolves, hybrid models combining AI-driven assessments with human judgment are becoming increasingly prominent in teacher education. While AI systems are excellent at handling large datasets, offering consistency, and providing quick feedback, they still face challenges when it comes to assessing more subjective aspects of education, such as creativity, emotional depth, and critical thinking. This subtheme explores how hybrid models can combine the best of both worlds: the efficiency, scalability, and objectivity of AI, along with the nuanced judgment and emotional intelligence of human evaluators (Shi & Xuwei, 2023). In teacher education, this hybrid approach could enable a more personalized and holistic assessment of student work, allowing human educators to refine AI-generated evaluations, provide feedback on aspects like creativity and cultural relevance, and ensure that the assessment process is contextually meaningful and fair.

These hybrid models are expected to evolve further as both AI capabilities and human evaluators' roles adapt to the changing landscape of education. For instance, AI could be used to pre-assess student work or provide initial feedback, while human educators could focus on interpreting this feedback in light of the broader educational goals, such as fostering critical thinking, ethical reasoning, and emotional intelligence. This collaboration will likely become a hallmark of future assessment practices in teacher education, offering a more balanced, reliable, and personalized approach to evaluating literary materials.

5.3. Predicting Future Educational Paradigms: AI and Human Insights in Effective Evaluation

The future of educational assessment is likely to be characterized by increasingly sophisticated interactions between AI technologies and human educators. As educational paradigms shift toward more personalized, learner-centered approaches, the role of AI in assessments will expand, particularly in higher education and specialized fields such as medical education (TAŞKIN BEDİZEL, 2023). These changes will be driven by advancements in AI, such as more robust predictive analytics, the ability to provide deeper insights into student progress, and the application of AI to foster collaborative learning environments.

In this evolving landscape, AI and human collaboration will become essential for effective evaluation. For example, AI may play a more prominent role in analyzing patterns in student performance and suggesting improvements, while human educators will retain the crucial role of interpreting these patterns in the context of broader pedagogical goals and values. This integration of AI and human insight will not only enhance the evaluation of literary materials but will also support the development of future educational models that prioritize both personalized learning and holistic educational outcomes.

The future of AI in education is not about replacing human educators but complementing and enhancing their roles. As AI continues to develop, its integration with human insights will be key to creating assessment models that are more effective, fair, and reflective of the diverse needs of students. The next phase of AI and education research will likely focus on refining these hybrid models, addressing the ethical and practical challenges associated with their implementation, and ensuring that they contribute positively to the educational experience for all learners. Emerging technologies offer significant potential for improving the efficiency, personalization, and scalability of assessments, while hybrid models promise to combine the strengths of both AI and human expertise. As these technologies continue to evolve, it will be essential to consider both the opportunities and challenges they present, including ethical concerns such as privacy and fairness, and to develop frameworks that ensure AI complements, rather than replaces, human intelligence in educational practices. With the continued integration of AI in educational assessment, future paradigms will likely offer more dynamic, responsive, and inclusive evaluation systems that better serve the needs of diverse learners.

SOLUTIONS AND RECOMMENDATION

In addressing the issues, controversies, and challenges identified in the previous sections, this chapter proposes several solutions and recommendations aimed at enhancing the integration of Artificial Intelligence (AI) in educational assessment. These solutions are designed to address concerns such as algorithmic bias, data privacy, and the limitations of AI in evaluating subjective aspects of student performance, while also optimizing the benefits of AI to improve the efficiency, accuracy, and consistency of educational evaluations.

Development of Hybrid Evaluation Models

Recent research underscores the potential of hybrid evaluation models that combine AI-driven assessments with human expertise in educational settings. These models leverage the efficiency of AI in handling large-scale tasks, such as grading and data analysis, while retaining human insight for subjective elements like creativity, critical thinking, and emotional depth (Zhou, 2024). AI has shown promise in addressing longstanding issues in traditional assessment practices, including difficulties with design and implementation and the inability to adapt assessments to individual learners' needs (Swiecki et al., 2022). While AI demonstrates high proficiency in evaluating objective components, such as total exam scores, its consistency varies across different exam types, indicating areas for improvement (Karademir Coskun & Alper, 2024). Furthermore, the integration of AI in online learning environments has been shown to enhance student engagement and learning outcomes. However, challenges such as data privacy concerns and algorithmic bias must be addressed to ensure ethical and fair practices (Lyanda et al., 2024).

Considering these findings, the adoption of a hybrid evaluation model emerges as a central solution. By combining AI's capacity for handling repetitive tasks with human evaluators' ability to assess nuanced and complex aspects of student performance, this model promises more comprehensive, fair, and personalized assessments. It ensures that the consistency and efficiency of AI are complemented by the critical judgment and contextual understanding of human educators. Educational institutions should prioritize training educators to effectively integrate AI tools into their assessment practices. This training will equip educators to collaborate with AI systems, maximizing the efficiency of evaluations while preserving the human expertise needed to ensure fairness, accuracy, and personalized feedback.

Ethical Frameworks and Algorithmic Transparency

The integration of AI in education presents several ethical concerns that demand careful consideration and proactive management. Key issues include algorithmic transparency, data privacy, fairness, and the potential for biases in AI systems (Florina Mihai Leta & Diane-Paula Vancea, 2023; M. Sywelem & Asmaa M. El-Sayed Mahklouf, 2024). One of the most critical aspects is ensuring the transparency and explainability of AI systems, as these are essential for fostering trust among educators, students, and other stakeholders (Mauricio Rojas Contreras & Jorge Omar Portilla Jaimes, 2024). Ethical guidelines and frameworks are necessary to address these concerns, ensuring that AI is used responsibly and equitably in educational settings (M. Sywelem & Asmaa M. El-Sayed Mahklouf, 2024). To mitigate the risks associated with AI in education, recommendations include the establishment of clear, transparent standards for algorithmic assessments, the implementation of robust privacy protection measures, and the creation of diverse teams for AI algorithm development to minimize societal biases (Zhenzhen Li, 2024). Regular audits of AI systems should be carried out to ensure adherence to ethical standards and the continued integrity of the system (Florina Mihai Leta & Diane-Paula Vancea, 2023).

Establishing clear ethical guidelines and ensuring transparency in AI systems is crucial for addressing concerns around data privacy and algorithmic biases. AI systems should be explainable, with their decision-making processes accessible to educators and students alike. This will foster trust in AI-driven assessments and ensure that their use is both equitable and responsible. Educational institutions, in collaboration with AI developers, should prioritize the development and implementation of ethical frameworks. These frameworks should focus on protecting student data, preventing biases in AI algorithms, and maintaining fairness in assessment practices. Additionally, regular audits of AI systems are necessary to ensure that these systems continue to meet the highest ethical standards, thereby promoting a more transparent, just, and trustworthy AI-driven educational environment.

Ongoing Professional Development for Educators

The integration of AI in education underscores the critical need for ongoing professional development for educators to ensure they can effectively utilize and critically evaluate AI tools (Brandão et al., 2024; Walter, 2024). Key components of such professional development include fostering AI literacy, providing hands-on experience with AI tools, and equipping educators with skills in prompt engineering (Brandão et al., 2024; Walter, 2024). As AI transforms assessment methods, educators must adapt to their evolving roles, which involve balancing the efficiency of AI automation with the irreplaceable value of human expertise. This balance is essential for maintaining educational integrity and ensuring equitable access to AI-driven resources (Miller, 2024). Moreover, AI's role in educational measurement raises important ethical considerations related to validity, fairness, and algorithmic bias. These issues require careful attention to establish responsible guidelines for AI use in education (Bulut et al., 2024). To address these challenges, educators must be equipped with critical thinking skills, enabling them to engage with AI tools thoughtfully and collaboratively. This collaborative effort across disciplines is necessary to reimagine curriculum development and engage students effectively in the AI-driven educational landscape (Miller, 2024; Walter, 2024).

The successful integration of AI into educational assessments requires educators to be more than just proficient in the technical use of AI tools. They must also be critical consumers of AI-generated content, able to assess the quality and fairness of AI-driven assessments. As such, professional development programs should focus on developing new competencies, including the ability to interpret AI-generated feedback, assess the ethical implications of AI in educational settings, and maintain pedagogical standards.

Professional development programs for educators should not only emphasize technical skills required for using AI tools but also incorporate training on the ethical, pedagogical, and critical thinking aspects necessary for evaluating and interpreting AI-generated assessments responsibly. These programs should empower educators to navigate the complexities of AI integration while upholding academic integrity and promoting equitable educational outcomes.

Addressing the Limitations of AI in Subjective Evaluation

AI tools, especially large language models (LLMs) like ChatGPT, have demonstrated considerable proficiency in objective assessments, such as grading tests or answering factual queries. However, when it comes to evaluating complex and subjective aspects of student work—such as creativity, cultural relevance, emotional engagement, and nuanced reasoning—AI faces significant challenges. These elements, which are often intrinsic to the evaluation of literary and artistic materials, require a deeper level of human insight that AI systems currently lack. Thus, while AI has the potential to support educational assessment, it must be continually refined to address these subjective dimensions. Recent studies have pointed out that AI, despite its growing capabilities, still struggles to capture the intricacies of student creativity and critical thinking (Kostic et al., 2024). While AI tools can effectively reduce the grading workload by automating objective evaluations, their performance in subjective evaluations is only moderately aligned with human judgments (Kooli & Yusuf, 2024). This discrepancy underscores the need for an integrated approach to assessment—one that combines AI's efficiency with the deeper contextual understanding that human evaluators can provide.

AI developers should focus on enhancing the capabilities of AI systems to evaluate subjective aspects of student work more effectively. This can be achieved by incorporating advanced natural language processing (NLP) techniques and training AI models on diverse, rich datasets that better capture a broad spectrum of creative expressions and cultural nuances. These improvements will enable AI to more accurately assess subjective elements like creativity and emotional engagement. However, despite these advancements, AI should not be relied upon exclusively for evaluating these aspects. Human evaluators must remain an integral part of the assessment process, as they are better equipped to interpret the subtleties and cultural context that AI may overlook.

To address the limitations of AI in evaluating subjective content, studies suggest the development of more structured grading criteria that include both objective and subjective dimensions. Furthermore, AI should be used as a tool to complement, rather than replace, human evaluators, especially when it comes to tasks requiring high-level cognitive skills and emotional intelligence (Nadeem et al., 2024; Ragolane et al., 2024). The evolving nature of AI necessitates ongoing research and refinement to improve its accuracy and reliability in educational assessment (Kostic et al., 2024). This hybrid approach, combining AI efficiency with human expertise, holds the potential to create a more balanced, effective, and fair system for evaluating both objective and subjective elements in student work.

Research and Collaboration between AI Developers and Educators

The successful integration of AI into education is not solely dependent on technological advancements but also requires ongoing collaboration between AI developers and educators. Educators, who are on the front lines of the classroom, can provide invaluable insights into the practical effectiveness and limitations of AI tools in educational assessments. Their feedback is crucial for refining AI systems to meet educational goals and ensure they align with pedagogical standards. AI developers, in turn, must work closely with educators to design tools that are not only technologically sophisticated but also ethically sound, pedagogically relevant, and culturally sensitive (Mohamad & Nazlan, 2024; Ogunsakin, 2024).

Moreover, the collaborative effort should extend beyond the development phase to include continuous evaluation of AI tools in real educational settings. This feedback loop will allow for the refinement of AI tools based on real-world usage, enhancing their effectiveness in personalized instruction, adaptive feedback, and real-time assessment (Mulally, 2024). Both parties must work together to ensure that

AI integration complements rather than replaces human judgment, preserving the critical role of teachers in shaping student learning experiences (Bulut et al., 2024).

Educational institutions should foster collaborations between AI developers, educational researchers, and teachers to ensure that AI tools are tailored to meet the practical needs of classrooms and educational assessments. These collaborations should prioritize not only the technical aspects of AI but also its ethical implications, ensuring that AI applications are responsible and equitable. Additionally, longitudinal research should be conducted to assess the long-term impacts of AI on educational assessment, student engagement, and learning outcomes (Mohamad & Nazlan, 2024). This research should explore both the benefits and the potential challenges of AI integration, providing valuable insights that can guide future educational policies and practices (Ogunsakin, 2024; Bulut et al., 2024). By investing in such research and collaboration, educators and AI developers can work together to create more effective, inclusive, and sustainable AI-driven educational environments.

Promoting a Balanced Approach to AI Integration

The integration of AI in education has the potential to significantly enhance educational assessment and improve learning experiences. AI can streamline administrative tasks, personalize learning experiences, and offer scalable solutions for assessment (Miller, 2024; Al Fraidan, 2024). However, it is crucial to maintain a balanced approach that acknowledges and preserves the irreplaceable role of human educators. While AI can assist in automating tasks and providing personalized feedback, human educators are essential for fostering critical thinking, creativity, and emotional intelligence—qualities that AI cannot replicate (Chan & Tsi, 2023; Liang, 2023). Thus, AI should be viewed as a tool that complements, rather than replaces, traditional teaching and assessment methods (Miller, 2024; Chan & Tsi, 2023).

A balanced approach to AI integration requires careful consideration of both the opportunities and challenges AI presents. Educators and policymakers must work together to ensure that AI is utilized in ways that support the core values of education, such as the development of critical thinking skills, the nurturing of creativity, and the promotion of emotional and social intelligence (Al Fraidan, 2024). Furthermore, AI tools should be designed to align with pedagogical goals and educational philosophies that prioritize holistic student development (Liang, 2023).

Policymakers and educators should collaborate to develop a clear and shared vision for the role of AI in education. This vision should emphasize the complementary relationship between AI technologies and human expertise, ensuring that AI enhances rather than detracts from the teaching process. Educational policies, curriculum design, and assessment practices should be aligned with this vision, encouraging a holistic approach to education that integrates both AI and traditional teaching methods. By creating an educational environment that values the strengths of both AI and human educators, we can achieve a more well-rounded, effective, and ethically sound approach to teaching and learning (Chan & Tsi, 2023). Such a balanced approach will not only optimize the benefits of AI but also ensure that the human aspects of education, which are vital for student development, are preserved.

FUTURE OF RESEARCH DIRECTION

The use of Artificial Intelligence (AI) in education is growing rapidly, offering many opportunities but also presenting challenges. AI has the potential to greatly improve how we assess students, personalize learning, and handle administrative tasks. One of the most promising trends in education is personalized learning powered by AI. With AI's ability to analyze large amounts of data, it can tailor lessons to meet the individual needs of each student, providing real-time feedback and adjusting learning paths. However, there are still many questions about how effective and scalable these AI-driven systems are in different educational settings. Future research should explore how AI can be adapted to various types of schools, from K-12 to universities, and how these systems can be used effectively across different education systems.

Another important trend is the development of hybrid assessment models. While AI is very good at automating certain tasks, such as grading and data analysis, it struggles with subjective aspects of student work, like creativity, critical thinking, and emotional engagement. For these aspects, human judgment is still needed. Combining AI tools with human expertise seems to be the best solution for this challenge. Future research should focus on designing assessment models that blend the strengths of AI with human evaluation. This way, we can make assessments more balanced, accurate, and holistic. Studies can look into how AI can be used for both formative and summative assessments and how teachers can be integrated into the process to improve the quality of the assessments.

The ethical concerns surrounding AI in education, such as data privacy, bias, and transparency, are another important area for future research. AI systems rely heavily on student data to provide feedback and assessments, so it's crucial that these systems are transparent and accountable. There is also concern about how AI might unintentionally introduce bias if the data it is trained on isn't representative of all student groups. Future research should focus on developing AI systems that are fair and inclusive. Research is needed to explore how AI can be developed and used ethically, particularly in ways that protect students' privacy and ensure that no group is disadvantaged by the technology.

For AI in education to work effectively, we need to overcome technical, logistical, and financial challenges. While AI holds a lot of promise, we have yet to fully realize its potential. One important aspect is how to integrate AI into existing teaching and learning frameworks. Researchers need to explore the infrastructure required to support AI in schools, how to manage the costs of implementing AI tools, and how educators can be trained to use these tools effectively. Research can also investigate how AI can be adapted for use in low-resource settings, where schools may not have access to the technology needed to use AI tools.

As AI becomes a bigger part of education, we also need to focus on how it can work alongside human teachers. AI is excellent at performing tasks that are repetitive or time-consuming, but it cannot replace the complex understanding and social-emotional skills that teachers bring to the classroom. In the future, AI will likely play a supportive role, helping teachers rather than replacing them. Research should explore how AI can complement teaching by providing personalized feedback, identifying struggling students, and adjusting learning paths to meet individual needs. Understanding how AI can enhance the role of teachers is essential in ensuring that AI supports and doesn't replace human interaction in the classroom.

To use AI effectively in education, teachers need to be trained in AI literacy. Teachers must understand how to use AI tools, interpret the feedback generated by AI, and know how to integrate AI into their teaching practices. Research is needed to find the best ways to provide professional development for teachers, whether through online courses, workshops, or collaborative learning communities. Studies should also look at how this training impacts teachers' perceptions of AI and how ready they are to use these tools in their classrooms.

There are many barriers that need to be addressed before AI can be fully integrated into education. One of the main challenges is the technology itself. Schools need access to the necessary hardware and software to run AI systems, and this can be a barrier, especially in less wealthy areas. Future research should look at how to make AI tools more affordable and accessible, particularly for schools in low-income areas. Data privacy and security are also major concerns. AI systems require vast amounts of student data, which raises the need to protect that data. Research must focus on developing secure AI systems that comply with privacy regulations. Another concern is the scalability of AI tools. What works well in one classroom or educational system may not work in another. Research can explore how AI tools can be designed to be flexible and adaptable to different educational settings.

AI also has the potential to transform educational research. As AI technologies continue to improve, new research opportunities will arise, particularly in the areas of student achievement, data analytics, and educational equity. For example, researchers can conduct longitudinal studies to track the long-term effects of AI-powered assessments on student performance. AI can also be used to identify learning gaps and provide personalized support for students with diverse needs, thus promoting inclusive education. It will be important to assess how AI affects student engagement, academic achievement, and overall well-being in the long run, to determine whether AI-driven assessment tools are truly effective and sustainable.

The future of AI in education holds great promise but also requires careful consideration of the challenges involved in its implementation. Research will play a critical role in addressing key issues such as creating hybrid assessment models, mitigating ethical concerns, and overcoming technical barriers. By fostering collaboration between educators, AI developers, and policymakers, we can ensure that AI is used in a way that benefits students and supports teachers. AI has the potential to improve educational assessments, create more personalized learning experiences, and enhance overall educational outcomes. But to achieve this, we must carefully study and understand its impact, refine its design, and ensure that its implementation is ethical and inclusive.

CONCLUSION

In conclusion, this chapter discussed how Artificial Intelligence (AI) is being used in educational assessments, especially in teacher education programs. AI has great potential to improve the accuracy, efficiency, and consistency of assessments. It can quickly process large amounts of student data, which allows for more precise evaluations. However, AI also faces challenges, especially when it comes to evaluating subjective aspects of student work, such as creativity, emotional engagement, and cultural understanding. These aspects are hard for AI to assess because they involve human judgment and understanding. Therefore, the chapter emphasizes that AI should not replace human evaluators but rather work alongside them to enhance the assessment process.

Through comparing AI-driven assessments with traditional human evaluations, the chapter pointed out both the advantages and limitations of AI. AI can standardize assessments and offer personalized feedback, but it struggles with evaluating subjective qualities like creativity and critical thinking. These qualities are difficult to measure with AI because they require human insight and context. In teacher education, where assessing these skills is crucial, human evaluators are needed to provide the necessary depth and understanding. Thus, the chapter suggests a balanced approach, where AI supports human expertise rather than replacing it.

Ethical concerns are also an important part of this discussion. The chapter explored issues related to data privacy, algorithmic bias, and the potential for AI to widen educational inequalities. AI systems collect large amounts of sensitive student data, so it's vital to ensure these systems are used responsibly. Bias in algorithms could unfairly affect certain students and create more inequality in education. Therefore, it's important to ensure that AI tools are fair, transparent, and unbiased. This requires continuous research, thoughtful policies, and training for educators who will be using these technologies.

Given the opportunities and challenges, the chapter supports a hybrid model of assessment, where both AI and human evaluators play essential roles. This model allows AI to handle tasks that involve processing large amounts of data and providing quick feedback. However, for complex and subjective evaluations, human evaluators are still needed. By combining AI and human expertise, assessments can be more accurate, fair, and personalized.

As AI continues to develop, its role in education will keep growing. However, its use must be carefully managed to ensure it supports, rather than replaces, human judgment. The chapter highlights that AI should be seen as a tool to enhance the educational experience, not as a replacement for teachers. Ongoing collaboration between AI developers, educators, and policymakers is crucial to ensure that AI systems meet educational needs and are used ethically. This collaboration will shape the future of AI in education, ensuring it benefits both students and teachers.

The future of AI in education depends on creating a balance between technology and human expertise. This balance will help create an educational environment where AI supports more efficient and personalized assessments, while human educators guide students through the more complex and subjective aspects of learning. The research and policies developed today will shape how AI is used in education in the future. It is important that these efforts focus on improving education for all learners, making it fairer and more effective. As AI in education continues to grow, the partnership between AI and human expertise will be key in shaping how technology can best be used to improve education.

ACKNOWLEDGMENT

The researcher would like to express sincere gratitude to all those who contributed to the successful completion of this work. Special thanks are extended to the students who participated in the study, as their insights, involvement, and constructive feedback played a critical role in enhancing the quality and relevance of the research.

Appreciation is also due to Isabela State University, particularly the College of Education, for its continuous support throughout the research process. The university provided the necessary resources, facilities, and a nurturing academic environment, all of which were essential for the accomplishment of this study.

Furthermore, the researcher acknowledges the invaluable guidance and encouragement received from academic mentors, colleagues, and peers. Their expertise and counsel significantly shaped the development and direction of the research.

Finally, the researcher would like to thank all those who, in one way or another, contributed to the completion of this work. Their support has been fundamental in bringing this research to its successful conclusion.

REFERENCES

Adel, A., Ahsan, A., & Davison, C. (2024). ChatGPT Promises and Challenges in Education: Computational and Ethical Perspectives. *Education Sciences*, *14*(8), 814. DOI: 10.3390/educsci14080814

Akinnagbe, O.B. (2024). Human-AI Collaboration: Enhancing Productivity and Decision-Making. *International Journal of Education, Management, and Technology*.

Al Fraidan, P.A. (2024). Anticipatory Thinking and AI-Driven Assessments: A Balanced Approach to AI Integration in Education Aligned with Saudi Vision 2030. *African Journal of Biomedical Research*.

Anjum, P. G., Choubey, P. J., Kushwaha, S., & Patkar, V. (2023). AI in Education: Evaluating the Efficacy and Fairness of Automated Grading Systems. *International Journal of Innovative Research in Science, Engineering and Technology*, *12*(6), 1–14. DOI: 10.15680/IJIRSET.2023.1206161

Appelganc, K., Rieger, T., Roesler, E., & Manzey, D. (2022). How Much Reliability Is Enough? A Context-Specific View on Human Interaction With (Artificial) Agents From Different Perspectives. *Journal of Cognitive Engineering and Decision Making*, *16*(4), 207–221. DOI: 10.1177/15553434221104615

Bearman, M., & Luckin, R. (2020). Preparing University Assessment for a World with AI: Tasks for Human Intelligence.

Benitta, G., Asha, H. J., & Josephine, J. A. (2024). An Integrated (Hybrid Based) Besuited Education System Design for the Better Models. *2024 4th International Conference on Advance Computing and Innovative Technologies in Engineering (ICACITE)*, 561-565.

Brandão, A., Pedro, L., & Zagalo, N. (2024). *Teacher professional development for a future with generative artificial intelligence – an integrative literature review*. Digital Education Review. DOI: 10.1344/der.2024.45.151-157

Bulut, O., Beiting-Parrish, M., Casabianca, J.M., Slater, S.C., Jiao, H., Song, D., Ormerod, C., Fabiyi, D.G., Ivan, R., Walsh, C., Rios, O., Wilson, J., Yildirim-Erbasli, S.N., Wongvorachan, T., Liu, J.X., Tan, B., & Morilova, P. (2024). The Rise of Artificial Intelligence in Educational Measurement: Opportunities and Ethical Challenges. *ArXiv, abs/2406.18900*.

Chan, C.K., & Tsi, L.H. (2023). The AI Revolution in Education: Will AI Replace or Assist Teachers in Higher Education? *ArXiv, abs/2305.01185*.

Contreras, M. R., & Jaimes, J. O. (2024). AI Ethics in the Fields of Education and Research: A Systematic Literature Review. *2024 International Symposium on Accreditation of Engineering and Computing Education (ICACIT)*, 1-6. DOI: 10.1109/ICACIT62963.2024.10788651

Cope, B., Kalantzis, M., & Searsmith, D. (2020). Artificial intelligence for education: Knowledge and its assessment in AI-enabled learning ecologies. *Educational Philosophy and Theory*, *53*(12), 1229–1245. DOI: 10.1080/00131857.2020.1728732

Esling, P., & Devis, N. (2020). Creativity in the era of artificial intelligence. *ArXiv, abs/2008.05959.*

Farooqi, M.T., Amanat, I., & Awan, S.M. (2024). Ethical Considerations and Challenges in the Integration of Artificial Intelligence in Education: A Systematic Review. *Journal of Excellence in Management Sciences.*

Han, S. (2021). AI, culture industries and entertainment.

Kadaruddin, K. (2023). Empowering Education through Generative AI: Innovative Instructional Strategies for Tomorrow's Learners. *International Journal of Business, Law, and Education.*

Kasneci, E., Seßler, K., Küchemann, S., Bannert, M., Dementieva, D., Fischer, F., Gasser, U., Groh, G. L., Günnemann, S., Hüllermeier, E., Krusche, S., Kutyniok, G., Michaeli, T., Nerdel, C., Pfeffer, J., Poquet, O., Sailer, M., Schmidt, A., Seidel, T., & Kasneci, G. (2023). ChatGPT for good? On opportunities and challenges of large language models for education. *Learning and Individual Differences*, *103*, 102274. DOI: 10.1016/j.lindif.2023.102274

Khademi, A. (2023). Can ChatGPT and Bard Generate Aligned Assessment Items? A Reliability Analysis against Human Performance. *ArXiv, abs/2304.05372.*

Kim, J., Haddadian, G., & Kim, M. K. (2023). An Investigation of Knowledge-Based AI vs. Human Evaluation in the Context of Academic Summary Evaluation: Similarities, Dissimilarities, and Being Toward Mutual Understandings. *Proceedings of the 17th International Conference of the Learning Sciences - ICLS 2023.*

Kooli, C., & Yusuf, N. (2024). Transforming Educational Assessment: Insights Into the Use of ChatGPT and Large Language Models in Grading. *International Journal of Human-Computer Interaction*, 1–12. DOI: 10.1080/10447318.2024.2338330

Lee, M. H., Siewiorek, D. P., Smailagic, A., Bernardino, A., & Badia, S. B. (2021). A Human-AI Collaborative Approach for Clinical Decision Making on Rehabilitation Assessment. *Proceedings of the 2021 CHI Conference on Human Factors in Computing Systems*. DOI: 10.1145/3411764.3445472

Li, Z. (2024). The shadow of the algorithm: the ethical blind spot of artificial intelligence education. *Journal of Education, Humanities and Social Sciences.*

Lyanda, J.N., Owidi, S., & Simiyu, A.M. (2024). Rethinking Higher Education Teaching and Assessment In-Line with AI Innovations: A Systematic Review and Meta-Analysis. *African Journal of Empirical Research.*

Mahamuni, D. A., Parminder, D., & Tonpe, D. S. (2024). Enhancing Educational Assessment with Artificial Intelligence: Challenges and Opportunities. *2024 International Conference on Knowledge Engineering and Communication Systems (ICKECS), 1*, 1-5. DOI: 10.1109/ICKECS61492.2024.10616620

Miller, W. (2024). Adapting to AI: Reimagining the Role of Assessment Professionals. *Intersection: A Journal at the Intersection of Assessment and Learning.*

Mulally, T. (2024). An Experiential Journey: A Year of a Professor Using AI in the Classroom and Research. International Journal of Studies in Education and Science.

Nadeem, M., Farag, W., & Helal, M. (2024). Rethinking Assessment Methodologies in the Era of Artificial Intelligence: Expanding Beyond ChatGPT's Scope. *2024 Mediterranean Smart Cities Conference (MSCC)*, 1-6. DOI: 10.1109/MSCC62288.2024.10697084

O'Cain, A., Fedoruk, B. D., Masri, Z., Frost, R. M., & Alahmar, A. (2023). A System for the Improvement of Educational Assessment Using Intelligent Conversational Agents. SSRN *Electronic Journal.* DOI: 10.2139/ssrn.4393234

Ogunsakin, I.B. (2024). Unlocking The Potential of Artificial Intellignce:. *International Journal of Research in STEM Education.*

Owan, V. J., Abang, K. B., Idika, D. O., Etta, E. O., & Bassey, B. A. (2023). Exploring the potential of artificial intelligence tools in educational measurement and assessment. *Eurasia Journal of Mathematics, Science and Technology Education, 19*(8), em2307. DOI: 10.29333/ejmste/13428

Ragolane, M., Patel, S., & Salikram, P. (2024). AI Versus Human Graders: Assessing the Role of Large Language Models in Higher Education. *Asian Journal of Education and Social Studies.*

Rane, N. L. (2023). Enhancing the Quality of Teaching and Learning through ChatGPT and Similar Large Language Models: Challenges, Future Prospects, and Ethical Considerations in Education. SSRN *Electronic Journal.* DOI: 10.2139/ssrn.4599104

Rane, N. L. (2024). *Enhancing the quality of teaching and learning through ChatGPT and similar large language models: Challenges, future prospects, and ethical considerations in education.* TESOL and Technology Studies.

Roshanaei, M., Olivares, H., & Lopez, R.R. (2023). Harnessing AI to Foster Equity in Education: Opportunities, Challenges, and Emerging Strategies. *Journal of Intelligent Learning Systems and Applications.*

Shi, J., & Xuwei, Z. (2023). Integration of AI with Higher Education Innovation: Reforming Future Educational Directions. [IJSR]. *International Journal of Scientific Research.*

Swiecki, Z., Khosravi, H., Chen, G., Maldonado, R. M., Lodge, J. M., Milligan, S., Selwyn, N., & Gašević, D. (2022). Assessment in the age of artificial intelligence. *Comput. Educ. Artif. Intell.*, *3*, 100075. DOI: 10.1016/j.caeai.2022.100075

Sywelem, M. M., & Mahklouf, A. M. (2024). Ethical Considerations in the Integration of Artificial Intelligence in Education: An Overview. *Education and Information Technologies.*

TAŞKIN BEDİZEL, N.R. (2023). Evolving landscape of artificial intelligence (AI) and assessment in education: A bibliometric analysis. *International Journal of Assessment Tools in Education.*

Walter, Y. (2024). Embracing the future of Artificial Intelligence in the classroom: The relevance of AI literacy, prompt engineering, and critical thinking in modern education. *International Journal of Educational Technology in Higher Education*, *21*(1), 1–29. DOI: 10.1186/s41239-024-00448-3

Weber, A.S. (2020). ETHICS CONCERNS IN ARTIFICIAL INTELLIGENCE USE IN EDUCATION.

Zhang, S. (2024). Chatgpt Assisted Teachers in Improving Formative Assessment. *Journal of Education, Humanities and Social Sciences.*

Zhou, N. (2024). *Evaluating Human and Machine Assessment: Introducing a Hybrid Approach for Enhanced Educational Evaluation.* Lecture Notes in Education Psychology and Public Media.

Chapter 8
AI-Assisted Storytelling for Young Learners: Innovations and Evaluations

Tri Pujiani
https://orcid.org/0000-0001-6009-9207
Universitas Harapan Bangsa, Indonesia

ABSTRACT

The limited availability of reading materials for children constitutes a big challenge to literacy development. This chapter utilizes expert reviews and comparative analyses in testing how AI storytelling meets this gap. With the application of AI in generating varied and interactive stories, customized reading resources can thus be made available to effectively meet the goals of beginning literacy in young learners for better engagement and comprehension. However, the quality of the storytelling by AI remains questionable. The chapter therefore compares quality, appropriateness, and educational effectiveness of the stories created by AI with those by a human from the perspectives of language experts and early childhood education professionals. Their feedback also raises the respective strengths and weaknesses of both approaches in support of literacy development. The chapter now explores where technology and education meet to reveal both the innovative possibilities and practical considerations involved in using AI to support young learners to develop literacy through storytelling.

DOI: 10.4018/979-8-3373-6330-1.ch008

Copyright © 2026, IGI Global Scientific Publishing. Copying or distributing in print or electronic forms without written permission of IGI Global Scientific Publishing is prohibited.

INTRODUCTION

Early childhood literacy is one of the foundational building blocks of education, as well as a pivotal predictor of future academic and lifetime success. Exposure to engaging and relevant reading materials at an early age significantly enhances children's cognitive, linguistic, and emotional development (Wirth et al., 2020). Storytelling, a traditional method for imparting cultural values and knowledge, remains an essential tool for fostering literacy. However, to be effective, reading materials must align with children's developmental stages, cultural contexts, and interests.

Despite this foundational role of literacy resources, disparities in access persist, particularly in under-resourced communities. This is because the availability of culturally relevant and interesting reading materials is usually limited, thus hindering literacy development and leading to inequalities in learning among young learners. According to Lee et al., (2023), traditional publishing processes are unable to meet the demand for customized content, and large gaps remain in the provision of suitable resources.

The lack of attractive and contextual literacy resources is a continuous problem for educators, parents, and policymakers alike. As the traditional ways have not helped to bridge these gaps, the recent technological development, especially in Artificial Intelligence (AI), has opened new avenues for innovating solutions. Advanced AI technologies, such as Natural Language Processing (NLP) and generative algorithms, have shown promise in generating various and personalized narratives. These AI stories overcame the limitation of traditional publishing by scaling up, adapting, and making the content interactive, which suits the needs of young learners. As stated by Kalantzis and Cope (2024) that AI, especially Generative AI, is capable of generating different types of texts and reading materials according to learner needs, thereby expanding access to previously limited literacy resources.

However, questions abound on the quality and educational impact of the AI-generated stories. Unlike human-written narratives embedded in cultural nuance and emotional depth, AI content lacks contextual relevance and authenticity. Additionally, most of the concerns about biases in the AI systems and ethical considerations when deploying them have not yet been fully addressed (Amirjalili et al., 2024). Equally underexplored is the question of the comparative effectiveness of stories generated by AI and human-written stories in supporting the development of literacy.

It is in this context that the chapter tries to fill the gaps by discussing how AI-assisted storytelling increases early childhood literacy development. Specifically, this would consider the diverse stories which are generated interactively by AI technologies and relevant to culture for the diverse learners through a comparative analysis of how quality, appropriateness, and educational values of stories generated by AI stack up against human-generated stories drawing on feedback provided by both language experts and early childhood education professionals.

This chapter will discuss the strengths and limitations of AI-assisted storytelling, drawing on both expert reviews and empirical evidence. From this, the chapter might indicate the roles that could be played by AI in tackling resource gaps in early childhood education, while human oversight is necessary to ensure cultural sensitivity and ethical integrity, among other issues, for educational effectiveness. That therefore means the chapter will contribute to the bigger discussion of integrating AI technologies into education through practical recommendations that may be useful to educators, policy-makers, and technologists.

The Challenges in Children's Literacy Development

In literacy development, children have to overcome a number of challenges that are critical in determining their future academic and social lives. These are multifaceted and involve the lack of access to reading materials, language and cultural issues, inadequacy of early exposure, non-provision of individual learning, issues related to instructional approaches, cognitive and developmental concerns, lack of motivation and engagement, socioeconomic elements, lack of adequate integration of technology, and psychological factors.

Limited Access to Quality Reading Materials

In poor communities, access to appealing and age-appropriate books related to the children's cultural backgrounds is usually highly limited. A lack of books negatively impacts literacy development; exposure to varied types of reading materials is crucial in vocabulary and comprehension building (Zucker et al., 2022). Economic disparities further worsen this by having fewer libraries and educational resources in rural and low-income areas. Moreover, the digital gap remains, and while these can enhance learning in themselves, a lack of equal opportunity in terms of access to technology is excluding many children from this very resource.

Language and Cultural Barriers

Materials containing vocabulary that is out of the child's reach bring about frustration and disengagement. Reading materials that do not depict a child's culture, experience, and values make the child disconnected from those materials (Scorer & Vardy, 2024). In multilingual communities, the children may have a challenge obtaining full literacy in their mother tongue and are taught to read and write in a second language, making it complicated.

Insufficient Early Exposure

Early exposure to books and storytelling is considered essential for early literacy development (Maureen et al., 2021). Unless the initial years of a child are invested in with literacy activities, chances are that they start formal schooling at a disadvantage and that the gap will be hard to cover later on. While parental involvement goes a long way, motivation or lack of awareness in terms of reading skills also hampers progress that a child may achieve.

Lack of Individualized Learning

Traditional systems of education have often utilized standardized ways of teaching that do not tend to address the learning needs or learning pace of every child. The passive modes of learning, such as rote memorization, actively do not engage children in the process that is an integral part of building comprehension and critical thinking among children. To diverse learning styles, diverse learning opportunities are required, personalized to interactive learning (Walkington & Bernacki, 2020).

Challenges in Instructional Approaches

Inadequately trained teachers may fail to use effective techniques for teaching skills of literacy. Knowledge of obsolete methodologies that are non-interactive does not appeal to children who have become accustomed to digital tools. Overcrowded classrooms are further obstacles in providing the required individual attention that students with problems of literacy need (Pramesty et al., 2022).

Cognitive and Developmental Issues

For others, there might even be an incidence of learning disabilities including dyslexia or ADHD complicating the process (Guimarães et al., 2022). Most children with delayed speech and language development are seriously deficient in phonemic awareness during the earliest years of literacy development. Early identification and targeted intervention help facilitate the learning process of such children.

Lack of Motivation and Engagement

Irrelevant materials of reading for a child may disengage him from reading (Tan & Mante-Estacio, 2021). With advancements in technology, children may prefer playing games and watching videos instead of reading; hence, it would further decrease their urge for motivating themselves to read texts. In this direction, relevant content development would be required in order to make someone love reading and motivating themselves.

Socioeconomic Factors

Families cannot invest money in books or educational toys or even enrolling in literacy programs during a financial crisis. At home, the parents with poorly developed literacy skills may not be of much help for the child in developing his or her own literacy. Socioeconomic status of a child does contribute in a big way towards this literacy journey (Salas & Pascual, 2023).

Insufficient Integration of Technology

Although technology has great potential for literacy learning, the reality often is that such potential seldom manifests within a traditional classroom. The resources may be inappropriate in terms of age or educationally ineffective and might distract rather than support learning (Taghizadeh & Hasani Yourdshahi, 2020). Appropriately embedded technological tools within the learning environment can facilitate both interactive and personalized opportunities for development in literacy.

Psychological and Emotional Factors

The fear of making mistakes may well discourage children from participating actively in reading or writing. Poor readers may get a poor self-image further debilitating them from practicing literacy skills (Tong, 2022). Such psychological impediments to literacy development call for supportive and confidence-building strategies.

These are challenges that need multilevel approaches in securing, developing, and distributing reading materials that are more accessible, engaging, and relevant to the culture. Some of the challenges, especially the limited access to appropriate qualified reading sources and cultural barriers, can be overcome by utilizing AI-generated materials. Teachers may generate stories matched to the students' characteristics, special needs, and interests. In this way, teachers will be supported in providing more effective reading materials and students will be more motivated and engaged in learning because of the relevant and accessible sources.

The Characteristics of Effective Reading Materials for Young Learners

Effective reading materials for young learners are those that can easily engage, motivate, and further develop literacy skills. The materials should be appropriate to the age of the children, culturally relevant, and serve to stimulate a positive interaction between the reader and the text. The integration of different kinds of strategy and types of content in a big manner provides large possibilities for giving effective reading experiences to young learners. The characteristics of effective reading materials for young learners would include the following:

Age and Language Appropriateness

Reading materials, prepared in consideration of the age and language proficiency level of the learners, help to retain their interest in and motivation for learning. When the texts are appropriately adjusted according to a child's stage of development, they present an optimum level of difficulty neither too hard to demoralize them from proceeding nor too easy to take away all interest in work (McBreen & Savage, 2020). Picture books work marvellously with young learners since they integrate both visual and textual elements within a supportive context, thereby enhancing comprehension while allowing for vocabulary development. The visuals in picture books not only provide one with a way to develop an understanding of complex ideas for children but also create an interest in reading by making the process more enjoyable (Khoirunnisak et al., 2024). With learners growing, their moving them onto texts that are progressively challenging to their linguistic and cognitive abilities secures progressive improvement in literacy skills.

Cultural Relevance and Interest

Culturally relevant and engaging materials are important in developing a relationship between the reader and the text. The use of folk literature, which contains universal themes and narratives most of the time, can engage the young reader while introducing him/her to their cultural heritage and values (Tan & Mante-Estacio, 2021). It is easier to relate more when stories reflect the learner's background and experiences, and reading, as such, becomes all the more interesting and pleasing (Novita et al., 2023). In seeing representations of their identities and day-to-day lives within texts, students are not only building an interest but also constructing some feelings of inclusion and validation. A significant finding is that the connection developed between the content and the reader is necessary to inculcate a lifelong habit of reading and to constantly engage in literacy practices.

Interactive and Multimodal Content

Reading materials with interactive and multimodal elements have the possibility to increase engagement and diversify learning styles. Elaboration of personal stories and creative visuals allow the learners to express and make contact with the material creatively and meaningfully (Fadhilah et al., 2020). Reading is considered to be dynamic and adaptative for auditory, visual, and kinaesthetic learners after videos and digital content had their entrance as multimedia tools into classrooms. These multimodal modes of approach keep interest going and create avenues for learners to engage themselves with concepts in varied formats for deeper understanding and knowledge retention. Thus, interactive elements help to bridge the gap between traditional and modern learning methodologies by making reading more immersive.

Encouragement of Reader-Text Interaction

An extremely reader-oriented approach to the interaction and interpretation of texts plays an essential role in critical thinking and reading. A deep and enhanced approach to working with texts affords the learners chances of connection, question, and reflection on materials beyond the superficial level of their understanding. Activities which engage students in reflecting on stories shared by peers or further investigating other people's point of views create ownership of one's experiences of reading (Fadhilah et al., 2020). To that end, the engagement not only sharpens the cognitive appetite of your children, but it also raises emotional and social learning through discussions and collaborations. Drawing the educator's emphasis on the reader-text interaction will afford them an opportunity to develop thoughtful reflective confident readers who can manage complex texts.

Effective reading material for young children must be age-appropriate, culturally relevant, multimodal, and interactive so that they engage, understand, and think critically. When children see themselves reflected in stories and are invited to interact meaningfully with texts, they learn to read as well as develop a lifelong love for reading. These materials not only teach but also foster emotional and social growth. However, there is still a gap in the current traditional reading approaches to the access of literacy material itself.

Gaps in Traditional Approaches to Developing Literacy Materials

The access to adequate reading materials for children is where the need for effective literacy materials in young learners reveals a big loophole that has existed in traditional approaches towards literacy development. Conventional ways of developing literacy materials have often failed to address the variant needs of young learners. Standardization alone may not consider cultural background, language, and experience variance in children. This may be the reason that makes them uninterested, thus less effective during the development of literacy. Another thing, conventional print materials are non-interactive due to their static nature. At times especially within the digital age, the inability of such material resources to be adaptive means not allowing for personalized learning that answers differentiated needs in learning style and tempo.

In addition, the preparation and distribution of traditional literacy materials may be very resource-intensive and slow; hence, it inhibits periodic updating of content or making adaptations according to particular learner needs. This condition is highly worse in under-resourced communities, where accesses to a variety of good quality reading materials are highly restricted (Zucker et al., 2022). This also means a reliance on traditional publishing processes, while the inclusion of feedback from educators and learners in materials is extremely time-consuming, making the resources difficult to improve in the shortest run.

Children's literacy development is faced with challenges that have to be approached from a multidimensional perspective, considering especially the use of appropriate and relevant reading materials. Literacy materials should reflect age and language appropriateness, contextual and cultural relevance, and interactivity in order to meet the needs of young, diverse learners. The identification of gaps in traditional approaches underlines the need for innovative approaches that make use of technology and inclusive practices in a bid to develop more effective and accessible literacy materials.

Innovations in AI-Assisted Storytelling

AI has already brought about highly innovative methods for improving learning experiences in many different sectors, from education to others. One such development is AI-assisted storytelling. Advanced technologies create a personalized, engaging, interactive experience for young children in developing their literacy skills. Such tools can enhance vocabulary, comprehension, and narration while contributing to cognitive-emotional development.

With these, endless possibilities in co-creating a story are possible, even by mere conversion of text into speech and even into visuals and music. Text-to-image and text-to-sound model integrations develop comprehension and language skills through multisensory learning. This dynamic storytelling approach nurtures cognitive development by engaging many senses at once and allows the young learner to make concrete and relatable some abstract ideas (Golwalker, 2024). AI-powered storytelling focuses on educational and cultural relevance, thus responding to the needs of modern classrooms.

Such applications are able to offer culturally specific content; hence they are particularly useful in bilingual and multicultural settings. Because AI-generated stories reflect backgrounds and experiences, building a sense of belonging is crucial to creating engagement and comprehension. More importantly, such a tool introduces them to applications and implications of AI-a dimension of technological literacy to be taken alongside the more traditional literacy skills that the curriculum should entail (Hazari, 2024). Beyond interactivity and cultural relevance, AI-assisted storytelling would provide unparalleled access to all forms of narratives.

AI systems can produce various stories across genres and topics, making sure that the learners have access to content that matches their interests. Such a plethora of materials becomes highly valuable in under-resourced situations where traditional publishing can't meet demand. Another advantage of AI-generated content is that it is very often multilingual, making it a priceless tool in bilingual education and global learning settings (Feng & Wang, 2023). These features further democratize storytelling and expand its possibilities.

Adaptability is yet another important strong point of AI-based storytelling. It is possible for such platforms to update story elements on the fly by considering the learners' feedback and performances in offering appropriate, individual learning pathways based on the learners' weaknesses and issues. AI can change the difficulty level in narratives, vocabulary, and themes according to a learner's requirements. This flexibility in training provides the necessary guidance to each child according to his individual needs and promotes effective skill development in creativity, construction of narratives, or critical thinking. Research evokes that students develop greater interest and creative skills from adaptive learning experiences than in the normal class process, hence making AI an essential tool in present times (Loughland, 2019; Zheng et al., 2020).

In conclusion, the AI-assisted storytelling allows literacy development with embedded interactive and multimodal literacy, cultural relevance, and accessibility, turning out to be adaptive. A systematic review conducted by (Chen, 2024) revealed that AI-driven storytelling in early childhood education improve language acquisition and literacy development, promoting cognitive and emotional development. This study shows that AI-assisted storytelling is promising in promoting young learners' language development, yet the quality of AI-generated and human-written stories is under researched.

Case Study 1: Comparative Analysis of AI vs. Human-Written Stories

Study Design

It uses a mixed-method approach in which the research experts conduct reviews and comparative analyses of the differences between AI-generated and human-created stories intended for young learners. The research methodology, therefore, incorporates two layers of qualitative evaluations by two groups of participants: language experts and early childhood education professionals. Participants will be asked to review a set of stories, according to the review criteria pre-specified for an all-rounded evaluation of the quality and suitability of those stories. The expert panel is very carefully composed with a blend of linguistic and pedagogical expertise to ensure sensitive insights are reflected in matters regarding language fluency, cultural relevance, and educational effectiveness.

To ensure rigorous data collection, the study applies a systematic framework for evaluation. Language experts focus on linguistic quality, including grammatical accuracy, fluency, vocabulary, readability and tone consistency, while early childhood educators assess the age-appropriateness, engagement potential, relevance, language clarity, and educational value of the stories. These are complemented by a comparative exercise in which participants try to identify the origin of the stories, AI or human, followed by feedback on strengths, weaknesses, and avenues for improvement. This triangulates the approach to validity by capturing diverse perspectives (Da Silva Santos et al., 2020).

Criteria for Comparison

The effectiveness of storytelling as produced by both AI and humans was analysed in three key areas: language quality, cultural appropriateness, and for learner engagement. For learners whose native language is not English, it is important to consider that grammatical accuracy is a key determining factor because if a learner experiences faulty syntax they struggle with comprehension. In recent years, while AI tools that use NLP have improved their accuracy in producing grammar correctly there remain instances where anomalies arise (Markowitz et al., 2023). On the other side, humans capitalize on language instinctively or intuitively. Another significant factor is cultural appropriateness; AI tools frequently produce storytelling artifacts that were trained on massive datasets that allow for generalized training datasets which bring an unacceptable number of stories without context that are culturally inappropriate (Peters & Carman, 2024). From a standpoint of the human experience, human storytelling does culturally appropriate value by capturing lived experience and cultural nuance. Lastly, in terms of engagement and education, human generated stories tend to contain strong elements of morality, emotion and motivation while AI-generated content is produced for relevance, flexibility, multimodality, and other features (Markowitz et al., 2023). Some of the areas we have discussed suggest a hybrid form of storytelling whereby AI can produce artifacts much faster than a human while combining the power of human storytelling.

Findings

In this research, eight stories were created as the learning sources to be implemented by using storytelling method. The stories were developed with many interactive activities inside the stories to enhance engagement and to keep the children focus on the learning process. Two types of stories were used as comparison to obtain the overview of the effectiveness of AI-generated and human-written stories. Language experts and young learners' pedagogy experts were involved to validate the stories created.

The language experts reviewed the stories based on the grammar and syntax, language fluency, vocabulary use, readability, and the consistency of the tone. Following is the summary of the language experts' validation.

Table 1. The summary of language experts' validation

No	Story Title	Grammar and Syntax	Language Fluency	Vocabulary Use	Readability	Tone Consistency	Total Score
1	Dewi Sri	5	4,33	4,33	4,67	5	4,67
2	Ten Hills	5	4,33	4,33	4,67	5	4,67
3	Bawang Putih	5	5	5	5	5	5
4	The Magic Tree	5	4,67	4,67	4,67	5	4,8
5	Malin Kundang	4,5	4,67	4,67	4,67	4,67	4,63
6	Keong Mas	4,83	5	5	5	5	4,97
7	Si Kancil	4,83	4,67	4,67	4,67	5	4,77
8	The Race	4,83	4,33	4,33	4,33	5	4,57

Table 1 summarizes the language experts' validation of eight stories with scores ranging from 4.33 to 5. "Bawang Putih" scored a perfect 5 in all categories, while "The Race" scored the lowest at 4.57. Overall, most stories achieved high ratings, indicating strong linguistic quality, with room for minor improvements in fluency and vocabulary. The validation confirms the stories are linguistically sound and suitable for educational purposes.

Meanwhile, the English for Young Learners experts reviewed the stories based on the age appropriateness, engagement level, relevance, clarity of language, and educational value. Following is the summary of the English for young learner experts' validation.

Table 2. The summary of English for young learner experts' validation

No	Story Title	Age Appropriateness	Engagement Level	Relevance	Clarity of Language	Educational Value	Total Score
1	Dewi Sri	5,00	4,67	5,00	4,50	5,00	4,83
2	Ten Hills	5,00	4,67	4,67	5,00	5,00	4,87
3	Bawang Putih	5,00	5,00	5,00	5,00	5,00	5,00
4	The Magic Tree	5,00	4,67	5,00	5,00	5,00	4,93
5	Malin Kundang	4,33	4,50	5,00	4,67	4,67	4,63
6	Keong Mas	5,00	5,00	5,00	5,00	5,00	5,00
7	Si Kancil	5,00	4,67	5,00	5,00	4,67	4,87
8	The Race	5,00	4,67	4,33	5,00	5,00	4,80

Table 2 summarizes the experts' validation of stories for young learners. Scores range from 4.33 to 5.00, with "Bawang Putih" and "Keong Mas" achieving perfect ratings across all aspects. "Malin Kundang" scored the lowest at 4.63, mainly due to slightly lower age appropriateness and engagement. Overall, the high scores indicate that most stories are well-designed for young learners, combining educational value and linguistic clarity effectively.

When being asked to identify the AI-generated and human-written stories, the language and English for young learner experts were varied. It indicated that the quality and the language structure of AI-generated stories were quite the same as the human-written ones. The following table shows the experts judgement of the stories.

Table 3. AI-generated vs. human-written stories: The experts' judgement on the stories

No.	Title	Expert 1	Expert 2	Expert 3	Expert 4	Correct Answer
1	Dewi Sri	Human	Human	AI	AI	AI
2	Ten Hills	Human	Human	AI	AI	AI
3	Bawang Putih	AI	Human	Human	Human	AI
4	The Magic Tree	AI	Human	AI	Human	AI

continued on following page

Table 3. Continued

No.	Title	Expert 1	Expert 2	Expert 3	Expert 4	Correct Answer
5	Malin Kundang	AI	AI	Human	Human	Human
6	Keong Mas	AI	AI	Human	Human	Human
7	Si Kancil	AI	AI	Human	AI	Human
8	The Race	Human	AI	AI	AI	Human

Table 3 displays expert judgments on whether stories are AI-generated or human-written, compared to the correct answers. While some stories, such as "The Magic Tree," were consistently identified correctly, others, like "Dewi Sri," had mixed evaluations. What this inconsistency points to is that it is not quite easy to differentiate between AI-generated and human-written stories, suggesting that AI-generated content is getting nearer to human thoughtfulness with respect to language use and narration. Therefore, AI-generated stories can be taken into consideration for use in adding variety to stories and making up for the shortage of proper reading resources for children.

DISCUSSION

Findings from this study indicate that the AI- and human-generated stories for young learners of English language were validated by examining the linguistic quality, pedagogical engagement, and the possibilities of comparison. Table 1 shows the scores provided by language experts, ranging from 4.33 to 5.00, suggesting a degree of linguistic quality. In particular, "Bawang Putih" received perfect scores across the linguistic categories, whereas "The Race" received 4.57 suggesting minor issues of vocabulary and readability. The findings here support Chomsky's (1968) that grammaticality and fluency should guide the principles in preparing the language learning materials. To this end, high grammar, syntax and vocabulary usages justify these principles, meaning that the stories are fit for pedagogical purposes. Furthermore, this readability and consistency of tone is in line with Krashen's theory of comprehensible input, stating that learners will pick up language much more effectively if the input is given at a point just beyond their current proficiency level but is still comprehensible notion of linguistic competence while espousing Krashen's theory of comprehensible input. Specifically, when acquiring a second language, learners need to decrease problems with grammar, syntax, and vocabulary (Scarcella & Perkins, 1987). Supportive studies, like Tang et al. (2023) solidified need for synaptic complexity and lexical diversity of development when children are acquiring a second language.

From a pedagogical perspective, Table 2 indicates high engagement and educational strength, with "Bawang Putih" and "Keong Mas" earning perfect 5.00 scores in each category. These stories had strong age-appropriateness, clarity, and relevance for the targeted audience. According to Isnaniah et al., (2024), good educational stories are the ones that at appropriate age, engaging, and relevant. "Malin Kundang" earned 4.63 in educational strength and engagement but lacked some age-level engagement, supporting Vygotsky's (1978) Zone of Proximal Development, which explains that learning is most effective when materials are just challenging and meaningful. The interactive features within the stories also support Mayer's Cognitive Theory of Multimedia Learning, which states that how visually appealing materials will engage the learner and enhance retention (Moreno & Mayer, 1999). In line, Abderrahim & González (2020) stated that digital storytelling also contributes to building motivation and participation in young learners.

Table 3 summarizes experts' judgments about story origin, but clearly there is not one clear answer. For example, "Dewi Sri" was categorized as AI by two experts but not by the other two of the four experts, while "Ten Hills" (also AI) was classified as neutral. "Malin Kundang" and "The Race" were most often listed as human. Our results seem to confirm the observations by Orwig et al. (2024) and Jakesch et al. (2022) that provide some evidence of the improvement of the sophistication of novel-length stories generated by AI that imitate aspects of human creativity, curiosity, and writing style. Furthermore, variability of expert judgement also captures the subtle ways human writers still have a clear advantage in terms of depth of feeling and cultural context. As Jarrahi (2018) noted that AI is more about human effort to support and not replace.

To summarise, the texts we examined have been highly creative and pedagogically valuable, and they can be used for early English language design. Our research indicated that AI-generated texts have the potential to inspire human creativity and be personalized and scaled, but purposeful human involvement is required to add cultural context and value the importance of emotion. Teachers are challenged to combine AI efficiencies with human knowledge to enable students to have variety, fun, and ultimately to provide more meaningful literacy experiences.

Expert Feedback: Perspectives on AI Storytelling

Given the potential of AI-generated stories to enhance young learners' literacy skills, the experts pointed out their perspectives on AI storytelling. Educational effectiveness and appropriateness become the consideration to leverage young learners' reading sources by utilizing AI without dismissing human-sense in the content.

Educational Effectiveness of AI-Generated Versus Human-Created Stories

Linguists and early childhood experts evaluated AI- and human-generated stories as teaching materials. They found that stories generated by AI exhibited strong grammar, vocabulary, and syntax, similar to stories produced by a human writer. As Jakesch et al. (2022) said that AI tools can produce linguistically complex and interesting content. AI text is clear, functional, and relatively concise, and systematically provides developmentally appropriate input for young children learning literacy. However, researchers discovered a neglect of emotions and cultural representation in AI stories vs. human stories that could be valuable contributors in promoting empathy and cultural knowledge (Karadoğan, 2023). This is illustrated in terms of emotionally rich content that was attributed to human agency and creativity in "Bawang Putih". In contrast other artificially generated stories by "Keong Mas" and "Si Kancil" were described as formulaic stories that relied on white washed values. Research by Chen (2024), Elmorsy (2024), and Yang et al. (2023) confirm and add support for the literacy benefits of AI, but, they emphasize that using AI should be together with the guidance of a teacher. Professionals agreed and added that AI-generated stories supplement, never replace, but even augment human-created educational materials (Jarrahi, 2018).

Appropriateness of Themes and Narratives for Young Learners

Experts considered AI-generated stories for young children pedagogically and developmentally appropriate although might target the different ages and learning goals. While there were many draws to having interactive components (questions, activities, or moral stories) that can tie into Mayer's Cognitive Theory of Multimedia Learning (Mayer, 2009), there were aspects that detracted from the overall product, especially some created stories without emotional resonance, or stories that contained no coherence as in one expert's thoughts on "The Magic Tree" which was simply copacetic but generic and "Ten Hills" was fine pedagogically, but still lacked emotional resonance, or a sense of empathy. Moreover, as Karadoğan (2023) pointed out that AI content can be grammatically correct and exact in every context, but still have not attended to empathy, emotion, and creativity. The experts suggested AI generated themes would need to be curated for age-appropriate and culturally sensitive parameters. Additionally, in reference to Vygotsky's Zone of Proximal Development (Barnett, 2019) experts noted the oversight of a human to aid in the appropriateness of the content.

Suggestions for Enhancing AI-Generated Storytelling

Several actionable recommendations were given by experts for enhancing the quality and effectiveness of AI-generated stories as an educational tool:

Incorporating Cultural and Emotional Depth. *Refinement to a story leading towards more relevant, emotionally resonating themes must include both educators and cultural consultants to circumvent such AI limitation. This collaboration can help bridge the gap between AI's technical capabilities and the nuanced requirements of effective storytelling. Recent studies, such as those by Baskerville (2011), emphasize the importance of culturally rich narratives in fostering inclusivity and empathy among young readers. Emotionally deep and culturally authentic stories such as "Malin Kundang" and "The Race" were identified, their merit again attributed to a human author.*

Enhancing Interactivity. *More interactive elements, like decision-making opportunities, puzzles, or discussion prompts, might also serve to make AI stories more interesting. Mayer's (2009) theory highlights the role of interactivity in enhancing learning outcomes, particularly for young learners who benefit from hands-on and participatory experiences. Experts also recommended integrating multimedia features, such as animations, sound effects, and illustrations, to create a more immersive storytelling experience.*

Refining Narrative Coherence. *This would be logically ensured in the storyline so that coherence keeps the readers glued and grasp what is written. Experts recommend more advanced models of NLP, which should be exploited to bring coherence and flow into AI-generated stories. Moreover, Spooren and Sanders (2008) emphasize that story coherence is necessary as it favours both language acquisition and cognitive development in children.*

Personalization and Adaptability. *Generative AI stories can adapt autonomously to the different learning needs, preferences, and levels of proficiency. In support of this, a story may have the ability for adaptive learning; it will suggest the right degree of challenge or offer supportive level exercise (Jauhiainen & Guerra, 2023).*

The Importance of Human Curation in Refining AI Outputs

Although artificial intelligence stories are becoming more advanced, researchers generally agree that human curation is necessary to ensure anything resembling minimum quality and educational intention. One aspect of human curation is ethics and cultural sensitivity, as AI systems are only as biased as the datasets on which they were trained. Without human supervision, AI-generated shared stories may inadvertently present some stereotypical behaviour or a lack of cultural sensitivity. Educators and cultural consultants will have to modify the outputs of AI, while also adhering to their own pedagogical and ethical bounds (Klimova & Chen, 2024; Kumar et al., 2024; Pack & Maloney, 2024).

While the human element is crucial for emotional richness and creativity, AI is not capable of adding the emotional nuance and cultural significance of a human storyteller. According to Horváthová (2022), emotionally engaging narratives develop empathy and social-emotional development capacity in young audiences. As well, experts have advocated continuously monitoring and user feedback that can emerge with AI, so AI systems can be improved. Jauhiainen and Guerra (2023) suggest that feedback loops be imbedded for improving adaptability and function of AI systems.

Case Study 2: Using AI-Assisted Structured Storytelling to Foster Literacy and Environmental Awareness in Preschoolers

Research Background and Setting

Lu et al. (2024) implemented AI-generated storytelling and pictures to educate children on sustainability in Taiwanese kindergarten. Sixty 5-6-year-old children were assigned to an experimental group and a control group; children in the experimental group received structured stories produced by ChatGPT, whereas the control group received unstructured stories. Children engaged with the stories over three weeks using a child-friendly digital platform. Learning gains were assessed using language rubrics, communication scales, usability ratings, and interviews.

Teaching Procedures

The digital storytelling sessions were done with a clearly defined process that emphasized both narrative content and use of the interactive system. Teachers first developed complex story templates, including themes, characters, environments, issues, sub-objectives, and conclusions. The templates were then used as prompts to get ChatGPT to generate full story content, ensuring that it was aligned with learning and environmental objectives. The system provided a children's interface with animation, sound effects, and simple navigation. Students engaged in two 30-minute sessions every week for three weeks. During each session, they read AI-generated stories using tablets, selecting titles such as The Adventures of Czech Rabbit *and* The Surprising Journey of the Explorer. *Teachers guided navigation, taught sustainability principles, and assisted students in learning the narrative framework. In follow-up sessions, children were asked to retell or make up their own stories on the topics using the digital technologies. Whole group discussion and storying scaffolds such as picture description, story mapping, and reflection activities were also supported by teachers to build comprehension and language use.*

Findings and Practical Recommendations

The study found that structured AI-generated storytelling enhanced children's language skills, creativity, and environmental consciousness. The experimental group was more proficient at creating stories and narrating pictures than the control group, and was more engaged and having positive attitudes toward technology. Though usability ratings were moderate, the method proved educationally effective when guided by teachers. Retrieved from this study, some practical recommendations for educators are proposed:

- Use teacher-developed story structures to guide AI-generated material (add theme, plot, and conclusion).
- Integrate graphics and animations to facilitate greater young learners' participation and comprehension.
- Present relevant and learning goal-oriented themes in rich narrative contexts.
- Request students to re-tell or create their own stories through technology to cultivate expressive and narrative abilities.
- Utilize group discussion and reflection to sustain learning and enhance communication.

Practical Considerations for Implementing AI in Literacy Development

Opportunities for Integrating AI into Educational Practices

AI supplements traditional literacy resources through dynamic, scalable and individualized content. Whereas textbooks are static resources, tools powered by AI can generate individualized reading materials for each learner. In addition, other adaptive systems can measure performance and make recommendations for targeted areas of individualized resources (Jauhiainen & Guerra, 2023). The ability of AI to generate stories, activities, and quizzes in various languages, will also promote inclusive education and begin to solve content knowledge gaps in developing or neglected communities (Kusmiatun et al., 2024).

AI also promotes opportunities for interactive and adaptive learning with the use of storytelling apps, chat-based conversation platforms, and gamification. Programs like Duolingo and Kahoot use adaptive functions to challenge the learner while simultaneously keeping them motivated (Pujiani et al., 2023). AI tools can provide instant feedback on language development in remembering and understanding capabilities (Rakya, 2023), and simulate conversations to promote fluency and confidence in learners.

AI can also keep a learner socially and emotionally engaged by discerning tone and classroom environment and adapting their teaching style to the needs of each learner, which promotes a socially inclusive, learner-centred space. The ability to assess the learning environment and provide individualized options reflects Vygotsky's notion of the Zone of Proximal Development and the understanding that scaffolding is important to support maximum leaning (Vygotsky, 1978). Overall, AI enhances early literacy through individualized perspectives on instruction, engagement, and access to quality culturally relevant documents.

Ethical Consideration and Challenges in Utilizing AI-generated Stories for Young Learners

When implementing artificial intelligence (AI) with a focus on literacy, it is important to recognize the ethical challenges, specifically bias and data privacy. AI systems trained through large datasets can reinforce stereotypes or cultural misrepresentations (Ghosh et al., 2024), and therefore need diversity within the dataset and people closely monitoring the implementation. Moreover, personalized learning with data offers an opportunity for questions and concerns with respect to how student data is stored, shared and protected. Educators and policymakers must take every step to ensure that their correct data management arrangements align with the privacy (Huang, 2023).

While AI can do many things, it is still imperfect. For example, AI can offer grammatically correct, contextually relevant stories without creativity or emotionality (Karadoğan, 2023). We cannot move into the future without human curation. Educators, linguists and cultural historians should read and refine AI content to guarantee that it is sufficiently culturally relevant and emotionally labour audience member could experience, and also has feedback mechanisms that improve the quality and relevance of the content (Rakya, 2023). The instructional pedagogy achieved by AI is probably so powerful that it should not go to waste but the learning mediation must combine human presence and insight with AI savviness to create an ethical, meaningful and pedagogically sound learning experience.

Recommendations for Educators and Policymakers

Educational practitioners should view AI as an addition to resources and not as a substitute. Utilizing AI tools like AI-generated stories or analytics for following student progress enhances current literacy programming; offering more depth and interactivity (Anggoro & Pratiwi, 2023). Teacher education and training is required; professional development needs to develop their skills in using and evaluating AI content including identifying bias or inaccuracy. Political policymakers need to create ethical policies for data subject protection that includes recognizing the ethics of data contributions and processes focusing on bias. Schools must create, protect, and secure their data with stakeholder negotiation among governments, tech corporations, and educators.

Collaboration by education practitioners and developers is paramount. Educators hold essential knowledge about the learners' needs and the developers can provide technical support in the field. Education practitioners need to showcase real-world experiences where the locus for using AI tools are located. Applied ongoing research and development is needed in AI settings (especially in multilingual story generation, speech recognition, and gamified learning settings). Longitudinal perspectives should be considered as researchers study if AI has any delayed or cumulative impact on literacy.

AI provides support for literacy that is personalized and interactive. Nevertheless, the ethical use of AI, and its appropriate application by humans and the developer will determine if AI mediations will attain expected effectiveness for these learner-level AI tools.

Implications for Future Research and Development

Exploring Advancements in AI Storytelling Technology

This has driven rapid development in AI-powered storytelling technology over the last couple of years. More research should be done to develop the capacity of AI in creating narratives that are not only linguistically correct but have depth in culture and emotion. Whereas current systems, like GPT models developed by OpenAI, demonstrate unprecedented capability in generating coherent and engaging content, they nevertheless very frequently fall short in terms of emulating the nuanced creativity of human authors (Karadoğan, 2023).

Another promising direction involves the development of multimodal storytelling. This can be in the form of text, images, and audio in a way that creates immersive narratives, allowing it to suit different learning styles. To this effect, Mastellotto (2021) give evidence on how multimedia significantly increases learner engagement and comprehension, especially early readers. Future AI systems could build on recent advances in computer vision and voice synthesis in order to create stories with customized illustrations and realistic narrations.

Another interesting development could be the building of adaptive storytelling algorithms that may interact in real time with the user's reactions and create the story that is tailored to the peculiar tastes, cultural backgrounds, and stages of development. Jauhiainen and Guerra (2023) note that the coming wave of adaptive learning technologies offers unparalleled opportunities to make education even more personalized because AI covers the peculiar needs of every learner.

Also, future ethics are highly recommended when developing AIs with respect to bias, stereotyping, and misinformation in generated content. Dataset curation and training algorithms should be presented in a very transparent manner with the view that these AI storytelling tools are to be inclusive, culturally sensitive, and so on. This is in line with Alshahrani et al. (2024), Huang (2023), Pendy (2023) who called for ethical AI use in education, emphasizing fairness and accountability.

Encouraging Collaboration Between AI Developers, Educators, and Linguists

AI storytelling in education will require serious involvement and collaboration among the developers of AI, educators, and linguists. Each has a certain expertise in important activities that are required for the fine-tuning and contextualizing of AI-generated narratives.

Although AI developers may possess technical expertise in developing intricate algorithms, most of them usually lack pedagogical and even cultural nuances in storytelling. Together with teachers, they will more accurately perceive the dynamics within the class and the needs of learners. For example, educators might consult on the appropriateness of themes, vocabulary difficulty, and the level of interactivity within stories produced by AI. Such collaboration will help ensure that this AI tool is useful, enjoyable, and suitable for educational purposes (Jarrahi, 2018).

Linguists on the other hand are set to elevate linguistic and cultural relevance for the content produced by way of AI. It might also lead to the development of various stories in a way that reflects the diversity of different languages and cultures. For example, linguistic input will probably help AI systems use idiomatic expressions, regional dialects, and culturally specific references that make stories more relatable for learners from diverse backgrounds.

Interdisciplinary research initiatives and partnerships will be encouraged to facilitate collaboration. Joint university-technology company-educational institution programs will engage AI experts, educators, and linguists in co-developing the AI storytelling tools. Funding agencies and policy makers should support such initiatives because of their revolutionary potential for literacy education.

Expanding Access to AI-Assisted Storytelling Globally

Ensuring that all communities have access to AI-assisted storytelling in disadvantaged communities is crucial to preventing educational disadvantages from growing. A key consideration is to create affordable, scalable AI tools such as mobile-based storytelling apps using lightweight story generation models and consider ways to provide these available to learners with limited access to resources. Cloud platforms support the delivery of interactive stories while only requiring a small amount of hardware for access

Multilingual AI tools are also a critical consideration. These AI powered tools can tell stories in different languages, and are trained on datasets of different languages, and local dialects, support mother-tongue education and contribute to language preservation (Ganuza & Hedman, 2019; Nakamura et al., 2023). Thus, AI powered storytelling has the potential to contribute to both literacy and language preservation.

Along with considering language, working with local community groups is also very important. Educational developers and educators should continue to work with the community to ensure that AI content is appropriate to the community's cultural values and educational goals, and that the community sees relevance and ownership of the content. In order to effectively scale AI storytelling solutions, systemic changes and investment in digital Infrastructure, and ed-tech subsidies from government; and operational from NGOs and/or international systems, and building content and funding that can scale and distribute widely.

With careful development, collaboration, and support, the incorporation of AI-powered storytelling has significant potential for transformational learning and literacy. It can support cultural diversity, inclusivity, and global equity to make education meaningful and accessible for all learners.

CONCLUSION

AI-driven storytelling can bring revolutionary transformation to early childhood education, particularly in addressing the literacy gaps and resource inequities. Its strengths lie in generating responsive, linguistically accurate, and engaging stories that facilitate customized and scalable learning, most importantly, in under-resourced contexts. However, AI alone is not sufficient; its current limitations in cultural sensitivity, emotional depth, and ethical transparency demand careful human oversight.

Educators and policymakers must work collaboratively with technologists to ensure AI content aligns with pedagogical goals, respects cultural contexts, and adheres to ethical standards. The collaboration alone can ensure the future of AI use in literacy by employing technology to optimize efficiency and preserve the human elements that foster good learning. Continued interdisciplinary research and development are essential to bringing the full potential of AI as a supplement, not a substitute, for the teacher's role in crafting inclusive and effective narrative experiences for early learners.

REFERENCES

Abderrahim, L., & González, D. (2020). The Impact of Digital Storytelling on the Motivation and Engagement of Young Foreign Language Learners. *Technology and the Psychology of Second Language Learners and Users*. https://doi.org/https://doi.org/10.1007/978-3-030-34212-8_20

Alshahrani, B. T., Pileggi, S. F., & Karimi, F. (2024). A Social Perspective on AI in the Higher Education System: A Semisystematic Literature Review. *Electronics (Basel), 13*(8), 1–27. DOI: 10.3390/electronics13081572

Amirjalili, F., Neysani, M., & Nikbakht, A. (2024). Exploring the boundaries of authorship: a comparative analysis of AI-generated text and human academic writing in English literature. *Frontiers in Education*. https://doi.org/https://doi.org/10.3389/feduc.2024.1347421

Anggoro, K., & Pratiwi, D. (2023). Fostering Self-Assessment in English Learning with a Generative AI Platform: A Case of Quizizz AI. *Studies in Self-Access Learning Journal*. https://doi.org/https://doi.org/10.37237/140406

Barnett, S. (2019). Application of Vygotsky's Social Development Theory. *Journal of Education and Practice*. https://doi.org/https://doi.org/10.7176/jep/10-35-01

Baskerville, D. (2011). Developing Cohesion and Building Positive Relationships through Storytelling in a Culturally Diverse New Zealand Classroom. *Teaching and Teacher Education, 27*(1), 107–115. https://doi.org/https://doi.org/10.1016/J.TATE.2010.07.007. DOI: 10.1016/j.tate.2010.07.007

Chen, G. (2024). The Impacts of AI-Driven Storytelling Applications on Language Acquisition and Literacy Development in Early Childhood Education: A Systematic Review. *Asian Journal of Advanced Research and Reports*. https://doi.org/https://doi.org/10.9734/ajarr/2024/v18i11770

Chomsky, N. (1968). *Language and Mind*. Harper and Row. https://doi.org/https://doi.org/10.1037/e400082009-004

Da Silva Santos, K., Ribeiro, M., De Queiroga, D., Da Silva, I., & Ferreira, S. (2020). The use of multiple triangulations as a validation strategy in a qualitative study. *Ciencia & Saude Coletiva, 25*(2), 655–664. https://doi.org/https://doi.org/10.1590/1413-81232020252.12302018 PMID: 32022205

Elmorsy, G. (2024). Using Generative AI Tools to Improve Children's Story Production Skills in Early Childhood: Suggested Standards. *Scientific Journal of King Faisal University: Humanities and Management Sciences*. https://doi.org/https://doi.org/10.37575/h/edu/230043

Fadhilah, N., Dewi, H., & Winata, W. (2020). Creativity of Creation and Story-Telling in Open-Ended Learning with Visual Art Media for Early Childhood Education. *Proceedings of the 2nd International Conference on Arts and Design Education (ICADE 2019)*. https://doi.org/https://doi.org/10.2991/assehr.k.200321.010

Feng, Y., & Wang, X. (2023). A comparative study on the development of Chinese and English abilities of Chinese primary school students through two bilingual reading modes: human-AI robot interaction and paper books. *Frontiers in Psychology*, *14*, 1200675. https://doi.org/https://doi.org/10.3389/fpsyg.2023.1200675. DOI: 10.3389/fpsyg.2023.1200675 PMID: 37860299

Ganuza, N., & Hedman, C. (2019). The Impact of Mother Tongue Instruction on the Development of Biliteracy: Evidence from Somali–Swedish Bilinguals. *Applied Linguistics*, *40*(1), 108–131. https://doi.org/https://doi.org/10.1093/APPLIN/AMX010. DOI: 10.1093/applin/amx010

Ghosh, S., Venkit, P., Gautam, S., Wilson, S., & Caliskan, A. (2024). Do Generative AI Models Output Harm while Representing Non-Western Cultures: Evidence from A Community-Centered Approach. *ArXiv*. https://doi.org/https://doi.org/10.48550/arXiv.2407.14779

Golwalker, A. (2024). Narration with Graphics: An AI Generated Story Teller. *Interantional Journal of Scientific Research in Engineering and Management*. https://doi.org/https://doi.org/10.55041/ijsrem32119

Guimarães, U., Schizzi, J., & Fernandes, D. (2022). Learning Difficulties and Disorders - A Psychopedagogical Approach. *Revista Científica Multidisciplinar*. https://doi.org/https://doi.org/10.47820/recima21.v3i10.2026

Hazari, S. (2024). Justification and Roadmap for Artificial Intelligence (AI) Literacy Courses in Higher Education. *Journal of Educational Research and Practice*. https://doi.org/https://doi.org/10.5590/jerap.2024.14.1.07

Horváthová, I. (2022). Social-emotional development to learners in primary level of education through "reading" wordless picture books. *Ducational Role of Language Journal*. https://doi.org/https://doi.org/10.36534/erlj.2022.01.03

Huang, L. (2023). Ethics of Artificial Intelligence in Education: Student Privacy and Data Protection. *Science Insights Education Frontiers*. https://doi.org/https://doi.org/10.15354/sief.23.re202

Isnaniah, I., Ramalia, T., Viona, I., Luthfiyandini, L., & Belina, T. (2024). Unlocking Young Minds: The Power of Storytelling in Teaching English for Young Learners. *Primacy Journal of English Education and Literacy*. https://doi.org/https://doi.org/10.33592/primacy.v3i1.5031

Jakesch, M., Hancock, J., & Naaman, M. (2022). Human heuristics for AI-generated language are flawed. *Proceedings of the National Academy of Sciences of the United States of America*, *120*, •••. https://doi.org/https://doi.org/10.1073/pnas.2208839120 PMID: 36881628

Jarrahi, M. (2018). Artificial intelligence and the future of work: Human-AI symbiosis in organizational decision making. *Business Horizons*. https://doi.org/https://doi.org/10.1016/J.BUSHOR.2018.03.007

Jauhiainen, J., & Guerra, A. (2023). Generative AI and ChatGPT in School Children's Education: Evidence from a School Lesson. *Sustainability*. https://doi.org/https://doi.org/10.3390/su151814025

Kalantzis, M., & Cope, B. (2024). Literacy in the Time of Artificial Intelligence. *Reading Research Quarterly*. https://doi.org/https://doi.org/10.1002/rrq.591

Karadoğan, A. (2023). A Bridge Between Technology and Creativity: Story Writing with Artificial Intelligence. *İnsan ve Sosyal Bilimler Dergisi*. https://doi.org/https://doi.org/10.53048/johass.1368950

Khoirunnisak, E., Fatirul, A., & Harwanto. (2024). How Educational Flipbooks and Learning Motivation Affect Early Reading Proficiency in First-Grade Kindergarteners. *Jurnal Komunikasi Pendidikan*. https://doi.org/https://doi.org/10.32585/jurnalkomdik.v8i2.5292

Klimova, B., & Chen, J. (2024). The Impact of AI on Enhancing Students' Intercultural Communication Competence at the University Level: A Review Study. *Language Teaching Research Quarterly*. https://doi.org/https://doi.org/10.32038/ltrq.2024.43.06

Kumar, A., Bhoyar, S., & Mishra, A. (2024). Does ChatGPT foster academic misconduct in the future? *Public Administration and Policy*. https://doi.org/https://doi.org/10.1108/pap-05-2023-0061

Kusmiatun, A., Efendi, D., Pansori, M., Judijanto, L., Sariasih, Y., & Saddhono, K. (2024). The Power of AI in Generating Novel Based and Impactful Character Development for Fiction Story. *2024 4th International Conference on Advance Computing and Innovative Technologies in Engineering (ICACITE)*, 1555–1561. https://doi.org/https://doi.org/10.1109/ICACITE60783.2024.10616700

Lavin, S. R. (2019). *Towards a useful conception of the ZPD for language education.* https://doi.org/https://doi.org/10.33422/2nd.2nd.icate.2019.12.840

Lee, J., Shin, D., & Noh, W. (2023). Artificial Intelligence-Based Content Generator Technology for Young English-as-a-Foreign-Language Learners' Reading Enjoyment. *RELC Journal*, *54*(2), 508–516. https://doi.org/https://doi.org/10.1177/00336882231165060. DOI: 10.1177/00336882231165060

Loughland, T. (2019). Adaptive Teaching for Students' Critical and Creative Thinking. *Teacher Adaptive Practices.* https://doi.org/https://doi.org/10.1007/978-981-13-6858-5_1

Lu, R. S., Lin, H. C. K., Yang, Y. C., & Chen, Y. P. (2024). Integrating Urban Mining Concepts Through AI-Generated Storytelling and Visuals: Advancing Sustainability Education in Early Childhood. *Sustainability (Basel)*, *16*(24), 11304. Advance online publication. DOI: 10.3390/su162411304

Markowitz, D., Hancock, J., & Bailenson, J. (2023). Linguistic Markers of Inherently False AI Communication and Intentionally False Human Communication: Evidence From Hotel Reviews. *Journal of Language and Social Psychology*, *43*(1), 63–82. https://doi.org/https://doi.org/10.1177/0261927X231200201. DOI: 10.1177/0261927X231200201

Mastellotto, L. (2021). Developing Young Learners' Multiliteracies through Multimodal Storytelling. *Pathways to Plurilingual Education.* https://doi.org/https://doi.org/10.26493/978-961-7055-36-8.251-265

Maureen, I., Van Der Meij, H., & De Jong, T. (2021). Evaluating storytelling activities for early literacy development. *International Journal of Early Years Education*, *30*(4), 679–696. https://doi.org/https://doi.org/10.1080/09669760.2021.193. DOI: 10.1080/09669760.2021.1933917

Mayer, R. E. (2009). *Multimedia Learning.* Cambridge University Press., https://doi.org/https://doi.org/10.1017/CBO9780511811678 DOI: 10.1017/CBO9780511811678

McBreen, M., & Savage, R. (2020). The Impact of Motivational Reading Instruction on the Reading Achievement and Motivation of Students: A Systematic Review and Meta-Analysis. *Educational Psychology Review*, *33*(3), 1125–1163. https://doi.org/https://doi.org/10.1007/s10648-020-09584-4. DOI: 10.1007/s10648-020-09584-4

Moreno, R., & Mayer, R. (1999). Cognitive Principles of Multimedia Learning: The Role of Modality and Contiguity. *Journal of Educational Psychology*, *91*(2), 358–368. https://doi.org/https://doi.org/10.1037/0022-0663.91.2.358. DOI: 10.1037/0022-0663.91.2.358

Nakamura, P., Molotsky, A., Zarzur, R., Ranjit, V., Haddad, Y., & De Hoop, T. (2023). Language of instruction in schools in low- and middle-income countries: A systematic review. *Campbell Systematic Reviews*, *19*, •••. https://doi.org/https://doi.org/10.1002/cl2.1351

Novita, D., Hamied, F., & Sukyadi, D. (2023). Effect of Culturally Familiar Text on Low-Proficiency Reader's Reading Comprehension. *NOBEL: Journal of Literature and Language Teaching*. https://doi.org/https://doi.org/10.15642/nobel.2023.14.1.115-132

Orwig, W. W., Edenbaum, E. R., Greene, J. D., & Schacter, D. L. (2024). The Language of Creativity: Evidence from Humans and Large Language Models. *Journal of Creative Behavior*. https://doi.org/https://doi.org/10.1002/jocb.636

Pack, A., & Maloney, J. (2024). Using Artificial Intelligence in TESOL: Some Ethical and Pedagogical Considerations. *TESOL Quarterly*. https://doi.org/https://doi.org/10.1002/tesq.3320

Pendy, B. (2023). Artificial Intelligence: The Future of Education. *Jurnal Indonesia Sosial Sains*, *2*(11), 2003–2012. DOI: 10.59141/jiss.v2i11.801

Peters, U., & Carman, M. (2024). Cultural Bias in Explainable AI Research: A Systematic Analysis. *Journal of Artificial Intelligence Research*, *79*, 971–1000. https://doi.org/https://doi.org/10.1613/jair.1.14888. DOI: 10.1613/jair.1.14888

Pramesty, N. S., Maghfiroh, A., & Mustikawati, D. A. (2022). Teachers ' Challanges in Teaching English to Young Learners in Rural Area at SDN 02 Sendang. *Jurnal Pendidikan*, 1–11.

Pujiani, T., Sukmawati, I. D., Bintang, A., & Pradana, A. (2023). Enriching EFL Classroom Activities with Online Games. *Conference on English Language Teaching*, 2023, *2023*, 65–83.

Rakya, Z. (2023). Exploring the Impact of Artificial Intelligence (AI) on Learner-Instructor Interaction in Online Learning (Literature Review). *International Journal of Emerging Multidisciplinaries: Computer Science & Artificial Intelligence*. https://doi.org/https://doi.org/10.54938/ijemdcsai.2023.02.1.236

Salas, N., & Pascual, M. (2023). Impact of school SES on literacy development. *PLoS One*, *18*(12), e0295606. https://doi.org/https://doi.org/10.1371/journal.pone.0295606. DOI: 10.1371/journal.pone.0295606 PMID: 38127961

Scarcella, R., & Perkins, L. (1987). Shifting Gears: Krashen's Input Hypothesis. *Studies in Second Language Acquisition*, *9*(3), 347–353. https://doi.org/https://doi.org/10.1017/S0272263100006720. DOI: 10.1017/S0272263100006720

Scorer, M., & Vardy, E. (2024). Children need to see themselves in their reading material: parental perspectives on the importance of ethnically and culturally diverse reading material. *Literacy*. https://doi.org/https://doi.org/10.1111/lit.12379

Spooren, W., & Sanders, T. (2008). The acquisition order of coherence relations : On cognitive complexity in discourse. *Journal of Pragmatics and Discourse Research*, *40*, 2003–2026. https://doi.org/https://doi.org/10.1016/J.PRAGMA.2008.04.021

Taghizadeh, M., & Hasani Yourdshahi, Z. (2020). Integrating technology into young learners' classes: Language teachers' perceptions. *Computer Assisted Language Learning*, *33*(8), 982–1006. DOI: 10.1080/09588221.2019.1618876

Tan, D., & Mante-Estacio, M. (2021). Eader-Text Connection: Reporting the Engagement of High School Students with Culturally Relevant Texts. *TEFLIN Journal - A Publication on the Teaching and Learning of English*. https://doi.org/https://doi.org/10.15639/teflinjournal.v32i2/342-361

Tang, T., Lau, D., & Leung, M. (2023). Corpus of Mandarin Child Language: A preliminary study on the acquisition of semantic content categories in Mandarin-speaking preschoolers. *Frontiers in Psychology*, *14*, 1234525. https://doi.org/https://doi.org/10.3389/fpsyg.2023.1234525. DOI: 10.3389/fpsyg.2023.1234525 PMID: 38022991

Tong, F. (2022). Psychological and pedagogical effects on engagement and achievement: Implications for literacy and maths learning. *Educational Psychology*, *42*(8), 931–933. https://doi.org/https://doi.org/10.1080/01443410.2022.2140275. DOI: 10.1080/01443410.2022.2140275

Vygotsky, L. S. (1978). *Mind in Society: The Development of Higher Psychological Processes*. Harvard University Press.

Walkington, C., & Bernacki, M. (2020). Appraising research on personalized learning: Definitions, theoretical alignment, advancements, and future directions. *Journal of Research on Technology in Education*, *52*(3), 235–252. https://doi.org/https://doi.org/10.1080/15391523.2020.1747757. DOI: 10.1080/15391523.2020.1747757

Wirth, A., Ehmig, S., Drescher, N., Guffler, S., & Niklas, F. (2020). Facets of the Early Home Literacy Environment and Children's Linguistic and Socioemotional Competencies. *Early Education and Development*, *31*(6), 892–909. https://doi.org/https://doi.org/10.1080/10409289.2019.1706826. DOI: 10.1080/10409289.2019.1706826

Yang, W., Hu, X., Yeter, I., Su, J., Yang, Y., & Lee, J. (2023). Artificial intelligence education for young children: A case study of technology-enhanced embodied learning. *Journal of Computer Assisted Learning*, *40*(2), 465–477. https://doi.org/https://doi.org/10.1111/jcal.12892. DOI: 10.1111/jcal.12892

Zheng, L., Liu, R., & Zhang, X. (2020). Effects of an interest-driven creation approach on students' mobile learning performance and creativity in learning science in a science museum. *Journal of Computers in Education*, *8*(2), 159–182. https://doi.org/https://doi.org/10.1007/s40692-020-00175-4. DOI: 10.1007/s40692-020-00175-4

Zucker, T., Oh, Y., Smith, K., & Baker-Finck, J. (2022). Low-Income Elementary Students Access to Books & Reading Motivation. *Reading Psychology*, *43*(3-4), 250–276. https://doi.org/https://doi.org/10.1080/02702711.2022.2094040. DOI: 10.1080/02702711.2022.2094040

KEY TERMS AND DEFINITIONS

AI (Artificial Intelligence): The capability of machines or software to perform tasks that typically require human intelligence, such as reasoning, learning, and problem-solving.

AI-Generated Stories: Narratives created using artificial intelligence algorithms without direct human authorship.

Chatbot: A computer program or AI system designed to simulate human conversation through text or voice interactions.

Cognitive-Emotional Development: The interconnected growth of cognitive abilities and emotional regulation in children or learners.

Cultural Awareness: An understanding of different cultural backgrounds, values, and perspectives.

Early Childhood Education Expert: A professional specializing in the principles, methods, and best practices of educating young children.

Early Childhood Literacy: The development of reading and writing skills in young children before formal schooling.

Human-Authored Narratives: Stories or content created by human writers rather than AI.

Language Expert: A professional specializing in language learning, teaching, or linguistics.

Language Literacy: The ability to read, write, and communicate effectively in a language.

Literacy Development: The process of acquiring reading and writing skills over time.

Low-Income Areas: Communities with limited financial resources affecting education and social development.

Mayer's Cognitive Theory: A theory of multimedia learning that explains how people process and retain information.

Multilingual Communities: Societies where multiple languages are spoken and used in daily life.

Multimodal: The use of multiple modes of communication, such as text, images, and sound, in learning and interaction.

NGO (Non-Governmental Organization): An independent organization that operates for social, educational, or humanitarian purposes.

NLP (Natural Language Processing): A field of AI that enables computers to understand and process human language.

Theory of Comprehensible Input: A language learning theory stating that learners acquire language best when exposed to input slightly beyond their current proficiency.

Under-Resourced Communities: Areas lacking adequate educational, financial, or technological resources.

Young Learners: Children typically in the early stages of education, often under the age of 12.

Zone of Proximal Development (ZPD): A concept in learning theory describing the difference between what a learner can do independently and what they can achieve with guidance.

Compilation of References

Abbas, N., Imran, A. S., Manzoor, R., Hussain, T., & Hussain, M. (2023). Role of Artificial Intelligence Tools in Enhancing Students' Educational Performance at Higher Levels. *Journal of Artificial Intelligence Machine Learning and Neural Network*, *35*(35), 36–49. DOI: 10.55529/jaimlnn.35.36.49

Abderrahim, L., & González, D. (2020). The Impact of Digital Storytelling on the Motivation and Engagement of Young Foreign Language Learners. *Technology and the Psychology of Second Language Learners and Users*. https://doi.org/https://doi.org/10.1007/978-3-030-34212-8_20

Abduh, A., Sakkir, G., Rosmaladewi, R., Andrew, M., & Yasdin, Y. (2022). Teachers' Perceptions of English Teaching Strategies in the Current Curriculum Change. *International Journal of Language Education*, *6*(4), 437–444. DOI: 10.26858/ijole.v6i4.25246

Abdulah, D. M., Zaman, B. A., Mustafa, Z. R., & Hassan, L. H. (2024). Artificial Intelligence Integration in Academic Writing: Insights from the University of Duhok. *ARO (Koya)*, *12*(2), 194–200. DOI: 10.14500/aro.11794

Acuña, O. L., & Carvajal, D. M., Bolanos-Barbosa, Angie D., & Reyes, L. H. (2025). Fostering Technical Proficiency and Professional Skills: A Multifaceted PO-PBL Strategy for Unit Operations Education. *Education for Chemical Engineers*, *51*(1).

Adel, A., Ahsan, A., & Davison, C. (2024). ChatGPT Promises and Challenges in Education: Computational and Ethical Perspectives. *Education Sciences*, *14*(8), 814. DOI: 10.3390/educsci14080814

Adıgüzel, T., Kaya, M. H., & Cansu, F. K. (2023). Revolutionizing education with AI: Exploring the transformative potential of ChatGPT. *Contemporary Educational Technology*, *15*(3), ep429. DOI: 10.30935/cedtech/13152

Agbor, U. I., Duke, O. O., Obaji-Akpet, I. O., Nwagboso, C. I., Eja, T. R., Awubi, E., & Ukume, G. D. (2024). Artificial intelligence and academic research: Understanding the potential and the threats to academic writing. *Ianna Journal of Interdisciplinary Studies*, *6*(2), 33–52. DOI: 10.5281/zenodo.11120274

Ahmed, A. (2022). Exploring silences in the field of computer assisted language learning. [HTML]

Ahsan, M. J. (2025). Cultivating a culture of learning: The role of leadership in fostering lifelong development. [HTML]. *The Learning Organization*, *32*(2), 282–306. DOI: 10.1108/TLO-03-2024-0099

Ajiye, O. T., & Omokhabi, A. A. (2025). The Potential and Ethical Issues of Artificial Intelligence in Improving Academic Writing. *ShodhAI: Journal of Artificial Intelligence*, *2*(1), 1–9. DOI: 10.29121/shodhai.v2.i1.2025.24

Akbarani, R. (2024). Use of Artificial Intelligence in English Language Teaching. *International Journal of English Learning and Applied Linguistics (Ijelal)*, *4*(1), 14–23. DOI: 10.21111/ijelal.v4i1.10756

Akimushkin, C., Amancio, D. R., & Oliveira, O. N. (2017). Text Authorship Identified Using the Dynamics of Word Co-Occurrence Networks. *PLoS One*, *12*(1), e0170527. DOI: 10.1371/journal.pone.0170527 PMID: 28125703

Akinnagbe, O.B. (2024). Human-AI Collaboration: Enhancing Productivity and Decision-Making. *International Journal of Education, Management, and Technology*.

Akpabio, E., Akpabio, I., & Akpabio, I. (2025). Leveraging AI for Personalized English Language Learning: Tailoring Instruction to Individual Needs. In AI Applications for English Language Learning (pp. 385-414). IGI Global Scientific Publishing. [HTML]

Al Fraidan, P.A. (2024). Anticipatory Thinking and AI-Driven Assessments: A Balanced Approach to AI Integration in Education Aligned with Saudi Vision 2030. *African Journal of Biomedical Research*.

Alam, A. (2023). Harnessing the power of AI to create intelligent tutoring systems for enhanced classroom experience and improved learning outcomes. In *Intelligent Communication Technologies and Virtual Mobile Networks* (pp. 571–591). Springer Nature Singapore. [HTML] DOI: 10.1007/978-981-99-1767-9_42

Aldalbahi, A., El-Naggar, M., El-Newehy, M., Rahaman, M., Hatshan, M., & Khattab, T. (2021). Effects of Technical Textiles and Synthetic Nanofibers on Environmental Pollution. *Polymers*, *13*(1), 155. DOI: 10.3390/polym13010155 PMID: 33401538

AlGerafi, M. A. M., Zhou, Y., Oubibi, M., & Wijaya, T. T. (2023). Unlocking the potential: A comprehensive evaluation of augmented reality and virtual reality in education. Electronics. mdpi.com

Alharbi, W. (2023). AI in the Foreign Language Classroom: A Pedagogical Overview of Automated Writing Assistance Tools. *Education Research International, 2023*, 1–15. DOI: 10.1155/2023/4253331

Ali, S. B., Haider, M., Samiullah, D., & Shamsy, S. (2024, July–September). Assessing students' understanding of ethical use of artificial intelligence (AI): A focus group study. *International Journal of Social Science and Entrepreneurship*, *4*(3).

Alkatheiri, M. S. (2022). Artificial intelligence assisted improved human-computer interactions for computer systems. [HTML]. *Computers & Electrical Engineering*, *101*, 107950. DOI: 10.1016/j.compeleceng.2022.107950

Al-khresheh, M. H. (2024). Bridging technology and pedagogy from a global lens: Teachers' perspectives on integrating ChatGPT in English language teaching. Computers and Education: Artificial Intelligence. sciencedirect.com

Al-khresheh, M. H. (2024). Bridging technology and pedagogy from a global lens: Teachers' perspectives on integrating ChatGPT in English language teaching. *Computers and Education: Artificial Intelligence*, *6*, 100218. DOI: 10.1016/j.caeai.2024.100218

AllahRakha, N.AllahRakha. (2024). UNESCO's AI Ethics Principles: Challenges and Opportunities. *International Journal of Law and Policy*, *2*(9), 24–36. DOI: 10.59022/ijlp.225

Allen, L. K., & Kendeou, P. (2024). ED-AI Lit: An Interdisciplinary Framework for AI Literacy in Education. *Policy Insights from the Behavioral and Brain Sciences*, *11*(1), 3–10. DOI: 10.1177/23727322231220339

Alnasib, B. N. M. (2023). Factors Affecting Faculty Members' Readiness to Integrate Artificial Intelligence into Their Teaching Practices: A Study from the Saudi Higher Education Context. International Journal of Learning. *Teaching and Educational Research*, *22*(8), 465–491. DOI: 10.26803/ijlter.22.8.24

Alotaibi, M. S. (2024). Game-Based Learning in Early Childhood Education: A Systematic Review and Meta-Analysis. *Frontiers in Psychology*, *15*, 1307881. Advance online publication. DOI: 10.3389/fpsyg.2024.1307881 PMID: 38629045

Alotaibi, N. S., & Alshehri, A. H. (2023). Prospers and Obstacles in Using Artificial Intelligence in Saudi Arabia Higher Education Institutions—The Potential of AI-Based Learning Outcomes. *Sustainability (Basel), 15*(13), 10723. DOI: 10.3390/su151310723

Alqahtani, T., Badreldin, H. A., Alrashed, M., Alshaya, A. I., Alghamdi, S. S., Bin Saleh, K., Alowais, S. A., Alshaya, O. A., Rahman, I., Al Yami, M. S., & Albekairy, A. M. (2023). The emergent role of artificial intelligence, natural learning processing, and large language models in higher education and research. *Research in Social & Administrative Pharmacy, 19*(8), 1236–1242. DOI: 10.1016/j.sapharm.2023.05.016 PMID: 37321925

Alshahrani, B. T., Pileggi, S. F., & Karimi, F. (2024). A Social Perspective on AI in the Higher Education System: A Semisystematic Literature Review. *Electronics (Basel), 13*(8), 1–27. DOI: 10.3390/electronics13081572

Alt, D., Naamati-Schneider, L., & Weishut, D. J. (2023). Competency-based learning and formative assessment feedback as precursors of college students' soft skills acquisition. [tandfonline.com]. *Studies in Higher Education, 48*(12), 1901–1917. DOI: 10.1080/03075079.2023.2217203

Aluko, H. A., Aluko, A., Offiah, G. A., Ogunjimi, F., Aluko, A. O., Alalade, F. M., Ogeze Ukeje, I., & Nwani, C. H. (2025). Exploring the effectiveness of AI-generated learning materials in facilitating active learning strategies and knowledge retention in higher education. [HTML]. *The International Journal of Organizational Analysis.* Advance online publication. DOI: 10.1108/IJOA-07-2024-4632

Al-Zahrani, A. M. (2024). Unveiling the shadows: Beyond the hype of AI in education. *Heliyon, 10*(9), e30696. DOI: 10.1016/j.heliyon.2024.e30696 PMID: 38737255

Amaliah, N., Sunarlia Limbong, Nur Ina Syam, Fahmi Room, & Khaliq Bashar. (2023). Using Technology as Learning Media to Enrich ESP Students' Speaking Skill for Indonesian Higher Education Students. *IJOLEH : International Journal of Education and Humanities, 2*(1), 43–51. DOI: 10.56314/ijoleh.v2i1.126

Amirjalili, F., Neysani, M., & Nikbakht, A. (2024). Exploring the boundaries of authorship: a comparative analysis of AI-generated text and human academic writing in English literature. *Frontiers in Education.* https://doi.org/https://doi.org/10.3389/feduc.2024.1347421

Andersson, R., Ringhagen, A., & Tapper, A. (2024). *Exploring the Integration of Artificial Intelligence Tools in English as a Foreign Language (EFL) Pedagogy.* Gothenburg University Publications Electronic Archive (GUPEA). https://gupea.ub.gu.se/handle/2077/79561

Andriessen, D., & Van Den Boom, M. (2007). East is East, and West is West, and (n)ever its intellectual capital shall meet. *Journal of Intellectual Capital*, *8*(4), 641–652. DOI: 10.1108/14691930710830800

Anggoro, K., & Pratiwi, D. (2023). Fostering Self-Assessment in English Learning with a Generative AI Platform: A Case of Quizizz AI. *Studies in Self-Access Learning Journal*. https://doi.org/https://doi.org/10.37237/140406

Anitha, V., & Reddy, C. K. K. (2025). Harnessing the Power of Deep Learning: Revolutionizing English Language Learning Applications. In AI Applications for English Language Learning (pp. 313-354). IGI Global Scientific Publishing. [HTML]

Anjum, P. G., Choubey, P. J., Kushwaha, S., & Patkar, V. (2023). AI in Education: Evaluating the Efficacy and Fairness of Automated Grading Systems. *International Journal of Innovative Research in Science, Engineering and Technology*, *12*(6), 1–14. DOI: 10.15680/IJIRSET.2023.1206161

Appelganc, K., Rieger, T., Roesler, E., & Manzey, D. (2022). How Much Reliability Is Enough? A Context-Specific View on Human Interaction With (Artificial) Agents From Different Perspectives. *Journal of Cognitive Engineering and Decision Making*, *16*(4), 207–221. DOI: 10.1177/15553434221104615

Arani, S. M. N. (2024). Navigating the future of language learning: A Conceptual review of ai's role in personalized learning. [callej.org]. *Computer-Assisted Language Learning Electronic Journal*, *25*(3), 1–22.

Arkkelin, D. (2014). *Using SPSS to Understand Research and Data Analysis*. Psychology Curricular Materials.

Asdar, Y. J., Natsir, T., Anggreani, A. V., Sasabone, L., & Kechik, T. N. B. T. (2023). Strengthening Character Education Based on Online Learning for University Students Pasca Covid-19. *IJOLEH : International Journal of Education and Humanities*, *2*(1), 35–42. DOI: 10.56314/ijoleh.v2i1.125

Asratie, M. G., Wale, B. D., & Aylet, Y. T. (2023). Effects of using educational technology tools to enhance EFL students' speaking performance. Education and Information Technologies. springer.com

Assael, Y., Sommerschield, T., Shillingford, B., Bordbar, M., Pavlopoulos, J., Chatzipanagiotou, M., Androutsopoulos, I., Prag, J., & De Freitas, N. (2022). Restoring and attributing ancient texts using deep neural networks. *Nature*, *603*(7900), 280–283. DOI: 10.1038/s41586-022-04448-z PMID: 35264762

Athanassopoulos, S., Manoli, P., Gouvi, M., Lavidas, K., & Komis, V. (2023). The Use of ChatGPT as a Learning Tool to Improve Foreign Language Writing in a Multilingual and Multicultural Classroom. *Advances in Mobile Learning Educational Research, 3*(2), 818–824. DOI: 10.25082/AMLER.2023.02.009

Attia, S., & Elsawy, E. (2024). Higher Education Students' Perceptions and Attitudes about Using ChatGPT in Oman: A Case Study of OCMT. *International Journal of Educational Sciences and Arts, 3*(4), 304–321. DOI: 10.59992/IJESA.2024.v3n4p8

Bachman, L., & Adrian, P. (2022). *Language assessment in practice: Developing language assessments and justifying their use in the real world.* Oxford University Press.

Bahr, A. (2024). Bridges Without Foundation? Why the Use of AI Tools in Academia Needs to Build on Ethics First. *Filozofia, 79*(5), 486–500. DOI: 10.31577/filozofia.2024.79.5.2

Baker, S. (2024). AI Narratives: A History of Imaginative Thinking about Intelligent MachinesImagining AI: How the World Sees Intelligent Machines. *Poetics Today, 45*(2), 363–366. DOI: 10.1215/03335372-11093003

Balci, S., Secaur, J. M., & Morris, B. J. (2022). Comparing the effectiveness of badges and leaderboards on academic performance and motivation of students in fully versus partially gamified online physics classes. Education and information technologies. springer.com

Barnett, S. (2019). Application of Vygotsky's Social Development Theory. *Journal of Education and Practice.* https://doi.org/https://doi.org/10.7176/jep/10-35-01

Barrot, J. S. (2022). Social media as a language learning environment: a systematic review of the literature (2008-2019). Computer assisted language learning. [HTML]

Baskerville, D. (2011). Developing Cohesion and Building Positive Relationships through Storytelling in a Culturally Diverse New Zealand Classroom. *Teaching and Teacher Education, 27*(1), 107–115. https://doi.org/https://doi.org/10.1016/J.TATE.2010.07.007. DOI: 10.1016/j.tate.2010.07.007

Baum, S. D. (2021). Artificial Interdisciplinarity: Artificial Intelligence for Research on Complex Societal Problems. *Philosophy & Technology, 34*(S1), 45–63. DOI: 10.1007/s13347-020-00416-5

Bearman, M., & Luckin, R. (2020). Preparing University Assessment for a World with AI: Tasks for Human Intelligence.

Bengsch, G. (2024). Redefining traditional pedagogy: The integration of machine learning in the contemporary language education classroom. In Pan, F. (Ed.), *AI in language teaching, learning, and assessment* (pp. 197–214). IGI Global., DOI: 10.4018/979-8-3693-0872-1.ch010

Benitta, G., Asha, H. J., & Josephine, J. A. (2024). An Integrated (Hybrid Based) Besuited Education System Design for the Better Models. *2024 4th International Conference on Advance Computing and Innovative Technologies in Engineering (ICACITE)*, 561-565.

Betaubun, M. (2023). Personalized Pathways to Proficiency: Exploring the Synergy of Adaptive Learning and Artificial Intelligence in English Language Learning. *Technium, 17*, 60–66. DOI: 10.47577/technium.v17i.10047

Bogach, N., Boitsova, E., Chernonog, S., Lamtev, A., Lesnichaya, M., Lezhenin, I., Novopashenny, A., Svechnikov, R., Tsikach, D., Vasiliev, K., Pyshkin, E., & Blake, J. (2021). Speech processing for language learning: A practical approach to computer-assisted pronunciation teaching. [mdpi.com]. *Electronics (Basel), 10*(3), 235. DOI: 10.3390/electronics10030235

Bolaños, F., Salatino, A., Osborne, F., & Motta, E. (2024). Artificial intelligence for literature reviews: Opportunities and challenges. *Artificial Intelligence Review, 57*(10), 259. DOI: 10.1007/s10462-024-10902-3

Bolsinova, M., Deonovic, B., Arieli-Attali, M., Settles, B., Hagiwara, M., & Maris, G. (2022). Measurement of ability in adaptive learning and assessment systems when learners use on-demand hints. [sagepub.com]. *Applied Psychological Measurement, 46*(3), 219–235. DOI: 10.1177/01466216221084208 PMID: 35528271

Brandão, A., Pedro, L., & Zagalo, N. (2024). *Teacher professional development for a future with generative artificial intelligence – an integrative literature review*. Digital Education Review. DOI: 10.1344/der.2024.45.151-157

Bulut, O., Beiting-Parrish, M., Casabianca, J.M., Slater, S.C., Jiao, H., Song, D., Ormerod, C., Fabiyi, D.G., Ivan, R., Walsh, C., Rios, O., Wilson, J., Yildirim-Erbasli, S.N., Wongvorachan, T., Liu, J.X., Tan, B., & Morilova, P. (2024). The Rise of Artificial Intelligence in Educational Measurement: Opportunities and Ethical Challenges. *ArXiv, abs/2406.18900.*

ButarButar, R., & Simatupang, E. (2020). The impact of technology hello English application in EFL classroom. *Lingual: Journal of Language and Culture, 8*(2), 11.

Carrió-Pastor, M. L. (Ed.). (2016). *Technology Implementation in Second Language Teaching and Translation Studies: New Tools, New Approaches*. Springer Singapore., DOI: 10.1007/978-981-10-0572-5

Casheekar, A., Lahiri, A., Rath, K., Prabhakar, K. S., & Srinivasan, K. (2024). A contemporary review on chatbots, AI-powered virtual conversational agents, ChatGPT: Applications, open challenges and future research directions. [HTML]. *Computer Science Review*, *52*, 100632. DOI: 10.1016/j.cosrev.2024.100632

Chan, C.K., & Tsi, L.H. (2023). The AI Revolution in Education: Will AI Replace or Assist Teachers in Higher Education? *ArXiv, abs/2305.01185.*

Chan, C. K. Y. (2024). Students' perceptions of 'AI-giarism': Investigating changes in understandings of academic misconduct. *Education and Information Technologies*. Advance online publication. DOI: 10.1007/s10639-024-13151-7

Chapelle, C. A. (2003). *English Language Learning and Technology: Lectures on Teaching and Research.* Cambridge University Press. DOI: 10.1075/lllt.7

Chapinal-Heras, D., & Díaz-Sánchez, C. (2024). A review of AI applications in human sciences research. *Digital Applications in Archaeology and Cultural Heritage*, *32*, e00323. DOI: 10.1016/j.daach.2024.e00323

Chen, G. (2024). The Impacts of AI-Driven Storytelling Applications on Language Acquisition and Literacy Development in Early Childhood Education: A Systematic Review. *Asian Journal of Advanced Research and Reports.* https://doi.org/https://doi.org/10.9734/ajarr/2024/v18i11770

Chen, Y. (2024, May). Enhancing language acquisition: The role of AI in facilitating effective language learning. In 2024 3rd International Conference on Humanities, Wisdom Education and Service Management (HWESM 2024) (pp. 593-600). Atlantis Press. atlantis-press.

Chen, L., Wang, H., & Zhang, Y. (2023). Reducing test anxiety through adaptive assessment in online language learning. *Journal of Educational Technology & Society*, *26*(4), 123–135.

Chomsky, N. (1968). *Language and Mind.* Harper and Row. https://doi.org/https://doi.org/10.1037/e400082009-004

Chookaew, S., Kitcharoen, P., Howimanporn, S., & Panjaburee, P. (2024). Fostering student competencies and perceptions through artificial intelligence of things educational platform. *Computers and Education: Artificial Intelligence*, *7*(September), 100308. DOI: 10.1016/j.caeai.2024.100308

Choukaier, D. (2024). Integrating AI In English Language Pedagogy: Innovations And Outcomes In Teaching English As Second /Foreign Language. *Educational Administration: Theory and Practice, 30*(5), 3811–3822. https://doi.org/Doi: DOI: 10.53555/kuey.v30i5.3538

Christou, D., & Tsoumakas, G. (2021). Extracting Semantic Relationships in Greek Literary Texts. *Sustainability (Basel), 13*(16), 9391. DOI: 10.3390/su13169391

Christou, P. (2023). How to Use Artificial Intelligence (AI) as a Resource, Methodological and Analysis Tool in Qualitative Research? *The Qualitative Report*. Advance online publication. DOI: 10.46743/2160-3715/2023.6406

Clark, E., Ross, A. S., Tan, C., Ji, Y., & Smith, N. A. (2018). Creative writing with a machine in the loop: Case studies on slogans and stories. *International Conference on Intelligent User Interfaces, Proceedings IUI, March*, 329–340. https://doi.org/ DOI: 10.1145/3172944.3172983

Conijn, R., Kahr, P., & Snijders, C. J. (2023). The Effects of Explanations in Automated Essay Scoring Systems on Student Trust and Motivation. *Journal of Learning Analytics, 10*(1), 37–53. DOI: 10.18608/jla.2023.7801

Contreras, M. R., & Jaimes, J. O. (2024). AI Ethics in the Fields of Education and Research: A Systematic Literature Review. *2024 International Symposium on Accreditation of Engineering and Computing Education (ICACIT)*, 1-6. DOI: 10.1109/ICACIT62963.2024.10788651

Cope, B., Kalantzis, M., & Searsmith, D. (2020). Artificial intelligence for education: Knowledge and its assessment in AI-enabled learning ecologies. *Educational Philosophy and Theory, 53*(12), 1229–1245. DOI: 10.1080/00131857.2020.1728732

Crafts, N. (2021). Artificial intelligence as a general-purpose technology: An historical perspective. *Oxford Review of Economic Policy, 37*(3), 521–536. DOI: 10.1093/oxrep/grab012

Creely, E. (2024). Exploring the Role of Generative AI in Enhancing Language Learning: Opportunities and Challenges. *International Journal of Changes in Education, 1*(3), 158–167. DOI: 10.47852/bonviewIJCE42022495

Creswell, J. W. (2013). *Educational research: Planning, conducting, and evaluating quantitative and qualitative research* (Fourth Indian edition). PHI Learning Private Limited.

Da Silva Santos, K., Ribeiro, M., De Queiroga, D., Da Silva, I., & Ferreira, S. (2020). The use of multiple triangulations as a validation strategy in a qualitative study. *Ciencia & Saude Coletiva, 25*(2), 655–664. https://doi.org/https://doi.org/10.1590/1413-81232020252.12302018 PMID: 32022205

Dabbagh, N., & Kitsantas, A. (2012). Personal Learning Environments, social media, and self-regulated learning: A natural formula for connecting formal and informal learning. *The Internet and Higher Education, 15*(1), 3–8. DOI: 10.1016/j.iheduc.2011.06.002

Dai, Y. (2024). Dual-contrast pedagogy for AI literacy in upper elementary schools. *Learning and Instruction, 91*, 101899. DOI: 10.1016/j.learninstruc.2024.101899

Dai, Y., Liu, A., & Lim, C. P. (2023). Reconceptualizing ChatGPT and generative AI as a student-driven innovation in higher education. *Procedia CIRP, 119*, 84–90. DOI: 10.1016/j.procir.2023.05.002

Darling-Hammond, L., Schachner, A. C. W., Wojcikiewicz, S. K., & Flook, L. (2024). Educating teachers to enact the science of learning and development. *Applied Developmental Science, 28*(1), 1–21. DOI: 10.1080/10888691.2022.2130506

Darwin, R., Rusdin, D., Mukminatien, N., Suryati, N., Laksmi, E. D., & Marzuki, . (2024). Critical thinking in the AI era: An exploration of EFL students' perceptions, benefits, and limitations. *Cogent Education, 11*(1), 1–18. DOI: 10.1080/2331186X.2023.2290342

Deng, L. (2018). Artificial Intelligence in the Rising Wave of Deep Learning: The Historical Path and Future Outlook [Perspectives]. *IEEE Signal Processing Magazine, 35*(1), 180–177. DOI: 10.1109/MSP.2017.2762725

Dergaa, I., Chamari, K., Zmijewski, P., & Ben Saad, H. (2023). From human writing to artificial intelligence generated text: Examining the prospects and potential threats of ChatGPT in academic writing. *Biology of Sport, 40*(2), 615–622. DOI: 10.5114/biolsport.2023.125623 PMID: 37077800

Di Mitri, D., Schneider, J., & Drachsler, H. (2022). Keep me in the loop: Real-time feedback with multimodal data. [springer.com]. *International Journal of Artificial Intelligence in Education, 32*(4), 1093–1118. DOI: 10.1007/s40593-021-00281-z

Di Vaio, A., Palladino, R., Hassan, R., & Escobar, O. (2020). Artificial intelligence and business models in the sustainable development goals perspective: A systematic literature review. *Journal of Business Research, 121*, 283–314. DOI: 10.1016/j.jbusres.2020.08.019

Dillon, S., & Schaffer-Goddard, J. (2023). What AI researchers read: The role of literature in artificial intelligence research. *Interdisciplinary Science Reviews*, *48*(1), 15–42. DOI: 10.1080/03080188.2022.2079214

Dimitriadou, E., & Lanitis, A. (2023). A critical evaluation, challenges, and future perspectives of using artificial intelligence and emerging technologies in smart classrooms. *Smart Learning Environments*, *10*(1), 12. DOI: 10.1186/s40561-023-00231-3 PMID: 40478141

Dindar, M., Muukkonen, H., & Järvelä, S. (2022). The Promises and Challenges of Artificial Intelligence for Teachers: A Systematic Review of Research. *TechTrends*, *66*(4), 616–630. DOI: 10.1007/s11528-022-00715-y

Dogara, M. M. The Use of Artificial Intelligence in Enhancing Teaching, Learning, Research and Community Service in Zoology Education. Role of AI in Enhancing Teaching/Learning, Research and Community Service in Higher Education, 76. researchgate.net

Dong, Y. (2023). Revolutionizing academic English writing through AI-powered pedagogy: Practical exploration of teaching process and assessment. *Journal of Higher Education Research*, *4*(2), 52. DOI: 10.32629/jher.v4i2.1188

Duncanson, J. (2024). Supporting L2 Writing Using QuillBot. *Gatesol Journal*, *33*(1), 30–36. DOI: 10.52242/gatesol.195

Dupps, W. J. (2023). Artificial intelligence and academic publishing. *Journal of Cataract and Refractive Surgery*, *49*(7), 655–656. DOI: 10.1097/j.jcrs.0000000000001223 PMID: 37390321

Ecclestone, K., Biesta, G., & Hughes, M. (2010). *Transitions and learning through the life course*. Routledge London.

Eguchi, A., Okada, H., & Muto, Y. (2021). Contextualizing AI Education for K-12 Students to Enhance Their Learning of AI Literacy Through Culturally Responsive Approaches. *Ki - Künstliche Intelligenz*, *35*(2), 153–161. DOI: 10.1007/s13218-021-00737-3

Elam, M. (2023). Poetry Will Not Optimize; or, What Is Literature to AI? *American Literature*, *95*(2), 281–303. DOI: 10.1215/00029831-10575077

Elkhatat, A. M., Elsaid, K., & Almeer, S. (2023). Evaluating the efficacy of AI content detection tools in differentiating between human and AI-generated text. *International Journal for Educational Integrity*, *19*(1), 17. DOI: 10.1007/s40979-023-00140-5

Ellikkal, A. & Rajamohan, S. (2024). AI-enabled personalized learning: empowering management students for improving engagement and academic performance. Vilakshan-XIMB Journal of Management. emerald.com

Elmorsy, G. (2024). Using Generative AI Tools to Improve Children's Story Production Skills in Early Childhood: Suggested Standards. *Scientific Journal of King Faisal University: Humanities and Management Sciences*. https://doi.org/https://doi.org/10.37575/h/edu/230043

El-Rashidy, M. A., Mohamed, R. G., El-Fishawy, N. A., & Shouman, M. A. (2022). Reliable plagiarism detection system based on deep learning approaches. *Neural Computing & Applications*, *34*(21), 18837–18858. DOI: 10.1007/s00521-022-07486-w

Enholm, I. M., Papagiannidis, E., Mikalef, P., & Krogstie, J. (2022). Artificial intelligence and business value: A literature review. *Information Systems Frontiers*, *24*(5), 1709–1734. DOI: 10.1007/s10796-021-10186-w

Erbas, İ., Çipuri, R., & Joni, A. (2021). The impact of technology on teaching and teaching English to elementary school students. *Linguistics and Culture Review*, 1316–1336.

Erler, A. (2023). Publish with AUTOGEN or Perish? Some Pitfalls to Avoid in the Pursuit of Academic Enhancement via Personalized Large Language Models. *The American Journal of Bioethics*, *23*(10), 94–96. DOI: 10.1080/15265161.2023.2250291 PMID: 37812096

Esling, P., & Devis, N. (2020). Creativity in the era of artificial intelligence. *ArXiv, abs/2008.05959*.

Eslit, E. R. (2023). Thriving Beyond the Crisis: Teachers' Reflections on Literature and Language Education in the Era of Artificial Intelligence (AI) and Globalization. *International Journal of Education and Teaching*, *3*(1), 46–57. DOI: 10.51483/IJEDT.3.1.2023.46-57

Evers, K., & Chen, S. (2022). Effects of an automatic speech recognition system with peer feedback on pronunciation instruction for adults. [HTML]. *Computer Assisted Language Learning*, *35*(8), 1869–1889. DOI: 10.1080/09588221.2020.1839504

Ezzaim, A., Dahbi, A., Aqqal, A., & Haidine, A. (2024). AI-based learning style detection in adaptive learning systems: A systematic literature review. [HTML]. *Journal of Computers in Education*, •••, 1–39. DOI: 10.1007/s40692-024-00328-9

Fadhilah, N., Dewi, H., & Winata, W. (2020). Creativity of Creation and Story-Telling in Open-Ended Learning with Visual Art Media for Early Childhood Education. *Proceedings of the 2nd International Conference on Arts and Design Education (ICADE 2019)*. https://doi.org/https://doi.org/10.2991/assehr.k.200321.010

Faragher, R., Chen, M., Miranda, L., Poon, K., Rumiati, , Chang, F.-R., & Chen, H. (2021). Inclusive education in Asia: Insights from some country case studies. [wiley.com]. *Journal of Policy and Practice in Intellectual Disabilities*, *18*(1), 23–35. DOI: 10.1111/jppi.12369

Farooqi, M.T., Amanat, I., & Awan, S.M. (2024). Ethical Considerations and Challenges in the Integration of Artificial Intelligence in Education: A Systematic Review. *Journal of Excellence in Management Sciences*.

Fattah, H. A., Vadivel, B., Shaban, A. A., & Shanmugam, K. (2023). Enhancing English Language Education: The Impact of AI Integration in the Classroom. *The Journal of Humanistic Education and Development*, *5*(6), 116–123. DOI: 10.22161/jhed.5.6.15

Feng, Y., & Wang, X. (2023). A comparative study on the development of Chinese and English abilities of Chinese primary school students through two bilingual reading modes: human-AI robot interaction and paper books. *Frontiers in Psychology*, *14*, 1200675. https://doi.org/https://doi.org/10.3389/fpsyg.2023.1200675. DOI: 10.3389/fpsyg.2023.1200675 PMID: 37860299

Ferk Savec, V., & Jedrinović, S. (2024). The Role of AI Implementation in Higher Education in Achieving the Sustainable Development Goals: A Case Study from Slovenia. *Sustainability (Basel)*, *17*(1), 183. DOI: 10.3390/su17010183

Fitria, T. N. (2021). Grammarly as AI-powered English Writing Assistant: Students' Alternative for Writing English. *Metathesis Journal of English Language Literature and Teaching*, *5*(1), 65. DOI: 10.31002/metathesis.v5i1.3519

Foka, A., & Griffin, G. (2024). AI, Cultural Heritage, and Bias: Some Key Queries That Arise from the Use of GenAI. *Heritage*, *7*(11), 6125–6136. DOI: 10.3390/heritage7110287

Fraidan, A. A. (2024). Integrating AI-Powered Library Systems to Enhance Research and Learning in English Language Departments: A Case Study of Faculty and Student Perceptions. *Library Progress International*, *44*(3), 12058–12065.

Franta, A., & Silver, S. (2024). Sentiment Analysis and the Sentimental Novel. *Critical Inquiry*, *50*(3), 402–424. DOI: 10.1086/728948

Fuchs, K., & Aguilos, V. (2023). Integrating Artificial Intelligence in Higher Education: Empirical Insights from Students about Using ChatGPT. *International Journal of Information and Education Technology (IJIET)*, *13*(9), 1365–1371. DOI: 10.18178/ijiet.2023.13.9.1939

Ganguly, D. (2020). The Global Novel: Comparative Perspectives Introduction. *New Literary History*, *51*(2), v–xviii. DOI: 10.1353/nlh.2020.0028

Ganuza, N., & Hedman, C. (2019). The Impact of Mother Tongue Instruction on the Development of Biliteracy: Evidence from Somali–Swedish Bilinguals. *Applied Linguistics*, *40*(1), 108–131. https://doi.org/https://doi.org/10.1093/APPLIN/AMX010. DOI: 10.1093/applin/amx010

Garcia, M., Rodriguez, F., & Martinez, E. (2024). The impact of an AI-powered adaptive language system on student motivation and proficiency gains: A large-scale study. *Computers & Education*, *190*, 104635.

Ge, L., Agrawal, R., Singer, M., Kannapiran, P., De Castro Molina, J. A., Teow, K. L., Yap, C. W., & Abisheganaden, J. A. (2024). Leveraging artificial intelligence to enhance systematic reviews in health research: Advanced tools and challenges. *Systematic Reviews*, *13*(1), 269. DOI: 10.1186/s13643-024-02682-2 PMID: 39456077

Gerlich, M. (2025). AI Tools in Society: Impacts on Cognitive Offloading and the Future of Critical Thinking. *Societies (Basel, Switzerland)*, *15*(1), 6. DOI: 10.3390/soc15010006

Ghanbari, N. & Nowroozi, S. (2021). The practice of online assessment in an EFL context amidst COVID-19 pandemic: Views from teachers. Language Testing in Asia. springer.com

Ghio, A. (2024). Democratizing academic research with Artificial Intelligence: The misleading case of language. *Critical Perspectives on Accounting*, *98*, 102687. DOI: 10.1016/j.cpa.2023.102687

Ghosh, S., Venkit, P., Gautam, S., Wilson, S., & Caliskan, A. (2024). Do Generative AI Models Output Harm while Representing Non-Western Cultures: Evidence from A Community-Centered Approach. *ArXiv*. https://doi.org/https://doi.org/10.48550/arXiv.2407.14779

Gianitsos, E., Bolt, T., Chaudhuri, P., & Dexter, J. (2019). Stylometric Classification of Ancient Greek Literary Texts by Genre. *Proceedings of the 3rd Joint SIGHUM Workshop on Computational Linguistics for Cultural Heritage, Social Sciences, Humanities and Literature*, 52–60. DOI: 10.18653/v1/W19-2507

Gill, K. S. (2020). Strange affair of man with the machine. *AI & Society*, *35*(4), 777–782. DOI: 10.1007/s00146-020-01078-9 PMID: 33071473

Goleman, D. (2005). *Emotional intelligence: Why it can matter more than IQ*. Bantam.

Golwalker, A. (2024). Narration with Graphics: An AI Generated Story Teller. *Interantional Journal of Scientific Research in Engineering and Management*. https://doi.org/https://doi.org/10.55041/ijsrem32119

Gralha, J. G., & Pimentel, A. S. (2024). Gotcha GPT: Ensuring the Integrity in Academic Writing. *Journal of Chemical Information and Modeling*, *64*(21), 8091–8097. DOI: 10.1021/acs.jcim.4c01203 PMID: 39438283

Gruenhagen, J. H., Sinclair, P. M., Carroll, J., Baker, P. R. A., Wilson, A., & Demant, D. (2024). Computers and Education : Artificial Intelligence The rapid rise of generative AI and its implications for academic integrity: Students ' perceptions and use of chatbots for assistance with assessments. *Computers and Education: Artificial Intelligence, 7*(November 2023), 100273. https://doi.org/DOI: 10.1016/j.caeai.2024.100273

Guimarães, U., Schizzi, J., & Fernandes, D. (2022). Learning Difficulties and Disorders - A Psychopedagogical Approach. *Revista Científica Multidisciplinar*. https://doi.org/https://doi.org/10.47820/recima21.v3i10.2026

Gültekin Talayhan, Ö., & Babayiğit, M. V. (2023). The Influence of AI Writing Tools on the Content and Organization of Students' Writing : A Focus on EFL Instructors' Perceptions T. *Current Debates in Social Sciences*, *6*(2), 83–93. DOI: 10.29228/cudes.71701

Guo, Y., & Wang, Y. (2024). Exploring the Effects of Artificial Intelligence Application on EFL Students' Academic Engagement and Emotional Experiences: A Mixed-Methods Study. *European Journal of Education*, *12812*. Advance online publication. DOI: 10.1111/ejed.12812

Gupta, D. P. (2024). Navigating the Future of Education: The Impact of Artificial Intelligence on Teacher-Student Dynamics. *Eatp*, 6006–6013. DOI: 10.53555/kuey.v30i4.2332

Hamamra, B., Mayaleh, A., & Khlaif, Z. N. (2024). Between tech and text: The use of generative AI in Palestinian universities - a ChatGPT case study. *Cogent Education*, *11*(1), 2380622. DOI: 10.1080/2331186X.2024.2380622

Han, S. (2021). AI, culture industries and entertainment.

Han, A., Zhou, X., Cai, Z., Han, S., Ko, R., Corrigan, S., & Peppler, K. A. (2024). Teachers, Parents, and Students' perspectives on Integrating Generative AI into Elementary Literacy Education. *Proceedings of the CHI Conference on Human Factors in Computing Systems*, 1–17. DOI: 10.1145/3613904.3642438

Hazari, S. (2024). Justification and Roadmap for Artificial Intelligence (AI) Literacy Courses in Higher Education. *Journal of Educational Research and Practice*. https://doi.org/https://doi.org/10.5590/jerap.2024.14.1.07

Hockly, N. (2023). Artificial intelligence in English language teaching: The good, the bad and the ugly. *RELC Journal*, *54*(2), 445–451. DOI: 10.1177/00336882231168504

Holmes, W., Porayska-Pomsta, K., Holstein, K., Sutherland, E., Baker, T. T., Shum, S. B., Santos, O. C., Rodrigo, M. M. T., Cukurova, M., Bittencourt, I. I., & Koedinger, K. R. (2021). Ethics of AI in Education: Towards a Community-Wide Framework. *International Journal of Artificial Intelligence in Education*, *32*(3), 504–526. DOI: 10.1007/s40593-021-00239-1

Horváthová, I. (2022). Social-emotional development to learners in primary level of education through "reading" wordless picture books. *Ducational Role of Language Journal*. https://doi.org/https://doi.org/10.36534/erlj.2022.01.03

Hosseinalipour, A., & Ghanbarzadeh, R. (2023). A novel metaheuristic optimisation approach for text sentiment analysis. *International Journal of Machine Learning and Cybernetics*, *14*(3), 889–909. DOI: 10.1007/s13042-022-01670-z

Hoter, E., Yazbak Abu Ahmad, M., & Azulay, H. (2024). Enhancing Language Learning and Intergroup Empathy through Multi-User Interactions and Simulations in a Virtual World. Virtual Worlds. mdpi.com

Hou, X., Omar, N., & Wang, J. (2022). Interactive Design Psychology and Artificial Intelligence-Based Innovative Exploration of Anglo-American Traumatic Narrative Literature. *Frontiers in Psychology*, *12*, 755039. Advance online publication. DOI: 10.3389/fpsyg.2021.755039 PMID: 35222140

Hou, Z. (2021). Research on adopting artificial intelligence technology to improve effectiveness of vocational college English learning. *Journal of Physics: Conference Series*, *1744*(4), 42122. DOI: 10.1088/1742-6596/1744/4/042122

Huang, L. (2023). Ethics of Artificial Intelligence in Education: Student Privacy and Data Protection. *Science Insights Education Frontiers*. https://doi.org/https://doi.org/10.15354/sief.23.re202

Hu, L., Li, D., Liu, H., Chen, X., Gao, Y., Huang, S., Peng, X., Zhang, X., Bai, X., Yang, H., Kong, L., Tang, J., Lu, P., Xiong, C., & Liang, H. (2024). Enhancing fairness in AI-enabled medical systems with the attribute neutral framework. *Nature Communications*, *15*(1), 8767. DOI: 10.1038/s41467-024-52930-1 PMID: 39384748

Hussain, S. A., Bresnahan, M., & Zhuang, J. (2025). The bias algorithm: How AI in healthcare exacerbates ethnic and racial disparities – a scoping review. *Ethnicity & Health*, *30*(2), 197–214. DOI: 10.1080/13557858.2024.2422848 PMID: 39488857

Hussein, M., Hassan, H., & Nassef, M. (2019). Automated Language Essay Scoring Systems: A Literature Review. *PeerJ. Computer Science*, *5*, e208. DOI: 10.7717/peerj-cs.208 PMID: 33816861

Hutson, J., Jeevanjee, T., Graaf, V. V., Lively, J., Weber, J., Weir, G., Arnone, K., Carnes, G., Vosevich, K., Plate, D., Leary, M., & Edele, S. (2022). Artificial Intelligence and the Disruption of Higher Education: Strategies for Integrations across Disciplines. *Creative Education*, *13*(12), 3953–3980. DOI: 10.4236/ce.2022.1312253

Imran, M. C., Khaliq Bashar, Budiarti Putri Uleng, Nina Ariani, Sukmawati, Suharti Siradjuddin, Sujarwo, & Irman. (2022). The Impact of Computer Assisted Language Learning (CALL) Technology on Indonesian Learners' Speaking Skills. *IJOLEH : International Journal of Education and Humanities*, *1*(2), 183–189. DOI: 10.56314/ijoleh.v1i2.83

Isnaniah, I., Ramalia, T., Viona, I., Luthfiyandini, L., & Belina, T. (2024). Unlocking Young Minds: The Power of Storytelling in Teaching English for Young Learners. *Primacy Journal of English Education and Literacy*. https://doi.org/https://doi.org/10.33592/primacy.v3i1.5031

Jakesch, M., Hancock, J., & Naaman, M. (2022). Human heuristics for AI-generated language are flawed. *Proceedings of the National Academy of Sciences of the United States of America*, *120*, •••. https://doi.org/https://doi.org/10.1073/pnas.2208839120 PMID: 36881628

Jarrahi, M. (2018). Artificial intelligence and the future of work: Human-AI symbiosis in organizational decision making. *Business Horizons*. https://doi.org/https://doi.org/10.1016/J.BUSHOR.2018.03.007

Jauhiainen, J., & Guerra, A. (2023). Generative AI and ChatGPT in School Children's Education: Evidence from a School Lesson. *Sustainability*. https://doi.org/https://doi.org/10.3390/su151814025

Javed, F. (2024). The Evolution of Artificial Intelligence in Teaching and Learning of English Language in Higher Education: Challenges, Risks, and Ethical Considerations. In The Evolution of Artificial Intelligence in Higher Education: Challenges, Risks, and Ethical Considerations (pp. 249-276). Emerald Publishing Limited. [HTML]

Jazbec, S. Š., & Kacjan, B. (2019). "Multilingualism Is the Real Thing": Multilingualism From the Parents' Perspective. *The New Educational Review*, *57*(3), 87–98. DOI: 10.15804/tner.19.57.3.07

Jensen, L. X., Buhl, A., Sharma, A., & Bearman, M. (2025). Generative AI and higher education: A review of claims from the first months of ChatGPT. *Higher Education*, *89*(4), 1145–1161. DOI: 10.1007/s10734-024-01265-3

Jiang, D., Pei, Y., Yang, G., & Wang, X. (2022). Research and Analysis on the Integration of Artificial Intelligence in College English Teaching. *Mathematical Problems in Engineering*, *2022*, 1–8. DOI: 10.1155/2022/3997573

Jockers, M. L. (2013). *Macroanalysis: Digital methods and literary history*. University of Illinois Press. DOI: 10.5406/illinois/9780252037528.001.0001

Jones, N. (2022). Experiential Literature? Comparing the Work of AI and Human Authors. *APRIA Journal*, *5*(5), 41–57. DOI: 10.37198/APRIA.04.05.a5

Joseph, A., & Eapen, N. G. (2023). Conversational agents and chatbots: current trends. In *Machine Learning and Deep Learning in Natural Language Processing* (pp. 17–52). CRC Press. [HTML] DOI: 10.1201/9781003296126-4

Kadaruddin, K. (2023). Empowering Education through Generative AI: Innovative Instructional Strategies for Tomorrow's Learners. *International Journal of Business, Law, and Education*.

Kalantzis, M., & Cope, B. (2024). Literacy in the Time of Artificial Intelligence. *Reading Research Quarterly*. https://doi.org/https://doi.org/10.1002/rrq.591

Kaltenbrunner, W. (2015). Scholarly Labour and Digital Collaboration in Literary Studies. *Social Epistemology*, *29*(2), 207–233. DOI: 10.1080/02691728.2014.907834

Karabayeva, I., & Kalizhanova, A. (2024). Evaluating Machine Translation of Literature Through Rhetorical Analysis. *Journal of Translation and Language Studies*, *5*(1), 1–9. DOI: 10.48185/jtls.v5i1.962

Karadoğan, A. (2023). A Bridge Between Technology and Creativity: Story Writing with Artificial Intelligence. *İnsan ve Sosyal Bilimler Dergisi*. https://doi.org/https://doi.org/10.53048/johass.1368950

Kara, S. (2018). Blended learning: A model to enhance engagement in reading class. *Abant İzzet Baysal Üniversitesi Eğitim Fakültesi Dergisi*, *18*(2), 953–970. DOI: 10.17240/aibuefd.2018..-431467

Karataş, F., Abedi, F. Y., Ozek Gunyel, F., Karadeniz, D., & Kuzgun, Y. (2024). Incorporating AI in foreign language education: An investigation into ChatGPT's effect on foreign language learners. *Education and Information Technologies*, *29*(15), 19343–19366. DOI: 10.1007/s10639-024-12574-6

Kasih, E. N. E. W., Suprayogi, S., Indriyanto, K., Amarudin, A., & Putra, A. V. L. (2024). Artificial Intelligence for Literature Class : Trends and Attitude. *10th International Conference on Education and Technology (ICET)*, 142–148. https://doi.org/DOI: 10.1109/ICET64717.2024.10778422

Kasneci, E., Seßler, K., Küchemann, S., Bannert, M., Dementieva, D., Fischer, F., Gasser, U., Groh, G. L., Günnemann, S., Hüllermeier, E., Krusche, S., Kutyniok, G., Michaeli, T., Nerdel, C., Pfeffer, J., Poquet, O., Sailer, M., Schmidt, A., Seidel, T., & Kasneci, G. (2023). ChatGPT for good? On opportunities and challenges of large language models for education. *Learning and Individual Differences*, *103*, 102274. DOI: 10.1016/j.lindif.2023.102274

Kato, M. (2016). Humanistic Traditions, East and West: Convergence and divergence. *Educational Philosophy and Theory*, *48*(1), 23–35. DOI: 10.1080/00131857.2015.1084216

Kelly, C. J., Karthikesalingam, A., Suleyman, M., Corrado, G., & King, D. (2019). Key challenges for delivering clinical impact with artificial intelligence. *BMC Medicine*, *17*(1), 195. DOI: 10.1186/s12916-019-1426-2 PMID: 31665002

Khademi, A. (2023). Can ChatGPT and Bard Generate Aligned Assessment Items? A Reliability Analysis against Human Performance. *ArXiv, abs/2304.05372*.

Khalifa, M., & Albadawy, M. (2024). Using artificial intelligence in academic writing and research: An essential productivity tool. *Computer Methods and Programs in Biomedicine Update*, *5*, 100145. DOI: 10.1016/j.cmpbup.2024.100145

Khan, W., Daud, A., Khan, K., Muhammad, S., & Haq, R. (2023). Exploring the frontiers of deep learning and natural language processing: A comprehensive overview of key challenges and emerging trends. [sciencedirect.com]. *Natural Language Processing Journal*, *4*, 100026. DOI: 10.1016/j.nlp.2023.100026

Khoirunnisak, E., Fatirul, A., & Harwanto. (2024). How Educational Flipbooks and Learning Motivation Affect Early Reading Proficiency in First-Grade Kindergarteners. *Jurnal Komunikasi Pendidikan*. https://doi.org/https://doi.org/10.32585/jurnalkomdik.v8i2.5292

Kholis, A. (2021). Elsa Speak App: Automatic Speech Recognition (ASR) for Supplementing English Pronunciation Skills. *Pedagogy Journal of English Language Teaching*, *9*(1), 1. DOI: 10.32332/joelt.v9i1.2723

Kholodniak, O. (2023). Comparative literary theory: A cross-cultural approach to English literature. *Research Journal in Advanced Humanities*, *4*(4). Advance online publication. DOI: 10.58256/rjah.v4i4.1317

Khosrow-Pour, M. (2008). *Encyclopedia of information science and technology* (Vol. 1). Igi Global.

Khurma, O. A., Albahti, F., Ali, N., & Bustanji, A. (2024). AI ChatGPT and student engagement : Unraveling dimensions through PRISMA analysis for enhanced learning experiences. *Contemporary Educational Technology*, *16*(2), 1–22. DOI: 10.30935/cedtech/14334

Kim, J., Haddadian, G., & Kim, M. K. (2023). An Investigation of Knowledge-Based AI vs. Human Evaluation in the Context of Academic Summary Evaluation: Similarities, Dissimilarities, and Being Toward Mutual Understandings. *Proceedings of the 17th International Conference of the Learning Sciences - ICLS 2023*.

Kim, N., & Kim, M. K. (2022). Teacher's Perceptions of Using an Artificial Intelligence-Based Educational Tool for Scientific Writing. *Frontiers in Education*, *7*, 755914. Advance online publication. DOI: 10.3389/feduc.2022.755914

Kitcharoen, P., Howimanporn, S., & Chookaew, S. (2024). Enhancing Teachers' AI Competencies Through Artificial Intelligence of Things Professional Development Training. *International Journal of Interactive Mobile Technologies (Ijim)*, *18*(02), 4–15. DOI: 10.3991/ijim.v18i02.46613

Klimova, B., & Chen, J. (2024). The Impact of AI on Enhancing Students' Intercultural Communication Competence at the University Level: A Review Study. *Language Teaching Research Quarterly*. https://doi.org/https://doi.org/10.32038/ltrq.2024.43.06

Klimova, B., & Pikhart, M. (2025). Exploring the effects of artificial intelligence on student and academic well-being in higher education: A mini-review. *Frontiers in Psychology*, *16*, 1498132. DOI: 10.3389/fpsyg.2025.1498132 PMID: 39963679

Klimova, B., Pikhart, M., Benites, A. D., Lehr, C., & Sanchez-Stockhammer, C. (2023). Neural machine translation in foreign language teaching and learning: A systematic review. [HTML]. *Education and Information Technologies*, *28*(1), 663–682. DOI: 10.1007/s10639-022-11194-2

Klopfer, E. (2008). *Augmented learning: Research and design of mobile educational games*. MIT Press. DOI: 10.7551/mitpress/9780262113151.001.0001

Kooli, C., & Yusuf, N. (2024). Transforming Educational Assessment: Insights Into the Use of ChatGPT and Large Language Models in Grading. *International Journal of Human-Computer Interaction*, 1–12. DOI: 10.1080/10447318.2024.2338330

Kruk, M. & Kałużna, A. (2025). Investigating the Role of AI Tools in Enhancing Translation Skills, Emotional Experiences, and Motivation in L2 Learning. European Journal of Education. [HTML]

Kuddus, K. (2022). Artificial intelligence in language learning: Practices and prospects. Advanced analytics and deep learning models. [HTML]

Kujundziski, A. P., & Bojadjiev, J. (2025). Artificial Intelligence in Education: Transforming Learning Landscapes. In Reimagining Intelligent Computer-Assisted Language Education (pp. 1-54). IGI Global. [HTML]

Kukulska-Hulme, A., & Shield, L. (2008a). An overview of mobile assisted language learning: From content delivery to supported collaboration and interaction. *ReCALL*, *20*(3), 271–289. DOI: 10.1017/S0958344008000335

Kumar Pandey, A., & Sekhar Roy, S. (2024). Extractive Question Answering Over Ancient Scriptures Texts Using Generative AI and Natural Language Processing Techniques. *IEEE Access : Practical Innovations, Open Solutions*, *12*, 101197–101209. DOI: 10.1109/ACCESS.2024.3431282

Kumar, A., Bhoyar, S., & Mishra, A. (2024). Does ChatGPT foster academic misconduct in the future? *Public Administration and Policy*. https://doi.org/https://doi.org/10.1108/pap-05-2023-0061

Kunjumuhammed, S. K. (2024). Artificial Intelligence in Addressing Educational Inequality Dimensions in Higher Education Institutions (HEIs): A Critical Review. Risks and Challenges of AI-Driven Finance: Bias, Ethics, and Security, 146-164. [HTML]

Kurtz, G., Amzalag, M., Shaked, N., Zaguri, Y., Kohen-Vacs, D., Gal, E., Zailer, G., & Barak-Medina, E. (2024). Strategies for Integrating Generative AI into Higher Education: Navigating Challenges and Leveraging Opportunities. *Education Sciences*, *14*(5), 503. DOI: 10.3390/educsci14050503

Kusmiatun, A., Efendi, D., Pansori, M., Judijanto, L., Sariasih, Y., & Saddhono, K. (2024). The Power of AI in Generating Novel Based and Impactful Character Development for Fiction Story. *2024 4th International Conference on Advance Computing and Innovative Technologies in Engineering (ICACITE)*, 1555–1561. https://doi.org/https://doi.org/10.1109/ICACITE60783.2024.10616700

Lai, Y. (2023). The Impact of AI-Driven Narrative Generation, Exemplified by ChatGPT, on the Preservation of Human Creative Originality and Uniqueness. *Lecture Notes in Education Psychology and Public Media*, *26*(1), 121–124. DOI: 10.54254/2753-7048/26/20230865

Lameras, P. & Arnab, S. (2021). Power to the teachers: an exploratory review on artificial intelligence in education. Information. mdpi.com

Lavin, S. R. (2019). *Towards a useful conception of the ZPD for language education*. https://doi.org/https://doi.org/10.33422/2nd.2nd.icate.2019.12.840

Leavy, P. (2017). *Research design: Quantitative, qualitative, mixed methods, arts-based and community-based participatory research approaches*. The Guilford Press.

LeClerc, T. (2024). Writing sensitively: Defining sensitivity in the literary sphere. *New Writing*, *21*(3), 288–298. DOI: 10.1080/14790726.2024.2325996

Lee, D., Kim, H.-H., & Sung, S.-H. (2022). Development Research on an AI English Learning Support System to Facilitate Learner-Generated-Context-Based Learning. *Educational Technology Research and Development*, *71*(2), 629–666. DOI: 10.1007/s11423-022-10172-2 PMID: 36533222

Lee, J., Shin, D., & Noh, W. (2023). Artificial Intelligence-Based Content Generator Technology for Young English-as-a-Foreign-Language Learners' Reading Enjoyment. *RELC Journal*, *54*(2), 508–516. https://doi.org/https://doi.org/10.1177/00336882231165060. DOI: 10.1177/00336882231165060

Lee, M. H., Siewiorek, D. P., Smailagic, A., Bernardino, A., & Badia, S. B. (2021). A Human-AI Collaborative Approach for Clinical Decision Making on Rehabilitation Assessment. *Proceedings of the 2021 CHI Conference on Human Factors in Computing Systems*. DOI: 10.1145/3411764.3445472

Lee, S., & Kim, B. (2024). Immediate versus delayed AI feedback on pronunciation: An empirical study. *Language Learning & Technology*, *28*(1), 45–60.

Levy, M., & Stockwell, G. (2013). *CALL dimensions: Options and issues in computer-assisted language learning*. Routledge. DOI: 10.4324/9780203708200

Li, Z. (2024). The shadow of the algorithm: the ethical blind spot of artificial intelligence education. *Journal of Education, Humanities and Social Sciences.*

Liao, X., Zhang, X., Wang, Z., & Luo, H. (2024). Design and implementation of an AI-enabled visual report tool as formative assessment to promote learning achievement and self-regulated learning: An experimental study. [HTML]. *British Journal of Educational Technology*, *55*(3), 1253–1276. DOI: 10.1111/bjet.13424

Li, B., Jiang, J., Ma, L., Huang, Y., & Wu, X. (2024). Mitigating university students' reliance on ChatGPT. In *Proceedings of the 2024 8th International Seminar on Education, Management and Social Sciences (ISEMSS 2024)* (pp. 245–251). Atlantis Press. https://doi.org/DOI: 10.2991/978-2-38476-297-2_31

Li, K. C., & Wong, B. (2023). Artificial Intelligence in Personalised Learning: A Bibliometric Analysis. *Interactive Technology and Smart Education*, *20*(3), 422–445. DOI: 10.1108/ITSE-01-2023-0007

Lin, C. C., Huang, A. Y. Q., & Lu, O. H. T. (2023). Artificial intelligence in intelligent tutoring systems toward sustainable education: a systematic review. Smart Learning Environments. springer.com

Lin, S., & Crosthwaite, P. (2024). The grass is not always greener: Teacher vs. GPT-assisted written corrective feedback. *System*, *127*, 103529. DOI: 10.1016/j.system.2024.103529

Liu, Q. & Khalil, M. (2023). Understanding privacy and data protection issues in learning analytics using a systematic review. British Journal of Educational Technology. wiley.com

Liu, L. (2024). Impact of AI gamification on EFL learning outcomes and nonlinear dynamic motivation: Comparing adaptive learning paths, conversational agents, and storytelling. [HTML]. *Education and Information Technologies.*

Liu, S., Liu, C., & Lang, C. (2024). Consumer Engagement in Fashion Circularity in China: Exploring Consumer Online Fashion Resale through the Lens of Social Practice Theory. *Sustainability (Basel)*, *16*(11), 4733. DOI: 10.3390/su16114733

Liu, W., & Wang, Y. (2024). The Effects of Using AI Tools on Critical Thinking in English Literature Classes Among EFL Learners: An Intervention Study. *European Journal of Education*, *59*(October), 1–12. DOI: 10.1111/ejed.12804

Lo, K., Chang, J. C., Head, A., Bragg, J., Zhang, A. X., Trier, C., Anastasiades, C., August, T., Authur, R., Bragg, D., Bransom, E., Cachola, I., Candra, S., Chandrasekhar, Y., Chen, Y.-S., Cheng, E. Y.-Y., Chou, Y., Downey, D., Evans, R., & Weld, D. S. (2024). The Semantic Reader Project. *Communications of the ACM*, *67*(10), 50–61. DOI: 10.1145/3659096

Longo, L., Brcic, M., Cabitza, F., Choi, J., Confalonieri, R., Del Ser, J., Guidotti, R., Hayashi, Y., Herrera, F., Holzinger, A., Jiang, R., Khosravi, H., Lecue, F., Malgieri, G., Páez, A., Samek, W., Schneider, J., Speith, T., & Stumpf, S. (2024). Explainable Artificial Intelligence (XAI) 2.0: A manifesto of open challenges and interdisciplinary research directions. *Information Fusion*, *106*, 102301. DOI: 10.1016/j.inffus.2024.102301

López-Meneses, E., Mellado-Moreno, P. C., Gallardo Herrerías, C., & Pelícano-Piris, N. (2025). Educational Data Mining and Predictive Modeling in the Age of Artificial Intelligence: An In-Depth Analysis of Research Dynamics. [mdpi.com]. *Computers*, *14*(2), 68. DOI: 10.3390/computers14020068

Lottu, O. A., Jacks, B. S., Ajala, O. A., & Okafor, E. S. (2024). Towards a conceptual framework for ethical AI development in IT systems. *World Journal of Advanced Research and Reviews*, *21*(3), 408–415.

Loughland, T. (2019). Adaptive Teaching for Students' Critical and Creative Thinking. *Teacher Adaptive Practices*. https://doi.org/https://doi.org/10.1007/978-981-13-6858-5_1

Lukman, R. A., & Aisy, R. (2023). Problematika penggunaan Artificial Intelligence (AI) untuk pembelajaran di kalangan mahasiswa STIT Pemalang. *Jurnal Madaniyah*, *13*(2), 242–255. DOI: 10.58410/madaniyah.v13i2.826

Luo, J. (2024). Research on Reconstruction and Cultural Inheritance of Ancient Literature under Digital Expression. *Applied Mathematics and Nonlinear Sciences*, *9*(1), 20242591. DOI: 10.2478/amns-2024-2591

Luo, Y. (2024). Innovative Research on AI-assisted Teaching Models for College English Listening and Speaking Courses. *Applied and Computational Engineering*, *69*(1), 155–160. DOI: 10.54254/2755-2721/69/20241493

Lu, R. S., Lin, H. C. K., Yang, Y. C., & Chen, Y. P. (2024). Integrating Urban Mining Concepts Through AI-Generated Storytelling and Visuals: Advancing Sustainability Education in Early Childhood. *Sustainability (Basel)*, *16*(24), 11304. Advance online publication. DOI: 10.3390/su162411304

Lyanda, J.N., Owidi, S., & Simiyu, A.M. (2024). Rethinking Higher Education Teaching and Assessment In-Line with AI Innovations: A Systematic Review and Meta-Analysis. *African Journal of Empirical Research.*

Mahamuni, D. A., Parminder, D., & Tonpe, D. S. (2024). Enhancing Educational Assessment with Artificial Intelligence: Challenges and Opportunities. *2024 International Conference on Knowledge Engineering and Communication Systems (ICKECS), 1*, 1-5. DOI: 10.1109/ICKECS61492.2024.10616620

Makeleni, S., Mutongoza, B. H., & Linake, M. A. (2023). Language Education and Artificial Intelligence: An Exploration of Challenges Confronting Academics in Global South Universities. *Journal of Culture and Values in Education, 6*(2), 158–171. DOI: 10.46303/jcve.2023.14

Malik, A. R., Pratiwi, Y., Andajani, K., Numertayasa, I. W., Suharti, S., Darwis, A., & Marzuki, . (2023). Exploring Artificial Intelligence in Academic Essay: Higher Education Student's Perspective. *International Journal of Educational Research Open, 5*, 100296. Advance online publication. DOI: 10.1016/j.ijedro.2023.100296

Marian, M., Borco i, I., Borco i, C.-A., Cusman, A., Toma, A., & Ionică, D. (2023). A Case Study on Extending the Use of Cloud-Based Services within two Romanian Higher-Education Institutions. *2023 22nd RoEduNet Conference: Networking in Education and Research (RoEduNet)*, 1–6. DOI: 10.1109/RoEduNet60162.2023.10274937

Markowitz, D., Hancock, J., & Bailenson, J. (2023). Linguistic Markers of Inherently False AI Communication and Intentionally False Human Communication: Evidence From Hotel Reviews. *Journal of Language and Social Psychology, 43*(1), 63–82. https://doi.org/https://doi.org/10.1177/0261927X231200201. DOI: 10.1177/0261927X231200201

Marzuki, W., Widiati, U., Rusdin, D., Darwin, , & Indrawati, I. (2023). The impact of AI writing tools on the content and organization of students' writing: EFL teachers' perspective. *Cogent Education, 10*(2), 1–17. DOI: 10.1080/2331186X.2023.2236469

Mastellotto, L. (2021). Developing Young Learners' Multiliteracies through Multimodal Storytelling. *Pathways to Plurilingual Education.* https://doi.org/https://doi.org/10.26493/978-961-7055-36-8.251-265

Matache, I.-C.The Impact of Ethics on the Quality of Higher Education Services. (2021). Ethics in academia: The impact of ethics on the quality of higher education services. *Perspective Politice, 14*(1-2), 77–84. DOI: 10.25019/perspol/21.14.6

Maureen, I., Van Der Meij, H., & De Jong, T. (2021). Evaluating storytelling activities for early literacy development. *International Journal of Early Years Education*, *30*(4), 679–696. https://doi.org/https://doi.org/10.1080/09669760.2021.193. DOI: 10.1080/09669760.2021.1933917

Mavidi, P. N. (2025). *Fluency Reimagined: AI and the Future of English Learning*. AI Applications for English Language Learning. [HTML] DOI: 10.4018/979-8-3693-9077-1.ch011

Mayer, R. E. (2009). *Multimedia Learning*. Cambridge University Press., https://doi.org/https://doi.org/10.1017/CBO9780511811678 DOI: 10.1017/CBO9780511811678

McBreen, M., & Savage, R. (2020). The Impact of Motivational Reading Instruction on the Reading Achievement and Motivation of Students: A Systematic Review and Meta-Analysis. *Educational Psychology Review*, *33*(3), 1125–1163. https://doi.org/https://doi.org/10.1007/s10648-020-09584-4. DOI: 10.1007/s10648-020-09584-4

McInnis-Dominguez, M. (2023). An AI Solution: Using ChatGPT to Counter Plagiarism and Boost Enrollments in Hispanic Literature Courses. *Middle Atlantic Review of Latin American Studies*, *7*(2), 127–182. DOI: 10.23870/marlas.444

Mehta, V., Thomas, V., & Mathur, A. (2024). AI-dependency in scientific writing. *Oral Oncology Reports*, *10*, 100269. DOI: 10.1016/j.oor.2024.100269

Mendes de Oliveira, M., Sporn, Z., Kliemann, L., Borschke, A., & Meyering, M. (2023). Online language learning and workplace communication: A study on Babbel's virtual-classroom solution. [tandfonline.com]. *Computer Assisted Language Learning*, *36*(8), 1501–1527. DOI: 10.1080/09588221.2021.2002364

Miller, W. (2024). Adapting to AI: Reimagining the Role of Assessment Professionals. *Intersection: A Journal at the Intersection of Assessment and Learning*.

Mishra, P. (2025). Revolutionizing Education With AI and ML. Internet of Behavior-Based Computational Intelligence for Smart Education Systems, 53-94. [HTML]

Mizumoto, A. & Eguchi, M. (2023). Exploring the potential of using an AI language model for automated essay scoring. Research Methods in Applied Linguistics. sciencedirect.com

Mohamed, A. M. (2024). Exploring the potential of an AI-based Chatbot (ChatGPT) in enhancing English as a Foreign Language (EFL) teaching: Perceptions of EFL Faculty Members. [HTML]. *Education and Information Technologies*, *29*(3), 3195–3217. DOI: 10.1007/s10639-023-11917-z

Moreno, R., & Mayer, R. (1999). Cognitive Principles of Multimedia Learning: The Role of Modality and Contiguity. *Journal of Educational Psychology*, *91*(2), 358–368. https://doi.org/https://doi.org/10.1037/0022-0663.91.2.358. DOI: 10.1037/0022-0663.91.2.358

Moretti, G., Sprugnoli, R., Menini, S., & Tonelli, S. (2016). ALCIDE: Extracting and visualising content from large document collections to support humanities studies. *Knowledge-Based Systems*, *111*, 100–112. DOI: 10.1016/j.knosys.2016.08.003

Mouboua, P. D.Patricia Diane MouboauaFadeke Adeola AtobateleOlateju Temitope Akintayo. (2024). Multilingual Education and Social Equity: A Comparative Study of Integration Policies in Multicultural Societies. *GSC Advanced Research and Reviews*, *19*(2), 32–42. DOI: 10.30574/gscarr.2024.19.2.0165

Moya, S., & Camacho, M. (2024). Computers and Education : Artificial Intelligence Leveraging AI-powered mobile learning : A pedagogically informed framework. *Computers and Education: Artificial Intelligence*, *7*(August), 1–12. DOI: 10.1016/j.caeai.2024.100276

Mulally, T. (2024). An Experiential Journey: A Year of a Professor Using AI in the Classroom and Research. International Journal of Studies in Education and Science.

Mustofa, A., & Hill, J. L. (2018). Understanding cultural context in responding to literature: Researching the teaching of literature in EFL classroom context. *English Language Teaching*, *11*(6), 108–115. DOI: 10.5539/elt.v11n6p108

Nadeem, M., Farag, W., & Helal, M. (2024). Rethinking Assessment Methodologies in the Era of Artificial Intelligence: Expanding Beyond ChatGPT's Scope. *2024 Mediterranean Smart Cities Conference (MSCC)*, 1-6. DOI: 10.1109/MSCC62288.2024.10697084

Nakamura, P., Molotsky, A., Zarzur, R., Ranjit, V., Haddad, Y., & De Hoop, T. (2023). Language of instruction in schools in low- and middle-income countries: A systematic review. *Campbell Systematic Reviews*, *19*, •••. https://doi.org/https://doi.org/10.1002/cl2.1351

Natsiuk, M., & Osidak, V. (2023). Multilingualism in Society and Education: The Ukrainian Context. *Ars Linguodidacticae*, *11*(11), 4–15. DOI: 10.17721/2663-0303.2023.1.01

Navaie, F., Panwar, K., & Asino, T. I. (2024). The impact of AI-based technology such as Chat-GPT on second language (L2) learners' academic writing. *Journal of Applied Instructional Design*, *13*(1), 259–262. DOI: 10.59668/1269.15645

Nazaretsky, T., Ariely, M., Cukurova, M., & Alexandron, G. (2022). Teachers' trust in AI-powered educational technology and a professional development program to improve it. [wiley.com]. *British Journal of Educational Technology, 53*(4), 914–931. DOI: 10.1111/bjet.13232

Ng, D. T. K., Leung, J. K. L., Su, J., Ng, R. C. W., & Chu, S. K. W. (2023). Teachers' AI digital competencies and twenty-first century skills in the post-pandemic world. *Educational Technology Research and Development, 71*(1), 137–161. DOI: 10.1007/s11423-023-10203-6 PMID: 36844361

Nikhil, V., Annamalai, R., & Jayapal, S. (2025). NLP-Driven Approaches to Automated Essay Grading and Feedback. In Adopting Artificial Intelligence Tools in Higher Education (pp. 99-117). CRC Press. [HTML]

Ning, B., Liu, F., & Liu, Z. (2023). Creativity Support in AI Co-creative Tools: Current Research, Challenges and Opportunities. 2023 26th International Conference on Computer Supported Cooperative Work in Design (CSCWD), 5–10. DOI: 10.1109/CSCWD57460.2023.10152832

Novita, D., Hamied, F., & Sukyadi, D. (2023). Effect of Culturally Familiar Text on Low-Proficiency Reader's Reading Comprehension. *NOBEL: Journal of Literature and Language Teaching*. https://doi.org/https://doi.org/10.15642/nobel.2023.14.1.115-132

Nsengiyumva, D. S., Oriikiriza, C., & Kalyango, S. (2021). Cross-Linguistic Transfer and Language Proficiency in the Multilingual Education System of Burundi: What Has the Existing Literature So Far Discovered? [Indonesian Journal of English Language Teaching and Applied Linguistics]. *Ijeltal, 5*(2), 387. DOI: 10.21093/ijeltal.v5i2.770

O'Cain, A., Fedoruk, B. D., Masri, Z., Frost, R. M., & Alahmar, A. (2023). A System for the Improvement of Educational Assessment Using Intelligent Conversational Agents. SSRN *Electronic Journal*. DOI: 10.2139/ssrn.4393234

Ogunsakin, I.B. (2024). Unlocking The Potential of Artificial Intellignce:. *International Journal of Research in STEM Education.*

Onderi, H. N. (2025). Artificial intelligence: Ethics and academic integrity in higher education. In Areba, G. N., Gisore, B. N., & Njurai, E. W. (Eds.), *Artificial intelligence, digital learning, and leadership: Redefining higher education* (p. 24). IGI Global., DOI: 10.4018/979-8-3373-0025-2.ch003

Onesi-Ozigagun, O. (2024). Revolutionizing Education Through Ai: A Comprehensive Review of Enhancing Learning Experiences. *International Journal of Applied Research in Social Sciences*, *6*(4), 589–607. DOI: 10.51594/ijarss.v6i4.1011

Orwig, W. W., Edenbaum, E. R., Greene, J. D., & Schacter, D. L. (2024). The Language of Creativity: Evidence from Humans and Large Language Models. *Journal of Creative Behavior*. https://doi.org/https://doi.org/10.1002/jocb.636

Ouyang, F., & Jiao, P. (2023). Artificial Intelligence in Education : The Three Paradigms. *Computers and Education: Artificial Intelligence, 2*(April 2021), 100020. https://doi.org/DOI: 10.1016/j.caeai.2021.100020

Ouyang, F., Wu, M., Zheng, L., Zhang, L., & Jiao, P. (2023). Integration of artificial intelligence performance prediction and learning analytics to improve student learning in online engineering course. [springer.com]. *International Journal of Educational Technology in Higher Education*, *20*(1), 4. DOI: 10.1186/s41239-022-00372-4 PMID: 36683653

Owan, V. J., Abang, K. B., Idika, D. O., Etta, E. O., & Bassey, B. A. (2023). Exploring the potential of artificial intelligence tools in educational measurement and assessment. *Eurasia Journal of Mathematics, Science and Technology Education*, *19*(8), em2307. DOI: 10.29333/ejmste/13428

Özdere, M. (2023). The Integration of Artificial Intelligence in English Education: Opportunities and Challenges. [LET Journal]. *Language Education & Technology*, *3*(2), 137–172.

Pack, A., & Maloney, J. (2024). Using Artificial Intelligence in TESOL: Some Ethical and Pedagogical Considerations. *TESOL Quarterly*. https://doi.org/https://doi.org/10.1002/tesq.3320

Pan, Y. (2024). Exploring the Subjectivity of English Academic Discourse in the Context of Big Data. *Applied Mathematics and Nonlinear Sciences*, *9*(1), 20240489. DOI: 10.2478/amns-2024-0489

Parker, J. L., Richard, V. M., Acabá, A., Escoffier, S., Flaherty, S., Jablonka, S., & Becker, K. P. (2024). Negotiating Meaning with Machines: AI's Role in Doctoral Writing Pedagogy. *International Journal of Artificial Intelligence in Education*. Advance online publication. DOI: 10.1007/s40593-024-00425-x

Pendy, B. (2023). Artificial Intelligence: The Future of Education. *Jurnal Indonesia Sosial Sains*, *2*(11), 2003–2012. DOI: 10.59141/jiss.v2i11.801

Pesovski, I., Santos, R., Henriques, R., & Trajkovik, V. (2024). Generative AI for Customizable Learning Experiences. *Sustainability (Basel)*, *16*(7), 3034. DOI: 10.3390/su16073034

Peters, U., & Carman, M. (2024). Cultural Bias in Explainable AI Research: A Systematic Analysis. *Journal of Artificial Intelligence Research*, *79*, 971–1000. https://doi.org/https://doi.org/10.1613/jair.1.14888. DOI: 10.1613/jair.1.14888

Pividori, M., & Greene, C. S. (2024). A publishing infrastructure for Artificial Intelligence (AI)-assisted academic authoring. *Journal of the American Medical Informatics Association : JAMIA*, *31*(9), 2103–2113. DOI: 10.1093/jamia/ocae139 PMID: 38879443

Polakova, P. & Klimova, B. (2024). Implementation of AI-driven technology into education–a pilot study on the use of chatbots in foreign language learning. Cogent education. tandfonline.com

Pramesty, N. S., Maghfiroh, A., & Mustikawati, D. A. (2022). Teachers ' Challanges in Teaching English to Young Learners in Rural Area at SDN 02 Sendang. *Jurnal Pendidikan*, 1–11.

Pujiani, T., Sukmawati, I. D., Bintang, A., & Pradana, A. (2023). Enriching EFL Classroom Activities with Online Games. *Conference on English Language Teaching*, 2023, *2023*, 65–83.

Putrawan, G. E., Mahpul, , Sinaga, T., Poh, S. K., & Dekhnich, O. V. (2022). Beliefs About Multilingualism With Respect to Translanguaging: A Survey Among Pre-Service EFL Teachers in Indonesia. *Integra Educativa*, *26*(4), 756–770. DOI: 10.15507/1991-9468.109.026.202204.756-770

Qu, S. (2024). A Thematic Analysis of English and American Literature Works Based on Text Mining and Sentiment Analysis. *Jes*, *20*(6s), 1575–1586. DOI: 10.52783/jes.3076

Ragolane, M., Patel, S., & Salikram, P. (2024). AI Versus Human Graders: Assessing the Role of Large Language Models in Higher Education. *Asian Journal of Education and Social Studies*.

Rainie, A. (2023). The Use of Digital Tools and Ai in Education. In *General Hospital Koprivnica* (Issue April). https://doi.org/DOI: 10.13140/RG.2.2.13438.87363

Rakya, Z. (2023). Exploring the Impact of Artificial Intelligence (AI) on Learner-Instructor Interaction in Online Learning (Literature Review). *International Journal of Emerging Multidisciplinaries: Computer Science & Artificial Intelligence*. https://doi.org/https://doi.org/10.54938/ijemdcsai.2023.02.1.236

Rane, N. L. (2023). Enhancing the Quality of Teaching and Learning through ChatGPT and Similar Large Language Models: Challenges, Future Prospects, and Ethical Considerations in Education. SSRN *Electronic Journal*. DOI: 10.2139/ssrn.4599104

Rane, N. L. (2024). *Enhancing the quality of teaching and learning through ChatGPT and similar large language models: Challenges, future prospects, and ethical considerations in education*. TESOL and Technology Studies.

Ratnasari, E., Nurhidayat, E., & Fakhruddin, A. (2019). Kahoot Application As Technology Resources in Teaching. [JELL]. *Journal of English Language Learning*, *2*(1), 1–6.

Ravichandran, K., Virgin, B. A., Patil, S., Fatma, G., Rengarajan, M., & Bala, B. K. (2024, July). Gamifying Language Learning: Applying Augmented Reality and Gamification Strategies for Enhanced English Language Acquisition. In *2024 Third International Conference on Smart Technologies and Systems for Next Generation Computing (ICSTSN)* (pp. 1-6). IEEE. [HTML] DOI: 10.1109/ICSTSN61422.2024.10670787

Redmond, P., Heffernan, A., Abawi, L., Brown, A., & Henderson, R. (2018). An Online Engagement Framework for Higher Education. *Online Learning : the Official Journal of the Online Learning Consortium*, *22*(1). Advance online publication. DOI: 10.24059/olj.v22i1.1175

Renacido, J. M. D., & Biray, E. T. (2025). Enhancing Peer Engagement and Student Motivation Through AI-Gamified Interactive Learning Tools. In Advancing Sustainable Development Goals With Educational Technology (pp. 277-342). IGI Global Scientific Publishing. [HTML]

Revell, T., Yeadon, W., Cahilly-Bretzin, G., Clarke, I., Manning, G., Jones, J., Mulley, C., Pascual, R. J., Bradley, N., Thomas, D., & Leneghan, F. (2024). ChatGPT versus human essayists: An exploration of the impact of artificial intelligence for authorship and academic integrity in the humanities. *International Journal for Educational Integrity*, *20*(1), 18. DOI: 10.1007/s40979-024-00161-8

Ritter, S., Anderson, J. R., Koedinger, K. R., & Corbett, A. (2007). Cognitive Tutor: Applied research in mathematics education. *Psychonomic Bulletin & Review*, *14*(2), 249–255. DOI: 10.3758/BF03194060 PMID: 17694909

Roshanaei, M., Olivares, H., & Lopez, R.R. (2023). Harnessing AI to Foster Equity in Education: Opportunities, Challenges, and Emerging Strategies. *Journal of Intelligent Learning Systems and Applications*.

Rosmayanti, V., Noni, N., & Patak, A. A. (2022). Students' acceptance of technology use in learning English pharmacy. *International Journal of Language Education, 6*(3), 314–331. DOI: 10.26858/ijole.v6i3.24144

Rosmayanti, V., Patak, A. A., & Noni, N. (2023). Integrating technology into ESP instruction: Teaching English for pharmacy students. *The Journal of AsiaTEFL, 20*(2), 475–484. DOI: 10.18823/asiatefl.2023.20.2.18.475

Roy, D., & Putatunda, T. (2023). From Textbooks to Chatbots: Integrating AI in English Literature Classrooms of India. *Journal of E-Learning and Knowledge Society, 19*(3), 65–73. DOI: 10.20368/1971-8829/1135860

Sabri, N., Sadeghian, S., & Bahrak, B. (2020). A cross-country study on cultural similarities based on book preferences. *Social Network Analysis and Mining, 10*(1), 86. DOI: 10.1007/s13278-020-00695-y

Saddhono, K., Nugrahani, F., & Syamsuri, A. S. Ermanto, Rahim, A. R., & Sarimanah, E. (2024). The Ethics of AI in Literature: Reflections On Representation and Responsibility. 2024 International Conference on IoT, Communication and Automation Technology (ICICAT), 755–760. https://doi.org/DOI: 10.1109/ICICAT62666.2024.10923247

Sajja, R., Sermet, Y., Cikmaz, M., Cwiertny, D., & Demir, I. (2024). Artificial intelligence-enabled intelligent assistant for personalized and adaptive learning in higher education. Information. mdpi.com

Sakkir, G., Al Amir, F., Atmowardoyo, H., Weda, S., & Rosmayanti, V. (2024). An analysis of translanguaging practices in an Indonesian EFL classroom : Teacher perception Geminastiti. *Xlinguae, 17*(2), 3–15. DOI: 10.18355/XL.2024.17.02.01

Salas, N., & Pascual, M. (2023). Impact of school SES on literacy development. *PLoS One, 18*(12), e0295606. https://doi.org/https://doi.org/10.1371/journal.pone.0295606. DOI: 10.1371/journal.pone.0295606 PMID: 38127961

Salman, H., Imran, A., Niazi, S., Rahat, A., Arif, A., & Anjum, S. (2024). Artificial Intelligence In Higher Education: Strategies For Fostering Creativity In Writing Instruction. *Migration Letters : An International Journal of Migration Studies, 21*(S8), 1089–1097.

Sarker, I. H. (2021). Machine learning: Algorithms, real-world applications and research directions. SN computer science. springer.com

Sasabone, L. (2023). Applying Google Classroom As An Instructional Technology Media In Improving Students' Reading For English For Specific Purposes (ESP). *EDULEC : Education. Language And Culture Journal, 3*(1), 110–119. DOI: 10.56314/edulec.v3i1.123

Sayers, D., Sousa-Silva, R., Höhn, S., Ahmedi, L., Allkivi-Metsoja, K., Anastasiou, D., ... & Yayilgan, S. Y. (2021). The Dawn of the Human-Machine Era: A forecast of new and emerging language technologies. hal.science

Scarcella, R., & Perkins, L. (1987). Shifting Gears: Krashen's Input Hypothesis. *Studies in Second Language Acquisition, 9*(3), 347–353. https://doi.org/https://doi.org/10.1017/S0272263100006720. DOI: 10.1017/S0272263100006720

Schwitzgebel, E. (2023). AI systems must not confuse users about their sentience or moral status. *Patterns (New York, N.Y.), 4*(8), 100818. DOI: 10.1016/j.patter.2023.100818 PMID: 37602213

Scorer, M., & Vardy, E. (2024). Children need to see themselves in their reading material: parental perspectives on the importance of ethnically and culturally diverse reading material. *Literacy*. https://doi.org/https://doi.org/10.1111/lit.12379

Selfa-Sastre, M., Pifarré, M., Cujba, A., Cutillas, L., & Falguera, E. (2022). The role of digital technologies to promote collaborative creativity in language education. [frontiersin.org]. *Frontiers in Psychology, 13*, 828981. DOI: 10.3389/fpsyg.2022.828981 PMID: 35222209

Selwyn, N. (2016a). *Is technology good for education?* John Wiley & Sons.

Selwyn, N. (2019). *Should robots replace teachers? AI and the Future of Education* (1st ed.). Solity Press.

Seo, K., Tang, J., Roll, I., Fels, S., & Yoon, D. (2021). The Impact of Artificial Intelligence on Learner–instructor Interaction in Online Learning. *International Journal of Educational Technology in Higher Education, 18*(1), 54. Advance online publication. DOI: 10.1186/s41239-021-00292-9 PMID: 34778540

Serpico, K. (2024). The Belmont Report doesn't need reform, our moral imagination does. *Research Ethics, 20*(3), 559–573. DOI: 10.1177/17470161241235772

Shadiev, R. & Wang, X. (2022). A review of research on technology-supported language learning and 21st century skills. Frontiers in Psychology. frontiersin.org

Shah, P. (2023). *AI and the Future of Education: Teaching in the Age of Artificial Intelligence*. Jossey Bass, Wiley.

Shah, P. S., & Acharya, G. (2024). Artificial intelligence/machine learning and journalology: Challenges and opportunities. *Acta Obstetricia et Gynecologica Scandinavica*, *103*(2), 196–198. DOI: 10.1111/aogs.14772 PMID: 38284152

Shao, Z., Zhao, R., Yuan, S., Ding, M., & Wang, Y. (2022). Tracing the evolution of AI in the past decade and forecasting the emerging trends. *Expert Systems with Applications*, *209*, 118221. DOI: 10.1016/j.eswa.2022.118221

Shidiq, M. (2023). The use of artificial intelligence-based chat-gpt and its challenges for the world of education; from the viewpoint of the development of creative writing skills. *Proceeding of International Conference on Education, Society and Humanity, 1*(1), 353–357.

Shi, J., & Xuwei, Z. (2023). Integration of AI with Higher Education Innovation: Reforming Future Educational Directions. [IJSR]. *International Journal of Scientific Research.*

Shirley, D. A., & Langan-Fox, J. (1996). Intuition: A Review of the Literature. *Psychological Reports*, *79*(2), 563–584. DOI: 10.2466/pr0.1996.79.2.563 PMID: 9148314

Shortt, M., Tilak, S., Kuznetcova, I., Martens, B., & Akinkuolie, B. (2023). Gamification in mobile-assisted language learning: A systematic review of Duolingo literature from public release of 2012 to early 2020. [tandfonline.com]. *Computer Assisted Language Learning*, *36*(3), 517–554. DOI: 10.1080/09588221.2021.1933540

Sim, I., & Cassel, C. (2024). The ethics of relational AI — Expanding and implementing the Belmont principles. *The New England Journal of Medicine*, *391*(3), 193–196. DOI: 10.1056/NEJMp2314771 PMID: 39007542

Singh, J. P., & Kaur, B. P. (2024). Academic integrity and ethics in higher education: A case study on the use of artificial intelligence in academic writing and tackling plagiarism. In Thanuskodi, S. (Ed.), *Exploring digital metrics in academic libraries* (pp. 172–195). IGI Global., DOI: 10.4018/979-8-3693-5807-8

Singun, A. J. (2025). Unveiling the barriers to digital transformation in higher education institutions: a systematic literature review. Discover Education. springer.com

Sinn, D., & Soares, N. (2014). Historians' use of digital archival collections: The web, historical scholarship, and archival research. *Journal of the Association for Information Science and Technology*, *65*(9), 1794–1809. DOI: 10.1002/asi.23091

Škobo, M., & Petričević, V. (2023). Navigating the Challenges and Opportunities of Literary Translation in the Age of AI: Striking a Balance Between Human Expertise and Machine Power. *Društvene i Humanističke Studije (Online)*, *8*(2(23)), 317–336. DOI: 10.51558/2490-3647.2023.8.2.317

Smith, J., & Jones, K. (2023). Effectiveness of personalized learning pathways in an AI-driven Spanish curriculum. *Journal of Applied Linguistics*, *44*(3), 321–338.

Sofi-Karim, M., Bali, A. O., & Rached, K. (2023). Online education via media platforms and applications as an innovative teaching method. [springer.com]. *Education and Information Technologies*, *28*(1), 507–523. DOI: 10.1007/s10639-022-11188-0 PMID: 35791317

Song, C., Shin, S. Y., & Shin, K. S. (2023). Optimizing foreign language learning in virtual reality: a comprehensive theoretical framework based on constructivism and cognitive load theory (VR-CCL). Applied Sciences. mdpi.com

Song, C., Shin, S. Y., & Shin, K. S. (2024). Implementing the dynamic feedback-driven learning optimization framework: a machine learning approach to personalize educational pathways. Applied Sciences. mdpi.com

Song, C., & Song, Y. (2023). Enhancing academic writing skills and motivation: Assessing the efficacy of ChatGPT in AI-assisted language learning for EFL students. *Frontiers in Psychology*, *14*, 1260843. DOI: 10.3389/fpsyg.2023.1260843 PMID: 38162975

Song, W., Zhao, C., & Liu, L. (2019). Multi-Task Learning for Authorship Attribution via Topic Approximation and Competitive Attention. *IEEE Access : Practical Innovations, Open Solutions*, *7*, 177114–177121. DOI: 10.1109/ACCESS.2019.2957152

Sperlich, B., Düking, P., Leppich, R., & Holmberg, H.-C. (2023). Strengths, weaknesses, opportunities, and threats associated with the application of artificial intelligence in connection with sport research, coaching, and optimization of athletic performance: A brief SWOT analysis. *Frontiers in Sports and Active Living*, *5*, 1258562. DOI: 10.3389/fspor.2023.1258562 PMID: 37920303

Spooren, W., & Sanders, T. (2008). The acquisition order of coherence relations : On cognitive complexity in discourse. *Journal of Pragmatics and Discourse Research*, *40*, 2003–2026. https://doi.org/https://doi.org/10.1016/J.PRAGMA.2008.04.021

Staples, S., Egbert, J., Biber, D., & Conrad, S. (2015). Register variation a corpus approach. *The Handbook of Discourse Analysis*, 505–525.

Straume, I., & Anson, C. (2022). Amazement and trepidation: Implications of AI-based natural language production for the teaching of writing. *Journal of Academic Writing*, *12*(1), 1–9. DOI: 10.18552/joaw.v12i1.820

Suissa, O., Elmalech, A., & Zhitomirsky-Geffet, M. (2022). Text analysis using deep neural networks in digital humanities and information science. *Journal of the Association for Information Science and Technology*, *73*(2), 268–287. DOI: 10.1002/asi.24544

Sujarwo, Abdul Hakim Yassi, & Abbas, Herawaty, & Harlinah sahib. (2024). An Interactive-Based E-Module of Translation Technology of Blended and Online Learning to Improve Autonomous Learning. [TSRJ]. *The Seyreport Journal*, *19*(06), 193–209. DOI: 10.5281/ZENODO.11547317

Sujarwo, S., Asdar, A., Sabillah, B. M., Sukmawati, S., Akhiruddin, A., & Muh. Syata, W. (2023). Innovation In English Language Learning Model Based Digital Literacy To Construct Young Learners' Character. *Ethical Lingua. Journal of Language Teaching and Literature*, *10*(2). Advance online publication. DOI: 10.30605/25409190.640

Sula, C. A., & Hill, H. V. (2019). The early history of digital humanities: An analysis of Computers and the Humanities (1966–2004) and Literary and Linguistic Computing (1986–2004). *Digital Scholarship in the Humanities*, fqz072. DOI: 10.1093/llc/fqz072

Sulviana, Muhammad Chairil Imran & Sulviana. (2022). Using BBC Web-Based Learning Courses to Improve Vocational High School (VHS) Students' Speaking Skill. *EDULEC : Education, Language, and Culture Journal*, *2*(1), 94–100. DOI: 10.56314/edulec.v2i1.34

Sun, W. (2023). The impact of automatic speech recognition technology on second language pronunciation and speaking skills of EFL learners: a mixed methods investigation. Frontiers in Psychology. frontiersin.org

Suresh Babu, S., & Dhakshina Moorthy, A. (2024). Application of artificial intelligence in adaptation of gamification in education: A literature review. [HTML]. *Computer Applications in Engineering Education*, *32*(1), e22683. DOI: 10.1002/cae.22683

Suryana, I., Asrianto, A., & Murwantono, D. (2020). Artificial Intelligence to Master English Listening Skills for Non-English Major Students. *Journal of Languages and Language Teaching*, *8*(1), 48. DOI: 10.33394/jollt.v8i1.2221

Swiecki, Z., Khosravi, H., Chen, G., Maldonado, R. M., Lodge, J. M., Milligan, S., Selwyn, N., & Gašević, D. (2022). Assessment in the age of artificial intelligence. *Comput. Educ. Artif. Intell.*, *3*, 100075. DOI: 10.1016/j.caeai.2022.100075

Sywelem, M. M., & Mahklouf, A. M. (2024). Ethical Considerations in the Integration of Artificial Intelligence in Education: An Overview. *Education and Information Technologies.*

Tafazoli, D. (2024). Exploring the potential of generative AI in democratizing English language education. Computers and Education: Artificial Intelligence. sciencedirect.com

Taghizadeh, M., & Hasani Yourdshahi, Z. (2020). Integrating technology into young learners' classes: Language teachers' perceptions. *Computer Assisted Language Learning*, *33*(8), 982–1006. DOI: 10.1080/09588221.2019.1618876

Tai, T. Y., & Chen, H. H. J. (2023). The impact of Google Assistant on adolescent EFL learners' willingness to communicate. [HTML]. *Interactive Learning Environments*, *31*(3), 1485–1502. DOI: 10.1080/10494820.2020.1841801

Tajik, A. (2025). Gamified and non-gamified AI tools in enhancing EFL listening comprehension: An analysis of Duolingo and Replika's impact on engagement, motivation, and …. [HTML]

Tammets, K., & Ley, T. (2023). Integrating AI tools in teacher professional learning: A conceptual model and illustrative case. *Frontiers in Artificial Intelligence*, *6*, 1255089. DOI: 10.3389/frai.2023.1255089 PMID: 38130325

Tan, D., & Mante-Estacio, M. (2021). Eader-Text Connection: Reporting the Engagement of High School Students with Culturally Relevant Texts. *TEFLIN Journal - A Publication on the Teaching and Learning of English.* https://doi.org/https://doi.org/10.15639/teflinjournal.v32i2/342-361

Tan, S. C., Lee, A. V. Y., & Lee, M. (2022). A systematic review of artificial intelligence techniques for collaborative learning over the past two decades. Computers and Education: Artificial Intelligence. sciencedirect.com

Tang, F. (2024). Understanding the role of digital immersive technology in educating the students of english language: does it promote critical thinking and self-directed learning for …. BMC psychology. springer.com

Tang, J., & Foley, J. (2022). A Case Study on the Effectiveness of Applying Content and Language Integrated Learning in an Artificial Intelligence English Reading Course. *Arab World English Journal*, *13*(3), 236–253. DOI: 10.24093/awej/vol13no3.15

Tang, T., Lau, D., & Leung, M. (2023). Corpus of Mandarin Child Language: A preliminary study on the acquisition of semantic content categories in Mandarin-speaking preschoolers. *Frontiers in Psychology*, *14*, 1234525. https://doi.org/https://doi.org/10.3389/fpsyg.2023.1234525. DOI: 10.3389/fpsyg.2023.1234525 PMID: 38022991

TAŞKIN BEDİZEL, N.R. (2023). Evolving landscape of artificial intelligence (AI) and assessment in education: A bibliometric analysis. *International Journal of Assessment Tools in Education*.

Tecuci, G. (2012). Artificial intelligence. *Wiley Interdisciplinary Reviews: Computational Statistics*, *4*(2), 168–180. DOI: 10.1002/wics.200

Tian, W., Ge, J., Zhao, Y., & Zheng, X. (2024). AI Chatbots in Chinese Higher Education: Adoption, Perception, and Influence Among Graduate Students—an Integrated Analysis Utilizing UTAUT and ECM Models. *Frontiers in Psychology*, *15*, 1268549. Advance online publication. DOI: 10.3389/fpsyg.2024.1268549 PMID: 38384353

Tomczyk, P., Brüggemann, P., & Vrontis, D. (2024). AI meets academia: Transforming systematic literature reviews. *EuroMed Journal of Business*. Advance online publication. DOI: 10.1108/EMJB-03-2024-0055

Tong, F. (2022). Psychological and pedagogical effects on engagement and achievement: Implications for literacy and maths learning. *Educational Psychology*, *42*(8), 931–933. https://doi.org/https://doi.org/10.1080/01443410.2022.2140275. DOI: 10.1080/01443410.2022.2140275

Tsai, S.-C. (2022). Learning With Mobile Augmented Reality- And Automatic Speech Recognition-Based Materials for English Listening and Speaking Skills: Effectiveness and Perceptions of Non-English Major English as a Foreign Language Students. *Journal of Educational Computing Research*, *61*(2), 444–465. DOI: 10.1177/07356331221111203

Tumbe, C. (2019). Corpus linguistics, newspaper archives and historical research methods. *Journal of Management History*, *25*(4), 533–549. DOI: 10.1108/JMH-01-2018-0009

UNESCO. (2021). *Recommendation on the ethics of artificial intelligence*. UNESCO.

Valdivieso, T., & González, O. (2025). Generative AI Tools in Salvadoran Higher Education : Balancing Equity, Ethics, and Knowledge Management in the Global South. *Education Sciences*, *15*(214), 1–31. DOI: 10.3390/educsci15020214

Van Der Sommen, F., & De Groof, J. (2024). Risks and rewards of AI democratization. *United European Gastroenterology Journal, 12*(4), 427–428. DOI: 10.1002/ueg2.12560 PMID: 38526950

Villegas-Ch, W., García-Ortiz, J., & Sánchez-Viteri, S. (2024). Personalization of Learning: Machine Learning Models for Adapting Educational Content to Individual Learning Styles. *IEEE Access : Practical Innovations, Open Solutions, 12*, 121114–121130. DOI: 10.1109/ACCESS.2024.3452592

Vygotsky, L. S. (1978). *Mind in Society: The Development of Higher Psychological Processes*. Harvard University Press.

Walkington, C., & Bernacki, M. (2020). Appraising research on personalized learning: Definitions, theoretical alignment, advancements, and future directions. *Journal of Research on Technology in Education, 52*(3), 235–252. https://doi.org/https://doi.org/10.1080/15391523.2020.1747757. DOI: 10.1080/15391523.2020.1747757

Walter, Y. (2024). Embracing the future of Artificial Intelligence in the classroom: The relevance of AI literacy, prompt engineering, and critical thinking in modern education. *International Journal of Educational Technology in Higher Education, 21*(1), 1–29. DOI: 10.1186/s41239-024-00448-3

Wang, C. (2024). *Exploring Students' Generative AI-Assisted Writing Processes: Perceptions and Experiences From Native and Nonnative English Speakers*. Technology Knowledge and Learning., DOI: 10.1007/s10758-024-09744-3

Wang, D., & Huang, X. (2025). Transforming education through artificial intelligence and immersive technologies: Enhancing learning experiences. [HTML]. *Interactive Learning Environments*, 1–20. DOI: 10.1080/10494820.2025.2465451

Wang, Q., Liu, C., & Lan, S. (2023). Digital literacy and financial market participation of middle-aged and elderly adults in China. *Economic and Political Studies, 11*(4), 441–468. DOI: 10.1080/20954816.2022.2115191

Wang, T., Lund, B. D., Marengo, A., Pagano, A., Mannuru, N. R., Teel, Z. A., & Pange, J. (2023). Exploring the potential impact of artificial intelligence (AI) on international students in higher education: Generative AI, chatbots, analytics, and international student success. *Applied Sciences (Basel, Switzerland), 13*(11), 6716. DOI: 10.3390/app13116716

Wang, X., Thompson, M., Yang, K., Roy, D., Koedinger, K. R., Rose, C. P., & Reich, J. (2021). Practice-based teacher questioning strategy training with ELK: A role-playing simulation for eliciting learner knowledge. *Proceedings of the ACM on Human-Computer Interaction, 5*(CSCW1), 1–27. DOI: 10.1145/3449125

Warschauer, M. (2004). *Technology and social inclusion: Rethinking the digital divide*. MIT press.

Washington, J. (2023). The Impact of Generative Artificial Intelligence on Writer's Self-Efficacy: A Critical Literature Review. In SSRN *Electronic Journal*. https://doi.org/DOI: 10.2139/ssrn.4538043

Watters, C., & Lemanski, M. K. (2023). Universal skepticism of ChatGPT : A review of early literature on chat generative pre-trained transformer. *Frontiers in Big Data*, *6*, 1–10. https://doi.org/https://doi.org/10.3389/fdata.2023.1224976. DOI: 10.3389/fdata.2023.1224976 PMID: 37680954

Weber, A.S. (2020). ETHICS CONCERNS IN ARTIFICIAL INTELLIGENCE USE IN EDUCATION.

Wei, L. (2023). Artificial intelligence in language instruction: impact on English learning achievement, L2 motivation, and self-regulated learning. Frontiers in psychology. frontiersin.org

Wei, L. (2023). Artificial Intelligence in Language Instruction: Impact on English Learning Achievement, L2 Motivation, and Self-Regulated Learning. *Frontiers in Psychology*, *14*, 1261955. Advance online publication. DOI: 10.3389/fpsyg.2023.1261955 PMID: 38023040

Wellek, R., & Warren, A. (1949). *Theory of Literature*. Harcourt, Brace and Company, Inc.

White, R., Davis, P., & Miller, S. (2024). Using AI for thematic analysis in undergraduate literary studies: A case study. *Journal of Digital Humanities*, *6*(2), 87–101.

Wiese, L. J., Patil, I., Schiff, D. S., & Magana, A. J. (2025). AI ethics education: A systematic literature review. *Computers and Education: Artificial Intelligence*, *8*, 100405. DOI: 10.1016/j.caeai.2025.100405

Williamson, B. (2017). *Big data in education: The digital future of learning, policy and practice*.

Wirth, A., Ehmig, S., Drescher, N., Guffler, S., & Niklas, F. (2020). Facets of the Early Home Literacy Environment and Children's Linguistic and Socioemotional Competencies. *Early Education and Development*, *31*(6), 892–909. https://doi.org/https://doi.org/10.1080/10409289.2019.1706826. DOI: 10.1080/10409289.2019.1706826

Wise, B., Emerson, L., Van Luyn, A., Dyson, B., Bjork, C., & Thomas, S. E. (2024). A scholarly dialogue: Writing scholarship, authorship, academic integrity and the challenges of AI. *Higher Education Research & Development*, *43*(3), 578–590. DOI: 10.1080/07294360.2023.2280195

Wong, L., Tan, G. W., Ooi, K., & Dwivedi, Y. K. (2023). The Role of Institutional and Self in the Formation of Trust in Artificial Intelligence Technologies. *Internet Research*, *34*(2), 343–370. DOI: 10.1108/INTR-07-2021-0446

Woolf, B. P., Lane, H. C., Chaudhri, V. K., & Kolodner, J. L. (2018). AI Grand Challenges for Education. *AI Magazine*, (Winter), 66–84.

Wu, X. (2022). Dynamic evaluation of college English writing ability based on AI technology. *Journal of Intelligent Systems*, *31*(1), 298–309. DOI: 10.1515/jisys-2022-0020

Yang, X. (2023). A historical review of collaborative learning and cooperative learning. TechTrends. springer.com

Yang, L., Wang, G., & Wang, H. (2024). Reimagining Literary Analysis: Utilizing Artificial Intelligence to Classify Modernist French Poetry. *Information (Basel)*, *15*(2), 70. DOI: 10.3390/info15020070

Yang, W., Hu, X., Yeter, I., Su, J., Yang, Y., & Lee, J. (2023). Artificial intelligence education for young children: A case study of technology-enhanced embodied learning. *Journal of Computer Assisted Learning*, *40*(2), 465–477. https://doi.org/https://doi.org/10.1111/jcal.12892. DOI: 10.1111/jcal.12892

Yeo, M. A. (2023). Academic integrity in the age of Artificial Intelligence (AI) authoring apps. *TESOL Journal*, *14*(3), e716. DOI: 10.1002/tesj.716

Yingsoon, G. Y., Zhang, S., & Chua, N. A. (2025). Empowering Educators in the Era of Next-Generation AI: Redefining the Teacher's Role in an AI-Enhanced Learning Environment. In Teachers' Roles and Perspectives on AI Integration in Schools (pp. 1-30). IGI Global Scientific Publishing. [HTML]

Yin, L., & Fathi, J. (2025). Exploring the motivational dynamics of chinese learners on tandem and hellotalk: A self-determination theory perspective. [HTML]. *Learning and Motivation*, *90*, 102113. DOI: 10.1016/j.lmot.2025.102113

Yu, H. (2024). The application and challenges of ChatGPT in educational transformation: New demands for teachers' roles. Heliyon. cell.com

Zamiri, M. & Esmaeili, A. (2024). Methods and technologies for supporting knowledge sharing within learning communities: A systematic literature review. Administrative Sciences. mdpi.com

Zhai, C. & Wibowo, S. (2023). A systematic review on artificial intelligence dialogue systems for enhancing English as foreign language students' interactional competence in the university. Computers and Education: Artificial Intelligence. sciencedirect.com

Zhai, C., Wibowo, S., & Li, L. D. (2024). The effects of over-reliance on AI dialogue systems on students' cognitive abilities: A systematic review. *Smart Learning Environments*, *11*(28), 1–37. DOI: 10.1186/s40561-024-00316-7

Zhai, X. (2024). An analysis of the value and linguistic features of contemporary literary texts based on knowledge graph. *Applied Mathematics and Nonlinear Sciences*, *9*(1), 20240493. DOI: 10.2478/amns-2024-0493

Zhang, S. (2024). Chatgpt Assisted Teachers in Improving Formative Assessment. *Journal of Education, Humanities and Social Sciences.*

Zhang, Z. (2024). Advancements and Challenges in AI-driven Language Technologies: From Natural Language Processing to Language Acquisition. *Applied and Computational Engineering*, *57*(1), 146–152. DOI: 10.54254/2755-2721/57/20241325

Zhao, D. (2024). The impact of AI-enhanced natural language processing tools on writing proficiency: An analysis of language precision, content summarization, and creative writing facilitation. *Education and Information Technologies*, •••, 1–32.

Zhao, Y., Zhao, M., & Shi, F. (2024). Integrating moral education and educational information technology: A strategic approach to enhance rural teacher training in universities. [HTML]. *Journal of the Knowledge Economy.*

Zheng, L., Liu, R., & Zhang, X. (2020). Effects of an interest-driven creation approach on students' mobile learning performance and creativity in learning science in a science museum. *Journal of Computers in Education*, *8*(2), 159–182. https://doi.org/ https://doi.org/10.1007/s40692-020-00175-4. DOI: 10.1007/s40692-020-00175-4

Zhou, N. (2024). *Evaluating Human and Machine Assessment: Introducing a Hybrid Approach for Enhanced Educational Evaluation.* Lecture Notes in Education Psychology and Public Media.

Zhou, X., Zhang, J., & Chan, C. (2024). Unveiling Students' Experiences and Perceptions of Artificial Intelligence Usage in Higher Education. *Journal of University Teaching & Learning Practice*, *21*(06). Advance online publication. DOI: 10.53761/xzjprb23

Zohny, H., McMillan, J., & King, M. (2023). Ethics of generative AI. *Journal of Medical Ethics*, *49*(2), 79–80. DOI: 10.1136/jme-2023-108909 PMID: 36693706

Zucker, T., Oh, Y., Smith, K., & Baker-Finck, J. (2022). Low-Income Elementary Students Access to Books & Reading Motivation. *Reading Psychology*, *43*(3-4), 250–276. https://doi.org/https://doi.org/10.1080/02702711.2022.2094040. DOI: 10.1080/02702711.2022.2094040

About The Contributors

Andi Asrifan, S.Pd, M.Pd, a distinguished figure in the realm of education, particularly in English Language Education, has made significant contributions through his extensive research, teaching, and leadership roles. As the Head of the Institute for Cooperation and International Affairs at Universitas Muhammadiyah Sidenreng Rappang and now a lecturer in Universitas Negeri Makassar (UNM), Dr. Asrifan's academic journey is marked by a rich tapestry of achievements, including a Doctor of Education in English Language Education. His work spans various facets of education, language, and technology, reflecting the diverse topics covered in his publications and research endeavors. These include, but are not limited to, the impact of the COVID-19 pandemic on educational practices, methodologies in English as a Foreign Language (EFL) classrooms, and the integration of technology in teaching and learning processes. Dr. Asrifan's commitment to advancing educational standards and practices is further evidenced by his active participation in international conferences, webinars, and workshops across countries like India, the Philippines, and Pakistan. These events, organized by various institutions and associations, underscore his role as a global educator and thought leader. His dedication to professional development is also highlighted through his involvement in numerous courses and certifications in personal branding, public speaking, and literacy teaching. Moreover, Dr. Asrifan's leadership extends beyond academia into organizational and educational development, where he has served in various capacities, including as an external examiner for Ph.D. dissertations and a reviewer for scientific journals. His accolades, memberships in professional organizations, and roles as an ambassador for international associations speak volumes of his influence and commitment to fostering educational excellence and sustainable development goals globally.

***

Anshari, M.Hum. is a prominent academic figure, currently serving as the Dean of the Faculty of Language and Literature at Universitas Negeri Makassar (UNM). Born on April 29, 1964, in Enrekang, he has developed a strong foundation in Indonesian Language and Literature, earning his Bachelor's degree from IKIP Ujung Pandang, followed by a Master's and Doctorate from Universitas Hasanuddin and Universitas Negeri Malang, respectively. With a rich teaching portfolio, Prof. Anshari specializes in subjects such as Nusantara Literature, Indonesian Language Learning Methods, and Literary Theory. His research contributions over the past five years include significant studies on local wisdom in literature and environmental perceptions among students, supported by funding from DIPA UNM. Prof. Anshari's commitment to community service is evident through various training programs aimed at enhancing writing skills among students in Makassar and surrounding areas. His scholarly work has been recognized nationally, evidenced by receiving the Satya Lencana award from the President of Indonesia in 2009 for his dedication to education. His recent publication, "Eksistensi Bahasa Indonesia Masa Pendudukan Jepang," reflects his engagement with historical and cultural contexts in language studies. Prof. Dr. Anshari's extensive experience and scholarly contributions position him as a leading figure in advancing the fields of language and literature in Indonesia.

Muhammad Asdam is an Indonesian Language Education lecturer. He has over 20 years of experience as an academic with the Universitas Bosowa, where he is currently an Associate Professor. His current research interest includes students' learning and development at various levels and areas of education. His publication topics include Digital literacy, curriculum development, and Indonesian language skills.

Asdar is a Ph. D in Indonesian Language Education from the State University Makassar, Indonesia. He has over 15 years of experience as an academic with the Universitas Bosowa, where he is currently an Associate Professor and the Dean of the Faculty of Education and Literature. His current research interest includes students' learning and development at various levels and areas of education. His publication topics include reading comprehension, online learning, learning models in language, Digital literacy, integrative approach in learning, and writing skills

Boyet L. Batang, PhD, is currently the President of Isabela State University (ISU), Echague, Isabela. He previously served as Vice President for Academic Affairs, Director for Academic Affairs and Quality Assurance, and Dean of the College of Education at Isabela State University, Cabagan, Isabela. Prior to his current designation, he was the Cluster Executive Officer of ISU–City of Ilagan Campus. He earned his Bachelor's degree in Education, major in English, with an undergraduate certificate in Reading, and his Master's degree in English Language Arts from the Philippine Normal University, Manila. He obtained his Doctorate degree in English Language Studies (*Cum Laude*) from the Royal and Pontifical University of Santo Tomas, Manila. Prof. Batang is a national senior accreditor of the Accrediting Agency of Chartered Colleges and Universities in the Philippines (AACCUP), Inc., a national assessor of the Commission on Higher Education (CHED) Institutional Sustainability Assessment, and a member of the Regional Quality Assessment Team (RQAT) of CHED Region II. He also serves as an accreditor during the Professorial Accreditation under the Philippine Association of State Universities and Colleges (PASUC) and the CHED–DBM Joint Circular No. 3. He is the founding President of the Applied Linguistics and Literature Association of the Philippines, Inc. He holds the highest academic rank of *University Professor*, one of the most prestigious titles conferred in State Universities and Colleges in the Philippines. Prof. Batang has presented scholarly papers in both national and international conferences, and has published extensively in national, international, and Scopus-indexed journals. He has authored 22 publications, 15 of which are indexed in Scopus, with a total of 126 research citations. He is one of the lead researchers of the National Policy Research on Literacy, particularly in the development of the *Framework on Analytic Scoring Rubric/Monitoring and Evaluation Tool for Exemplary Community-Based Literacy Programs and Engagement in the Philippines*, which has been approved and adopted by the Literacy Coordinating Council (LCC) of the Philippines, Department of Education (DepEd). He also served as a faculty exchange lecturer at Rajamangala University of Technology Thanyaburi, Thailand. Currently, he is pursuing his second doctorate degree in Public Administration at the National College of Public Administration and Governance (NCPAG), University of the Philippines Diliman.

Rozel Sales-Batang is an Associate Professor at the College of Education, Isabela State University–Cabagan Campus. She earned her Bachelor's degree in Secondary Education, major in Filipino, and her Master of Arts in Education, major in Filipino, from the same university where she currently teaches Filipino courses focusing on language and literature, as well as major courses in Filipino. She is presently pursuing a Ph.D. in Filipino (Translation) at the College of Arts and Letters, University of the Philippines–Diliman.

Ramratan Guru is an Assistant Professor Level III, School of Design (SOD) at Mody University of Science and Technology, India. His research interests include new materialism, Smart Fabric Technology: Weaving UX design into Wearable Textiles, sustainability in fashion and textiles; circular fashion; waste management; technical textile, green composite materials and ethical fashion, Material Science and Industry Engineering. His Postdoctoral research was completed at the School of

Engineering, Department of Textile Engineering, University of Minho, Portugal, Europe. His Ph.D., M. Tech, and B. Tech were completed in the Department of Textile Technology at the National Institute of Technology (NIT) Jalandhar, Punjab, India. Dr. Ramratan has authored six books, published over 180 high-impact journal and conference papers, and contributed to more than 16 book chapters. He holds five granted patents and has filed more than 30 patent National and International applications. Dr. Ramratan has developed over eight innovative cellulosic fibers, earning recognition for his research in various countries, including Canada, the USA, Europe, the UK, and Brazil. He actively collaborates with universities across Brazil, Europe, Canada, the USA, and Asia. He has extensive publications in high impact journals as well as books and book chapters.

Kristiawan Indriyanto holds Ph.D. in American Studies from Universitas Gadjah Mada on the topic of postcolonial ecocriticism in Hawai'ian-American literature. His main research interests are analyzing indigenous literature with a postcolonial ecocriticism perspective, primarily focusing on Native Hawaiian literature and the decolonizing discourse of Hawaiian indigene through Aloha 'āina. He is the author of over 50 publications on various topics, a number of which are indexed in Scopus or Web of Science.

Elisabeth Ngestirosa Endang Woro Kasih is an Assistant Professor of Literature in the Master of English Language Studies program, Faculty of Arts and Education, Universitas Teknokrat Indonesia. She earned her doctoral degree in American Studies from the Faculty of Cultural Sciences, Universitas Gadjah Mada. She was also a visiting researcher at the Department of English, College of Liberal Arts and Sciences, Northern Illinois University. Her research focuses on Teaching English, pedagogy, minority literature, popular literature, and American literature, with several publications in various academic journals.

Sulmi Magfirah is an English literature lecturer from Universitas Khairun, Ternate, Indonesia. She has over 10 years of academic experience and is an associate professor. Her current research interest includes students' learning and development at various levels and areas of education and literature. Her publication topics include English literature, Learning-based digital, and English language skills

Sandi Pradana, was born in Lampung in December 1990. From a young age, they developed a deep interest in language and education. They completed their undergraduate studies in English Language at STKIP PGRI Bandar Lampung, an institution that provided a strong academic foundation in the English language. Their desire to further their knowledge led them to pursue a Master's degree in English Language at Universitas Negeri Yogyakarta. Currently, the author serves as a lecturer in the Education Program for Islamic Elementary School Teachers (PGMI) at the Sekolah Tinggi Ilmu Tarbiyah Tanggamus in Lampung Province. In this role, they focus on curriculum development and English language teaching, dedicating themselves to educating the next generation with enthusiasm and commitment. The author can be contacted via email at: sandi@stittanggamus.ac.id.

Mark-Jhon R. Prestoza, PhD is an assistant professor at the Cauayan City campus of Isabela State University. He graduated from the Polytechnic University of the Philippines – Open University with a Doctor of Philosophy in Education Management. He has a great quantity of national and international experience in curriculum development, instructional leadership, and teacher preparation. Filipino language, curriculum management, language and literacy, and the creation educational materials are among his areas of interest.

Tri Pujiani, M.Pd is an English lecturer of Harapan Bangsa University, Purwokerto and also a doctoral student of Language Education Science Department, Language and Art Faculty of Universitas Negeri Semarang. She obtained her master and bachelor degree from Sebelas Maret University. With a passion for English language education, her research interests lie in Teacher Professional Development, Teaching English to Young Learners, and Language Teaching Media. She is a member of APSPBI, TEFLIN, IELA, AISEE, and PELTIN.

L. Dyah Purwita Wardani SWW, received my master degree in American studies from Gadjah Mada University (2014). I have been becoming a lecturer of English department Faculty of Humanities in Universitas Jember for almost twenty years. My research focuses on young adult literature, feminism, gender and social humanities. I am the journal manager of Journal Feminism and Gender Studies and also the head of the research board at Center of Gender Studies at Universitas Jember.

Ramli is a lecturer at the English Education Department, Faculty of Teachers Training and Education, Universitas Borneo Tarakan, North Kalimantan, Indonesia. He pursued his doctorate at Universitas Negeri Malang, funded by the Indonesian Minister of Research and Technology (2019). He received the Sandwich Scholarship at the Ohio State University (OSU) in 2017. He sustainably explores his knowledge and competence as a lecturer by doing community services, teaching, and writing articles published in internationally and nationally accredited journals. Since 2023, he has been selected as a facilitator of Sekolah Penggerak batch 3 Kalimantan Utara as his pathway to contributing to education development, and in 2024, he was an awardee of Microcredential Scholarship in Western Sydney University Australia from GTK Kemendikbudristek in enhancing literacy education. Besides, he intensively attends conferences, workshops, and seminars/webinars for continuous professional development.

Vivit Rosmayanti, S.Pd.I., M.Pd was born in Botta on June 26, 1987. She has over 10 years of experience teaching at the University. She obtained a bachelor's degree in English Education from Alauddin State Islamic University. She completed her master's and doctoral degrees in English Education from Makassar State University. She is currently a lecturer in the Post Graduate Program, Department of English Education at Makassar State University, South Sulawesi, Indonesia. She is also actively writing research articles to be published in nationally and internationally accredited journals. She has written in some chapter books, monographs, and reference books. She is interested in teaching methods for teaching English. Her research interests include language teaching methodology, ICT instruction, and ESP teaching.

Sriwahyuni is a lecturer in the Bachelor's Program of Sociology Education at Universitas Megarezky. She earned her Bachelor's and Doctoral degrees from Universitas Hasanuddin and completed her Master's degree at Universitas Negeri Makassar.

Sujarwo is a Ph.D in English Language Studies (ELS) from Hasanuddin University, Indonesia. He has over 11 years of experience as an Academician with the Universitas Megarezky, where he is currently an Assistant Professor and the Secretary of the English Education Department Faculty of Teacher Training and Education. His current research interest includes EFL students' learning and development at various levels and areas of education. His publication topics include translation, ESP, online learning, learning models in ELT, and Research and Development (R & D) in Education

Andi Annisa Sulolipu is a lecturer in the Doctoral Program in Economics Education at Universitas Negeri Makassar. She earned her Bachelor's degree from Universitas Negeri Makassar and completed both her Master's and Doctoral studies at Universitas Negeri Malang.

Andi Meinar Dwi Rantisari Thayeb is a lecturer in the Pharmacy Program at Universitas Megarezky. She earned both her Bachelor's and Master's degrees from Universitas Hasanuddin.

Areski Wahid is currently a lecturer at Postgraduate Program in English Education Department of Universitas Negeri Makassar, Indonesia. She got her doctoral degree at Universitas Negeri Makassar and her master's degree at

Universitas Muhammadiyah Parepare. Her research interests include technology in language teaching, curriculum & material development, and ICT in language teaching.

Index

A

C

D

E

S

T

www.ingramcontent.com/pod-product-compliance
Lightning Source LLC
LaVergne TN
LVHW080856300926
849162LV00003B/437